THE POVERTY OF STRUCTURALISM

Foundations of Modern Literary Theory

Already published:

The Poverty of Structuralism: Literature and Structuralist Theory

Forthcoming titles in the sequence:

The Dematerialisation of Karl Marx: Literature and Marxist Theory

The Poverty of Structuralism

Literature and Structuralist Theory

Leonard Jackson

Longman
London and New York

Longman Group UK Limited,
Longman House, Burnt Mill, Harlow,
Essex CM20 2JE, England
and Associated Companies throughout the world.

Published in the United States of America
by Longman Inc., New York

First published 1991

British Library Cataloguing in Publication Data

Jackson, Leonard
    The poverty of structuralism : literature and
    structuralist theory. – (Foundations of modern literary
    theory).
    1. Linguistics. Structuralism. Theories
    I. Title   II. Series
    410.1

    ISBN 0–582–06697–2
    ISBN 0–582–06696–4 pbk

Library of Congress Cataloging in Publication Data
Jackson, Leonard.
    The poverty of structuralism : structuralist theory and literature
    Leonard Jackson.
        p. cm. -- (Foundations of modern literary theory)
    Includes bibliographical references and index.
    ISBN 0–582–06697–2 (cased). -- ISBN 0–582–06696–4 (paper)
    1. Structuralism (Literary analysis)   2. Literature, Modern--20th
century--History and criticism.   I. Title.   II. Series.
PN98.S7J33   1991
801'.95'0904--dc20   90–49916
                                                                          CIP

Set in Bembo

Produced by Longman Singapore Publishers (Pte) Ltd.
Printed in Singapore

Contents

Acknowledgements

I really owe too many debts to acknowledge any; but I am particularly grateful to my colleagues Peter Ryan, Ian Birchall, David Grylls, Jonathan Rée and Peter Widdowson for setting me thinking on literary theory, or reading and commenting on parts of this manuscript, or reacting to oral presentations of parts of it. My closest colleague, who has read the whole thing with a critical eye, is my wife Eleanor Jackson. My debt to her is obviously incalculable. None of these is necessarily to be taken as agreeing with any of the book, or as responsible for its defects.

Preface
Problems in the Foundations of Modern Theory

Modern literary theory is founded on the work of Marx, Saussure and Freud; but on that work has been erected a vast and baroque superstructure of theory and paradox, about society, language, and human subjectivity, which would have greatly surprised all three of them. The new radical literary theory arouses passionate commitment in some, but baffles and irritates, as much as it fascinates, the uncommitted among us; is this metaphysics of paradox necessary for the understanding of literature, we ask; is it true; does it even make sense?

Nowadays, as Marxism disappears from its Eastern European homelands, a darker question arises: was this body of radical protest ever a serious theory of literature at all? Did it ever even attempt (as serious theory in the social sciences should) to explain how literature works? Did it not rather use literary, and film and cultural studies to build up a theoretical-sounding ideology of opposition to capitalism, Western metaphysics, and science? An ideology of Western intellectual dissidence – very potent in the 1960s, but now beginning to date and look shabby?

This book and the two which follow offer both an introduction to this set of ideas and a fundamental critique of them. The critique is fundamental in the sense of going back to the historical and logical foundations of the theory: it rejects post-structuralist anti-foundationalism. This first book, *The Poverty of Structuralism*, is a critical introduction to the structuralist foundations. It is followed by a book on Marxist foundations, and a book on Freudian ones. Each of these has the same plan. It explains the basic theoretical model involved – in this case the structuralist model of language – and gives an account of the way that model has been developed – or twisted, distorted, rejected, lied about or transformed into its opposite – to become a part of the language contemporary literary and cultural theoreticians use. I hope that anyone who reads all three books will thus have to consider some of the fundamental issues about language, society and the mind that are presupposed by, and often hidden in, the difficult language of modern literary and cultural theory. But the books are not written in that difficult language, and do not presuppose that any of that theory is correct.

Each book is written at a level which ought to be comprehensible to an undergraduate or a serious general reader. Any technical or philosophical background that is needed for this purpose has been provided – often, naturally, in summary form, and with a minimum of technical terminology. Thus, any reader of this first book should be able to grasp what major claims Saussure made about human language, and what would count as a reasonable extension of these to literature. Perhaps even more important, the reader will also know what major claims, widely attributed to Saussure today and used as the foundation of literary theory, he did not make, and would probably have thought absurd. I hope something comparable is true about the main positions of Roland Barthes, and about the very small part of the work of Jacques Derrida that I discuss, and indeed about the many thinkers such as Roman Jakobson, Claude Lévi-Strauss and Jacques Lacan whom I introduce more briefly.

The general argument that I am putting forward is this. Structuralism – by which I mean mainly the attempt to apply the structuralist model of language, which dominated early twentieth-century linguistics, to the human sciences in general and to literature in particular – began as a rational research strategy in the work of Jakobson and others in the late 1920s. This strategy had a fundamental flaw, which arose from what I have called the 'logical poverty' of the underlying model of language – its inadequacy to account even for the facts of language, let alone those of literature or society. Nevertheless, it remained a rational scientific strategy when it was picked up by Lévi-Strauss in the 1940s; it was forced off course in France in the 1960s in a confrontation with what I have called French philosophy of the subject. The French are responsible, not (as is widely supposed in Britain and America) for the invention of structuralism, but for its death.

The various post-structuralisms are the lineal ancestors of contemporary literary theory, and many, though not all of them seem to me irrationalist in tendency, and, as I have suggested, to be explained rather as a movement of protest against capitalism, science, Western metaphysics, patriarchy and of anything else that the theorists dislike, than as serious theories about literature or culture. This is obviously a large and controversial question, and I deal with only a part of it in this volume. To be precise, I concern myself with the validity of Derrida's criticism of Saussure, and with what I call the 'textual mysticism' that his work has induced in later critics; I also discuss the strange philosophy I have called 'linguistic and discursive idealism', which seems to me to be found in many Anglo-American critics of the 1970s and 1980s, though they called themselves materialists. This philosophy, in which almost magical powers of world and mind-construction are supposed to be possessed by language, has often, absurdly, been attributed to Saussure; one of the later chapters of this book tries to show that it is false in itself, and has nothing to do with him.

I also make some positive suggestions both about the treatment of language and that of literature. I suggest that there are exciting lines of empirical, rather than metaphysical, enquiry in investigating the way in which complex concepts are built up in language, and the way in which a systematic underlying picture of the world is revealed by studying the structure of standard metaphors in a language. I suggest that a broadly realist philosophical framework is far more useful than contemporary relativism both for the empirical study of language and of literature. It offers a better account of the relationship between language and thought; and a better account of the nature of complex and half-material objects like works of literature. I even suggest that there are some merits in an objective functional theory of literary value.

The second book in this sequence, entitled provisionally, *The Dematerialisation of Karl Marx*, discusses the Marxist foundations of modern theory; it argues for the permanent value of the materialist and scientific elements of Marxist theory for cultural explanation; and the obsolescence of the rest of that theory, including all the revolutionary part. It claims that most modern theory on the Left is what Marx would have called idealist; as such, it is intellectually inadequate to explain the phenomena, objectively reactionary and, paradoxically, partly responsible for the triumph of right-wing regimes. The third book: provisionally called *Making Freud Unscientific*, discusses the Freudian foundations of modern theory; it argues for the value of certain Freudian theories as parts of scientific psychological explanations of cultural phenomena; against the tendency to reformulate Freud in unscientific, non-objective ways: humanistic,

Heideggerian, Lacanian, or whatever; and against the tendency to see him, within literary theory, merely as one more text to be set against all the other texts.

The books are written for two audiences: undergraduate and general readers who wish to know what claims structuralist theories and some post-structuralist theories have made; and specialists who are prepared to consider some of the arguments against those claims. I hope that the second group will not be put off by the fact that I have written in plain English, with supporting explanations also in plain English of any material in linguistics or philosophy that may be required. It is sometimes argued that merely to write about modern theory in clear language shows a fundamental incomprehension of its significance, and an ideological bias into the bargain. Obviously, I don't believe this: it strikes me as élitist bullying. In any case, literary theory is really a bundle of specialisms; the linguists don't understand the philosophers, the philosophers don't understand the linguists, and nobody understands Jacques Lacan. We ought to be engaged in co-operative attempts to understand each others' specialities, not in overtrumping each other.

So I have tried throughout to write in language which a first-year undergraduate will understand, while presenting arguments about the history of structuralism, about language and linguistics, about representations of meaning and about the reality of abstract objects like languages, works of literature (and even in one case the objects of mathematics) that I think a specialist ought to take seriously. After all, it is always open to the specialist to translate these arguments into language difficult enough for him to understand; the non-specialist cannot make the opposite translation.

The introduction gives a summary of the book, in a greatly simplified and rather overgeneralized form, and without qualifications, supporting arguments, explanations, or references. These are all to be found in the body of the book. There is also a brief summary of its argument at the beginning of each chapter and a very short reading list for beginners at each chapter end.

Men and movements

Some of the lines of connection between the ideas underlying contemporary literary theory

In the early twentieth century, the following five intellectual movements were fairly separate: German idealism, Marxism; phenomenology and existential phenomenology; psychoanalysis; and linguistics-based structuralism. In the 1950s and 1960s in France, they came together in an inextricable knot often called, misleadingly, French structuralism.

What is called 'post-structuralism' is, I think, a complex response to the failure of these five movements to cohere into a single philosophical framework and general theory of the human sciences. The response is to argue that we cannot have such general theories: they self-destruct; they exist only through the imposition of structure and the suppression of dissenting voices. This view can lead to an extreme relativism and perspectivism.

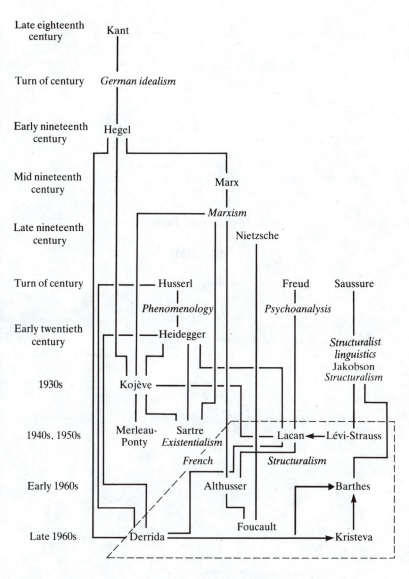

Late eighteenth century	Kant
Turn of century	*German idealism*
Early nineteenth century	Hegel
Mid nineteenth century	Marx
Late nineteenth century	*Marxism* — Nietzsche
Turn of century	Husserl — Freud — Saussure
	Phenomenology — *Psychoanalysis*
Early twentieth century	Heidegger — *Structuralist linguistics*
	Jakobson — *Structuralism*
1930s	Kojève
1940s, 1950s	Merleau-Ponty — Sartre — Lacan ← Lévi-Strauss
	Existentialism
	French — *Structuralism*
Early 1960s	Althusser — Barthes
Late 1960s	Derrida — Foucault — Kristeva
1970s, 1980s	'*Post-structuralism*' – otherwise post-phenomenology, post-Freudianism, post-Marxism

To

My Beloved Family

LJ   IMJ

and

EJ

Introduction
From Social Science to Textual Mysticism and Back: the World of Modern Theory

1. THE FOUNDATIONS OF MODERN THEORY IN MARX, FREUD AND SAUSSURE AND THE POVERTY OF THE STRUCTURALIST MODEL

Modern literary theory is very strange. If we went by the standards that normally apply to theories in the sciences and in philosophy we would expect theories of literature to be attempts, within the framework of ordinary rational argument, to explain how poems, plays and stories work: why they have the linguistic structures they do, what their psychological effects are and what relations they have to society and history. And we would expect some attempt to make these theories self-consistent and consistent with the evidence. To our surprise – certainly to mine – we find that much of modern theory isn't like that. In scientific terms it makes no sense and doesn't explain anything. Or, to put the point more politely, much of it is a domain of conscious paradox which eschews reductive and mechanistic explanations, and it looks very odd by comparison not just with chemistry or physics, but with academic psychology, say, or linguistics, or philosophical logic. Sometimes, indeed, it makes quite radical criticisms of these sciences and of the framework of rationality in which they are argued. It sees this rationality as an expression of Western capitalism, or Western metaphysics, or of the name of the father – of patriarchy. Literary theory thus becomes an alternative metaphysics, or an alternative to metaphysics, or an oppositional ideology. That is why it is so popular.

My purpose in *Foundations of Modern Literary Theory* is to trace how such theory developed in a philosophical re-reading of Marxism, psychoanalysis and structuralism; to discuss some of the claims that it makes; and to ask whether it actually offers a better account of

1

literature (or metaphysics) than more realist, materialist and commonsensical theories do. Most theorists will have little doubt on this score. The philosophical sophistication of modern theory – the way it draws on Nietzsche, on Heidegger, on Derrida – is seen as one of its major titles to respect. By comparison with the conceptual framework of the modern theorist, that of the traditional literary critic seems almost Neanderthal: an inherited set of emotive grunts. That is why modern theorists devote little attention to the passionate objections of traditional critics: what is the point of trying to refute a grunt? I am going to argue, however, that underlying traditional literary criticism is a sophisticated realist and materialist theory of the world; while much modern textual theory is idealist textual mysticism, aimed at evading serious intellectual or political problems.

Here is a brief and rather tendentious account of my position. The modern theory that I am concerned with developed in France in the 1950s and the 1960s out of a rethinking of the ideas of Karl Marx, of Sigmund Freud and of Ferdinand de Saussure. It became the ideology of a marginal group of intellectuals, poised somewhere between a very large Stalinist Communist party and an even larger bourgeoisie. It developed under the intellectual influence of French philosophy of the subject – drawing on the ideas of Husserl and Heidegger and in tension with those of Merleau-Ponty and Sartre. Under the misleadingly limited name 'structuralism' it briefly succeeded existentialism as a group of popular philosophies; and when the structuralist model collapsed in about 1967, a variety of post-structuralisms succeeded it and were exported to marginal and lonely literary intellectuals all over the world. Hence our present discontents.

Like all capsule accounts this one oversimplifies and misses the variety and complexity of what went on. The word 'developed' is in many ways too weak to capture the process of creative transformation in which Marx, Freud and Saussure were turned into their own opposites. The modern left-wing theorist is more likely to be influenced by Michel Foucault – and therefore, ultimately, by Nietzsche – than he is by Karl Marx; he is more interested in theorizing the way in which 'power' produces 'knowledge' than in class conflict or the influence of the economy. The modern Lacanian, though often immensely scholarly in using Freud's original papers, is utterly remote in spirit from the scientific, mechanistic and biological orientation of Freud. And the real Saussure has wholly disappeared behind an idealist philosopher of language retrospectively constructed for their own purposes by the Tel Quel group and Jacques Derrida.

But although they have been transformed, these great originals have not been left behind. It is a mark of modern theory that the major contributors – Jacques Lacan in psychoanalysis, Louis Althusser for Marxism, Jacques Derrida for textual anti-theory – have tended to be commentators. They re-read the sacred texts rather than refute them. So in the most advanced modern theories, the original categories of Marxism, psychoanalysis and linguistics pop up to subvert our conclusions. The ghosts of Marx, Freud and Saussure haunt modern theory saying: 'That is not what I meant at all!' When a modern theorist calls himself a materialist, the ghost of Marx says indignantly: 'I was talking about the economy.' When a modern Lacanian gives a presentation, the ghost of Freud protests: 'This is unscientific gibberish.' And whenever I read Derrida's book, *Of Grammatology*, I hear the ghost of Saussure howling 'Liar!'

The thesis that I want to advance in this book is in some ways a defence of Marx, Freud and Saussure against their modern followers. I argue that the theories of all three have great merits, as well as great weaknesses, and that something like them is necessary if ever we are to have a theory of literature of real explanatory power. But in the development of modern literary theory the merits of these thinkers have been dropped and the weaknesses built upon. And this is a consequence of the fact that modern literary theory does not in general aim at offering explanations of how literature works. It offers instead large, cloudy, negative ideological aspirations. It offers critiques of capitalism, and Western metaphysics, and patriarchy, and of the very possibility of reading. It metaphorically removes the ground from beneath our feet in every area of bourgeois intellectual life – a dizzying sensation and rather pleasant when you get used to it. But it does not explain anything.

Marx, Freud and Saussure had one important thing in common. They all thought themselves to be scientists. Marx thought that he had put socialism on a scientific basis; Freud thought he had done the same for psychology; Saussure attempted to provide a scientific basis for the study of language – and, more generally, of signs. In the development of modern theory out of the work of these three the main thing that has been lost – lost round about 1967 actually – is the scientific intention. It seems to have been agreed that we cannot hope, and should not try, for scientific theories of culture. No sufficient grounds have ever been given for this view, but it flows naturally enough from certain 'revolutionary' or therapeutic aims, or from the predominance of certain kinds of philosophy: the philosophy of Heidegger, for example. Walter Biemel puts the point succinctly, in his book *Martin*

Heidegger (1973): the term 'explanation' 'may safely be left to refer to the activity of grasping natural processes'. There is here a principled opposition to the very idea of explanatory theory when applied to human beings; this opposition lives on in much modern work and is often expressed at a high theoretical level. I, however, find it fundamentally superstitious: a remnant of a prescientific world view.

In this book I assume that one of the things we want literary theory to do is to offer more or less scientific explanations of literature as a phenomenon in the world; and that these explanations do not hinder and may actually help our understanding of particular works of literature. I don't take this point for granted, but argue it at many stages in the book. And I argue also that certain central elements in the work of Marx, Freud and Saussure – possibly in a changed or updated form – play an essential part in cultural explanation. We can't do without them.

Thus the central element in Marx's theory, in my view, is his historical materialism: his picture of human society as based on the forces and relations of production – i.e. on how material things are produced and who controls this. It leads to explanations of high culture as a reflection, and also as an integral part, of economic processes, and to analysis of cultural artefacts in terms of the light they throw on these processes. We can't, in my view, do without this mode of explanation and the corresponding mode of analysis, so we need Marx's theory of historical materialism even if we reject his views on revolution as romantic nonsense. (Typically, however, it is historical materialism that the modern left has moved away from, while retaining a quite unfounded affection for the language of imaginary revolutions. The modern 'materialist' is often somebody who believes the class struggle is a contest over the control of the production of new meanings for literary texts. This point is examined in volume II: *The Dematerialisation of Karl Marx*.)

The central element of Freudian theory is its account of the dynamic effects of the unconscious: of the way in which repressed processes in the unconscious emerge, in a transformed way, in forms varying from neuroses and slips of the tongue to dreams. It leads to explanations of literary production and response as the outcome of similar processes. These are among the oldest literary applications of these theories, but seem to me to remain indispensable, at least while scientific explanations of cultural phenomena are what we are looking for.

It doesn't do to reply to this, as some critics will: 'I am not interested in scientific explanation, which is reductive and dry, but with interpretations of texts, which are rich and exciting: my purpose is hermeneutic rather than scientific.' As with Marx, so with Freud, we find that there is no competition between looking for explanations and looking for cultural or textual analyses. On the contrary, they reinforce each other. It is because we have an explanation of literary production in terms of unconscious processes that we are justified in analysing particular works in terms of their unconscious contents.

Typically, however, the modern tendency has been away from scientific psychoanalysis toward a humanistic, phenomenological, existential or Lacanian type; and modern critics see Freud or Lacan as offering not explanatory theories, but just texts, to be set in contrast to literary texts. One is bound to ask 'What is the theoretical point of contrasting one arbitrary set of texts, which happen to be by Freud, with another arbitrary set, which happen to be called literature?'. The point seems to be to contest the very notion of 'theory' in this area; and I examine this contest in volume III: *Making Freud Unscientific*.

The major figure in this volume is Saussure. The central element in his theory was his conception of a language (*langue*) as a structured system, which underlies any particular use-of-that-language (*parole*), whether in speech or writing. A second element is the essential arbitrariness of the relationship between the sounds of language and the concepts that those sounds express (the fact that there is nothing pig-like about the word 'pig', for example). He calls this 'the arbitrariness of the sign'. Other elements include the distinction between the historical (or *diachronic*) study of language change and the (*synchronic*) study of its internal structure at a particular time; the distinction between the *syntagmatic* axis of language, by which signs are chained together, and what he calls the *associative* axis by which each sign recalls numerous others which are not present; and the systems of oppositions between sounds and oppositions between concepts, which help to limit the arbitrariness of the sign. Saussure's model of language was enormously influential in twentieth-century linguistics and retained some influence up to the mid-1950s, when structuralist models were superseded by Chomsky's generative grammar.

It is clear, with hindsight, and it was already pretty clear to Jakobson in the 1940s, that there are quite fundamental weaknesses in the Saussurean model of language: weaknesses so severe that we can say, merely by inspecting that model, that it is logically impossible that it should provide an adequate theory of human languages. I call weaknesses of this very fundamental kind, '**Logical Poverty**'. As a consequence of its logical poverty, it was impossible for the structuralist model of language to be satisfactory in the other areas, like anthropology, psychoanalysis, etc., for which it would be used in France. The weaknesses are these: Saussure's model has an inadequate conception of syntax; it has a confused notion of its fundamental category, the sign; and above all, it is conceived as a 'system of pure oppositions with no positive terms'. On this view, signifiers like the sound pattern of the word 'cat' only have meaning by contrast with other signifiers like the sound pattern of the word 'dog'. We cut up what would otherwise be a vague conceptual field of cogs into cats and dogs because we have the signifiers for them. This theory sounds attractive to some, but there are quite simple arguments to show that it is a logical impossibility for any working sign system.

We can show that at the level of syntax, the structuralist model can't account for the structural relationship between active sentences and passive ones, or questions and the corresponding answers; at the level of semantics it can't account for the meaning of simple words like 'aunt' and 'uncle'. I call this inadequacy 'the logical poverty of structuralist theory', or 'the poverty of structuralism' for short. (Typically, radical literary theorists have tended to reject the indispensable parts of structuralist theory, such as the *langue/parole* distinction, and have tried to build upon the parts that can be proved not to work, such as the notion of language as a system of pure oppositions. They have also questioned the very idea – central to Saussure's intentions – of having a 'science' of language.)

2   THE DEVELOPMENT OF THE STRUCTURALIST MOVEMENT AND ITS AFTERMATH

The argument I put in this volume is that structuralism was a rational research strategy, but was fatally flawed by the logical inadequacies of the structuralist model of language: what I call 'the poverty of structuralism' renders it, in my view, finally incapable of giving an adequate account of human language, let alone providing an adequate analogical model for other human sciences or for literary theory. But it might well be that a more adequate formal model – something like the transformational-generative model of language, or, more likely, some formal model more specific to society or the mind – might actually work. I make no judgement on this. The last thing I would want to do is to make inferences from the impracticability of the structuralist programme, to the impracticability of scientific theories of culture in general.

The various post-structuralisms, on the other hand, have always contained elements of irrationalism, aggressive paradox, textual mysticism, linguistic idealism and infantile leftism in Lenin's sense of the phrase, though this is not the whole story about them. The logical poverty of the model of language they sometimes adopt is the least of their demerits. I would therefore criticize structuralism and the various post-structuralisms on different grounds and see the former as redeemable into a practical research programme, while the latter remain mere philosophical gestures. I explain this rather summary account below and of course I give it in more detail, with supporting arguments, in the body of the book.

The first concern of this volume is to discuss the stream of ideas that flowed from Saussure: an intellectual movement which can be labelled semiological structuralism. Structuralism can be defined for our purposes as the attempt to apply the structuralist model of language, developed by Saussure and others at the beginning of the twentieth century, to the human sciences in general. Semiology, or semiotics, is a putative science of signs which might in principle extend to the whole of human culture, so far as that is seen as being based on an exchange of meanings. Structuralism and semiology are not identical: it is possible to have a theory of signs that is not based on the structuralist model of language. But historically they have been intertwined. Semiological structuralism is an appropriate name for a science of signs based on the structuralist model of language and that is my main topic here.

I begin by giving an account of what Saussure's model of language was. I am afraid the teaching of Saussure in many English departments today is rather unreliable. Often the original text of the *Course in General Linguistics* is not read, either in French or English; and the secondary sources used read back into the Saussure of around 1910 positions which were actually invented in Paris in the 1950s and 1960s. The history of ideas is thus distorted. The reason for this, I think, is a fundamental hostility to the science of linguistics itself and to any scientific or empirical approach to language. This is an attitude which can be documented for a wide range of critics from Leavisites to post-Marxists. They prefer to treat language from the point of view of a T.S. Eliot, a Mallarmé, a Heidegger or a Lacan, rather than a Bloomfield or a Chomsky; and the reading they give of Saussure puts him much closer to the former than to the latter group. My account in chapter 1 is concerned with the real Saussure; I discuss the new improved Saussure and the philosophy of linguistic idealism which he is held to support, later in the book.

I argue that, just as the theories of Marx and Freud contain elements of truth which are an essential part of any scientific sociology or psychology, so there are elements of truth about Saussure's model of human language which are necessary parts of any scientific linguistics. One cannot in scientific linguistics do without functional equivalents of the concepts of *langue* and *parole*, or synchronic and diachronic study, or, greatly revised, what Saussure called the syntagmatic and associative axes of language. One probably can't do without the phoneme – which in my view Saussure did describe, though there are proposals, which I touch on in the Appendix, for taking this discovery away from him.

One can manage, curiously enough, without a concept of the sign, as combination of signifier and signified. This is Saussure's most famous contribution, but is actually a very confusing category. It has played little part in Anglo-American linguistics, though a great one in continental linguistics. I think myself it should be dropped.

The extension of the Saussurean model of language to other realms, such as literature and mythology, was authorized by Saussure himself in his concept of semiology; and I would argue that it was a perfectly sensible research strategy at the time, however unhopeful it looks nowadays. It might well have been the case, as Jakobson and Tynjanov hoped in 1928, that one could usefully extend the concept of *langue* to literature and begin to derive both synchronic and diachronic laws of literature. Prague School structuralism of the 1930s is clearly one of the major theoretical schools of the twentieth century and should be recognized as such. It is described briefly in chapter 2 of this book, along with a few of the developments that took place in the structuralist model of language in the 1920s and 1930s and are described by Jakobson in 1942.

Structuralism became French when Claude Lévi-Strauss, the anthropologist, attended Roman Jakobson's lectures on linguistics in 1942. Lévi-Strauss was so impressed that he spent most of the 1940s trying to make anthropology scientific by modelling it on structuralist linguistics. French psychoanalysis, in which Freud had already been re-read in Hegelian and Heideggerian ways by Jacques Lacan, picked up some Saussurean terminology in 1953; though Lacan's structuralism, in my view, never went any deeper than that. Other famous figures of the 1960s, like the Marxist theoretician Louis Althusser and the historian of ideas Michel Foucault, were labelled 'structuralists' without having been influenced by structural linguistics at all. By this stage the label was a journalistic one and had lost the precise sense it has when one speaks of 'structuralist linguistics'. Hence the period is confusing. I try to sort out some of this confusion in chapter 3.

The really exciting thing that was happening at this stage was the attempt to replace philosophies like Sartre's existentialism, as accounts of the human world, by an austerely scientific 'structuralist' philosophy, calling on the anthropology of Lévi-Strauss, the psychoanalysis of Lacan, the rethought Marxism of Althusser and so on. The general idea was that human subjectivity would turn out to be not something coherent and central, as humanists supposed, but a consequence or side-effect of the 'structures' studied by these disciplines. For this purpose it was necessary to rethink, or rather reconstruct, Saussure as a philosopher of language, stressing precisely the weaker, logically inadequate side of his model of language as a system of pure oppositions in order to do so. The new Saussure, as Jonathan Culler points out, offers better evidence for the unconscious than Freud does. It is, however, naturally Lacan's much-revised linguistically structured version of the Freudian unconscious that this imaginary philosopher advocates (see chapter 3).

The high structuralist project collapsed with great speed. By 1968 it would have been hard to find anybody who thought it possible to provide a formal structural theory of the human subject. Some of the most influential criticism of the project came from Jacques Derrida; I discuss his critique of Lévi-Strauss. The new improved Saussure was now a pillar of the structuralist project; Derrida produced an influential critique of him as well. If we accept that the structuralist project effectively collapsed in 1967, then the whole French structuralist period was actually quite short. There were, however, those who never abandoned the label 'structuralist', or who went on writing within this paradigm. Lévi-Strauss was the most important of them. He did, however, in the 1970s, abandon his scientific claims (see chapter 3).

The most important structuralist literary critic, and one of the most important critics in modern France, was Roland Barthes, one of the founders of French semiology. By taking a look at his career as a whole, it is possible to see how a man could begin as a conventional literary critic, cultural journalist and theorist, with no particular knowledge of linguistics; could then read Saussure and other linguists and, in what he later described as a 'dream of scientificity', attempt to engage in empirical investigations in structuralist semiology – for example, a very thorough investigation of the language of fashion magazines; could then, under the influence of Derrida, Kristeva, and others, repudiate and mock the scientific goal and move, on the one hand, into a very personal belles-lettres-ism and on the other, into a mysticism of the text that rejects any form of systematic empirical enquiry. The journalistic term 'post-structuralist' has no uniform sense; but it must apply at least to Roland Barthes, who once called himself a structuralist and now had moved beyond that (see chapter 4).

Structuralism and 'post-structuralism' were exported to Britain and America in the 1960s, travelling in the same ships; they have never been sorted out since, despite having quite opposite characteristics. Jacques Derrida is the name most people think of when confronted with the word 'post-structuralism'. Yet it would be an inaccurate term for him: he was never a structuralist and his relation to structuralism was always an external and critical one. What Derrida is is a post-phenomenologist. That is to say, he is a philosopher who has developed a powerful method of internal critique in the philosophical sub-tradition of which Edmund Husserl and Martin Heidegger are the culmination. The method is a way of reading texts – not necessarily philosophical ones – which to my taste is all too easily successful in finding a 'metaphysics of presence' creeping in everywhere. Certainly Derrida found it in the new improved Saussure, thus proving that structuralism and phenomenology were fruit of the same tree: I examine this argument in chapter 5.

Derridan 'deconstruction' is a philosophical practice in which the rhetorical features of texts – the precise terms and metaphors used for example – are examined and shown, often by rhetorical techniques that resemble those of modernist writing, to undermine the texts' intended meaning and reference. Philosophers are divided about this technique; some think it simply a licence for bad arguments and rhetorical self-display, while others appear to be entirely taken over by it, treating it as the method by which to revalue the entire history of philosophy. My own concern with it is a limited one; I criticize one or two early arguments, particularly associated with Saussure. Derrida's deconstructive method has been widely adapted, particularly in America, by literary critics; my own view is that what it produces in them is, just as in the case of Barthes, an aggressive textual mysticism, rather at odds with the special kind of rigour characteristic of Derrida's earlier philosophy, though congruent enough with his later extravagant practices of writing.

3   THE NEW LINGUISTIC 'PHILOSOPHY' OF THE 1970s

In Britain in the 1970s the new criticism was domesticated into a kind of radical orthodoxy, best represented perhaps by the Coward and Ellis textbook *Language and Materialism*. Here Roland Barthes coalesced with Althusser, Lacan, Kristeva and Derrida to provide a blueprint for the new revolution: the production of a revolutionary human subject, by way of a revolution of the word. I have added, to represent this period, something from Tony Bennett and an influential statement of Kristeva; but thousands of examples could have been given, for we are dealing with a time when a politically radicalized post-structuralism became the common dialect.

Bliss was it in that mid-morning coffee-break to be alive, if you were a literary theorist and did not think it an absurd project to smash capitalism now. But to know any linguistics was merry hell, for at the heart of the new theory was an outrageously silly philosophy of language. I call this philosophy linguistic or discursive idealism. Its central claim appears to be that there is no language-independent reality; reality, or our reality at any rate, is linguistic through and through; our concepts of it are limited by, or are a product of our language. Ideas such as this have been common in twentieth-century thought and were now received uncritically: as if they were revelatory and new and yet needed no particular backing from evidence. On my view, what this philosophy does is to replay many of the claims of nineteenth-century idealism – that the world is a mental or ideal construct – replacing the notions of 'the mind' and 'ideas' with the notions of 'language' and 'discourse'. But the same arguments that hold against traditional idealism hold against the new linguistic or discursive form of idealism.

The new philosophy was attached to what was, for anybody who had recently been doing linguistics in Britain, an ancient and august name: Ferdinand de Saussure. Actually, as one can see from reading Coward and Ellis or Bennett, it had a composite relationship to Saussure. Some of it came from the weaker side of his model, that I have characterized as exhibiting 'logical poverty': the notion of a semantics of pure oppositions. It was genuine Saussure, but it was Saussure when he was plainly wrong. Some of it had nothing to do with Saussure; it was an illusion about what he thought. And some of it was a bold attempt to correct Saussure – often in a Lysenkoist spirit because his political line was supposed to be wrong – on occasions when he was plainly right. All of it, however, appeared to have been constructed in willed ignorance of the not inconsiderable work on language recently done by generative grammarians and some philosophers of language.

There is something very strange about this. If you look at language from a purely scientific point of view, Saussure and Chomsky belong to the same history, the history of linguistics; and the whole work of Saussure had been incorporated into linguistic theory, developed, and partially superseded by the time Chomsky gave that history its next decisive turn. For a theorist of language to go back from the theories of Chomsky to those of Saussure is as odd as if a chemist, writing in an age when cylinders of liquid oxygen are regularly sold, were to reject the theory that fire involves combination with oxygen and go back to the eighteenth-century theory that it involves the loss of a mythical substance called phlogiston. Or to put the point more strongly still: if literary theorists were interested in scientific questions about language they could no more return from Chomsky to Saussure than NASA could rely on pre-Galilean dynamics for calculating rocket trajectories.

What sort of 'scientific question about language' could a literary theorist be interested in? Well, one might ask what goes on when one reads a novel. From one point of view, it is a massively complex, but extraordinarily uniform and reliable process of perception and of cognitive transformation. Ask a million people to read the novels of Ian Fleming and they will all agree, confronted with these black marks on paper, that they have been reading about the adventures of a secret agent called James Bond. People sometimes say, very foolishly, that there is no kind of agreement about works of literature; but in fact there is massive and unanimous agreement, except on trivial points of interpretation and evaluation. You simply don't get a case where 50 per cent of the readers think they have been reading about the history of Tittlebats and the rest think they have been studying a hire-purchase schedule. They all recognize what they have read as a novel about James Bond and most of them could give you some account of the story.

The problem of explaining this remarkable and nearly universal skill is actually beyond the powers of natural science at the present time. The combined resources of cognitive psychology, artificial intelligence research using computer simulations, and generative linguistics (the three most promising contributory sciences) are not enough to produce convincing hypotheses about what psychological mechanisms the reader of a book uses to work out the plot from the words on the page. (At least, they weren't enough when I last looked.) But it is safe to say that nobody is going to propose going back to Hartleian associationist psychology, clockwork robots and Saussurean structuralism. What cognitive scientists will do is to go on, beyond present concepts in grammar, psychology and AI, in explaining the mechanisms of language use and in particular in explaining how language is used to build up complex concepts: reading a book, whether fact or fiction, is in my view merely a special case of this very general cognitive linguistic process. We have here potentially a progressive scientific research programme; and the mystery of mysteries is why more literary theorists are not interested in it.

What is marked about the radical literary theorist, however, is a massive and intellectually philistine lack of interest in any questions of this kind. In their attitude to language, the shiny new literary theorists are often like the old literary critics writ large. They are not interested in the banal workings of ordinary sentences, as studied by the grammarian or psycholinguist; but in what is strange, different, mystical or philosophical and can be used to underpin an oppositional world view. The revival of Saussure is not then the revival of an obsolete science. It is a gesture against science – against the whole mode of understanding that science represents. So Saussure emerges, not as an obsolete scientist, but as a magical philosopher: a philosopher who explains how language, on the basis of a few simple oppositions, can create a psyche and a world.

I argue here that language probably does play an important, even an essential part, in the way we construct and represent complex concepts, and that certain features of our vocabulary give an insight into underlying metaphorical structures of thought; but that is as far as we can go. Language is not a theory of reality nor an epitome of a culture, nor a mode of being; at best it is an instrument of thought. If we find ourselves attributing mystical or political properties to it, that is because we are projecting on to it properties that really belong to the messages it is used to convey, or to the art that is produced in it, or to its social context: as one might find Jacobean English religious in flavour because it is the language of the Bible, or as the upper classes used to find Cockney a vulgar dialect, because they found Cockneys vulgar people. Language for me is fundamentally an instrument, the workings of which should be approached in the same spirit as we describe a car engine; it would for me be a wonderful thing if we could provide a scientific description of what goes on when one asks for a cup of coffee to be passed, and I discuss briefly some of the fearsome complexities that I think are involved in that difficult feat.

Chapter 6 has then two purposes. In parts of it I try to sort out what bits of his 'philosophy' Saussure may reasonably have been supposed to believe. But most of the chapter is concerned with substantive issues: that is, what claims about the relationships between our language, the concepts we use and reality may reasonably be supposed to be true. The point is important; on my reckoning about half of modern literary theory rests on general claims about language, discourses and texts. These claims are usually not formalized as a full philosophy; they are, rather, scattered about in the course of arguments on other subjects. The Bennett, Kristeva and Coward and Ellis extracts illustrate this: I have put them in chapter 7 after the general discussion of language in chapter 6 to give them some context.

4   A REALIST ALTERNATIVE TO CONTEMPORARY RELATIVISM

The final chapter of this book is an attempt to show that there is a rational alternative to the type of theory now generally on offer. What I am arguing is that literary theory, like scientific enquiry, is best pursued within a framework of philosophical realism: that is, on the assumption that we are investigating the properties of real entities. In my view there are ways of making this position as intelligible for *Hamlet* as it is for a table or chair, though the conditions of existence are not quite the same for *Hamlet* as for a table or a chair. What I am arguing against is the extreme relativism and idealism which is characteristic of present-day literary theory and is often tacitly supported by the absurd linguistic philosophy discussed in chapter 6.

It seems to me that much contemporary theory – not all, but enough of it to be worth criticizing – can be described as a combination of textual mysticism and radical chic, based on a very curious counter-metaphysics. A major part of this theory is a mystique of the text. 'Text' in literary studies ought to be a neutral word that refers to the poems, plays and novels that we study without presupposing any particular method of study or special metaphysical status. The mystical concept of textual theory derives from writers like the later Barthes, Derrida and De Man. It expresses itself at the anthology level in titles like *Textual Strategies, Untying the Text, The Question of Textuality* – good anthologies these, I am not criticizing them. Its principles can be found, not so much in a worked out, systematic form – that would be difficult – but in *obiter dicta*, thrown off, often with a fine sense of brave paradox, by post-structuralist critics in their flight: as Catherine Belsey throws off a remark about meanings being an effect of interpretation in the course of a short book on Milton (Belsey 1988).

The theory has as its central principle how terribly difficult it is to read a book: difficult, that is, not because the language or the subject matter happens to be difficult, but in some fundamental, metaphysical way that springs from the nature of textuality itself. It makes unlikely claims about the nature of literary meaning, arguing that meanings are indeterminate products of interpretation, rather than pre-existing public constraints upon it: as if the word 'boy' can easily mean 'girl' if we work hard enough at it; or as if *Paradise Lost* could readily be interpreted as a realist novel of the Glasgow slums. It argues that texts inhabit a vast and essentially unspecifiable intertextuality; this is both more and less than the commonplace point that they make allusions to other texts and partly have to be understood in terms of other texts. It argues that human subjectivity itself is a side-effect of textuality; this would be a very bookish conception if it was meant as a theory of human psychology and presumably 'textuality' here is a metaphor: but for what? It argues that texts create worlds rather than refer to them, since there is no real world outside the text and independent of any text to refer to. This last claim if it is literally made (and otherwise, what does the metaphor mean?) is a pure linguistic or discursive idealism; and it makes 'textuality' or 'writing' into alternative names for God.

I call these doctrines 'textual mysticism', because it becomes apparent that something larger is in question than an attempt to determine the approximate meaning of the actual texts of particular books in particular historical contexts by ordinary processes of research. The text has become a figure for something like 'meaningful human experience' or 'life'. Despite the strenuously anti-metaphysical gestures of its founders, the true attraction of this position is a philosophical or even a religious one (see chapter 5).

This approach is taken to its limit in a clear and amusing article by Danto (1989), who actually manages to incorporate natural science (and, *a fortiori*, every possible empirical study) inside textual theory. He argues that while the content of natural science is highly unstable, the criteria of a good theory are not; these form part of a world of human understanding and intellectual hanging-togetherness figured by the text. Textual theory thus offers the pattern of a future metaphysics that will be queen of the sciences again. This is literally what Danto predicts; one can see why textual theory is becoming so popular if it offers the promise of a universal knowledge; if the student who has failed O-level physics can get an insight into all the sciences with the aid of Literary Theory.

This gorgeous metaphysics is founded on the work of anti-metaphysicians. The aim of the philosopher Jacques Derrida in his early works was slightly less than Danto's because it was negative: it was to shake the entire metaphysical structure of Western thought. Before him, Jacques Lacan the psychoanalyst had done something similar with a new reading of Freud that casts doubt on the very capacity of the ego for rational negotiation with reality: psychoanalysis extended from a psychological theory into a philosophical position that offers no place for rationality: a kind of surrealist epistemology. In turn, the procedures of historical analysis stemming from the work of Michel Foucault offer different forms of rationality in different historical periods: rationality becomes a historical construct, an effect of power structures and so forth. The modern critic drawing upon such sources as these and surpassing them, can really feel that he is shaking the intellectual ground beneath our feet. Here is something much more radical than a merely political revolution; and all achieved by a new style of *explication de texte*.

There are obvious objections to this style of radicalism. The traditional Marxist objection would be that it is idealist. That is to say, it aims to transform systems of ideas first, in the hope, presumably, that the economic and political structure of society will be transformed by them. It makes revolutions in the head, or at least in discourse. This of course makes it attractive to literary intellectuals, who are very much better at transforming the way we see the world than they are at transforming the actual world. My objection is that it is unscientific in areas where it is possible to be scientific, and it commits us to scientific and philosophical theories – of language, of the mind, of society, of the material world, of knowledge and even of value – that are inherently implausible and not supported by the facts.

In many areas – linguistics and psychology, for example – I don't see an answer to these objections. But there is a standard answer to them in the woollier social sciences and in literary theory, and it is an idealist answer. It is that in social reality the facts themselves are constituted in discourse. Literature, for example, is what critical discourse constitutes as literature; there is no literary reality, independent of critical discourse, to study. This has the advantage that the revolutions that are within our power are the very ones needed to change the realities we are interested in. I can abolish Shakespeare if only I can get him off the bloody syllabus. There is no independent Shakespearian cultural fact.

A typical relativist claim is that of Catherine Belsey here quoted, that 'meanings are an effect of interpretation, not its origin'. What is wrong with this as a general principle will be evident from the counter-examples I have given already: or from the fact that no effort of interpretation will enable us to read *Paradise Lost* fluently as the story of Cathy and Heathcliff, or, let's say, as a catalogue of spare parts for IBM-compatible personal computers. These readings are eliminated by preconscious linguistic and cognitive processes which Belsey and other critics of this persuasion simply leave untheorized. I argue that this claim is false and not only false, but incoherent: the very concept of interpretation only makes sense on the assumption that there are some meanings that exist prior to interpretation. In practice, interpretation is always based on pre-existing codes of meaning and could not be carried out if there were no such codes. Deconstructive arguments can of course readily be devised which shake assumptions like these; but one cannot coherently even state the opposite assumption.

Most relativist claims about literature, when made clear, seem to me to collapse in the way this one does; they presuppose a tacit objective understanding of the world and the critic herself which the critic is merely pretending not to notice. If one turns one's attention to describing this tacit understanding (and this is very much what the original structuralist project was attempting to do) it is possible to extend realist and objectivist theories a long way; though obviously not to the point where one is offering objective theories about the totality of culture – including one's own attempts to theorize. But there is no reason to think that the idea of formulating partial objective scientific theories of human cultures is exploded or absurd, however distasteful some may find it.

The puzzle is why anybody should find it distasteful. Why is there this absurd campaign to show that there is something nasty in the idea of formulating objective scientific theories about human beings? That the very idea of objective theory is racist, imperialist, and sexist, as well as being logocentric? I have heard it put as axiomatic that the desire for objective theory in sociology is an expression of a will to power over people: though in fact all knowledge confers power and non-objective, intimate, I–thou knowledge of the kind a mother has of her child, or a husband of his wife, can be used for quite desperate oppression. There seems to be no objective basis for the notion that objectivity is oppressive; any more than there is truth in the claim that truth is a product of power. These ideas are, rather, parts of a general oppositional stance towards an advanced industrial capitalist society, in which the discourses of science and engineering have a triumphal and central role, while those of the humanities are marginal and ineffective. They could even be seen as a counter-attack by a relatively unsuccessful group of intellectuals upon the ideology of a much more successful group: a radical politics and a radical anti-metaphysics go hand in ghostly hand into this sham battle.

So it is a curious, but undeniable and by no means incomprehensible fact that in the last twenty years literary theory has been very largely professed by people who do not wish to construct scientific or objective theories of literature or anything else. Some of them have devoted enormous ingenuity to constructing arguments to show that such theories are in principle impossible; and that those who propose them are naïve. Since the waning of the class war of the 1970s, much recent theoretical discourse has been a triumphal celebration of the impossibility of theory. As a literary intellectual, however, I am something of a traitor to my class. I find in both the radical politics and the radical anti-metaphysics that have dominated modern theory something profoundly oppressive and profoundly unliberating; as well as a great deal of wishful thinking.

I find hope in the development of modern science: not just for its great interest in itself, but as a model for rational unoppressive thinking about the world, to which current literary theory has nothing to contribute, but from which it might well learn. We might conceive it as the goal of literary theory to investigate the objective relationships of literature to language and its performance, to society in its material basis and its historical developments and to the biologically determined permanent objective structures of the human mind. Such an enquiry would draw upon modern linguistics, anthropology, cultural history and hard psychology and also provide a very serious test of the adequacy of those disciplines. There is a clear sense in which the human sciences must be regarded as inadequate, as long as they fail to give an adequate account of literature. There is also a clear sense in which literary theory must be regarded as inadequate, as long as it draws not upon the modern human sciences, but upon a metaphysical and idealist rehashing of Saussure, Marx and Freud.

BOOKS

There is no special book recommended for beginners for the preface and introduction. All topics discussed are taken up in later chapters.

FURTHER READING

For general and advanced readers there is a selection of source works in the main bibliography, on the major theoretical frameworks discussed and on modern critiques or variants of them, under the following names, listed in historical order under each topic:

Historical Materialism: Marx, Engels, Lenin, Althusser, Foucault.
Anthropology: Lévi-Strauss, Marvin Harris.
Psychoanalysis: Freud, Lacan, Eysenck.
Phenomenology and Existentialism: Husserl, Heidegger, Sartre, Derrida.
Logic and Language: Frege, Russell, Strawson, Searle.
Linguistics: Saussure, Bloomfield 1933, Jakobson, and Chomsky.
The Status of Scientific Theories: Popper, Lakatos.

There is a great deal of material in these references: a reader starting more or less from scratch would need several years to assimilate it. Moreover, each name listed represents only part of the development of a complex intellectual tradition: thus there are many different Marxisms and Freudianisms, many approaches to the pheno-menological and existential traditions in philosophy, and many models in linguistics. None of these theories is directly about literature; they are the material that literary theorists call upon and apply, with more or less principled opportunism. Opinions differ in the literary critical community on how far it is necessary to understand these theories before applying them; some hold as I do that one should understand the source theory fully, and others that it is sufficient to pick up the appropriate critical language by osmosis – that is, by unconscious assimilation.

The three books in this sequence *Foundations of Modern Literary Theory* offer only a highly selective guide to the theories of these writers, but should make it possible to use these theories critically, and with a degree of historical awareness about their origins.

CHAPTER ONE

Structuralism and the Real Saussure

Structures, Functions, and the Saussurean Model of Language

SUMMARY

Structuralism, in a broad sense, is the practice of studying phenomena as different as societies, minds, languages, literatures and mythologies, as total systems, or connected wholes – that is, **structures** – and in terms of their internal patterns of connection, rather than in terms of their historical sequence of development. It is the study of how the structures of these entities affect the way they **function**.

Structuralism, in the more familiar narrow sense, is an attempt to find a model for both the structure and functioning of societies, minds, etc in the structuralist model of language, developed in linguistics in the early twentieth century. Language is studied from many points of view, by philosophers, sociologists, literary critics, etc., all of whom make a point of having some axe to grind. Linguists study it for its own sake, to find out its intrinsic structure, and are sometimes roundly condemned for doing so. An influential early version of the structuralist model of language is to be found in the *Course in General Linguistics* (1916), by Ferdinand de Saussure, the basic principles of which are explained in this chapter. Attempts to apply the model to literature date at least from 1928, in the programme of Jakobson and Tynjanov. This was the start of literary structuralism.

1 THE BROAD SENSE OF STRUCTURALISM: A CULTURAL MECCANO

1.1 The elementary concept of structure

Here is a possible definition of a structure:

A structure is a set of parts which are connected together.[1]

In this sense, a containerful of spares is just a set; but if they are connected together to make a car, that car will be a structure. Similarly, there was once a popular children's engineering toy called Meccano, nowadays displaced by Lego. You bought a box of Meccano parts – small pieces of metal of various shapes, drilled with a regular pattern of holes so that they could be bolted together, which was called, with mathematical correctness, a Meccano set. From your set you took parts and bolted them together to make model cars, or cranes. These are structures. Adult engineers make prefabricated houses on this principle too; and polytechnic administrators make modular degree courses. The main advantage is the enormous number of different structures you can make, not all at the same time of course, out of the same limited kit of parts. This is also the main advantage of structuralist theories.

The general principle of structuralism is to extend this idea – of the standard kit of parts out of which you can make particular structures like cars and cranes – as far as it can possibly go; to extend it, in particular, outside the limits of the physical, or even biological worlds and into the contents of the mind.

How far is it possible to see objects as structures when we don't actually construct them ourselves? Obviously it is possible. In this sense – which is definitely one of the senses employed in common speech – almost every material object in the world is a structure. A tree can be seen as a structure and so can a geological formation; meteorologists even think of clouds as structures. The whole of physical science, in this sense, is based on explaining the behaviour of the world in terms of its physical structure.

But structures do not have to be material objects. An argument can be a structure – the parts being two premises and a conclusion and the connection being that the conclusion follows logically from the premises. A mind can be a structure made up of ego, superego and id. A society can be a structure: made up, say, of a set of statuses or positions like father, son; employer, employee – with connections between them; or of connected classes: bourgeoisie and proletariat.

The Meccano analogy is useful here, though it is necessary to keep it as a conscious analogy and to wonder just how far it can be pressed. Anybody who has ever played with a Meccano set has grasped the essential principle of structuralism. (Though not, of course, some of the more complex derivative notions like those of 'structural transformation'.) A structuralist, on the Meccano model, is a person who puts together some pieces from what he takes to be a pre-existing kit of parts (material or otherwise), to make a model of some aspect of the material, social or mental world. But if we are talking of societies, or minds, how far can we think of them as made up of parts that could possibly exist separately?

There is an equally common sense of structure which is slightly more abstract; here is a definition:

A structure is the set of connections between parts, in a set of parts which are connected together.

In this sense we should say that a car **has** a structure rather than that it is a structure; similarly that we build a crane **with** a certain structure out of our Meccano set; similarly that a tree, a hill, a cloud, an argument, a mind, a society **have** structures. In this sense of the word, to specify the structure of something, you specify the connections between the parts; you do not have to say what the parts are, beyond what is necessary to identify them. Hence different objects, made out of different parts, might have the same structure. (We can build a crane of the same structure out of Meccano or out of one of the numerous imitations.)

Claude Lévi-Strauss attaches a great deal of importance to this distinction between the more concrete and the more abstract sense of structure: he distinguishes them as **structure** and **form** respectively. In 'Structure and Form: Reflections on a Work by Vladimir Propp' (1960), he writes:

> The supporters of structural analysis in linguistics and in anthropology are often accused of formalism. This is to forget that formalism exists as an independent doctrine from which structuralism – without denying its debt to it – separated because of the very different attitudes the two schools adopt toward the concrete. Contrary to formalism, structuralism refuses to set the concrete against the abstract and to recognise a privileged value in the latter. Form is defined by opposition to material other than itself. But structure has no distinct content; it is content itself, apprehended in a logical organisation conceived as property of the real.
>
> (Lévi-Strauss, 1976)

For Lévi-Strauss, then, if he accepts the Meccano analogy at all[2], a model car made out of Meccano will be a structure; while the specification in the instruction book of how the parts fit together will specify the form of that structure.

If we accept either of the notions of structure defined above it is possible to offer a definition of a very broad concept of structuralism:

Structuralism is the practice of studying phenomena as different as societies, minds, languages, literatures and mythologies as total systems, or connected wholes – that is, structures – and in terms of their internal patterns of connection, rather than as sets of isolated items and in terms of their historical sequence.

Under this heading we can include at least the following: accounts of social structure in sociology and anthropology, by anthropologists of the Anglo-American schools just as much as by Lévi-Strauss; accounts of mental structures from the diverse points of view of Freud, of Piaget and of Chomsky; accounts of human language of the kind due to de Saussure, Sapir and the whole tradition of modern general linguistics; accounts of literature from formalist points of view, ranging from Northrop Frye through the Russian Formalists and into Structuralism in the narrower sense which is explored in the next section; accounts of mythology and legend from a similar range of points of view; and some recent approaches to history. In this account of general structuralism language has no particular privilege – it is one object of structuralist enquiry along with many others.

Some of the wilder claims for the importance of structuralism – the claim, for example, that it is the key movement of the modern period – probably have this very broad conception at the back of them. So also has the metaphysical structuralism of which Jacques Derrida (1967b) offers a critique. '. . . for it would not be difficult to show' (he says, without actually showing) 'that a certain structuralism has always been philosophy's most spontaneous gesture' (p.159). And, 'It would be easy enough to show that the concept of structure and even the word "structure" itself are as old as the *episteme* – that is to say, as old as Western science and Western philosophy . . .' (p.278).

It is worth asking, however, whether one is saying anything worth while about these very diverse thinkers and bodies of thought by labelling them all 'structuralist'. I think in fact that one is: one is saying something extremely simple about them and making a very weak claim, but it is a genuine claim and it is true. The claim is that in all these domains it is necessary to recognize significant structural patterns – where a structural pattern is defined as a pattern of connections between parts. One cannot simply reduce these domains to unordered sets of elementary parts and treat holistic properties as common

23

properties of each individual part, or even as general properties of the whole collection.

Here are three examples of this weak structural property, ranging from the banal to the slightly contentious.

(1) The properties of a building are not those of its bricks; you can build a square building forty feet high out of bricks nine inches long and rectangular.

(2) The properties of a passage of text are not those of the words in it; its meaning is not the meaning of any individual word, nor of all the words heaped together, but of a particular linear structure built out of them; and is dependent also on the structural patterns in the language from which the words come.

(3) The properties of a social institution cannot be reduced to properties of the people who take part in it. The Prudential Assurance Company is not identical with any or all of its employees, or with its articles of association; its purposes and functions are not necessarily identical with theirs; there is no collective consciousness to have purposes and functions; and yet the company does exist, and does have purposes and functions of a quite straightforward kind which depend on its own structure and the legal and social structure of society.

Is this claim too weak to be of any interest or importance? Many would assume that it is. Piaget, for example, in his book, *Structuralism* (1968), (which is less an introduction to the field than an attempt to re-found it) adopts a much stronger definition. As is common in this literature, it is unclear. According to him:

> a structure is a system of transformations . . . the structure is preserved or enriched by the interplay of its transformation laws, which never yield results external to the system, nor employ elements that are external to it. In short, the notion of structure is comprised of three key ideas: the idea of wholeness, the idea of transformation and the idea of self-regulation.

Piaget thus replaces the simple concept of a structure with the much more complex concept of a self-regulating system. It is not clear precisely what he means, since he never defines the key concept of **transformation**. But the obvious definition is:

a transformation is a change from one structure to another

where the word 'structure' bears the simpler sense defined earlier.

Piaget, of course, is interested in what might be called the self-generation of complex structures out of simpler ones; something which is important in itself, especially in biology, where this is a characteristic mode of physical development. It had been Piaget's life-work to show that it was a characteristic mode of cognitive development, too; in his empirical studies of **cognitive epistemology** (Piaget and Inhelder 1963), he had attempted to show how the capacity to recognize basic logical structures develops in children.

Piaget tries to show the importance of his concept in every field from mathematical logic to the social sciences. It is an idea to which it will be necessary to return when considering the possible philosophical consequences of structuralism. But it remains a complex and derivative concept, often most confusing in just those central areas of structuralist thought, like linguistics, where such notions as 'transformation' are most precisely defined.

Thus generative grammar is concerned with tree-structures, which are, as the name suggests, structures made out of parts of speech connected together like the twigs and branches of a tree. A 'transformation' here means a mapping from one tree-structure to another.[3] We need the concept of structure in order to define the concept of transformation, not the other way round! There seems little point in defining a sense for 'structuralism' that doesn't fit any model of linguistics very well and is better adapted to cybernetics.

I return therefore, to the very weak claim made above: that is that all these things that the structuralists consider contain significant patterns of connection between their parts; and it is these that need to be studied rather than – or at least as well as – the substantive elements of which things are made. Curiously enough, even from a claim as weak as this we can deduce a number of worthwhile consequences. Some of them are obvious; some are more subtle; but they are all capable of leading to confusion if they are forgotten; and they have often been forgotten in structuralist writing. By spelling them out at the start of my account, before getting on to structuralism in the narrower and more important sense of the linguistics-based model, I hope to avoid these confusions later on.

1.2 *Structure and real existence*

My first point is a blindingly obvious one.

Except in pure mathematics, which I discuss immediately below, every structure is a structure of something. If we use the word 'structure' in a concrete sense, so that we would say a Meccano model of a car is a structure, then we mean that it is a structure of – that is, made of – Meccano parts. If we use it in the abstract sense, then we mean that the structure of the Meccano model is the pattern of connection of the parts. We can specify this structure – in the abstract sense – without actually making it; this might be done by a diagram in the Meccano set's owner's manual. But if we want to make the actual model, we need more than a structural diagram to make it from. We need actual Meccano parts.

You cannot make a real object out of an abstract structure alone; only out of a structure of parts which are themselves real. As I said, the point is obvious when you are talking of material things like Meccano models. But it is quite often neglected by people talking in sophisticated ways about, say, the structure of the mind; and contriving to suggest that the mind is merely a structure, made out of nothing in particular. Still less would it be possible for language or the mind or society to be made out of something even more abstract, like 'metastructures' or 'transformations'; or, as Althusser suggests, for the structures of society to exist 'only in their effects' (1968 p.189). This proposal would make the structure of society something purely ideal, that existed only for the analyst; but such structures can't have any effects, except in the mind of the analyst.

These idealist positions are no necessary part of structuralism; but they abound in the last, French phase of it, when structuralism encountered French philosophy of the subject; and they abound in modern academic descriptions, even of the hard sciences. Even the popularizers of quantum mechanics sometimes seem to suggest that all you need to make an electron is a set of equations. This seems to be a revival of the old, magical view of the scientist: intone the right formula and computers work, screens glow. It isn't true; whether you are studying atoms or the anthropology of folk-tales (as Lévi-Strauss's argument implies), to make real objects you need real parts. The equations only tell you how the parts are put together, and how the parts are modified within the whole.

One can take this point slightly further. There are definite ways in which the parts constrain the structures that can be built out of them. This is not a matter of numerical limitations. It is sometimes suggested that if there are only a few kinds of part, that limits the number of structures that can be built out of them. But of course it doesn't. Provided we have enough identical bricks we can go on building houses for ever and every one different. The real limitation is of kind: you can't use Meccano parts to make a jelly; and you can't make much of a mechanical crane out of parts that are made of jelly. This points to certain radical limitations in structuralist principles; and it leads to the first **post-structuralist** point in this book. One view of post-structuralism would be that it involves the continual discovery that the nuts and bolts of our conceptual systems are actually made out of jelly.

One ought to add that any real object may have more than one structure. There may be many ways of dividing it into parts, and many different ways in which these sets of parts are connected. But however many structures it may have, the object is not exhausted by its structures. A combination of fifty abstract structures is no more a real object than is a single abstract structure. Real objects are made out of real parts: this goes for cranes, societies and people. Take the real parts away and there is nothing left: when every part of the Cheshire cat has gone, there is not even the structure of a grin; though as the logician, Lewis Carroll, demonstrated, it is still possible to **talk** about that non-existent abstract structure.

The discipline that talks about abstract structures is called logic and mathematics.[4] I am going to discuss this further when I consider Derrida's account of Husserl's *Origin of Geometry* in chapter 5; but for the moment I will offer the analogy of the Meccano instruction book. If we think of the universe as a Meccano set then it is possible to imagine a book which is something less than an instruction book and something more than a catalogue. The book – mathematical logic – is an account of **the infinite set of all possible structures.**

As an actual artefact, realized in the world by the publications of mathematicians, this book is a rather curious one. It is not fiction; indeed, it is true throughout and if we examine any part, then as soon as we understand it we shall find it is self-evidently true (or reject it as no part of mathematics). Though self-evident it is not subjective, and it applies throughout the objective universe. But it is incomplete; and that is because we are still writing it, taking care to preserve the remarkable properties listed above; yet knowing that the next chapter of the book may overturn our understanding of everything that went before.

For Husserl, it must be said, the analogy of the book is taken very seriously. For him, mathematics is only objective because you can write it down. And it is out of this account that Derrida seems to develop his extraordinarily strange concept of an *arche-writing* which, for all that he denies it is a metaphysical concept, appears to have the power to construct a world. Despite Derrida's sophistication, I think that he has here fallen back into the magical view of nature: for me, even mathematics can do no more than describe the objective world, not create it; and writing is merely a phenomenon within that world.

But a Derridean deconstruction of my own account might fasten on the analogy of the book I have just used and argue that it subverts the very point I am making.

On my view, however, we need to distinguish between the principles of logic and mathematics themselves, which specify the possible structures of the world, and the books we write, which merely offer a partial and developing approximate representation of those principles. The shapes of nature have always been partially governed by the principles of fractal geometry; though fractal geometry as an academic subject is only a few years old. This probably means one has to take a Platonist view of logic and mathematics as a set of wholly transcendental principles. It doesn't mean, however, that one has to take the same view of human reasoning processes which are carried out by means of rough linguistic categories in finite and faulty brains. The point is developed in chapters 5 and 6.

1.3   Structure and function

The second point raised by the structural model is just as obvious, but very different.

There are many types of description you can offer, besides structural descriptions, of both real and abstract objects. An obvious example of a type of description which is not a structural description and does not reduce to a structural description, is a functional description. Thus you can describe a car as a body with four wheels and an engine connected to the rear wheels. That is a structural description. Or you can describe it as a device for enabling people to move fast along roads. That is a functional description, and is quite different.

We sometimes get confused, because most descriptions of mechanical objects move easily between the structural and the functional, as they explain both what the machine consists of and how it works. Thus we say that a car is driven (functional description) by an engine connected to the rear wheels by a drive-shaft and differential (structural description) and steered (functional) by a wheel attached to a shaft (structural) operating (functional) a rack-and-pinion mechanism (structural).

We can make exactly the same distinction for non-mechanical artefacts. We can describe a detective story as a novel in which a crime is committed – usually a murder – and in which one of the characters – sometimes a professional detective – discovers who committed the crime. That is a structural description. We can also describe it as a device for undemandingly filling the time of a tired teacher at the end of the day and giving him a bit of cosy social reassurance. That is a functional description.

As with mechanical devices, most descriptions of non-mechanical artefacts that we produce are a mix of structural and functional description. For example, it is the function of a detective to discover the criminal. That is what detectives are for; just as a rack-and-pinion system is for steering the front wheels. But the two sorts of description are different all the same and have quite different properties. Value judgements, for example, seem to arise in functional descriptions. A good detective story is one that performs the function described above well and doesn't harrow the poor teacher too much (as a serious novel might). On this view, value judgements can't apply to pure structures; which raises some interesting questions about the basis of judgements about abstract art.

We can also apply both structural and functional descriptions to human language. Take one of the simplest possible sentences of English:

The boy kicked the ball.

We can say that its parts are five words – an article 'the', two nouns and a verb. An article, or determiner, is connected to one or other noun to make a verb phrase: 'the boy', 'the ball'; a verb is connected to one of the noun phrases to make a verb phrase: 'kicked the ball'; one of the noun phrases is connected to the verb phrase to make the whole sentence; and so we can say the sentence as a whole has a structure

$(_s(_{np}(_dthe)(_nboy))(_{vp}(_vkicked)(_{np}(_dthe)(_nball))))$,

which is perhaps more understandable when drawn (either way up) as a tree:

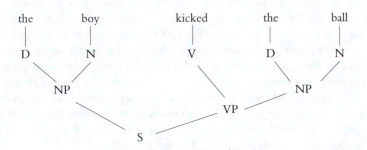

We can also say that the first noun phrase functions as the **subject** of the sentence and the verb phrase as the **predicate**, with the second noun phrase as the **object** of the verb. These are purely grammatical functions, but they seem to correlate intuitively in this case with notions like who is acting, what his action is, and what he is acting on. The whole sentence is an **indicative** one, which seems to correlate with making a statement.[3]

The parallel here to the structural and functional analysis of the way a motor car works is fairly obvious: linguistics is a fairly mechanistic study. And there is another parallel in the variability of what might be called the higher functions of both objects: that is, the different ways in which they can be used in society. A motor car seems to have a basic function of transport, but it can also be used as a status symbol, or a road-block, or an advertising hoarding. An indicative sentence seems to have a basic function of making a statement; but it can also be used as a linguistic example, as above; or to test out a microphone; or as a coded message to arrange for the assassination of the prime minister of Singapore.

It is sometimes argued that the existence of what I have called the variable higher functions of a sentence casts doubt upon the basic ones; or at least, that there is no reason to say that functions like making statements and asking questions are more basic than writing poems or delivering coded messages. The same argument would of course hold for cars: there is no reason to hold the transport function as more basic than the status-symbol one. I find this implausible in both cases. It would be almost impossible to make the structural design of a car, or of a sentence, intelligible, without assuming a basic set of engineering or of linguistic functions. Structure and function do not reduce to each other; but in these cases they do very strongly interact. There are certain functions of a car, or a sentence, that are, as it were, implicit in its structure and cannot be changed by the conscious or unconscious intentions of its user.

It is clear that one can easily extend structural–functional description to, say, the human body, or to human societies, though the ultimate function or purpose is not as clear in these cases as it is in the case of a man-made machine or other artefact. Perhaps it is merely to keep going. Most of the structures present in the body function in order to preserve the body in functioning existence, in a complex and often dangerous environment. This seems to be true both of physical structures and mental ones. It is an impressive insight, and this is no doubt what tempted Piaget to apply the word 'structure' to those special kinds of structure which function mainly to maintain and develop themselves.

Structural-functional descriptions of society are common forms in sociology and anthropology. Some would-be hard scientists object to them because they seem to attribute purpose or usefulness to social institutions; they are teleological and insufficiently mechanical. This seems odd in view of the naturalness of structural–functional descriptions for machinery, and there are evolutionary and selectional mechanisms for bringing about functional systems in societies, just as much as in the biological world. (The obvious Marxist objection – that what is functional from the point of view of one class looks very dysfunctional from the point of view of another is not really an objection to the principle of structural-functional description, but to the way in which it is carried out.)

There are others who find structural and functional explanations alike far too mechanical. They wish to give accounts of society or the mind in terms of meaning, intentionality or significance; and there is no logical bar to applying descriptions of this kind to societies, or for that matter to human bodies, or even to motor cars. Nor is there any *a priori* case for saying that these descriptions must always reduce to structural or functional ones, though they may be in some way related. Later on I shall examine the very dubious structuralist claim that meaning, personal identity and a whole range of reasonably familiar aspects of human experience can be reduced to effects of structures; even, as in the mystificatory Althusserian case, to structures which exist only in their effects. Despite my scepticism about the particular proposals made by structuralists, I would not want to rule out this claim in principle.

1.4 Structure and function in natural language

My third point about structure in general is the last of the really obvious ones.

Almost everything in the world, material or immaterial, is made out of parts with some connections between them and is therefore a structure. Even a glass of water has a structure, though the water in it perhaps has not, at least until you analyse it at the molecular level. Therefore to say that a particular thing X has a structure is to say very little about it indeed. To say anything interesting you have to say what particular structure(s) it has.

To say that societies, or myths or works of literature 'have a structure' is only to say that they are made out of parts and the parts are connected. That is not interesting. To say something interesting about them one has to say what the parts are, and how they are connected, and what is the result, or the function, or significance of those parts being connected in that way.

A real structuralist, in the narrower sense that I shall be exploring, says something much more specific than this. He says that societies, myths, works of literature and so forth 'have the structure of a language' – or sometimes 'have the structure of individual expressions from an underlying language'. This is to take the structure of one fairly well understood domain as the model for the structures of many others that are less well understood; it is a very strong and therefore very interesting claim. It is particularly interesting when one has a suspicion that the domain being modelled also has functions resembling those of language – that is, it is concerned with conveying or encoding meaning. The main thrust of the structuralist movement – particularly in the 1930s, when it was at its best – has been to explore such claims as these; in particular the possible connections between structure and meaning.[5]

Structuralism proper, then, in the narrow sense with which I shall be concerned throughout the rest of this book, is based on the insight that objects as diverse as societies, minds, myths and works of literature exhibit some of the structure and perform some of the functions, of human languages.[5] In order to understand the movement one must know what this structure is and what these functions are.

It is obvious that a language – French, for example, or German – has a function; it is what one French or German speaker uses in order to communicate with another French or German speaker and probably what they use to think with. It is not so obvious, at first sight, that a language has a structure. A sentence from that language clearly has a structure: it has a fixed order, for example, and if we changed the order of the words it would usually be nonsense. And a word obviously has a structure. It has a definite series of recognizable sounds, and if we changed the order of sounds it would usually be gibberish. But what do we mean by saying that the **language** has a structure? If we think of a language as a mere collection of words it seems a clear example of something that does **not** have a structure.

But as soon as we examine them we find that these words are not independent, unconnected entities that are merely collected together. Words have definite relationships with each other, which govern the way they can be used in sentences. Sounds in a language have definite relationships with each other, which govern the way in which they fit into syllables and words. It is the existence of these fixed relationships which makes a language into a structure with parts rather than a collection of bits; and which determines the nature of the small structures – sentences, noun-phrases and so forth – which can be made out of the bits. One line of development within the structuralist tradition is to show the existence of relationships of this kind, which both facilitate and constrain what people can do and think, in distant areas like kinship systems in anthropology, or the episodes of folk-tales.

Another line of development is logically rather different, though it sometimes gets confused with the first. Language has a function, as a communication system; certainly the most important communication system used by man, but equally certainly not the only one. It is perfectly possible to look at many other cultural systems, whatever their apparent primary purpose, as systems of communication. Thus you can talk about marriage, as Lévi-Strauss does, as a way in which kinship groups exchange women, and add that this is the way in which they **communicate** with each other. Just how useful this approach is cannot be determined in advance; maybe it will give us new insights into the human world, and maybe it will not. But it is important to notice that it is quite a different analogy from the first. Societies or books or human minds might be structurally analogous to languages without being functionally like them; or they might be functionally like human languages without being at all structurally similar.

Some of the most confused passages of structuralist analysis occur when it is not clear, even to the writer, which analogy is being claimed. Later in this book (chapter 7), I have analysed an example from Julia Kristèva, which is by no means the worst I could have found. There is, of course, a good deal of excuse for this confusion since, as we have seen, there is a strong relationship between grammatical structure and basic linguistic function – between indicative sentences and statements, and interrogative sentences and questions, for example. But there is still a fundamental logical difference, and it would have made for clarity in this field if there had been a general convention to reserve the word **structuralist** for the first analogy and **semiological**, or **semiotic**, for the second. It is, however, probably too late to hope for clarity now.

In the later French period, when structuralism was crossed with the philosophy of the subject and confusion began to abound, a rather bizarre variant of semiological theory grew up: that it was language, or perhaps the structure of language, that imposed structure upon the world, or perhaps the human world. This seems to be a combination of the idealist philosophical principle: that the structure of the world of phenomena proceeds from the mind, with the principle that the mind – the 'subject' – is an effect of language. I call this position 'Linguistic Idealism'. It has nothing to do with the structuralism of, say, Jakobson in 1928 or 1942, but sits well with Lacan. After it was manufactured in France, this position was projected backwards into the text of de Saussure, who thus became an idealist philosopher; one of the few philosophers who has made his major innovations when forty years dead.

I discuss this historical transformation of de Saussure in chapter 3, and in chapter 6 I consider various forms of linguistic idealism attributed to him, examining his text to decide whether he actually held these positions and formulating them as simply and precisely as I can, so that it is possible to decide whether they are true. (My tentative conclusion is, that most of these positions he did not hold, and the rest are not true.)

2 THE NARROW SENSE OF STRUCTURALISM: THE FIVE PRINCIPLES OF DE SAUSSURE

2.0 *Scientific linguistics as objective science*

In this section I am going to explain, in a way that assumes no specialist knowledge, the major Saussurean principles which I believe entered into the structuralist model of linguistics, and in due course influenced early structuralism, when it was in its scientific stage. This ought to be a non-controversial thing to do. Student readers may be surprised – though staff probably won't – to know that it is the site of a shooting war. Merely by saying these uncontroversial things, I am taking up an embattled position in a major controversy.

The trouble is that there are several different professional ways of taking an interest in language: those of the linguist, of several different varieties of philosopher, of the psychoanalyst, of the literary critic, of the teacher; and almost every one of them leads to a fiercely proprietorial view of what language is, and a feeling sometimes that the other people simply don't know what they are talking about. Like everybody else I share this feeling at times, but will try to do justice to the opposition. I ask them in turn – any post-structuralist who feels that the whole concept of objective scientific linguistics is a mistake, for example – to do me the same courtesy; not that I claim to speak for linguistics particularly – it doesn't need my advocacy – but I do want to argue rationally **about** it.

Linguists are interested in the nuts and bolts of language. They are interested in questions like 'what are the smallest distinctive sound elements in a language and how are they related to each other?'; or 'what is the structure of the auxiliary verb?' in some particular dialect. Some astonishingly impressive formal theories have been advanced in linguistics, for example those of Chomsky (1957; 1965); but the theories are all ultimately related to questions like these; and to be a linguist you have got to find these questions interesting. It is in this respect that linguistics most closely resembles the hard sciences, which also erect important general theories on rather trivial kinds of data, and in which the scientist has to be interested in getting the data right, even though it is the theory that renders the data important. My first, totally non-controversial but highly embattled position is that Saussure was a linguist. His philosophical positions – and he had some – were all part of his methodological discussions of linguistics. **He had no other explicit philosophical positions of any kind**.

Philosophers, poets and literary critics tend to have a very different kind of interest in language. Here is late Heidegger:

> To discuss language, to place it, means to bring to its place of being not so much language as ourselves: our own gathering into the appropriation.
> We would reflect on language itself, and on language only. Language itself is – language and nothing else beside. Language itself is language. The understanding that is schooled in logic, thinking of everything in terms of calculation and hence usually overbearing, calls this proposition an empty tautology. Merely to say the identical thing twice – language is language – how is that supposed to get us anywhere? But we do not want to get anywhere. We would like only, for once, to get to just where we are already.
>
> (Heidegger 1971, p.190)

This is a philosophical mantra, an invitation to reflect upon the languageness of language as a way into being.

What I have to do in this section, and what anybody would have to do merely in order to say what Saussure meant, is to adopt 'the understanding that is schooled in logic, thinking of everything in terms of calculation'. That is the sort of subject linguistics is; and Saussure was inaugurating modern scientific linguistics. That is also, to a surprising extent, what early structuralism was: after all, the greatest of the early structuralists was also one of the greatest linguists, Roman Jakobson. But it is not what post-structuralism is. The various post-structuralisms, which might just as well be called post-phenomenological, post-Marxist and post-Freudian, are much

The poverty of structuralism

closer in spirit to Heidegger than to Saussure, certainly in terms of their philosophical interests. Language appears in them much more as a philosophical metaphor than as it is for a linguist, the object of exact descriptive theories that are realized ultimately in the form of dictionaries and grammars (cf chapter 5 on de Man).

Heidegger is perhaps an extreme case. Other philosophers have been less rhapsodic, more suspicious of language; worked on it in more (though still philosophical) detail. They have seen it as a source of bewitchment by metaphysical pseudo-problems; under which heading many of them would have included all of Heidegger's own philosophical concerns. Some of them have tried to get rid of these problems by inventing new, artificial languages, composed entirely of the formulae of logic, in which metaphysical problems would be impossible to formulate (Carnap 1937); and some by critically examining our use of real languages (Wittgenstein 1953; Austin 1962a & b); or by inventing philosophical fictions about language, such as Wittgenstein's fictions about language-games (1953), or Derrida's concept of Writing (Derrida 1967b). Philosophers thus have a vast literature about language, which is largely independent of anything in linguistics. Often, their conception of what language is is also independent of anything in linguistics. This may actually be legitimate, but it is certainly dangerous: imagine a philosopher who had a theory about the nature of the material world that ignored physics and chemistry.

Other disciplines too have their own proprietary interest in language; producing, in the end, a vision of language which the linguist, stuck with his syntax and morphology, can hardly recognize. Jacques Lacan, the psychoanalyst, identifies language with the realm of the symbolic, which appears to equate with the whole of human culture. For him, the unconscious is an effect of language; indeed, major aspects of human subjectivity seem to be effects of language (Lacan 1953–54). Poets like Eliot and Pound have seen language as something to be cultivated and purified as an instrument of spiritual exploration; though it was perhaps socially tactless to speak of purifying the dialect of the tribe (Eliot T.S. 1944 p.39: *Little Gidding).* Some critics have followed them, seeing the maintenance of, say, English in its Englishness as a high cultural duty (Thompson, Denys *The Use of English, passim).* English teachers traditionally had a prescriptive view at a rather lower level; they taught some forms of language as correct, and classed others as incorrect, illogical, or vulgar; thus maintaining the polite frontiers of the class system. The collapse of this position, partly under the impact of descriptive linguistics, left many of them quite unclear whether language has a teachable structure, and very ready to encourage a self-expression unconscious of underlying structure. Some Marxists see language as a site of class and ethnic struggle; and are suspicious of any attempt to describe it objectively. Every one of these groups will have a vision of language, which seems to them, often correctly, to be urgent and profound; and which makes a description of German irregular verbs seem a rather trivial matter. Their vision will usually have little to do with objective linguistics.

Saussure's view – and that of most linguists since – would be that linguists are interested in the objective structure of language and its most basic functions, studied for their own sake; and that all the others are interested in one or another more or less high level **use** of language which they may well confuse with language itself (Saussure 1916, chapter 5 & *passim*). Many academics of other disciplines would agree with this. They would take it, as I do, that there is no possible legitimate conflict between the scientific investigation of language structure and basic function, and the study of larger questions of politics, metaphysics and poetry, in which language appears as a weapon, a mantra, a tool, or a metaphor of meaningful human experience, which is what it often seems to be for the post-structuralists.

But there is a significant minority – particularly among literary critics and theorists – who are surprisingly hostile to the very concept of scientific linguistics. This hostility is not new; and although it tends to take a hard-left form nowadays, it may actually come from any part of the political spectrum, from left to right, and from Leavisite to post-structuralist. I will give six examples, which happen to lie ready to hand, of a phenomenon which any teacher of literature and linguistics will have noticed.

The first is an article by Raymond O'Malley in *The Use of English* (Summer 1964) on structural linguistics in the classroom, called simply: 'One More Irrelevance'; the title displays the argument. The second is a book by Ian Robinson (1975), *The New Grammarian's Funeral: A Critique of Chomsky's Linguistics*, dedicated significantly to F.R. Leavis 'who twelve years since encouraged me to publish an essay on the state of linguistics'. Here is an extract:

> Linguistics can sometimes be the 'underlabourer' of criticism, or of other disciplines.* The 'linguistics and . . .' studies all go astray at present and are not as useful as they might be because they follow Chomsky in trying to move the linguistics part away from use, and because they exalt linguistics unduly. In the case in point, literary critics are often exhorted

to learn from linguists; but I never hear linguists told to learn from critics. Such a lesson is much needed, as I shall conclude by showing.
*Linguistics, in a wide sense, can offer help to criticism when linguistics is kept in its properly subordinate place. Every year in tutorials we waste time when bright pupils fumble around for grammatical terms that would have been commonplace thirty years ago . . .

(Robinson 1975, p.168)

The hostility of Leavisites of twenty-five or fifteen years ago, or today, is paralleled by the hostility of the contemporary far Left. Here are two examples heard at conferences. One well-known critic, speaking impromptu, commented upon the concept of 'rule-governed creativity' in generative grammar that it resembled 'the reformist concept of freedom under the law' (which the critic found detestable); somebody who believed in that ought to be a member of the SDP! (a centre party well known in Britain in the early 1980s, now almost defunct). I made enquiries afterwards as I couldn't believe the point was seriously intended: after all there is no logical connection whatever between descriptive grammar and the criminal law. But it **was** seriously intended: belief in grammar was thought to be like belief in law and order. (This apparent absurdity is not unprecedented or unsurpassed in the philosophical literature; Nietzsche thought belief in grammar was like belief in God.)

Another scholar, at another conference, argued that the concept of the 'ideal speaker–hearer' in linguistics suppressed ethnic conflicts and power relationships: what the linguist ought to investigate was a black South African in front of a white judge. A linguist (not me) intervened mildly to suggest that, when describing linguistic competence, one tried to do the simple things first; but the point was not taken. (The point is that in the case described at least four ideal speaker–hearers are present in two human bodies: the judge speaks Afrikaans and English, the black South African a different dialect of English and a Bantu language; the power-relationships present are not reflected in the structure of any of these languages though sociolinguistics can have a lot to say about them. This point is taken up a few pages on, in the discussion of *langue*.)

I won't give references to these two cases since they were not fully reported; but my fifth and six examples are published. Deleuze and Guattari in their book *Mille plateaux* (1980) provide a full theory to back the suggestion that my second conference speaker made (that to study grammar is somehow to suppress non-standard languages) and as one would expect, this turns out to involve a hostility to the whole universalizing scientific approach of linguistics. It is interesting that Deleuze is an authority on Nietzsche: we do have a philosophical tradition here, and not merely individual eccentricities; though my personal view is that it is an obscurantist and irrationalist tradition. Julia Kristeva (1980 p.25) is in some ways the most menacing of the lot: she argues on ethical grounds for 'compelling linguists to change their object of study' and become more like Heidegger or the poet Mallarmé. Here the source of hostility is a Lacanian or hermeneutic rather than a Marxist or anarchic Leftist ideology. (But see also Kristeva 1989, which is not considered here.)

I will go beyond the examples I have given here and venture on a generalization. Many people are opposed to scientific linguistics because it seems to threaten the ideology – Leavisite, Marxist, psychoanalytic, hermeneutic or whatever – in terms of which they teach literature, or live. Each of these ideologies has its own proprietorial view of language, and this is cast in doubt by the very existence of another model of language, based on scientific evidence.

Their positions are perhaps defensible, though difficult to defend and, I think, wrong. What is not possible to defend – it will probably shock any students who are reading these words as much as it shocks me – is that in many, though not all, literature and theory departments Saussure's scientific approach to the structure of language is effectively suppressed **even when his text is taught**; he is taught, not as a linguist with some interesting philosophical claims to make about the proper methodology for linguistics, but simply as a philosopher of language and as the originator of a baroque and impossible theory of meaning. The effect of this is a distortion of the history of ideas. Structuralism as the dominant theoretical mode in linguistics for forty years disappears from the face of Europe. The long history of literary structuralism based on the linguistic model is truncated into a brief French prelude to the wonders of post-structuralism. Students are not asked to consider what was in fact one of the more successful theoretical models of the twentieth century.

Why is a harmless science like linguistics – the study of the objective structure of human languages – found to be so threatening, so subversive, to such a range of ideologues? What do they fear? There is one important thing that the *Course in General Linguistics* was originally intended to do for students; and that it can still do for some students: and that is to give them a vision of an objective science of language; which is in turn a model for a possible range of objective human sciences. Compared with that vision, Saussure's theory of meaning is of quite marginal importance, and is in any case false (see chapter 6). The same vision, of the objective study of language as a model for the objective study of the human sciences in general, can of course be provided by other seminal linguistics texts, even from other schools of linguistics: I found it in Chomsky (1957) *Syntactic Structures*, when I first read this in 1963. Some people – most importantly in anthropology, Marvin Harris (1968) – have been influenced by Kenneth Pike's tagmemics (1967). Perhaps the best possible text, from the point of view of understanding the European structuralist tradition, would be Roman Jakobson (1976) *Sound and Meaning*. Anyone who doubts my account of the vision of structural linguistics, and its importance for structuralism, will perhaps believe the writer of the preface to that book, who was Claude Lévi-Strauss. (See chapter 3.)

There is an interesting contrast between the subjective, even religious overtones of one of the words I have repeatedly used here, 'vision', and the correlative phrase 'objective science'. It is possible to have a vision of objectivity: and that is an ideology, though one that the sciences adopt. As an ideology, it can come into conflict with other ideologies: for example, socialism; though I don't think it needs to, and it didn't, in my view, for Marx. But most post-structuralisms have moved against the ideology of objectivity as such. They have moved against the 'ideology' of universal and uniform reason that underlies the sciences. They expect to find, and expose, ideological and metaphysical assumptions wherever they go. And that makes it very difficult for them to handle scientific discourses, like the details of chemistry or large parts of linguistics. But to deny, or not give access to, the objectivist vision of structural linguistics and most structuralism, simply because post-structuralism has rejected it, would be more than a mild bit of anti-objectivism. It would be an act of suppression, and a lie about the main tradition of structuralism.

Ferdinand de Saussure's view of language was set out in a series of lecture courses that he gave between 1906 and 1911. A version of these lectures was published posthumously as the *Course in General Linguistics*, (Saussure 1916), edited by two of his students; this is the prime source for Saussure's arguments, and the book that has shaped the whole tradition; but for those who want to go back behind it, there is a critical edition based on the original notebooks (Saussure 1967). There are two English translations of the *Cours* available in 1989 and they are not equivalent; in fact they give a quite different account of the history of linguistic ideas and the discovery of the phoneme! I have made a comparison of them in Appendix A. The French text cited below as Saussure 1916a is the critical edition prepared by Tullio de Mauro, and published by Payot, Paris in 1973. The Baskin translation, published by McGraw-Hill, is cited as Saussure 1916b. The general methodological principles of linguistics that

Saussure put forward are five in number, and I shall consider them in order of importance.

2.1 *Langue and parole (language structure v. speaking in a language)*

First of all, Saussure picked out as the object of study for linguists the system or structure of the language – which he called **langue** – as opposed to the activity of speaking it, which he called **parole**. He thus offered a model for all later structuralist theories.

This distinction is so basic that it is essential to get it clear. Saussure intends that, within the whole field of linguistic activity (**langage**), we should distinguish between the language system (**langue**) and speaking or writing the language (**parole**). There are problems in this three-way distinction which are not so much problems of translation as of technical terminology. The point is that there is a conceptual distinction, absolutely necessary for doing linguistics, which the ordinary layman finds no difficulty in understanding, but which is not exactly reflected in the vocabulary of either English or French – or, as Saussure points out, German or Latin either. The English word 'language' is multiply ambiguous. We can say:

(1) 'What distinguishes man from the animals is language.'
'Language' here refers to a human capability, **and** the way it is used. The word here has its full ambiguity. Or we can say:

(2) 'One language I have learnt is German.'
'Language' here means vocabulary, principles of construction, idioms etc., which we may learn formally, or merely pick up from conversation.

(3) 'Shakespeare's language is brilliantly inventive.'
This means Shakespeare's use-of-language is inventive. The French word 'langage' would also mean use-of-language in this context.

These three examples correspond roughly to the technical categories *langage, langue,* and *parole*.

Of these three, there is no doubt that most people would find *langue* quite the least interesting. *Langage* – language as the general capacity that distinguishes man from the animals, as the dress of thought, as a mode of self-construction – that interests everyone; *parole* – language as the plays of Shakespeare or the sayings of one's mother – that too; but who can be interested in *langue* – language as grammar, vocabulary and sound patterns? The answer is, linguists can. Dictionaries and grammars are what they write. When Saussure gave his lectures he did not negate this point in any way. On the contrary, he made *langue*, which is what dictionaries and grammars describe, the basic object of study, and said that every other type of language study depended on the study of this.

Before leaving this point – which is a quite fundamental one – I shall give an example of the intimate practical relationship, and the absolute logical distinction, between *langue* – a language – and *parole* – speech or writing. The relationship between the two is this: you speak in a language. An easy way of grasping the distinction is to consider the difference between the speeches of Hitler and the German language, which Hitler spoke in. A historian – or a psychologist – might be interested in the speeches of Hitler; a linguist is interested in the language he speaks, and for him the speeches merely provide evidence about the language. If you want to speak German, what you learn is the language – which consists of vocabulary, grammar, rules of pronunciation and so forth. Then, using this knowledge, you make up your own speeches.

The distinction between *langue* and *parole*, taken as that between the systematic structure of a language and the particular things said in it, remains to this day, as it was millennia before Saussure drew attention to it, basic to linguistics as a science and to language learning; odd individuals have denied it in theory, but, if they have done any linguistic work at all, they have accepted it in practice. Strictly speaking, if you deny the distinction between language and speech in this sense, you deny the very existence of, say, the German language (as distinct from the speeches of German people) and it is then very difficult to find a logical place for statements about, say, German irregular verbs. Strictly speaking, you couldn't even say: 'Hans was speaking German but I couldn't understand him, so he switched to English.'

Although everybody agrees with Saussure that the study of language systems has to be central to linguistics, few people would accept his account of the status of *langue*. For Saussure, *langue* is something that is at once social – *langue* is the possession of the community of speakers – and constraining – *langue* is something fixed, *parole* is the realm of freedom. But these two aspects are not necessarily the same – indeed, they are not necessarily even consistent with each other. The concept of *langue* is thus open to two quite different kinds of objection.

The first is political. The notion of *langue*, it is said, presupposes a uniform speech-community with a common, fixed linguistic resource. But real communities are riven with conflict. They contain many different *langues*, side by side; the *langue* (dialect) that you speak is linked with racial and class affiliations. Should we not (in the example given above) study a South African judge confronting a black protestor, rather than some mythically uniform speech-community?

It is obviously true that different dialects are associated with different social groups, and differential access to structures of power; and Saussure was well aware of this, though he considers it explicitly mainly in connection with the problem of national and minority languages. But some scholars have jumped from this to the extraordinary conclusion that to study the grammatical structure of a dialect is to gloss over the social conflicts between speakers of different dialects; and that is not so at all. From the linguist's point of view, there are, either on an ethnic or a class basis, many *langues* to study within the same community, to which different social values are attached; and in terms of which, bitter social wars may well be waged. (Hymes 1964; Fishman 1968; Williams 1970, etc. For a general history of *The Politics of Linguistics*, see Newmeyer 1986.)

But each *langue* still has to be studied as a coherent linguistic system. Social value is not the same as value as a language. To the linguist, all dialects are equal; and this is perhaps the most important contribution linguistics has made to the politics of class and minority culture. To give a crude example: it was in fact the linguists who first pointed out that the lower classes in class societies have dialects of their own, and are not merely making a bad shot at speaking a standard language (cf. e.g. Labov 1969). In saying this they offered a severe critique of one of the standard ideological defences of class privilege: the gut feeling that members of the dominant class are likely to have, that their inferiors 'can't speak properly'. A similar point could be made about the languages of tribal peoples: it is the linguists who pointed out that these are fully as complex and sophisticated as those of civilized peoples: there are no primitive languages.

The second objection to *langue* is linguistic and philosophical. How can a speaker be constrained in his linguistic behaviour – his own spontaneous speech, that is – by *langue*, if *langue* is merely a social fact, external to himself? By the time a person has learnt to speak a language, the structure of that language has become a part of the very self that speaks. Modern linguists (like most teachers of language, ancient and modern) think of a language as a structure which a speaker has learned, usually by picking it up as a child from the speech heard then (Chomsky 1957; 1980). Their orientation is thus toward psychological processes in the individual rather than social facts; and what they stress is that the structure thus learned is not a fixed inventory of resources from which to choose, but a set of principles for making up new expressions. Language is what enables the individual to say new things, and have new thoughts, not an inventory of fixed expressions. This is a definite advance over Saussure.

But nothing could be more absurd than to set this psychological and creative viewpoint against Saussure's sociological viewpoint. Nobody denies that the structure the child learns must be one of those implicit in the speech the child hears. In this sense it must be a social fact, before the individual can learn it. Equally, the language must be a psychological fact – an internalized structure, something that has been learnt – before a person can speak it in society. There is nothing mutually contradictory in this pair of propositions. They follow directly from the fact that we learn a language by hearing our elders speak it, and our children learn it from us.

For the modern linguist, then, the situation is roughly as follows. There may be many different *langues* – different dialects, or even different languages – in the same community, and to them different social values will be attached: some will have high prestige, and some low, some will be required for entry to high office, and some effectively debar the speaker from such office. But these differences are the result of the working of social forces, and in particular of class or ethnic conflicts, and have nothing to do with the internal structure of each dialect, or its productive potential. Children learn their language from their elders; but they can then use it creatively producing *parole* – particular speeches in that *langue* – which they have never heard from anyone.

There is no difference in creative power between a high and low prestige *langue*; there may, however, be a difference in vocabulary content – particularly technical vocabulary – and availability of books. This affects the usefulness of particular *langues*, especially in education. You can't learn nuclear physics in the language of the Hopi Indians; there are no books, and even if there were, the necessary vocabulary has not yet been imported. But of course it could be; and according to Whorf (1956), the grammatical structure of their language is actually better adapted to the content of nuclear physics than English is!

One further point needs to be made about *langue*, for it can lead to some confusion. Differences of dialect, even minor ones, are, like differences of language, a matter of having a different *langue*. But not all differences we observe in language are differences of *langue*. We can, for example, talk formally or informally within the same *langue*. Thus I can say, without changing my dialect or language, either 'I cannot do this' or 'I can't do this'. Differences in tone of this kind, like differences of subject-matter, are differences produced within *parole*, using the same *langue*. Only in those rare cases where a person uses different dialects for formal and informal purposes is a difference of *langue* involved. Some people conduct a successful professional career in some standard world language, but can only make love in the peasant dialect of their childhood. Here the individual finds it necessary to switch between two *langues*, in order to find the appropriate tone within his own *parole*. This is psychologically a very complex situation; but it in no way casts doubt on the *langue/parole* distinction; on the contrary, only in terms of that distinction, or some other distinction like competence/performance which plays a corresponding part, can this and all the other cases of linguistic heterogeneity be exactly described.

The concept of *langue* is quite crucial for literary structuralism. Indeed, literary structuralism arises from an analogical extension of it. There is an important distinction to make here. Literature, as an imitative art using language as a medium, exploits many of the features of language including differences of dialect, of style and so forth; and critics and theorists have always studied these from the time of Plato on. But that is not what literary structuralism is about. Literary structuralism is based on finding an analogy between the cultural norms on which artistic forms are based, and the systematic structure of languages.

The birth of literary structuralism can be given a precise date in the winter of 1928, when Jakobson and Tynjanov put forward the theory that there were synchronic literary systems closely analogous to *langue*. Here is part of the sixth thesis of their short manifesto: *Problems in the Study of Language and Literature* (in Jakobson 1985):

> (6) The assertion of two differing concepts – *la langue* and *la parole* – and the analysis of the relationship between them (the Geneva school) has been exceedingly fruitful for linguistic science. The principles involved in relating these two categories (i.e the existing norm and individual utterances) as applied to literature must be elaborated. In this latter case, the individual utterance cannot be considered without reference to the existing complex of norms.

This poses a question which is crucial for the whole development of semiotics. Does the *langue-parole* distinction apply to sign–systems in general – with the arts as particular examples of sign-systems – or is it strictly confined to languages? Jakobson and Tynjanov extend it to literature, and seem to regard particular works of literature as utterances – items of *parole* – within a system of artistic conventions corresponding to *langue*. If this works at all it ought to work for all the arts. Is there a *langue* for music, for example; and if there is, are individual works of music part of the corresponding *parole*; or is it rather that individual performances are part of *parole*?

Or are we dealing with a loose analogy which can't be pressed too far? If this last is the case, then a structuralist semiotics looks impossible to construct, or at least loses most of its theoretical interest. Roland Barthes (1964a p.10) came to the conclusion that semiological systems were actually parasitic upon language, and couldn't exist apart from it, rather than being independent *langues* in their own right. This is a point to which it will be necessary to return.

2.2   *The diachronic and the synchronic (history versus structure)*

There are two quite different ways in which the linguist can be interested in *langue*. The approach which was dominant in de Saussure's day was a historical one. Linguists were philologists. Their main work was the study of texts written in dead languages. One of the things they studied those texts for was to trace the history of languages, and the changes they had gone through. Philologists were especially interested in tracing the history of sound changes; but of course they studied changes in grammar and vocabulary as well, and established historical connections between languages – in the end, building up elaborate family trees connecting languages like French, Spanish and Italian, which derive from Latin, and languages like English, Dutch and German, which have a Germanic ancestor, and projecting them back to a common proto-Indo-European ancestor that may have been spoken in Hungary or the Ukraine or Iran, several thousand years ago (Parret 1976). Saussure called this **diachronic** linguistics.

Another way – quite traditional in language study over the millennia, but rather neglected in the nineteenth century and down to de Saussure's own day – is to study a language as a total entity, as it exists at one point in time – it might be modern England or the Augustan period in Rome: to write its grammar, its phonology and its lexicon. The earliest work of this kind that we know about was done in ancient India. It was practised by the Greeks and Romans, and in mediaeval and renaissance Europe. In a sense it cannot be avoided if you want to teach a language in a school or university system; though at the higher intellectual levels, by the beginning of the twentieth century, historical philology had rather eclipsed it.

De Saussure called this **synchronic linguistics**. The distinction between the synchronic and the diachronic – both of them, be it noted, ways of studying *langue* – is our second principle. (Saussure 1916a p.139; Saussure 1916b p.98)

Jakobson and others have been sceptical about the complete separation of the synchronic and the diachronic. He points out that archaic and modern forms may actually lie side by side in a language, and even appear within the speech of a single person (Jakobson and Pomorska 1980). Indeed, in a sense this is inevitable. A person who learns a language in 1900 may still be alive in 1960 when the language has substantially changed. It would be very surprising if he and his contemporaries did not have the use of the 1900 and of the 1960, and of all the intermediate synchronic states of language that there had been. People who read books, of course, come to have a degree of passive access to much older forms of the language; some schoolchildren come to read Chaucer without much difficulty.

This means that our theory of *langue* ought to be more sophisticated; we ought to recognize multiple *langues*, present and archaic, governing the speech of one individual. Jakobson went beyond most linguists in his account of this phenomenon. He claimed that the tension between distinct language systems simultaneously present was one of the factors causing language change. (Old- and middle-English specialists will be likely to have a good deal of sympathy with this view, I should think.)

Indeed, from 1926 onward, Jakobson was toying with the notion that linguistic changes 'were systematic and goal-oriented, and that the evolution of language shares its purposefulness with the development of other sociocultural systems'. (Jakobson 1985, p.16). Thus emerges the notion that one might write a rational history of language change, comparable to the Marxist or the Hegelian account of history in general. Needless to say, it has never been written; though everybody nowadays would agree that the history of a language is the history of a succession of language-systems.

With this in mind, we shall be less surprised that the majority of the Jakobson–Tynjanov theses are about diachronic, not synchronic issues. Far from structuralism being an essentially static model, it was, in the eyes of its originators, directed at the discovery of historical laws of development, in literature as well as in language. I shall come back to this point in chapter 2.

2.4 *The arbitrariness of the sign*

Saussure's third principle is that language is best viewed as a system of **signs**, where a sign is defined as an essentially arbitrary linkage between a **signifier** and a **signified**. The signifier is a sound-image. The signified is a concept. When we learn a language it is this arbitrary pairing of sound-images and concepts that we learn. The empirical point of this claim is that there is no necessary connection between sound and meaning – nothing particularly pig-like about the word 'pig', or authoritarian about the word 'policeman', or plural about the noun-ending '-s'. All linguists accept this; onomatopoeia for example is a quite marginal aspect of language.

The principle that signs are arbitrary is easy enough to grasp; it is not so easy to rid oneself of the feeling that there is something natural about them: that there is something elephantine about the word 'elephant'. The reason is probably that we actually think by using signs; so the relationship between signifier and signified is continually reinforced, and comes to seem natural. In semiotics, the notion of the arbitrariness, or conventionality of the sign is often taken right outside language, into realms like film and general culture; and here it can have an extraordinarily liberating effect; no longer does one have to take the conventional images of women, for example, as natural facts; one can see these images as conventional signs, within a sign system rather like a language.

Saussure himself authorized some such extension to his ideas, by saying that he could foresee a new science of **semiology**, of which linguistics would only be a proper part. But one can take the point too far. Linguistic signs are actually much more arbitrary than other kinds of sign, which usually rest on some kind of natural resemblance, even if only a very partial one. Words are wholly arbitrary, and, in the overwhelming majority of cases, have no natural resemblance at all either to the objects they refer to, or the qualities they connote.

Roland Barthes (1957, trans. 1973) was very impressed by the political significance of the principle of the arbitrariness of the sign. In fact he got this insight (from Brecht) before he found semiology as a theoretical framework to put it in. In many of his early essays in *Mythologies* and elsewhere he works to denaturalize conventional images, and he has an explicitly political purpose in this: he thinks that the bourgeoisie hold power partly because of the sway of these images. The newspaper image of a French negro soldier happily saluting makes the French Empire seem merely a natural fact about the world, rather than a definite and revocable political enterprise. Similarly, modern feminists work to expose a process that they call 'gender construction' – the construction in the media and in discourse generally of a stereotype of feminine personality which is then taken as a natural fact about women.

This tradition is left-wing; but there is nothing left-wing about the basic insight. The American movement called General Semantics, based on the work of Alfred Korzybski in the 1930s had exactly the same insight: the word is not the thing. But its political orientation was fairly right-wing, and it was very popular among businessmen (see Hayakawa 1939). What is common to both the left-wing and right-wing tradition here is the feeling that we are somehow being fooled by signs; that something artificial and constructed is pretending to be natural and real. I think that in both cases what we have is an exciting half-truth. (And both camps tend enormously to overvalue the political significance of signs.)

2.4 The oppositional structure of language according to de Saussure

Saussure's fourth major principle is that the arbitrariness of the sign is limited by the systematic nature of sign systems. The signs that make up a language stand in opposition to each other; and this has two effects: on the way we perceive the signifier, and on the way we conceive, or understand, the signified. This point is still accepted today; but it is in articulating it that almost the whole development of modern linguistics has taken place. Saussure suggested a fairly limited number of systematic relationships; and these have been taken up and discussed within semiotics, as possible models for the structure of semiotic systems. One famous programmatic statement that he made was that language is a set of oppositions without positive terms. I include in chapter 6 some arguments that show that this is a logical impossibility for a working sign system. Modern linguistics would suggest a system at once more complicated, and less metaphysically removed from the empirical world.

2.4.1 *The phoneme is the minimal unit.* Consider an individual sign – say, a word in a language. It will, according to Saussure, consist of two parts, indissolubly joined to make one sign: the signifier, which is a sound-image, and the signified, which is a concept. 'Each sound-image is nothing more than the sum of a limited number of elements or **phonemes**' (In English, sounds like /p/,/b/,/t/,/d/,/k/,/g/, etc. There is a very rough correspondence with the alphabet). (Saussure 1916a, p.32; b, p.16)

What is the character of these minimal elements, the phonemes? They have of course a certain phonetic realization (i.e. they are pronounced in a certain definite way), but that is not the linguistically essential thing about them. The essential thing is that they should be different from each other. /b/ is different from /p/, /k/, /t/, /v/, etc.; and this difference is all that matters about the phonemes; they have no meaning, or even perceptual reality apart from their differences from each other. Every language has a finite set of phonemes (from about thirteen to about eighty in number), which are the minimal units from which sound-images are constructed; and their sole property is to be different from each other.

2.4.2 *The sound-image is a chain of phonemes.* How are these sound-images constructed? '. . . in contrast to visual signifiers (nautical signals, etc.) which can offer simultaneous groupings in several dimensions, auditory signifiers have at their command only the dimension of time. Their elements are presented in succession: they form a chain.' Each sound-image is therefore a chain of phonemes, which are purely differential elements. (Saussure 1916a, p.103; b, p.70)

2.4.3 *The sound-image is delimited by the concept.* What is it that delimits this chain? What is it that tells us, as we proceed along a chain of phonemes, that we have left one word and started on another? There is no physical marker of the end of one word and the beginning of another in the course of a simple sentence (say, 'The boy kicked the ball'). What marks the gap between words is the transition between one concept and another. The two phonemes in 'boy' are associated with one concept; the four in 'kicked' with another; but there is no concept associated with 'boyk' or 'icked'. (My examples here replace Saussure's.)

2.4.4 *The concept is delimited by the value of the sign in the language system.* What of the other side of the sign, the concept with which the sound-image is associated? If this were detached from its signifier it would be something purely psychological; and

> Psychologically our thought – apart from its expression in words – is only a shapeless and indistinct mass. Philosophers and linguists have always

agreed in recognising that without the help of signs we would be unable to make a clear-cut, consistent distinction between two ideas. Without language, thought is a vague, uncharted nebula.There are no preexisting ideas, and nothing is distinct before the appearance of language.

(Saussure 1916a, p.155; b, pp.111-2)

Saussure borrows the idea of 'value' from economics and claims that the concept associated with each sign is limited, or determined (the point is not clear) by the value of the sign in the language system as a whole. **Value** is to be distinguished from **signification**, or reference to objects. Thus the English word 'sheep' has a different value from the French word 'mouton', even when they have the same signification; for English has the word 'mutton' to contrast with 'sheep', and French has no corresponding opposition. Similarly French plurals – which cover two or more objects – mean something different from Sanskrit plurals; for Sanskrit possesses a dual case – a plural to cover pairs of objects only – as well as its ordinary plural, which is therefore used to cover three or more objects (Saussure 1916a pp.160-1; b, pp.115-7).

2.4.5 *Language is a system of pure oppositions*. These examples may seem limited in their implications, but Saussure draws very far-reaching conclusions:

> The characteristic role of language with respect to thought is not to create a material phonic means for expressing ideas, but to serve as a link between thought and sound, under conditions that of necessity bring about the reciprocal delimitations of units . . . (Saussure 1916b p.112).
> . . . The conceptual side of value is made up solely of relations and differences with respect to the other terms of language, and the same can be said of its material side . . .(pp.117-18).
> Everything that has been said up to this point boils down to this: in language there are only differences. Even more important: a difference generally implies positive terms between which the difference is set up; but in language there are only differences **without positive terms. (**p.120)

He naturally concludes '. . . language is a form and not a substance.' p.122 (Saussure 1916a, pp.156-169; b, pp.112-122).

2.4.6 *Signs are combined linearly in* **syntagms.** So much for the internal nature of linguistic signs; what about the relations between them? There are two main types: the **syntagmatic**, and the **associative**. (Saussure does not use the category 'paradigmatic' here, though it is often falsely attributed to him.) Syntagmatic relationships are linear ones: words are chained together in fixed phrases and combinations – as in the phrases 'I am . . .' or 'you are . . .', and get their force partly by standing in opposition to what precedes or follows them in discourse. On the face of it, the ideal type of syntagm would be a **sentence**; but Saussure does not think this is possible, because sentences are freely composed and not fixed. They must, therefore, belong to *parole* and not to *langue*. (Saussure 1916a, pp.172-3; b, pp.122-5).

2.4.7 *Signs gain some of their force from their **associations**, material or conceptual.* Outside discourse, words take their meaning from a wide range of associations held in the brain: associative relations. Thus the word 'education' would be associated with the word 'educate' and also with more distantly associated words like 'apprenticeship'. All sorts of similarities can produce associations; Saussure includes under this title both what later linguists would regard as close linguistic relationships like the possession of a common morpheme – 'painful, delightful, frightful, etc'. and purely intellectual associations like an analogy between concepts – 'education' and 'apprenticeship'. (Saussure 1916a p.175; b, p.126).

One example of an 'associative' relationship given by Saussure is the inflectional paradigm – e.g. Latin *dominus, domini, domino* etc. In later linguistics – not in Saussure – the usual opposition is not syntagmatic versus associative, but syntagmatic versus paradigmatic – a narrower concept. See chapter 2, section 5.3.

2.5   The priority of speech over writing

The other famous distinction Saussure made is that between speech and writing; and it does not really belong at the same level as the rest. It is not, that is to say, a fundamental parameter of Saussure's theory; it is, rather, factual observation about the world, coupled with some vigorous advice to his students. Like all linguists, Saussure stressed the importance of the spoken language, as the primary object of study for linguistics, rather than of writing, as its mere derivative.

The point here is that speech came before writing historically, and there are plenty of languages that don't have writing systems; and historical laws about sound changes, of the kind philologists put forward, obviously apply to the spoken, not the written language.

Students from literate cultures always need reminding of these facts; the written form is easier to pin down, so it comes to seem more real than the spoken one; and this trap is easy for philologists – students of dead languages – to fall into, since they exclusively study written evidence, and never hear their language of study spoken.

The point would hardly be worth mentioning in a study on this scale if it had not been for an extraordinary historical development. The philosopher Jacques Derrida (1967c) seized upon Saussure's remarks and interpreted them as the expression of a profound metaphysical prejudice that has dominated the entire Western world, at least since Plato, in favour of speech and against writing. The nature of the prejudice is this: that thought is supposed to be immediately present in speech, but not in writing.

Derrida developed this interpretation by way of a very careful and subtle analysis of Husserl's theory of signs (Derrida 1962). He then projected it onto the whole Western philosophical tradition, reading everything through it. It doesn't seem to be Plato's reason for preferring speech to writing as a medium for philosophy – he was more concerned with the possibilities of arguing and asking questions. And whatever may be the case in philosophy, this metaphysical doctrine seems to be totally irrelevant to anything that ever concerned Saussure. Yet Derrida has been very widely believed.

His position is easier to understand, if not accept, when one realizes that by the 1960s Saussure had been thoroughly reinterpreted, to become a philosopher rather than a linguist, and to offer the basic model for an imperialistic semiological structuralism that covered every field of intellectual life. Derrida's 'deconstruction' of Saussure was directed at that Saussure rather than the real one; but it remains a puzzle: how can he have read Saussure that way? (There is no puzzle about the efforts of later commentators; they have simply read Saussure through Derrida's eyes. As a result, this muddle has spread through half the literature by now.) I will return to this point.

These, then, are the five main principles of Saussure for the analysis of languages, which as we shall see were both developed and criticized by later linguists. He left also a hint that his model would apply to a wider class of sign systems, in a new science of semiology; and we shall need to consider briefly how this actually came about.

NOTES

1. Mathematically, one could I suppose say that a structure is merely a set, with a mapping from members of the set to members of the set. The nature of the mapping specifies what the structure is. In this book I work exclusively in concrete examples of structures, with only a few references to mathematical treatments of language structure which I happen to know about, like Chomsky (1956).
2. Lévi-Strauss was actually thinking of Russian formalism and its successor school, Prague School structuralism; presumably he took his characterization of their differences from Roman Jakobson, a leading figure in both schools.
3. See Chomsky (1957; 1965 chapter 2). For mathematical treatments at a high level of rigour, Chomsky (1956), Chomsky and Miller, in Luce, Bush and Galanter (1963). My account is a gross simplification and takes no heed of post-1960s work, but will do for the purposes of this discussion.
    It is important to realize that trees in linguistics are pure mathematical structures and that they have only the properties that they are defined to have. Literary critics and some philosophers treat linguistic structures in a quite fantastic way. According to Deleuze and Guattari (1980), the tree structure set out here is in some sense a hierarchy of authority! Now it so happens that while grammarians have been diagramming sentences with tree structures for centuries, the trees have in general had S, or its equivalent, drawn at the top only since Chomsky. For convenience, I have drawn this tree with S at the bottom. We have thus both reversed the hierarchy. This must be the easiest social revolution either Chomsky or I have ever achieved! In fact, it doesn't matter a damn which way up the tree is drawn; and both forms are exactly equivalent to the flat form with labelled brackets, which on Deleuze and Guattari principles ought to be an egalitarian form.
4. The analogy here is a crude one, but makes a serious point which is made again, without the analogy, in chapter 5. I am proposing a realist ontology of mathematics and logic, and trying to explain all three of its characteristic properties: internal validity, self-evidence and applicability to the real world, while recognizing that it is an unfinished human construction. Merely referring to the materiality of the practices of mathematicians, of course, would do nothing to block a Platonist theory of their object. On my view they are talking about the real world, but about its possibilities.
5. What I have in mind when I speak of a 'real structuralist' is someone like, say Jakobson or Tynjanov in 1928, when they proposed literary structuralism. (See next section for their definition and next chapter for discussion.) I am afraid some real structuralists of more recent vintage have proposed much odder claims than this. One post-structuralist who read my first chapter with intense disapproval because of its mechanistic approach suggested that the strong claim of structuralists was actually that 'Things have structures' and that 'Language is a meta-structure which itself structures these objectal structures.'

I was cross with him when I read this; because as a claim this is hopelessly confused and idealist, and I wouldn't admire structuralism if that was what it meant. But on reflection it does fairly represent positions that were being taken in France at about the time of the death of structuralism in the late 1960s. So I am grateful to my unknown benefactor.

BOOKS

De Saussure, F. 1916a,b,c *Course in General Linguistics*

Only one reference for basic reading is given for this chapter; but that is more important than any other reference in the book. The 1916 version of the *Cours de Linguistique Générale* is, unlike much structuralist and post-structuralist writing, immediately comprehensible to the undergraduate or general reader. It is best read in French, but perfectly satisfactory in English: there is a discussion of the two available translations in the Appendix to this book.

Beginners are strongly advised NOT to read any general introduction to Saussure before reading the *Course* itself. All those I have read commit the serious error of reading back into the text of 1916 ideas which really belong to the 1950s or 1960s. The context in which to read a general introduction to the interpretation of Saussure in the 1950s and 1960s is chapter 3, and I have recommended one there. But under no circumstances should a serious reader regard it as satisfactory to replace the original work by any popular introduction or commentary, including mine, half the nonsense currently talked about Saussure comes from making such a replacement.

FURTHER READING

Structuralism: Lévi-Strauss 1958, Hawkes 1977, Merquior 1986, Pettit 1977, Piaget 1968, Runciman 1969.
Philosophy of Language: Austin 1962a,b, Carnap 1937.

Linguistics: Saussure, Jakobson, and Chomsky passim; Bloomfield 1933, Hockett 1958, Luce, Bush and Galanter 1963, 1964, Pike 1967, Sapir 1921.

Historical Linguistics: Barber 1964, Lehmann 1967, Malmberg 1983, Parrett 1976.

Sociolinguistics and Politics of Language: Bernstein 1971, Fishman 1968, Hymes 1964, Jackson 1974, Labov 1970, Newmeyer 1986, Open University 1971, 1977, Pateman 1983, 1988, Pécheux 1975, Pratt 1977, Williams 1970.

Language and Literature: Easthope 1983, Eliot 1919, 1944, 1951, Leavis passim, Lodge D 1972, 1988, O'Malley 1964, Riffaterre 1978, Robinson 1975, Thompson 1964.

For titles and publishers, see main bibliography.

CHAPTER TWO
The Creative Phase of Structuralist Theory

Panini to Roman Jakobson: a Science of Language from Ancient India to Modern Prague

SUMMARY

This chapter provides a very brief sketch of the history of structuralism, and is intended mainly to correct the common assumption that the creative phase of structuralism occurred in France in the 1960s. In fact, the structuralist model of language lasted from the time of Saussure to the mid-1950s; when it was superseded by the generative model. Literary structuralism began in Prague in 1928 and many important structuralist studies of literature were made, particularly in the Prague school, in the 1930s. A good account of a later form of the structuralist model of language is given by Jakobson (1976) *Lectures on Sound and Meaning*; these lectures influenced Lévi-Strauss. Some of Jakobson's criticisms of the standard structuralist model are considered here: curiously, these often undercut the whole later development of structuralist theory in France that was built on Jakobson's work.

1 STRUCTURALISM AS CULT: THE MYTH OF THE 1960S AND THE TRUE HISTORY

Most people I meet, who have any conception of structuralism at all, have a curiously foreshortened and distorted view of its history. De

Saussure is there – or at least, one book of his, published after his death, in 1916. And so are certain famous French writers of the 1960s: Barthes, Lévi-Strauss, Althusser, Foucault, Derrida and Lacan, probably in that order; with Kristeva coming up hard on and off the rails and needed anyway as the statutory feminist. But there is nothing in between these epochs. A recent book – *Theories of Discourse* (Diane MacDonell 1986, p. 8) – puts this view of intellectual history very concisely: 'The seminal work of structural linguistics was Saussure's *Course in General Linguistics* (1916, trans. 1974); this was taken up by structuralism in the 1960s.'

The sceptical reader will be rightly suspicious of this brief story. 'Did nothing happen in the forty-four years between 1916 and the golden decade?' she will ask. Well, yes actually, quite a lot did. Structuralism was the main framework for work in theoretical linguistics, on both sides of the Atlantic, from about 1916, when de Saussure's *Cours* was published, to the publication of Chomsky's *Syntactic Structures* in 1957. Literary structuralism, as we have seen, dates from the Tynjanov–Jakobson theses, in 1928. And when, for example, was the following passage written, with its astonishing claim that structuralism is the central principle of all modern science?

> Were we to comprise the leading idea of present-day science in its most various manifestations, we could hardly find a more appropriate designation than structuralism. Any set of phenomena examined by contemporary science is treated not as a mechanical agglomeration but as a structural whole, and the basic task is to reveal the inner, whether static or developmental, laws of this system. What appears to be the focus of scientific preoccupations is no longer the outer stimulus, but the internal premises of the development; now the mechanical conception of processes yields to the question of their functions. Therefore immanent considerations of language and literature were predestined to take a prominent place in the debates of . . .

The answer, of course, is 1929. The debates were those of the First International Conference of Slavists; the author of the passage was Roman Jakobson, who recalled it forty years later in a little book called *Main Trends in the Science of Language*, which he dedicated to his colleague and occasional pupil, Claude Lévi-Strauss.

For Jakobson in 1929, structuralism was not a movement whose time would come in thirty years or so. On the contrary, it was the dominant movement in contemporary science in general and the central theoretical issue both in linguistics and literary theory. And this movement already had a substantial history in the work of the Russian formalists. These debates had begun, as far as Jakobson was concerned, fourteen years before, with the founding of the Moscow Linguistic Circle in 1915. The other platform of the Russian formalists, the Opojaz (Society for the Study of Poetical Language) was established in St Petersburg in 1916. Jakobson moved to Prague in 1920, partly to escape from developing political pressure; the Linguistic Circle of Prague was founded in 1926, and this – the base of Jakobson, Trubetskoy and Mukarovsky – became the main centre for the development of structuralist theory between the wars; though there were also centres in Copenhagen and Geneva.

The main development of modern structural linguistics and the first phase of structuralist literary theory thus came in the 1920s and 1930s, before it was disrupted by the Second World War. At the outbreak of war Trubetskoy died; Jakobson fled, eventually to America; work was interrupted by Nazi pressure, by economic pressure, and in due course by Stalinist pressure. The publication of the fourth volume of Mukarovsky's collected works was delayed for twenty years, for political reasons, and it came out eventually on his seventy-fifth birthday. As Galan (1985) points out, the tragedy was that nobody in the West noticed; it was the golden decade of the 1960s, and all eyes were currently fixed upon Paris.

What, then, of the French, who are so widely supposed to have invented structuralism in the 1960s? Lévi-Strauss learnt his linguistics, partly from Jakobson, around 1942; if scientific creativity is at issue, his best period was the 1940s. (See section 3.) Jacques Lacan was throwing the name of Saussure around in 1953. His best period was the 1950s (Clément 1983). All that we had to wait till the 1960s for was popular enthusiasm – 'cocktail-party gossip' of the kind Piaget (1968, p. 1) refers to – and of course, for Roland Barthes, Foucault, Derrida and an exciting student revolution. Unfortunately, many of us were young at the time of that revolution. Bliss was it in that dawn to be alive; I remember having that feeling myself, in a mild sort of way. (I wasn't quite young enough.) But it distorts one's historical perspective.

It is no part of my purpose here to attack MacDonell. Indeed, I think that she has captured and expressed an important truth. It is not historical truth. But it is the truth of what students are taught about structuralism in many literature departments; and it is the truth of an underlying value judgement: that structuralism is to be seen as a brief French prelude to post-structuralism and to modern theory, which are what really matter. It is of course, against that value judgement that this book is being written. In my view, modern theory is an ideology of opposition that can only be maintained in being by these vast selective blindnesses to whole academic subjects – like linguistics or materialist anthropology – and to whole periods – forty years in this case! – of intellectual history.

2   LINGUISTICS AS HARD SCIENCE: THE TRUE ROLE OF DE SAUSSURE

Nor is this the only suppression. Theorists often go back further than the beginning of the twentieth century in search of the foundations of sign theory. They go back, quite properly, to the mid-nineteenth century to C. S. Pierce (semiotician and metaphysician – see Esposito 1980); to Locke (1689); to the Stoics; to Plato and Aristotle. For Julia Kristeva (1971), in one of her grandest visions, semiotic activity 'marks our Western episteme from its Greek beginnings to its positivist apotheosis'. For her it is the semiotic enterprise that actually founds science, by developing the concept of the sign, which is basic to scientific abstraction. And it is semiotics, or at least her version of it, semanalysis, which is now (1969) about to put in question science and metaphysics. Other theorists seize on the world-old battle between philosophy and rhetoric, which starts with Plato, sways about uneasily through the Middle Ages and the Renaissance; which rhetoric was supposed to have lost for ever at the time of the rise of science, and which now has been renewed in the English departments.

What these visions foreclose is the possibility of science as an empirical enquiry into structures independent of the investigator and objectively present in the world. So it is natural that the one aspect of language study that is never referred to is the 2,500-year history of empirical linguistics. People talk as if Saussure were the founder of synchronic linguistic description, and as if this were some sort of philosophical idea of his; actually, in the form of Grammar, it has always been the staple of Western education. Descriptive generative phonology, on lines not unlike those of Chomsky and Halle (that is, including the postulation of hypothetical intermediate forms to explain observed forms), was practised by the Sanskrit grammarian Panini before Plato was born (Robins 1967). Linguistics became scientific before the natural sciences did; it is a willed ignorance of this long tradition of objective description of language structures that leads people to see Saussure as primarily a philosopher.

The linguistic science of the nineteenth century was neither rhetorical nor philosophical in character. It was, rather, a hard empirical science, strictly comparable to chemistry or Darwinian biology in its concern to provide theories that would explain a vast mass of factual detail. But these theories were, like those of palaeontology, historical. Linguistics was then overwhelmingly dominated by philological investigations of the language of old texts. These were used to build up a history of four thousand years of linguistic development and change, and what they offered in the end was a set of historical 'laws' governing sound changes, and a set of family trees connecting the major languages (see Lehmann 1967 for the major papers).

In this context the change to a synchronic point of view in the twentieth century was in a sense inevitable; no further theoretical development in the subject, even within historical linguistics itself, would have been possible without such a change. Most language study has always been synchronic; we can, after all, only speak, write or read a language as it exists at one point in time; and real linguistic history is the history of successive language-states. The linguistics of the twentieth century – of Mathesius, of Jakobson, of Hjelmslev, of Sapir and of Bloomfield – would have had to re-emphasize the synchronic aspect of language, its existence as a simultaneous structure, even if Saussure had never written a word.

Ferdinand de Saussure gave his account of the nature of human language and the proper methods for its study in lectures delivered in Geneva at the very end of his career. That career was in historical philology – the history of languages – not general linguistics; general linguistics in its modern form was effectively founded by these lectures. They must be thought of as the attempt of a great historical linguist, who thought that his subject had come to an impasse, to shift the emphasis of study in it from the historical to the contemporary, and from the study of individual items – particular sounds undergoing sound changes – to that of global structural relationships between signs.

Saussure was by no means the only linguist who was thinking along these lines. Vilem Mathesius, founder of the Prague Linguistic Circle, pointed out that he himself had declared his allegiance to synchronic, rather than diachronic study, by 1909, several years before Saussure's lectures were published. According to Jakobson (1976), the concept of the phoneme had been proposed, by the Polish linguist Jan Baudouin de Courtenay, in 1870, at the beginning of the Neo-Grammarian period, the most strict and radical period in historical philology! According to Josef Vachek (1966), the young Trubetskoy and Jakobson were led to a synchronic approach as much by the Polish and Russian tradition of Baudouin de Courtenay and L.V. Scerba as by any message brought from Geneva. Phoneme theory always remained at the heart of structuralist linguistics.

When the first International Congress of Linguists was held at Leiden in 1928, it was a joint programme of linguistic analysis from members of the Prague circle (Jakobson, Mathesius, Trubetskoy) and the Geneva School (Charles Bally, A. Sechehaye) which was accepted as policy. This gave almost official status to a broad 'structuralist' model in European linguistics. Saussure's lectures must be seen therefore, as offering not an isolated or personal philosophical schema, but the theoretical framework for urgently needed linguistic research; and this research programme was actually carried out by the next generation of scholars in Geneva, Prague, Copenhagen and elsewhere (Vachek 1966).

Modern expositions of 'Saussurean' theory often fail to note that Saussure's lectures were originally given by a philologist, to students of philology, and are packed with linguistic illustrations. To such students Saussure was mainly offering a more systematic and intellectually satisfying framework within which to study languages. The 'philosophy' of Saussure at this stage was no more than a discussion of linguistic methodology. He was not offering a scheme of general philosophy, idealist or otherwise. But in the course of these lectures he did suggest that the study of language was only a part of a larger science of signs in general – semiology. The content of this larger science was as yet unknown, but its place was already marked out for it. The study of language offered a model for the larger science to come (Saussure 1916).

Saussure's influence later divided into two streams, of utterly different character. From the main body of his lectures descends the European tradition of modern general linguistics. One must not underestimate the philosophical sophistication of this tradition. Jakobson (1973) records discussions of Husserl in the early 1920s in the Moscow Linguistic Circle, and later in the Prague, and Copenhagen linguistic circles. But linguistics is on the whole a sober, classificatory discipline, much given to detail, and with few of the crazy, disturbing philosophical implications of post-structuralist semiotics. For a long time this was also true of linguistics-based structuralism, the achievements of which can be represented by, say, Jakobson's analyses of poems by Baudelaire and by Shakespeare (De George and De George 1972; Jakobson and Jones 1970).

In the long term, however, Saussure's views had a completely different fate within linguistics and within the intellectual movement which began as structuralism and finally reversed itself into post-structuralism. For linguists he is a scientific classic. They read his work as an early study of language that has been very influential and is still well worth reading; though many of its theories are now superseded. For the later structuralist movement he is more like a literary classic or even a sacred text; they interpret him in the light of their own concerns, often misunderstanding, misrepresenting, or even plain lying to bring him in line with current questions.

A post-structuralist treatment like that of Jacques Derrida in *Of Grammatology* (1967c) is I think incomprehensible to a linguist even as a joke, since it is not clear within linguistics what is the point of the joke.

This process has come about gradually. One cannot understand the fundamental research strategy that characterized structuralism at its most promising on the basis of the modern, partly fictionalized Saussure. One has to go back to what he actually said, or is reported by his students as saying. Fortunately, the *Course in General Linguistics* is a fairly clear (though composite) book.

3 THE CREATIVE PHASE OF STRUCTURALISM: THE 1930s

There were four main phases in the structuralist movement; though the division between them is not chronologically tidy. The first, and longest, was, as I have said, a phase in the history of linguistic theory. Structuralism provided the framework for the most interesting theoretical discussions in linguistics from the time of Saussure to the coming of generative grammar in the late 1950s. It is one of the many ironies of the history of the movement that this framework for linguistics – the one on which almost all the non-linguistic structuralist developments were based – had been decisively overthrown just before structuralism became a popular craze in France.

The second phase, which we can date from the late 1920s, was an ambitious attempt to apply structuralist principles across the whole field of linguistics and literature as well. The ancestry of this movement on the literary-critical side was in Russian formalism. A Russian formalist like Shklovsky in 1914 resembles in some ways a figure like Ezra Pound in England in the same period. In the background are modern movements of Symbolist and of Futurist poetry; part of the critical problem is coming to terms with these. An essential move seems to be to reject all those things which are extraneous to the literary work itself: history, society, personal psychology of the author; and to look at the art work for its own sake, and as a thing made. This need becomes all the stronger when a revolution in society begins: making a new art is no longer mere propaganda for making a new society; it is a part of making a new society; a new world needs to contain new things.

Thinking in this way, one may also want to differentiate between the immense artistic significance of the art work, the thing made, and the artistic irrelevance and unimportance of the psychological or political, thematic or motivic material it is made out of. One may even, more radically, argue that everything, including subject matter, and perhaps especially personal and political subject matter, as soon as it enters a work of literature becomes a literary device, to be judged as such: there is no separable subject matter in a work of art. What was central to formalism (and the similarity to the ideas of, say, T. S. Eliot (1919) is remarkable) was the intuition that 'a work of art was an aesthetic unit obedient to its own laws' (J. E. Bowlt in Bann and Bowlt 1973). But what were those laws? Or as Jakobson put it, in 1919: what constituted literariness?

What structuralism offered was the possibility that somewhere in the structure of language were suggestions for what those laws might be; and for where literariness might reside. Now these two questions are in principle equivalent; but there is an important difference of emphasis between them, which led in the end to entirely different types of answer being given. If you look for a quality of literariness, you are very likely to look for it in the language of literature. That was on the whole Jakobson's route. It is a broad highway paved with detailed studies of phonology and versification, grammar and versification, and so forth. It is a route that leads to the development of linguistic stylistics. It led Jakobson himself, in the end (that is, in 1958, when he was established in America), to claim that Poetics was a proper branch of the science of linguistics (Jakobson 1958, in Sebeok 1960).

The other form of the question leads one to look first at the large-scale 'syntax' of a work: at its construction. Then at its semantics; what, and how, it means; how it functions. In the case of literature, as we shall see, we are rapidly forced to abandon the purely synchronic approach, the view of each work isolated against a background of synchronic literary conventions, and to see each one alluding to the earlier ones in a kind of dialogue conducted across historical time. We thus re-establish a literary history. Finally, there emerges a kind of pragmatics: works of literature are in dialogue not only with other works of literature, but with what is not literature: with history, even perhaps, with the individual psychology of the author. This, at least in large part, seems to have been the trajectory of Mukarovsky.

The original structuralist manifesto: 'Problems in the Study of Language and Literature' (in Matejka and Pomorska 1971; Jakobson 1985) was written in Russian, during a visit by Tynjanov to Jakobson in Prague in 1928. At that time formalism was under some political pressure. Jakobson himself had left Moscow for Prague in 1920; he was a founder-member of the Prague Linguistic Circle, itself a successor to the Moscow Linguistic Circle. The manifesto looks in many ways like a political document: a defence of the autonomy both of literary structure and literary history, from the Russian Marxist insistence that both are reflections, in a fairly crude way, of an economic base.

With this in mind we shall be less surprised that the majority of the Jakobson-Tynjanov theses are about diachronic, not synchronic issues. Thus, here are theses 2 and 3.

(2) The history of literature (art) being simultaneous with other historical series, is characterised, as is each of these series, by a complex network of specific structural laws. Without an elucidation of these laws, it is impossible to establish in a scientific manner the correlation between the literary series and other historical series.

(3) The evolution of literature cannot be understood until the evolutionary problem ceases to be obscured by questions about episodic, non-systemic genesis, whether literary (for example, so-called 'literary influences') or extraliterary. The literary and extraliterary material used in literature may be introduced into the orbit of scientific investigation only when it is considered from a functional point of view.

In the background of these declarations is probably a desire to distance literary history from close dependence on official Marxist history of society. Nonetheless, it is interesting (in view of the usual charge against structuralism that it doesn't reckon with history) that for Jakobson and Tynjanov,

(7) An analysis of the structural laws of language and literature and their evolution inevitably leads to the establishment of a limited series of actually existing types (and correspondingly, of types of structural evolution).

And that they look forward to

(8) A disclosure of the immanent laws of the history of literature (and language) . . .

Needless to say, this disclosure hasn't yet been made; but Prague School structuralists did make interesting contributions to literary history, which are briefly discussed below.

It was the later, French school that reverted to a more Saussurean, and less historical position; and gave some support to the claim that structuralism was anti-historical. But – despite Althusser's general lack of interest in linguistic questions – there are some interesting parallels between some of Jakobson's speculations about time (Jakobson 1985), and Althusser's notion of differential historical time, which was also evolved when Althusser was trying to distance himself from a crudely unilinear Marxist model of history. (Althusser 1965; Althusser and Balibar 1968).

One must not, however, overemphasize the political reasons for having a diachronic structuralism, at least in the study of literature. There are very good intellectual reasons as well; or at least, there are reasons why a purely synchronic structuralism will not work for literature. One can begin to get at these by asking a very fundamental question: why should there be any relationship between the structure of language and that of literature, over and above what is involved in one being the medium for the other?

The fields of language and literature probably did not appear quite as distinct in the time of the Russian formalists as they perhaps do today. Many of the scholars in the Moscow and Prague Linguistic Circles took a lifelong interest in both. Jakobson himself was a major linguist, a minor poet and an important critic; his account of the poets of his generation is powerfully moving ('On a Generation that Squandered its Poets', in Jakobson 1985). Moreover, one of the central topics that the circles investigated was Slavonic versification. There are no topics in the whole of literary and linguistic theory closer together than verse form and phonology.

But the pure structuralist approach was not equally successful for linguistics and for literary theory. The attempt to apply synchronic structural principles within linguistics itself was largely successful. The main reason for this is that it really is the case that languages have a synchronic structure. People who speak a language do speak within a describable linguistic structure currently prevailing, and not within some other structure, equally definite and describable, which prevailed two or three hundred years before. The task of the descriptive linguist is therefore a feasible one. Structuralist linguistics, in the hands of such people as Jakobson and Trubetskoy, produced results – such as the full development of the theory of the phoneme, and then the decomposition of the phoneme into distinctive features – which have been incorporated into linguistics and later modified but not wholly superseded.

Structuralist literary theory was not, and could not be, equally successful. The main reason for this is that it is based on a **metaphorical** adaptation of Saussurean principles. The notion is that literary conventions are a rough equivalent of the structural principles of a language; literary works are then equivalent to words, or sentences, or other expressions of that language. Alternatively one might see each work as an embodiment of a unique set of conventions – its language – and see the task of structuralist analysis as showing what that unique language is. There are evidently other possibilities; it is obvious that all of them are metaphorical, and this goes for all versions of structuralist literary theory that I have seen.

In a brilliant Anglo-American work published in 1975, and based on French rather than Czech structuralism, Jonathan Culler extracted the essential metaphor behind linguistics-based literary structuralism, and rebased it on modern generative linguistics. Literary theory should be the study of literary competence, he claimed, just as Chomsky's linguistics is the study of linguistic competence. How would this work? A person's linguistic competence is his tacit knowledge of the rules of construction and vocabulary of a language, which enables him to recognize and produce expressions of that language. His literary competence would therefore be his tacit knowledge of the synchronic literary conventions that enable him to recognize, and to produce if he produces, works of literature. The problem is, that this theory is as metaphorical as the earlier one. There is no precisely defined and explicitly listable set of synchronic literary conventions, comparable to the rules of a generative grammar.

On the contrary, literature works just as much by tacit reference to particular past works as to current norms; and a work of literature will communicate as much by significantly varying from the expectations set up either by past works or current norms as it will by conformity with them. This is as if, on the linguistic analogy, we were to produce new sentences by echoing, with significant changes, particular sentences we have heard in the past, and communicate our ideas mainly by deliberate grammatical errors.

The impressive thing about Prague School literary structuralism is that it actually faced up to some of these problems. It is useful, for this purpose, to consider the history of Russian formalism and of Prague School structuralism as a continuous process. As we have seen, certain key figures, like Jakobson, are common to the two schools; and Russian formalism can be seen as having set up, at an intuitive level, a problem to which Prague School structuralism offers a solution.

There is a fine study of this solution in F. V. Galan, *Historic Structures*, on which I am heavily dependent here. But I think I disagree with Galan's evaluations. Here is Mukarovsky's sophisticated definition of structure: 'The reciprocal relationships of all the poetic work's elements, actualised as well as nonactualised, create its structure. This structure is dynamic, containing both the tendencies of convergence and divergence, and is an artistic phenomenon which cannot be taken apart since each of its elements gains value only in a relationship to the whole' (Galan 1985, p. 30).

Galan celebrates this definition as: 'dynamic itself, for it embraces at once the langue–parole antinomy and . . . that between synchrony and diachrony'. That is true. But what is the point of structuralism as an analytical method, if it is based on a purely phenomenological and subjective concept of structure, as 'an artistic phenomenon which cannot be taken apart'?

And here is Mukarovsky coming to terms with literary history:

> It is clear that the value of respective parts does not depend on *a priori* norms but is given by their relationship to the whole. The value of the entire work, then, is determined by the degree to which it is able to fulfil the structural principle that underlies it. Structure, in other words, is a phenomenological and not an empirical reality; it is not the work itself, but the set of functional relationships which are located in the consciousness of a collective (generation, milieu, etc.). Several distinct structures with distinct dominants and distinct hierarchies among their parts can gradually be realised, in different times or, as the case may be, milieux, on the basis of the same work of art. Thus, the nature of structure is not univocally given by the work. The structure becomes explicit, however, once we perceive the work against the background of a vital tradition from which this work diverges and which it reflects. If the background of the tradition shifts, the structure changes too – the dominant is altered, etc. Owing to such a change the work assumes a completely new appearance. (Galan 1985, p.35)

As Galan quite reasonably points out (p. 58), Mukarovsky's own pretensions to scientific objectivity have now disappeared. 'The work of art comes close to resembling a Kantian noumenon, perceptible and knowable only through its appearances.'

This brings out the powerful tendencies toward idealism that were present in literary structuralism from very early on. It is worth remembering that in the history of philosophy, there was a next step directly after Kant (1790) had claimed that we could never know the thing-in-itself. The German idealists of the nineteenth century denied that there was a thing-in-itself. The world, for them, was constructed in the head – possibly the collective head of a developing Absolute Mind whose life was human history. This is the idealism that Marx explicitly repudiated. Ironically, it is a step corresponding to this – the denial of the existence of any objective work of art – that has been taken by many modern structuralist critics; and, more recently, even by critics who have called themselves Marxist, and who follow remotely in the train of Althusser (cf. Eagleton 1983).

Where Mukarovsky differs from such critics, and retains a strongly objective and scientific approach, is in his handling of lower-level phenomena. When it comes to phonology and to versification, his work is hard and objective, and bristles with diagrams and statistical tables. When he draws the large-scale picture of relationships in history and with society, he is broad, suggestive and phenomenological, as we can see above. And this is not, I think, simply his fault. On the contrary, it is inherent in the nature of the phenomena. The sound patterns of a language actually are structured in regular ways; versification works as a device by virtue of its relation to these natural properties of the language. If we look at the level of history and society, such patterns, at such a level of regularity and precision, are simply not to be found.

This is an important point, because it implies that not only the triumph of structuralism, but also the first sign of failure, came in the early 1930s. Consider what success would have meant. If there had really been a strong analogy between the norms under which works of art are produced, and the synchronic structure of a natural language, such that one could write an explicit 'grammatical' or 'phonological' description of the norms under which works of art are produced – can one imagine that Mukarovsky and Jakobson would not have written and published that description? At least in a crude and early form? Have there ever in all history been men better qualified to do this? Compare them, for example, with the major figures of a later generation, Lévi-Strauss, Lacan and Barthes, all of whom, whatever their expertise in their primary discipline, preserved a strictly amateur status in linguistics.

But, as we have found in our own day, if structuralism doesn't work, there is always semiotics. For Galan, the triumph of the later Prague School was to build up a consistent view of the work of art as a sign. The 'work-thing' or material datum, corresponds here to the Saussurean signifier; the 'aesthetic object' or immaterial signification (which seems to mean that which is phenomenologically present as an actually experienced work of art) is the signified. Galan points to some problems here arising from the inapplicability of the principle of the arbitrariness of the sign, and the question of whether a work of art can reasonably be taken to correspond with a single word of a language. My own objection would be different – I don't see how a semiotic position can ever lead to anything but a philosophical account of the work of art. The scientific goal of explanatory theory seems to be abandoned. I wonder if I am the only living person who is worried by this.

That, of course, does not and did not stop important interpretations being produced in this phase. Jakobson and Mukarovsky even produced an exciting innovation in subject-matter – extending their treatment from the purely language-based arts to cinema. That too didn't have to wait for *Screen*.

4   THE LINGUISTIC MODEL OF JAKOBSON

French structuralism was born in New York in 1942. Jakobson had fled from the Nazis first to Scandinavia, then to America; where he found the linguistics establishment sunk 'in the most vulgar period of behaviorism', and less than totally welcoming to a distinguished foreign scholar. The newly established Free School of Advanced Studies – staffed by French and Belgian exiles from occupied territories and Vichy France – offered him a chair in general linguistics; and he set to work to prepare lectures in French on *Sound and Meaning* (Jakobson 1976).

This series of lectures has great importance for the development of the French phase of structuralism, for it was what first introduced Claude Lévi-Strauss to structural linguistics; as he acknowledged in a grateful, and graceful preface, when they were published thirty years later. It is ironic therefore to find that Jakobson dismisses as obvious errors certain Saussurean points that we take for granted in a later structuralist tradition, though that tradition stems in part from Jakobson's work.

Jakobson was at that time at the height of his powers. A great linguist, and the creator of distinctive feature theory in phonology, in the course of a very long career he also did work on metaphor and aphasia (mental disorder, often due to brain damage, affecting the use of language) as well as on folk-tales and on the analysis of poetry.

Linguistics and Poetics, his paper for the Style in Language conference at Indiana, 1958 (Sebeok 1960) remains perhaps the most influential paper in linguistic stylistics that has yet been written. It seems strange to say this of the inventor of literary structuralism; but in the end he seems to me much more a linguist and stylistician than a structuralist thinker: the greatest of all students of the poetry of grammar; but no more successful than anybody else in producing a generative grammar of poetry.

But he was certainly among the most powerful propagandists for structuralism that there have ever been: for not only had he made great claims about its possibilities, but his own multifarious achievements suggested that those possibilities were really there. Without Jakobson, Lévi-Strauss would never have become a structuralist; and without Lévi-Strauss, the French would probably never have heard of the idea. They might have taken up Marshall McLuhan or Wittgenstein instead.

The *Lectures on Sound and Meaning*, however, were not propagandist at all; they were a straightforward critical introduction to linguistics. And this was exactly what was needed at that time. For it was the scientific prestige of structural linguistics – not just the insights of de Saussure – that formed the basis of the next phase of structuralism. The success of linguistics showed that Saussurean ideas could be worked out in detail, and in a rigorous theoretical way, to order masses of empirical data. The material itself was fairly trivial; no one but a linguist can get very excited about sound-patterns in natural languages. But the success of the method suggested its application to more intrinsically interesting material.

The third phase of structuralism can accordingly be characterized as an attempt to apply the principles of structural linguistics in other fields, in effect building up the science of semiology that de Saussure had postulated, but on the basis of the sophisticated linguistics available in the 1940s and 1950s. For linguistics does not stand still. All seven of the Saussurean points of structure I listed in chapter 1 have had to be modified or abandoned in the light of modern linguistics; and a number of cogent criticisms had already been made forty years ago.

4.1 The splitting of the phoneme

Perhaps the most important technological achievement of the twentieth century has been the splitting of the atom. Jakobson's feat was less than this: he split the phoneme, which was the atom of linguistics. Phonemes, said Jakobson, are constructed of smaller units, called distinctive features.

Jakobson's point is that the phoneme is not the unanalysable smallest unit of language; and the contrast between one phoneme and another is not the contrast between one unanalysable unit and another. Take the English phonemes /s/ and /z/. They differ in one significant feature of pronunciation: /z/ is voiced; that is, the vocal cords are allowed to buzz while it is pronounced; /s/, on the other hand, is not voiced. The same difference distinguishes the pair /p/ and /b/ and the pair /f/ and /v/. (One can test this difference out by pronouncing each pair in turn, resting a finger on one's Adam's apple.)

It is possible, says Jakobson, to isolate all the features which distinguish one phoneme from another – the distinctive features – and describe each of them, both in terms of articulation by the vocal organs, and in terms of acoustics. Thus one distinctive articulatory feature is closing the vocal tract at one end – front or back – as in p,b,k,g – rather than in the middle – as in t,d. It has as an acoustic correlate a low rather than a high resonance in the vocal tract. It is units like these – each one a special way of articulating a sound, accompanied by a characteristic quality of sound – which are the true smallest units from which all the languages in the world are built up.

When we pronounce a phoneme, what we are really doing is to combine several distinctive features of articulation, and produce a sound combining several distinctive acoustic features. A phoneme is, therefore, a bundle of distinctive features; and it is the distinctive feature that is the smallest unit of language. It is also no longer true to say that we cannot say more than one thing at a time. We can, indeed we must, pronounce several distinctive features at the same time; they are not separately pronounceable. So language is not a simple, linear thing. Closing our lips, voicing and letting the sound explode are all part of producing a single phoneme /b/.

Now this is obviously a major technical advance for the linguist; but does it – or should it – make any difference at all for the general structuralist tradition? I think it should have made a major difference, and it is one of the curiosities of that tradition that it did not. Pure phoneme theory – in which phonemes are only perceived as distinct because of their opposition to each other, and also only function in the language in terms of that opposition, is something abstracted altogether from the material world, and idealist. It encouraged the tendency which Saussure and some later structuralist linguists showed – Hjelmslev (1943) for example – to see language as a wholly abstract structure; and therefore offered a model for structuralists in other fields to build systems of pure abstract oppositions. Distinctive feature theory, on the other hand, is fairly concrete. It relates phonemes to physical features of the vocal tract, and to physical sound patterns.

Nevertheless it is the phoneme principle – the principle of pure opposition inducing meaning in otherwise meaningless signs – which was influential in the later French structuralist tradition and its associated semiotics. The distinctive feature principle was not influential as a model. This illustrates how an idealist intellectual tradition will give an idealist sense to any scientific model offered to it.

4.2   The critique of the phoneme

Jakobson in 1942 had another criticism of the phoneme, which cuts even deeper – he himself does not seem to realize quite how deep it goes. The phoneme, he says, differs from all other linguistic units precisely in that it has no signification other than its difference from other phonemes. De Saussure, says Jakobson, understood this; but he hastily overgeneralized this property and applied it to other linguistic elements as well, grammatical forms and words. These too, thought de Saussure, exhibit only differences from one another, and there were no positive terms (terms with a definite meaning of their own outside the language system).

This, says Jakobson, is simply a mistake. Even in the case of an opposition like German *Nacht* (night) and *Nächte* (nights) it is not true that the members have no meaning in isolation. 'For all speakers *Nächte* is an independent and direct designation of a concrete plurality.' (*Sound and Meaning* 1978, p. 64.) The point directly translates into English; 'night' designates a single night; 'nights' designates several nights. The contrast between /a/ and /a/ on the other hand (or in English, between no phoneme and the phoneme /s/), which is a contrast between phonemes within the words, is a pure opposition, between items that have no signification save in their opposition.

Jakobson's argument, presented here so early in the development of structuralism, undercuts the whole later development of the radical semiotic tradition (cf. chapters 6 and 7). This tradition builds on the theory of the empty phoneme to propose a theory of the empty signifier – the signifier without a signified. The idea seems to be that the signifier actually creates meaning. There is no 'transcendental signified' – or as I should put it, no world of experience which is even partly independent of language. Jakobson's critique removes the first basis for this extension. A radical semiotician would of course have the option of rejecting Jakobson's criticisms as positivist, empiricist or idealist, and I imagine this is what most do. But it is the radical semiotician who is the idealist here.

A sophisticated criticism might be that the word 'nights' designates a concrete plurality only when someone uses it; i.e., when it occurs in *parole*, not when it is merely lying in the dictionary unused. As part of *langue*, it merely has the potential to be used to designate a concrete plurality; and it gets that potentiality from the position it has in a system of differences. But as we shall see in chapter 6, even this ingenious defence won't actually work.

I said that Jakobson himself doesn't seem to realize how deep his criticism cuts. The phoneme is, according to him, unique among signs in that it has a signifier (a sound pattern) but no signified (no meaning). One cannot therefore generalize from it to other signs. But the obvious interpretation of his position (since the original definition of 'sign' is 'signifier–signified pair') is that the phoneme is not a sign at all. The phoneme is a recognizable unit of sound that makes a perceptual difference between one word and another, but is not associated with an idea. The whole word, on the other hand, is a sound pattern made up of these recognizable units; and it is associated with an idea. There is not the slightest point in applying the same word 'sign' to both these entities; and it is very confusing. It is the word that fits the original definition of 'sign': the phoneme does not. By itself it is not even a signifier; for it does not signify anything.

If this is correct, Saussure's position, and the whole of the radical semiotics that was later based on it – the whole theory of the priority of the signifier, with its mystificatory assumption that a world of meaning can be brought into existence just by speaking or writing – is based on a simple mistake; the mistake of supposing that the phoneme is a sign. And we ought to think seriously about abandoning the whole 'sign–signifier–signified' terminology, since it obviously won't fit even very simple cases.

The whole phoneme question was later to be transformed by the coming of **Generative Grammar**. By about 1965, a generative grammarian would have said that a speaker of a language has learnt a set of rules of construction and a set of vocabulary items; the rules enable him to construct sentences incorporating the vocabulary items, and assign to each sentence a pronunciation (specified as a sequence of units, each of which is a bundle of Jakobsonian distinctive features) and a set of meaning-elements, often set out as 'semantic features' attached to a grammatical tree-structure. In this model the Jakobsonian distinctive feature survives; the phoneme does not. And the question whether the phoneme, or the word, should be classified as a 'sign' simply disappears.

4.3 The syntagmatic and paradigmatic axes of language

I have said that de Saussure recognized two modes of organization in linguistic expressions: the syntagmatic and the associative. In the former, elements of language are arranged in linear order. In the latter, each element has meaning through its associations. Now it was very quickly realized that this latter category confuses several different kinds of structure. Consider the sentence:

He is mad.

For the phrase (syntagm) 'He is' we could substitute 'she is', 'I am', 'you are', 'they are' or anything else in what the older grammar books would call the 'paradigm' or pattern of the verb. Any of these phrases is related to the one in the sentence by being **inter-substitutable** for it. We can therefore speak of a 'paradigmatic' mode of organization in language, characterized by the existence of classes of elements – phrases, words, etc. – which are intersubstitutable. Some of these classes are small, like the three pronouns 'he', 'she', and 'it'; some are very large, like the class of adjectives which might be substituted for 'mad' – beautiful, angry, unpleasant, elephantine, etc. etc. We usually call the first type a 'closed' substitution class, and the second an 'open' class.

We can thus speak of two distinct axes of linguistic organization, which are, as it were, at right angles to each other, and operate independently: the syntagmatic, and the paradigmatic. They have been given several different names. Jakobson, in *Fundamentals of Language* 1956, speaks of the axes of combination and selection. M. A. K. Halliday (Halliday, McIntosh and Strevens 1964) used to speak of the axes of chain and choice. The notion of a paradigmatic, or substitutional or choice relationship is much tighter than that of an associative one. Modern linguists would regard mere associations of ideas or resemblances of sound, and so forth, as not being properly part of the language structure in the way that syntagmatic and paradigmatic relations are. There are, of course, other relationships which are a genuine part of the synchronic linguistic system, but are neither paradigmatic nor mere associations of ideas – the relationship between 'right' and 'righteous', for example, or 'policy' and 'political'.

One cannot complain that this development of linguistic theory has gone unrecognized in the structuralist tradition; indeed many structuralists, over-generously, credit the syntagmatic/paradigmatic distinction to Saussure himself. And this is natural; for the notion of paradigmatic relations – choice relations – systems of oppositions among morphemes, words, etc. – fits perfectly with the received structuralist model of phoneme theory. (The word 'morpheme' is modelled on the word 'phoneme'; it means a minimal meaning-bearing element like 'judge-' or '-ment' in the word 'judgement'.)

And this approach underpins the simple and symmetrical structuralist theory of meaning: that, for phonemes and morphemes alike, meaning derives simply from having a place in a system of oppositions. It will be noted that in arriving at this simplification, the other elements that Saussure included under his 'associative' axis – associations of ideas, synchronic derivational relationships, etc. – have simply been dropped; though they must have some relationship to meaning. What is beginning to emerge is that the linguistic model underlying the later versions of structuralism offers an enormous oversimplification of the facts of language, and is likely to produce grossly oversimplified models in any other realm of meaning to which it is applied.

This simple 'chain and choice' model of syntax turned out to be one of the first casualties of the generative revolution. Consider the example I gave. There is a sense in which the sentence 'He is mad' corresponds to the sentence 'The man is suffering from delusions' not merely semantically, but structurally. We can substitute 'The man' for 'He' and 'suffering from delusions' for 'mad'. But that implies that a **word** is sometimes intersubstitutable with a **phrase**. We can explain this fact simply enough by saying that speakers of a language have a tacit knowledge of rules for the construction of phrases out of smaller phrases – what are called **phrase-structure rules**.

Moreover sometimes substitution must be accompanied by systematic changes: 'He is mad' must be replaced by 'You are mad', not (in this dialect) by 'You is mad' or 'He are mad'. It is perfectly possible to represent structural relationships like these by grammatical rules; that is what old-fashioned grammarians had been doing for thousands of years before generative linguistics formalized them algebraically. But it is not possible to represent them within the limitations of structuralist 'chain and choice' grammars. The point is that a single choice – of the pronoun 'you' or 'he' – is represented twice in the syntagmatic chain. To represent this, we probably need rules of the kind technically called 'transformations': hence the full name of the new linguistic model **'transformational generative grammar'**. Although later models in linguistics, not considered in this book, have reduced the role of transformations as formal devices (see, e.g. Radford 1981) there is no question of returning to the simple structuralist 'chain and choice' model of syntax. It cannot describe the most elementary facts of language.

4.4 *Metaphor and metonymy*

Jakobson of course is writing well before the generative revolution and doesn't have the machinery to give a formally adequate account of rules of agreement, etc. He is, however, perfectly clear about the syntagmatic and paradigmatic aspects of language structure; and he goes on to make two very important and famous speculative extensions of them, one into the realm of abnormal psychology – to be specific, speech disorders; and the other into that of rhetoric and stylistic analysis. The theory is published in the second part of his book *Fundamentals of Language* (Jakobson and Halle 1956), the first part being devoted to phoneme theory. But he had the ideas much earlier.

Jakobson claims that there are two types of linguistic disorder, one – which he calls similarity disorder – corresponding to loss of control of the substitutive axis of language, the paradigmatic axis; and the other, which he calls contiguity disorder, corresponding to a loss of control of the syntagmatic axis – chaining and sentence construction. These two types of disorder, he claims, are closely related to the inability to handle two types of rhetorical process: metaphor, which is related to substitution on the paradigmatic axis, and metonymy, which is related to movement along the syntagmatic chain.

In a psychological test, the stimulus 'hut' might produce the **metaphoric** response 'den' or 'burrow', or the **metonymic** response 'thatch', 'litter' or 'poverty'. One type of aphasia would affect the capacity for a metaphoric response, while leaving that for metonymic response untouched; another might have the reverse effect. But the way in which these two aspects of language are used is also an important feature of personal literary style, or the stylistics of certain literary forms. 'In Russian lyrical songs, for example, metaphoric constructions predominate, while in the heroic epics the metonymic way is preponderant.'

Thus Jakobson rather grandly unites the principles of psycholinguistic pathology and those of literary criticism; just as in an early part of the same book he had united phonemics with the order of acquisition of language and its loss in aphasia. It has not proved possible to confirm this theory of language acquisition; and this syntactic identification of the sources of metaphor, metonymy and aphasia looks a good deal less compelling once one has started to doubt the primacy of the 'chain and choice' model of syntax.

Little of this grand unification, therefore, has survived later critical scrutiny. But it had an important influence on Jacques Lacan, who borrowed it wholesale for the foundations of his own theory of the unconscious as an effect of language, getting it wildly wrong, I am afraid, but retailing it with his usual brilliant surrealist dogmatism (Lacan 1966). The case is discussed in chapters 3, 6, and 7.

The metaphor/metonymy opposition has had a fine career in American post-structuralism, too. De Man (1979a) uses it in *Allegories of Reading* to show how Proust 'deconstructs' himself – a passage in Proust written in praise of metaphor relies heavily on the opposed figure of metonymy. De Man reaches quite grand conclusions about the unreliability of language itself on the basis of such deconstructions as these; but he takes the metonymy/metaphor opposition in terms of which he is working entirely for granted, and even supposes that it involves fundamental oppositions in epistemology.

However, once one abandons the 'chain and choice' model of language structure, the linguistic reasons for taking the metaphor/metonymy opposition as fundamental disappear. One has to look at the logical structure of the two, and ask whether there is all that much difference in the way they function. One might think that there is a good case for arguing that metonymy is merely a particular type of metaphor. Here is an example: To the same meeting, one Mafia boss brought with him three **guns**; the other brought three **soldiers**. In personnel they were evenly matched: both phrases mean 'men with guns'. In Jakobsonian terms I think you would have to call one of these metonymy, and the other metaphor; but there is little difference in the way they function, and I cannot believe there is the slightest difference in the epistemological principles at stake. (I suspect epistemology raises its head when you use a metaphor from physical experience to represent abstractions. See Lakoff 1987, chapter 6 for a plausible theory.)

These examples show two things: first how Jakobson retains his influence in more recent rhetorical theory; second, how that theory is much less secure than it believes itself to be. It cannot be regarded as (in the words of one practitioner) 'the most rigorous' form of rhetorical analysis. Mediaeval rhetoric was much more rigorous. For one thing it distinguished more carefully between rhetoric, linguistics (which it called grammar) and logic. As a result, it did not make hasty inferences from figures of speech to epistemology.

NOTES

1. Jakobson's actual words were: 'Bloomfield lived in the most vulgar period of behaviorism.' (Aslib conference on classification in linguistics and botany(!) Cambridge 1963). This is the only occasion I ever heard him; it would need high expertise in phonetic transcription to show why this remark has lived in my memory ever since.

BOOKS

Jakobson, Roman and **Tynjanov, Jurij** 1928 'Problems in the Study of Language and Literature'.

The original 'structuralist manifesto'.

Jakobson, Roman 1976 *Six Lectures on Sound and Meaning.*

This is the second most important reference in this book: the lectures of 1942 which led Claude Lévi-Strauss to invent French structuralism. They give a clear account of structural linguistics in the form it had then reached, and are clear and comprehensible to the undergraduate or general reader.

Galan, F. V. 1985 *Historic Structures: the Prague School Project 1928–1946.*

An excellent study of Prague-School literary structuralism, though not light reading.

FURTHER READING

History of Philosophy and Ideas: Copleston 1946, 1963, Lewis 1954, Locke 1689, Peters 1972.

History of Structural Linguistics: Halliday, McIntosh and Strevens 1964, Hjelmslev 1943, Hockett 1958, Holenstein 1976, Jakobson and collaborators passim, Humboldt 1836, Joos 1957, Lehmann 1967, Malmberg 1983, Martinet and Weinreich 1954, Mohrmann, Sommerfelt and Whatmough 1961, Parrett 1976, Robins 1967, Vachek 1966.

Russian Formalism etc: Bann & Bowlt 1973, Bennett 1979, Matejka and Pomorska 1971, Shukman 1983.

Literary Structuralism and Stylistics: Culler 1975, Galan 1985, Garvin 1964, Merquior 1986, Sebeok 1960.

For titles and publishers see main bibliography.

CHAPTER THREE

The French Phase: Structuralism Collapses

Lévi-Strauss, Lacan, Althusser, Foucault and Derrida: the Appropriation of Saussure, Freud and Marx by French Idealism

SUMMARY

The French phase of structuralism begins with Lévi-Strauss's appropriation of Jakobson's work for anthropology in the 1940s and perhaps Lacan's appropriation of some of Saussure's terminology for his own version of psychoanalysis in the 1950s. At its height in the early 1960s it was an intellectual craze that covered every possible subject from history to mathematics and cannot be summarized here (or perhaps anywhere). The linguistic elements in this phase were often little more than a sprinkling of jargon. (See Piaget 1968 for discussion.) The development most interesting for literary theory was marked by an attempt to synthesize the linguistic model with French philosophy of the human subject: the mind, and society, were explained as the effect of structures, often linguistic ones. It was in this period that Saussure was reconceived as a philosopher. The structuralist enterprise collapsed around 1967, under the influence of Lacan, Derrida and others and of political developments; and was succeeded by a variety of disparate post-structuralisms which have spread over Europe and America.

1   THE FIRST FRENCH STRUCTURALIST: CLAUDE LÉVI-STRAUSS

1.1   *The revelation of structural linguistics*

One of the staff who attended Jakobson's New York lectures was Claude Lévi-Strauss; formerly a philosopher, now an anthropologist and to become (as we shall see) a kind of philosopher again. He had a severely practical purpose in coming: but what he got was an intellectual vision:

> Still keenly aware of the difficulty which, as a result of my inexperience, I had met with three or four years earlier in trying to find an adequate notation to record the languages of central Brazil, I promised myself to acquire from Jakobson the rudiments which I lacked. In fact, however, what I received from his teaching was something quite different and, I need hardly add, something more important: the revelation of structural linguistics, as a result of which I would later be able to crystallise into a body of coherent ideas visions inspired by the contemplation of wild flowers somewhere near the border of Luxemburg at the beginning of May 1940 . . .

and (Lévi-Strauss adds with a calculated return to the empirical) certain technical problems in Marcel Granet's treatment of the ethnography of old China that were preoccupying him at the time (see Lévi-Strauss: Preface to Jakobson, *Sound and Meaning*, 1976, pp. xi–ii).

What gets the stress here is the revelatory power of the vision of intellectual order and system that linguistics provides. It is this revelation, rather than any actual applicability of the linguistic model or any major results that were produced, that was to be the principal driving force of linguistics-based structuralism in its third phase: the phase of global intellectual ambition and, by the 1960s, of cult. At the beginning, however, this is a distinctly scientific vision. Later, as we shall see, the vision remained; but the science began distinctly to crumble, and mythopoetics took over.

Lévi-Strauss at this stage was greatly inflenced by the linguistics which he had learned from Jakobson's lectures and he followed them up by fairly extensive reading. His preface to Jakobson's *Sound and Meaning* explains what he took from the lectures. The first four chapters of *Structural Anthropology*, Vol. I are articles from the 1940s and early 1950s (one of them, 'Structural Analysis in Linguistics and Anthropology', originally published in a linguistics journal, Word, 1945) and they explore the possible uses of linguistic models in anthropology. It is a sophisticated analysis, which looks beyond the simple importation of linguistic techniques like the componential analysis of kinship terms, and asks for a deeper type of influence.

What impressed Lévi-Strauss in the 1940s was the scientific rigour of linguistics and its explanatory successes.

> The anthropologists are in a very peculiar situation in relation to linguistics. For many years they have been working very closely with the linguists, and all of a sudden it seems to them that the linguists are vanishing, that they are going on the other side of the borderline which divides the exact and natural sciences on the one hand from the human and social sciences on the other. All of a sudden, the linguists are playing their former companions this very nasty trick of doing things as well and with the same sort of rigorous approach that was long believed to be the privilege of the exact and natural sciences. Then, on the side of the anthropologist there is some, let us say, melancholy and a great deal of envy. We should like to learn from the linguists how they succeeded in doing it, how we may ourselves in our own field, which is a complex one – in the field of kinship, in the field of social organisation, in the field of religion, folklore, art and the like – use the same kind of rigorous approach which has turned out to be so successful for linguistics.
>
> (*Structural Anthropology*, written 1952, chapter 4, p. 69)

There are many passages of this type in Lévi-Strauss's earlier work and they reveal the fundamental motive behind the original French structuralist movement. It was the hope of making the humanities scientific, in an age when scientific progress could still be seen as one of the few unquestionably desirable things. This hope, and a great deal of the optimism that goes with it, lasted until the 1960s; it was then succeeded by a wave of anti-scientific feeling: a feeling that not only was it not possible for the humanities to become scientific in this fashion, but that it was very undesirable that they should. The journalistic name 'post-structuralism', so far as it applies to anything clearly, applies to the intellectual products of this anti-scientific and in my view anti-rationalist wave of feeling, which still continues.

Lévi-Strauss himself was never a post-structuralist. But he too came to qualify his scientific claims almost out of sight. By the 1970s he was to regard mythography as the construction of a myth about myth; just as post-structuralists have come to regard 'theory' as a form of literature about literature rather than as a set of empirically testable explanations. And the introduction to the second volume of *Structural Anthropology* (1973), published fifteen years after the first volume and twenty-one years after the essay just quoted, has a very different tone:

> We may even wonder if this criterion of 'falsifiability' can truly be applied to the human sciences. Their epistemological status is not at all like those which the physical and natural sciences can claim for themselves. These are characterised by a harmony which at all times has reigned among

those who practice them at the level considered relevant to the contemporary state of the research. But such is not at all the case for the human sciences. With these, there is little or no discussion on the validity of such and such hypotheses. The discussion bears instead on the choice of a certain level of reference implied by this hypothesis, and not of another level which an opponent might favour.

It is exceptional for structural anthropologists to be told: 'Your interpretation of this phenomenon or group of phenomena is not the one which best accounts for the facts.' Rather, they are told: 'The way you break down the phenomena is not the way which interests us; we choose to break them down another way.' The subject of the human sciences is man, yet the man who studies himself as he practices the human sciences will always allow his preferences and prejudices to interfere in the way he defines himself to himself. What is interesting in man is not subject to scientific decision but results and always will result from a choice which is ultimately of a philosophical order.'

So we must recognise that the hypotheses of the human sciences cannot, now or ever, be falsified . . .   (Ibid, pp. viii–ix)

It will be seen that the early, scientific goal Lévi-Strauss proposed to himself has in the end been abandoned; and Lévi-Strauss takes it for granted that practitioners of the human sciences largely agree on this. In saying this, he is casting a sharp light on French cultural conditions, which are still significantly different from Anglo–American ones. In fact there have been a number of quite blistering attacks on Lévi-Strauss, from English and American anthropologists, on grounds of empirical inadequacy and fanciful interpretation. Some of these are documented in Neville Dyson-Hudson (1970) – a paper given at the conference in 1966 (Macksey and Donato 1970) which largely introduced post-structuralism to the United States.

To this day, there are still plenty of Western social scientists who take it that they are practising science in the full traditional sense; that they must confine themselves to hypotheses that are falsifiable in the light of empirical data and that have their value chiefly in explaining empirical data. There is a sophisticated critique of Lévi-Strauss's work, from this point of view, in Marvin Harris's vast history of anthropology: *The Rise of Anthropological Theory* (1968). Harris is a cultural materialist. This is a theoretical position in anthropology (not to be confused with the cultural materialism of a literary critic like Raymond Williams); Harris agrees with traditional Marxists that all the varieties of human cultures are to be explained on the basis of economic pressures; but he also adds population pressure and ecological variables, and rejects the Marxist dialectic. This gives him a thoroughgoing and fully scientific materialist basis for criticizing the idealism of Lévi-Strauss's approach to his subject, with its exclusive interest in mental representations. Nor is Harris the only critic on these lines.

1.2 Lévi-Strauss and the phoneme

We can see the kind of thing that can be at issue by considering Lévi-Strauss's handling of the phoneme concept and the fundamental distinction that linguists make between the phonetic or material level of a language and the phonemic or systematic level. As we have seen, he had heard of this first from Jakobson, who was concerned to reduce phonemes to relatively solid and material distinctive features. One would expect an anthropologist working on the basis of this analogy to show a keen interest in the material conditions of social life and in biology; particularly as the anthropologist concerned claimed to be interested both in Marxism and in the natural sciences, especially geology. And perhaps one might have expected him to develop some notion of -etic and -emic levels of society (that is, material versus socially meaningful), on the analogy of phonetics and phonemics. This is what was done by the American linguist Kenneth Pike, when he attempted an anthropological generalization of linguistics (*Language in Relation to a Unified Theory of the Structure of Human Behaviour*, 1964). The -emic, -etic terminology is picked up by Marvin Harris.

But this, notoriously, was not the orientation Lévi-Strauss took. What struck him was the principle of the phoneme itself: the principle of pure opposition among contentless signs; and the possibility of breaking down these opposed signs to underlying binary oppositions of which the subject is quite unconscious. Later, he applied the principle to myth: he proposed to analyse myths in terms of meaningless fundamental units he called mythemes (Lévi-Strauss, Preface to Jakobsen 1976). We shall meet this ending '-eme' several times more; it has often been borrowed. It always denotes a metaphor based on the phoneme; and always needs cautious examination.

It is hard to overstate the significance of Lévi-Strauss's move; it deserves to be quoted as the founding moment of French (idealist) structuralism. What Lévi-Strauss believes he has found, in the phoneme, is a unit that is in itself meaningless, but that, when placed in relationship with other units of the same kind, can build up structures of meaning. These structures are based ultimately upon binary oppositions to be found in the human unconscious. In the

1950s Lacan adopted a position related to this, though differing in detail, about the Freudian unconscious.

It is fairly clear that both of them were wrong, both in their actual theories and in the interpretation they gave to their sources. Saussure did not consistently hold the theory attributed to him; Jakobson roundly criticized it; and it is in any case logically impossible. These points are discussed in chapter 1, in the last section of chapter 2 and in chapter 6. They are very important; the mistakes that were made then have been made again and again by lesser people and are still found in the literature of the 1980s.

1.3   The elementary structures of kinship

Anthropologists usually consider that the central institutions of the kinds of society they study are kinship systems; and Lévi-Strauss's first book, *The Elementary Structures of Kinship* (1949) was on this topic. The striking insight in this book is that society is built upon the incest taboo – the prohibition against sex within the family, which forces men to exchange women, from one family to another, in order to marry. This is what creates an overall social structure larger than the nuclear family.

There are in such societies three main forms of exchange, that hold them together: the exchange of gifts, which corresponds to what in a more sophisticated society would be the economic structure; the exchange of women, according to very complex and sophisticated rules that create a kinship structure; and the exchange of verbal messages through language, that creates most of the culture of the society – which in the later work of Lévi-Strauss is a symbolic structure, or system of signs.

The effect of the rules that force marriage to be outside the nuclear family and within certain prescribed groupings is that the most elementary structure of kinship is not the nuclear family of husband, wife and children, but includes the husband, wife, children and wife's brother (maternal uncle) or corresponding male figure on the woman's side, who originally controls the woman and gives her away. This structure takes various forms and is associated with various attitudes held by one member of a kinship structure for another (attitudes that are independent of the personal character of the individuals involved, but depend solely on their place in the family structure). Thus in some societies a male child will have a severe, unapproachable respected father, but a familiar, joking relationship with his maternal uncle; in some the relations might be reversed.

Anthropologists have to explain such kinship rules and attitudes; one obvious kind of explanation would be an economic one, of the kind that Marx or Harris favour: to show that such rules have an ultimate economic function and enable the societies that adopt them to survive. Lévi-Strauss does not offer this kind of explanation. Another kind is a historical one: to show that certain phenomena exist because they have evolved historically. When applied to anthropology, which is mainly concerned with illiterate societies whose history is largely irrecoverable, there are problems with this approach, and it sometimes leads to an entirely speculative history. A structural explanation concentrates on what can be explained in terms of the relationships between the parts of the existing structure, without historical speculation. The analogy to synchronic linguistic study is obvious.

It is not for someone trained in linguistics and literature to judge the success, or even gauge the logical status, of Lévi-Strauss's explanatory hypotheses about kinship systems. This is one of the most technical areas of anthropology, where only specialists dare tread. And the difficulties of interpretation here are fearsome. Lévi-Strauss had a public dispute with his own translator, the distinguished anthropologist Rodney Needham, about what exactly his book meant; it is chronicled in Lévi-Strauss's second Preface and Needham's rather bewildered editorial note to his translation. But one thing stands out, at least from the point of view of a generative grammarian. From the beginning, Lévi-Strauss seems to have been interested not so much in the facts as outside observers see them, as in certain mental representations of reality in the minds of the participants. This special point of view carried over into his next work, on the ancient anthropological problem of *Totemism* (1962); and also into what was described as an extension of that work, the study of *The Savage Mind* (1962).

1.4 Investigating mental structures

The main concern of both *Totemism* and *The Savage Mind* is the way in which the mind organizes data. Earlier anthropologists had suggested, for example, that taking totem animals to represent social groups was a historical reminiscence of days when the groups ate that animal (now forbidden to them); or had offered innumerable other external explanations. Lévi-Strauss treats the whole problem of totemism, as so far described, as an illusion. We look instead at a system of relationships; a system of oppositions between totem animals becomes a way of culturally organizing the world. What is being investigated is a way of thinking by means of a system of categories, embodied in the totem animals. It is a way of approach with curious similarities to that of certain cognitive scientists, who are interested in prototype effects in thinking (Lakoff 1987).

All of Lévi-Strauss's work is oriented toward the study of representations of structures in the mind, just as the work of the generative grammarian is; and to increase the resemblance still further, he constantly aspires to push this to the point where he can uncover unconscious universal features of the mind. Unlikely as it would seem to those who are familiar with the very different styles of both thinkers, Chomsky and Lévi-Strauss appear, each in his own discipline and in his own continent, to be engaged in the very same quest for mental universals, though there has never been any question of either influencing the other, and Chomsky (1989) thinks Lévi-Strauss's work rather empty.

One major difference between the two is the gulf between the intellectual traditions in which they started working. Chomsky in America in the early 1950s was confronted with a triumphal behaviourism – exemplified by the work of the great behaviourist psychologist, B. F. Skinner (1957) – which attempted to reduce even human language to '*Verbal Behavior*' and denied that mental phenomena could be the subject of scientific enquiry at all. The dominant philosophy, though more sophisticated than this, was empiricist; perhaps the most significant philosopher for crude empiricism to confront was Quine, a follower of Russell; but philosophy itself was far less significant for linguistics than a generalized behaviourism which made investigation even of semantics seem an unscientific and pointless activity for linguists to engage in.

Lévi-Strauss, on the other hand, was confronted by Sartrean existentialism. For this philosophy, scientific and objective views of man have no interest at all: they are 'entomology'. Consciousness – 'being-for-itself' – is a kind of nothingness or lack of being which nonetheless creates a world of objects out of the otherwise undifferentiated plenitude of being-in-itself. It is necessarily connected to the world and its own past; but still free to make its choices now. To deny that would be bad faith. In existential humanism a man makes himself what he is and makes himself anew in every moment, in a freedom of consciousness essentially unfettered by social structure, material circumstances, unconscious motivations or his own biology. This is the philosophy which Sartre later attempted to reconcile with Marxism (Sartre 1943, p. 60).

This is perhaps unfair. It doesn't do justice to the subtlety of Sartre; and it is certainly wrong to identify Sartre's thought with French philosophy as a whole. But it would not be wrong to say that French philosophy takes an extraordinarily arrogant view of its own superior relation to the empirical sciences of man and often comes close to strangling them at birth. The point is amply documented by one of the few Francophone social scientists whose international stature is comparable with that of Lévi-Strauss: Jean Piaget, in his book *Insights and Illusions of Philosophy* (1965). This is a record of a lifelong battle to get acceptance of the bare legitimacy of empirical investigations into the development of logical categories in the child's mind, against an establishment which regarded any such investigation merely as evidence of a fairly obvious philosophical mistake. His experience runs parallel with that of Lévi-Strauss; but Piaget never gave up his empirical claims.

1.5   A new philosophy of man

It was probably inevitable that structural anthropology should have been interpreted as an alternative philosophy of man. Perhaps it would be truer to say that either structural anthropology had to become a new philosophy of man, or a new philosophy of man had to be constructed to accommodate it; for neither Sartre's philosophy nor any other within the phenomenological and existential traditions could do this. But, as is indicated in the extract from Lévi-Strauss (1976) quoted above, the pressure of the philosophical battle has changed the nature of his conception of anthropology. If you are only asked philosophical questions – and Lévi-Strauss has sometimes had to remind his public that he is actually interested in ethnographic data and did some field-work once – you are very strongly pushed into becoming a philosopher. And of course, philosophy is the subject Levi-Strauss started in anyway.

What has structuralism to offer as a **philosophical** position? A society can be seen in this framework as determined by a set of unconscious mental representations shared by the individuals in it. But in an important sense the system of mental representations has a logical priority over both the society and the individuals. Individual subjectivities are formed by the insertion of the individual into such a system; society is formed by the way such a mental system processes social behaviour that would otherwise be quite meaningless. There is no objective social world outside mental representations of it; and no free subjectivity not formed by such representations. This is the core of a new Kantian idealism. It also formed the starting point of the thought of Lacan, Althusser and Foucault.

1.6 Myth about myth

Much of Lévi-Strauss's later work is devoted to the analysis of myth; the influence of the linguistic model is still there and still profound, but he is working with extremely loose analogies. Thus different myths, told by different peoples in the same continent, are presented as in some sense part of the same *langue*, and become evidence for universal categories. There is a sense in which this is as loose as Jung's explorations of the collective unconscious, though less readable. His own description of his work as a mythology about mythology seems accurate enough.

Despite their large scale, these works seem to me to follow essentially the same principles of analysis as the 1955 paper 'The Structural Study of Myth'. Lévi-Strauss had a lifelong interest in literature and mythology. He collaborated with Jakobson in structuralist analyses of the former: the most famous example being an analysis of Baudelaire's *Les Chats* (De George and de George 1972). Jakobson seems to be the dominant partner here; the analytic technique greatly resembles that of Jakobson alone, dismembering a Shakespeare sonnet to show the grammatical and phonological oppositions it employs and their putative significance (Jakobson and Jones 1970).

Lévi-Strauss's own hand is responsible for an analysis of the Oedipus myth; though an early work, it shows both the strengths and weaknesses of his approach. He cuts the myth into episodes and arranges them on a two dimensional grid, to bring out the significant oppositions that the myth is supposed to be about. The myth without its grid runs as follows:

> Cadmos seeks his sister Europa, ravished by Zeus. He kills a dragon. The Spartoi, rising from its teeth, kill each other. Labdacos, Laios's father, is lame(?). Oedipus kills his father, Laios. Laios means left-sided(?). Oedipus kills the Sphinx. Oedipus means swollen-footed(?). Oedipus marries his

mother, Jocasta. Eteocles kills his brother Polynices. Antigone buries her brother Polynices despite a prohibition.

This is a fairly arbitrary division into episodes, with many that are present in the original sources, and seem important to most readers, arbitrarily left out. Lévi-Strauss now places the episodes in four columns, illustrating the following criteria:

> overrating blood relations (Cadmos seeks Europa; Oedipus marries Jocasta; Antigone buries Polynices) : underrating blood relations (Spartoi kill each other; Oedipus kills father; Eteocles kills brother) : slaying monsters (Cadmos kills dragon; Oedipus kills sphynx) : and having difficulty in standing upright (Labdacos is lame; Laios perhaps left-sided; Oedipus swollen-footed).

These criteria also seem highly arbitrary.

Lévi-Strauss then interprets his last two categories – killing a monster and being unable to stand properly – as meaning respectively the denial of the autochthonous origin of man and the persistence of the autochthonous origin of man. So the myth turns out to have a relational meaning: 'the overrating of blood relations is to the underrating of blood relations as the attempt to escape autochthony is to the impossibility to succeed in it'. It has to do, we are told, with 'the inability, for a culture which holds the belief that mankind is autochthonous . . . to find a satisfactory transition between this belief and the knowledge that human beings are actually born from the union of man and woman'.

I must say that I do not believe a word of this tall story. What I don't believe, in particular, is that this is a scientific method of investigation. There are far too many points at which the investigator can make arbitrary decisions about the content of the myth or the classification of the units, so that the results confirm whatever he wants them to confirm. He can cook the books as much as he likes. Indeed, it is not clear that there is such a thing as an uncooked book about myths.

1.7 Structure, sign and play in the discourse of the human sciences

This response of mine will strike the modern literary theorist – and perhaps the reader of this book – as astonishingly raw. The drive against scientific method, which Lévi-Strauss chronicles, has now progressed so far that advanced critics talk quite another language. The crucial change came in 1967, with Derrida's paper: 'Structure, Sign and Play in the Discourse of the Human Sciences', delivered at the same conference as Dyson-Hudson's empirical critique, but belonging to another intellectual world. Dyson-Hudson finds Lévi-Strauss not empirical enough and is distinctly suspicious of the imaginative, literary and philosophical flavour of introductions to his work by such anthropological illiterates as George Steiner and Susan Sontag; indeed, he is equally suspicious of the extensive philosophical ancestry claimed by Lévi-Strauss himself.

But for Derrida, Lévi-Strauss is stuck with a problem of an **essentially** philosophical kind, which Lévi-Strauss is, in a sense, not philosopher enough to solve. Ethnology (anthropology) is a European science employing traditional European concepts (including, of course, every concept that Dyson-Hudson and all the other empirical anthropologists employ). Yet to the extent that it is a study of non-European societies it must offer a critique of all ethnocentric categories – including those concepts of scientificity on which it is itself founded. It therefore, even in the hands of a highly sophisticated practitioner like Lévi-Strauss (and much more, it goes without saying, in the hands of crude empiricists like Dyson-Hudson) undermines its own scientificity.

Thus Lévi-Strauss is quite right to try and transcend the traditional metaphysical opposition between the sensible and the intelligible, which so perplexes the human sciences with such questions as: are they studies of material things, physical behaviour, etc., or are they studies of meaning? But he does it by situating himself, from the beginning, at the level of the sign. Yet the very concept of the sign as signifier–signified pair is determined by the opposition between the sensible and the intelligible, and is unintelligible without it. Ethnology, as a critique of Western thinking, cannot function except through a fundamental concept of Western metaphysics.

Similarly Lévi-Strauss makes a famous distinction between two types of thinking. One – implicitly that of the modern theorist – is that in which new concepts are forged to explain the world, in the way that an engineer makes a machine out of new, properly designed parts. The other – that of the primitive society which thinks in mythical terms – is that where ready-made classifications like that between one species of animal and another, are used for quite different cognitive purposes like social classification of people, as in what used before Lévi-Strauss to be called totemism. This intellectual method resembles the work of a rough handyman (*bricoleur*) who makes his objects of any old pieces left over from other work. But Derrida points out that all our concepts are left over from other work. We all start with ready-made concepts, produced originally for other purposes, and modify them for what we are doing now. It is not that there is a special kind of primitive thinking that is like *bricolage*. All thinking is *bricolage*.

And Derrida is very pleased that this should be so. What he likes about *bricolage* is not its scientific, but its mythopoeic power. What he likes about Lévi-Strauss's treatment of Bororo myth, in that late and so appropriately titled work, *The Raw and the Cooked*, is that there is no privileged reference-myth, that you can start the analysis from anywhere, there is no 'centre', no founding principle you can take for granted. You have for this purpose to forego scientific or philosophical discourse; structural discourse on myths is mythomorphic – the production of myth about myth.

I shall discuss the metaphysical anti-metaphysics that underlies Derrida's position later in this book. For the moment I am concerned only with his influence. So influential has this anti-scientific mode of interpretation become that it has in some quarters, particularly literary ones, quite occulted the original assumptions of Lévi-Strauss's work. Here is a comment from 1982 on the treatment of the Oedipus myth:

> Yet this displacement and the search for a latent content, or a 'deep-structure', cannot presuppose an ultimate meaning any more than it can assume a literal one. If Lévi-Strauss discovers that the Oedipus myth finally brings into play the opposition of parthenogenesis versus bisexual reproduction, the conclusion does not imply that the myth may be reduced to this particular signification. The value of the analysis must lie primarily in the deconstruction of the text's semiotic relations at all levels, just as the interest of the opposition autochthony/bisexual reproduction lies in the role it plays in the entire system of cultural codes – communicational, legal, economic – where it becomes merely another signifier. (Alwin Baum: Spanos et al. 1982, p. 91)

Baum, it may be said, is by no means a 'wild' deconstructionist, and claims to 'share in the pursuit of a structural poetics, or a semiotic theory generally'. But notice how loose and metaphorical he assumes the theory is going to be. He borrows the technical phrase 'deep structure' from 1965 generative grammar, but uses scare quotes to indicate that he doesn't mean it in the technical sense. His main anxiety is not to explain things, but to avoid being reductive about them. In the context of a discourse like this it begins to seem old-fashioned to ask that a theory in a social science should be empirically grounded, explanatorily adequate, and reductive in the sense that it is simpler than the facts it purports to explain; and positively vulgar to require that we should recognize something as a 'discovery' only if we believe it to be true.

1.8 Anthropology and generative grammar

Modern assumptions therefore hide from us both the true character of the work of the 1940s and 1950s and its true potential. It was, to begin with, largely scientific in character and aims despite the traditionally humanistic nature of much of its material. Success for it would have consisted, in the first instance, in the production of systematic structural descriptions of kinship relations, myth, folk-lore, poetry, etc. At a higher level, success would have consisted in the discovery of a set of universal categories in the operation of the human mind: a biological rather than a philosophical Kantianism. (Lévi-Strauss accepted the description of his own position as 'Kantianism without the transcendental subject'.)

There is an exact analogy here with Chomsky's generative grammar, whose development started more than ten years later than that of Lévi-Strauss's anthropology. Again we have a self-consciously – and I think justly – scientific stance; no social science has more carefully examined its own scientificity. We have an immense flowering of linguistic description – far more successful than anything provided by modern anthropology, partly because of the technical discoveries Chomsky had made about the mathematical structures exhibited by languages, and partly because languages are simpler than societies to describe. Again we have the quest for linguistic universals that are properties of the human mind; and this time it is possible to argue that some such properties are now known: for example that no languages are, or ever could be structured on a simple 'chain and choice' (finite-state grammar) model.

What distinguishes generative grammar from structuralist anthropology is its relationship to the empirical. Both these disciplines had rejected the empiricist notion that the subject matter of the social sciences is actual behaviour, in favour of the view that it is mental representations. Both, therefore, were subjected to severe attack by older, empiricist schools. But generative grammar proved incomparably more successful in providing comprehensive and testable descriptions of empirical reality. Far more generative grammarians than structuralist anthropologists did the equivalent of extensive fieldwork (e.g. by describing various languages in detail). Structuralist anthropology, on the evidence of its own leading figure, did not move toward the condition of scientific linguistics; it remained or became once again, a philosophical position. As such it was vulnerable, in a way that generative grammar is not, to the purely philosophical arguments of a Derrida.

It ought to be said that in principle Derrida's arguments apply just as much to generative grammar as to structuralist linguistics; indeed they seem to me to apply equally to all rational enquiry into matters of fact. But a purely philosophical critique of a science has quite a different force when the science has extensive results to offer and when it does not.

Where then, when it is satisfactory science, does work with this cognitive orientation lead? It is not surprising to find it associated with three flourishing types of modern scientific research: cognitive studies in psychology, neurophysiological research and the computer simulation of human behaviour in Artificial Intelligence research. (Chomsky's early theorems about language are standard parts of computer science texts.) Such research seems to me among the most interesting currently to be found in the world; and it is a puzzle to me why literary theorists are typically not interested in it. (Has any significant literary theorist been interested in hard psychology since the time of I. A. Richards?) In any case it is, I think, the cognitive sciences that are the true successors to the aims of early structuralism.

Modern semioticians are often uneasy about aims like these, seeing them as naïvely positivistic or politically reactionary, and perhaps as denying human freedom; and they give quite unconvincing metaphysical reasons for thinking them impossible to achieve. Derrida's work has become the Bible for this school. But there is no point in denying that the early structuralists wanted to bring hard scientific method to the humanities and thought they had a good model of it to work with, provided by structural linguistics.

Lévi-Strauss's earlier papers are quite decisive on this point. But his later ones equally decisively chronicle a move away from this strictly scientific, to what in the end became a self-confessedly mythological approach. Whether the controversy with Sartre – so hostile to an objective anthropological approach to man – led to a gradual re-philosophization of the whole enterprise; or whether Lévi-Strauss's early work on kinship simply didn't stand up empirically and had to be retrospectively reinterpreted in an idealist direction; or whether there are deep-rooted forces in French culture, or perhaps in the marginalized social position of literary intellectuals in any modern country, which are hostile to empirical studies of man, is very difficult to determine.

Whatever the reason, it is in this third stage, as we move on to ambitious attempts to order whole realms of enquiry on principles either derived ultimately from linguistics or paying some lip-service to it, that structuralism was converted from a research strategy in the social sciences, to a philosophical position opposed to humanism in general and Sartrean existentialism in particular and inadequate, careless, or even disdainful, in its treatment of the empirical. And it was for this purpose that de Saussure, now recognized (partly because he wrote in French) as the sole ancestor of structural linguistics, was retrospectively reinterpreted as a philosopher, concerned mainly with the nature of subjective experience, or even with the status of the unconscious mind. This is a role which would have greatly surprised him, and needs another section to describe.

2 HIGH STRUCTURALISM: THE THEORY OF THE SUBJECT AND THE NEW, IMPROVED SAUSSURE

2.1 *The encounter with philosophy*

The great adventure that happened to structuralism in France was its encounter with French philosophy − by which I mean mainly phenomenological and existential philosophy, along with a Hegelian element that descends from the pre-war lectures of Kojève − and with philosophically sophisticated versions of Marx and of Freud. I don't want to claim an epic, or world–historical scale for this intellectual battle. To say that it was the state of French philosophy in the late 1950s that produced the structuralism of Roland Barthes is surely to suggest that the foothill laboured to produce a mouse. The mountains in the background of this analogy are Husserl and Heidegger. They seem to me to be genuinely great philosophers, who succeeded in raising fundamental questions about the nature of knowledge and of existence respectively, and hence about the nature of philosophy itself. It is no slight on Sartre and even Merleau-Ponty to suggest that, though both important and original, their work was to domesticate the philosophy of being and phenomenology in a French habitat and form.

To this domesticated version of existentialism and phenomenology, structuralism emerged as an almost native competitor. As far as literary theory goes, the best known French structuralist and semiologist is Roland Barthes; I have devoted a chapter of this book to him. But if one is mainly interested in representing the dialogue between philosophy and structuralism, one probably shouldn't choose Barthes to represent the latter. A more obvious choice might be Lévi-Strauss, whose *La Pensée Sauvage* is dedicated to Merleau-Ponty and has a final chapter directed at the philosophy of Sartre. Another choice would be Lacan, deeply influenced by Hegel and by Heidegger and slightly by Lévi-Strauss, who provided a supposedly structuralist version of the Freudian unconscious to set against Sartre's effective repudiation of the unconscious. Another would be Louis Althusser, who offers a 'structural Marxism' as a counterpoise, *inter alia*, to the later, Sartre's existential variety of Marxism.

Barthes is, in my view, not in this league. As a theoretician he is perhaps the least philosophically interesting of the major structuralists. Of his two major theoretical works, *Elements of Semiology* was influential among semioticians, but is philosophically a rather dull adaptation of Saussure; *S/Z*, as I shall try to show, is in many ways closer to a modernist work of literature than to either philosophy or science. Barthes' dealings with theory are to some extent – not wholly, but to a significant extent – those of a literary critic with a yearning for academic respectability. They were his central interests at one time; but it would be a mistake to see them as his major achievements.

Yet even for such a man's work, in the environment of French culture in the late 1950s and the 1960s, it is necessary to provide a philosophical framework in order to see what there was to react against. He was never indifferent (as English critics used to be) to the philosophical fashions of the day, or to what specialists in anthropology, psychoanalysis or Marxist philosophy were making of them. Lévi-Strauss, Lacan and Althusser, in their development of theories of culture, the subject and ideology, cast multicoloured shadows on semiology and literary theory as well. It is, after all, in this intellectual environment that Saussure is taken up and re-read, not as a scientific linguist, but as a semiological philosopher with things to say about subjectivity and even the unconscious.

By 'French philosophy' I mean something broader than the work of Merleau-Ponty and Sartre, though including that work. The principles of this tradition are perhaps most clearly foreshadowed by Alexandre Kojève, in his extraordinarily influential lectures on Hegel's *Phenomenology of Spirit* in the 1930s; this passage comes from a translation and commentary on chapter 4, on the dialectic of master and slave:

> Man is Self-consciousness. He is conscious of himself, conscious of his human reality and dignity; and it is in this that he is essentially different from animals, which do not go beyond the level of simple Sentiment of

self. Man becomes conscious of himself at the moment when – for the first time – he says 'I'.

What leads to that is not the mere passive knowledge, of a pure subject confronting some object. This couldn't lead to self-consciousness; it could only leave the subject rapt out of himself, knowing only the object. What leads to self-consciousness is some kind of human desire (if only the desire to eat) that recalls the subject to himself.

> Desire is what transforms Being, revealed to itself by itself in (true) knowledge, into an 'object' revealed to a 'subject' by a subject different from the object and 'opposed' to it. It is in and by – or better still, as – 'his' Desire that man is formed and revealed – to himself and to others – as an 'I', as the I that is essentially different from and radically opposed to, the non-I. The (human) I is the I of a Desire or of Desire.

2.2 Lacan's philosophical re-reading of Freud

The Heideggerian and half-Marxist Hegelianism that Kojève offers (whether directly taken from him or not) had enormous influence on French thought in the 1940s and 1950s. Jacques Lacan, who attended Kojève's lectures, was already re-reading the whole work of Freud and rigorously rethinking it, in the light of such philosophical positions as this, as early as 1936. In Lacan's re-reading the mechanistic aspects of Freud's doctrine drop away; the Freudian reality principle comes under question; the object of the science becomes psychical rather than objective reality; the subject matter of psychology is limited to 'Facts about Desire' (Benvenuto and Kennedy 1986).

The distinction that Lacan comes to draw, between the human **subject** and the Freudian **ego** is, I think, a product of this type of analysis. Lacan takes an extreme position on the Freudian ego. Freud gave the ego the valuable function of negotiating with external reality. Lacan sees the ego as the product of misrecognition and false objectification in early childhood. The child, for Lacan, goes through a 'mirror phase' of development (recognized neither by Anna Freud nor Melanie Klein, nor, I think, by any paediatricians outside the Lacanian school). It then first learns to recognize itself, or at least imagine itself, through its reflection, as a unitary being. The ego remains an imaginary entity (i.e. one existing in fantasy) which is in turn the agent of misrecognition and false objectification later on. Lacan is directly opposed to those schools of analysis which take it as a goal of analysis to strengthen the ego and to improve adjustment to external social reality. All this predates Lacan's 'structuralist' period.

When structuralism entered into the French philosophical environment, something radically new happened to it; it changed from being merely a theory about language, literature, society or whatever and became a theory of the structure of the '**subject**' that experiences these objects. We have already seen the Kantian tendencies of Lévi-Strauss; the drive toward discovering universal structures of the human mind. Lacan took up certain Lévi-Straussian ideas, in a rather unclear way, and made them Freudian.

It seems reasonable enough to relate the passage through the Oedipal stage of development (the stage of wishing to kill the father and marry the mother) which in Freudian theory is the gateway to human adulthood, with the Lévi-Straussian incest-taboo, which is what produces human culture. Both serve to differentiate the animal from the human. The Lévi-Straussian world of culture, as opposed to nature, became the Lacanian world of '**the symbolic**', and this seems to be wholly or partially coextensive with the world of language. Entry into this world is what moves the organism beyond the animal stage and produces the human subject.

There is a conceptual gap here which may not have been apparent to Lacan, but which I find troublesome. Lacan's concern as an analyst is with speech. The early Lacan makes a distinction between a full speech which belongs to the subject and empty speech, which comes from the ego and belongs to the domain of the imaginary. It is a distinction rather similar to that of Heidegger, between discourse that articulates 'the intelligibility of Being-in-the-World' and 'idle talk' that offers mere social gossip. Empty speech is something that the analyst interprets rather than responding to its content; the appearance of full speech seems to be the nearest thing an early Lacanian would recognize to the patient being cured. These distinctions are very important to Lacan. But to a linguist – to Saussure or to Jakobson – both are simply ways of using the same language. So the linguist's concept of language won't really do for him. Yet it is the linguist's concept of language that seems to be needed for the construction of the all-important realm of the symbolic, where the subject is to be formed.

It is very difficult to argue questions like this. Lacan's public writings even of the 1950s, and still more later on, are gnomic and programmatic, as well as dogmatic, and sometimes give the impression of being demonstrations of the processes of unconscious thought. (Lacan had links with, and sympathies with, the Surrealists.) The seminars of the 1950s are much clearer; but it is hard to find even in them a clear statement of these, or any other hypotheses, let alone a consideration of the evidence for and against hypotheses. I personally know of no evidence that (for example) language acquisition has any relation to passage through the Oedipus complex, though both have been very extensively studied. And so obscure are Lacan's formulations that it is not clear to me, even at this moment, whether this lack of evidence has any bearing on his claims. It seems impossible to work out whether Lacanian claims about the name-of-the-father and language have anything to do with psycholinguistic studies of language acquisition. But if Lacan was actually engaged in scientific work relating to child development, presumably they should have some connection. This lack of connection with hard linguistic science is something that is still worrying if one attends seminars on Lacan in the 1990s. (Chomsky, who met Lacan rather late in life, described him as a conscious charlatan playing games with the Parisian intellectual community to see how much absurdity he could get away with (Chomsky 1989).)

2.3   The structuralist theory of the human subject

Nevertheless it was not irrational, in the 1950s, to see Lévi-Strauss and Lacan as providing the basis of a new science of man, which should at the same time be objective and yet provide a structural account of human subjectivity. It was even possible to see these as representing a 'scientific' account of human nature, in opposition to the unscientific existentialists; though an American behaviourist would probably have regarded both sides in the controversy as mad. If we construct, on a crude do-it-yourself basis, a kind of archetypal existentialist and phenomenological viewpoint, it will serve (much better than a scholarly study of Sartre or Merleau-Ponty would) to show what it was that structuralism was contradicting.

Central to this crude position then is the concept of the human subject, which is also identified with consciousness and with the self. This 'subject' is not just the passive viewpoint from which subjective experience is had, but the place where value-judgements and choices of action are made. It is also unitary and free. It finds itself thrown into a world which it did not construct; but it is free to act in that world and it constructs itself in the course of such action. There is no unconscious determination of the choices of the subject; it is bad faith to claim that.

This philosophical position (which, I repeat, I am not attributing to any one philosopher, but which I think is a reasonable representation of a general philosophical climate) is not a coherent one. The concept of the *subject*, which properly speaking arises as the pole opposite to the objective one in an analysis of experience into subject–object relationships – cannot really be identified with that of **consciousness** – which seems to imply some degree of awareness of thought-processes – or with **the self**, which according to psychoanalysts includes a large unconscious component. It would be logically possible for one of these – the subject – to be unitary, while the other two, consciousness and the self, were both complex constructions.

The structuralist challenge has, however, usually proceeded as if evidence about the complexity of consciousness, or of the self, was evidence for the disunity, or the constructedness, or even for the death, of something called 'the human subject'. What kind of evidence could this be? As Socrates pointed out in *The Republic*, simple introspection will show that there are conflicts within consciousness; and all psychological schools agree that the self is a complex construction that takes a person's whole life to produce. What has structuralism to offer that is at all new?

It has two kinds of consideration to offer, both of which can be given a perfectly general form, but both of which can be best introduced by considering aspects of the use of language. The first of these concerns the structuring of perception and of action. Consider one's dealings with the flow of speech. People who do not know a particular language **at all** (even in the sense of knowing some closely related language) actually hear the stream of sounds that a speaker of that language produces in an entirely different way from people who do know that language. They cannot hear the individual sounds of the language; they cannot hear the breaks within the words. Their actual perceptions of sounds are controlled by the structure of the language they know.

Any psychological theory of perception has to take account of this; and this is relevant to French philosophy not least because Merleau-Ponty's philosophy often reads as an elaborate and extended theory of perception. Perception here becomes something like an unmediated ground for knowledge; but the example of language suggests that no such unmediated perception exists. It suggests a radical critique of the whole notion of perception. (In the Baltimore conference in 1966, Derrida remarked: '. . . I don't know what perception is and I don't believe that anything like perception exists' (Macksey and Donato 1970, p. 272).)

Now in this special case, much of our relevant knowledge of a language seems to be reducible to a set of structural patterns; and in the case of a first language, this knowledge is normally unconscious and was acquired at a very early stage in the development of the self. Indeed, it is impossible to imagine a human self that did not have this much knowledge of at least one language. One might say that the self is partly **constructed** from this piece of code; i.e. the mind organizes its basic perceptions in terms of this piece of code.

But if this happens in the special case of language, why should it not happen generally? Suppose **all** our perceptions are handled in terms of structural codings, either built into us at birth, or learnt by social conditioning? (There is, one may add, a good deal of recent evidence that this is the case.) Would it not be true to say that the self which perceives is merely the locus of all these codes? When we perceive anything, the coded patterns of which we are partly made, process the stimuli received from the external world, into perceptions of an object.

What is true of perception is also true of action. When we speak, we speak words, made of the sounds we recognize as being part of our language. But it is the structural patterns built into ourselves when we first learnt the language that translate these into actual muscular actions that produce physical sounds which a microphone would receive. If we generalize these two cases, we may suppose that all our perceptions, and all our actions, are mediated by structures of which we are not conscious, but which are preconditions of consciousness.

So far I have not mentioned **symbolization**. I have been dealing with language simply as an example of the structured nature of human perception and action; we are in the world of structuralism but not yet in that of semiology. Even at this level we encounter evidence that the self is built out of structures; and that these exist in social codes before the self comes into existence.

But language is not merely a structured form of behaviour and experience. It is also a means of symbolization. Our thoughts are represented in language as in a medium; and for most of them, it is not obvious that there is any other possible medium. How could we represent a concept like that of 'the British economy' or 'the metaphysical poets' except in language? Even if there were any other medium than language that could represent thoughts, it would have to function like a language; and it might in some respects have to be structured like a language. It may be possible to have a concept that is not represented in language; but is it possible to have a concept that is not represented by some sign or other? It begins to look as if all concepts may be studied by studying the sign-systems in which they are represented; and this is the business of semiology.

Now concepts are a substantial part of the actual content of consciousness. The term covers pretty well everything in the mind except perceptions, impulses to action and so forth. But if this is the case, then semiology, the study of sign systems, will also be the study of the concepts that are in the mind; and to that extent, it will be a study of the constitution of the self. In so far as sign systems can be seen as internalized codes, the mind can be seen as partly constituted by those codes.

It may occur to the reader that there is a modern, positivist version of this theory that can easily be assimilated to the natural, rather than the human sciences. This is the view of the computer scientists working in what is called **artificial intelligence**. For them, the codes are actually computer programmes running in the brain – here seen as a computer. I rather like this theory, which seems to me attractively reductive. But no structuralist of the classical period would have thought in this way, though it is obviously what their theories lead to. The grip of philosophy was far too strong. Indeed, it still is far too strong; now that structuralism is dead, most post-structuralists will still find me hopelessly naïve for accepting the computational view of the mind.

What **was** obvious at this stage was the close connection of sign systems to the study of communication in **society**. Indeed this was, already, the older, Saussurean conception of semiology. The point is that the codes which carry meaning are acquired from society. At this point we begin to see that the study of individual consciousness can to a large extent be replaced by the study of socially available codes.

The human subject, that unitary phantom, has thus died twice at the hands of structuralism. It was already the locus of a set of perceptual codes, which are what enable it to perceive the world. It now becomes the locus of a set of symbolic codes, which give it its knowledge and its value systems. Society is no longer – if it ever was – a convenient arrangement made by a collection of autonomous human selves. On the contrary, each supposedly autonomous self is made out of pre-existing social codes. Only the unsocialized human body exists before social determination; not the person. (Which is presumably why, when Barthes started to move away from structuralism, he began to ground his writing on the body and its desires.)

This analysis of the subject, in some people's eyes, has a political significance. Althusser, for example, uses this approach (relying on Lacan for his structuralist theory of the subject) to build a theory of the way the individual human subject is constituted in ideology, and thus comes freely to accept as if they are his own choices, the options society offers to him, which Althusser believes to be oppressive. Some very important contemporary criticism descends from this Althusserian theory of ideology; though it often tends to reject its origins and look to someone like Foucault instead.

I must say I have never quite been able to understand why structuralist analysis was seen as an attack on the unity or individuality of the subject. To say that something is a structure made out of pre-existing parts is not to say that it does not exist, or is not a unit. And this remains true if the parts are pre-existing social codes or symbolic structures. And there could be hundreds of millions of unique individual selves made out of the standard parts a complex society provides. After all, everybody on earth except a few identical twins has a unique gene pattern; and they are assembled from only four different chemical units; why not for minds, as for bodies?

2.4 The Rewriting of Saussure as a philosopher

It is in the context of this philosophical controversy, between a structuralist and a phenomenological or existential conception of man, that there occurred the great rewriting of Saussure.

The Saussure encountered so far in this book belongs very much to what is sometimes called – always, I think, with hostile intention – the 'positivist' school of thinkers. He is the Saussure of the English and American linguistics departments: the great historical philologist whose final act was to found a new synchronic linguistics; a scientist making a decisive new development in his science. This Saussure never lost his interest in the nuts and bolts of language study: a very substantial proportion of the *Course in General Linguistics* is printed in the italic type that indicates linguistic examples, illustrating points of grammar, phonology and occasionally historical semantics. And for this Saussure semiology was an addition, a frill, a hopeful possibility, a suggestion somewhere in the margin of developments that probably ought to take place.

This is not at all the Saussure of the later structuralist tradition: the model for Roland Barthes and the dummy attacked by Derrida. That

Saussure is essentially a semiologist; a theoretician of the social sciences; and a philosopher from whom are to be derived theories alternative to those of Sartre and Co. on the constitution of the self. The new Saussure's work is read and read, it must be admitted, with extraordinary intensity and care, first as a model for the development of new non-linguistic branches of semiology and then for the metaphysical problems supposed to be revealed, to commentators like Jacques Derrida, by its own internal contradictions. In the course of this, every theoretical distinction that Saussure made is taken up, enlarged upon, analysed and transferred into other contexts in which it often means something entirely different. But the linguistic examples that pin down these theoretical distinctions are usually ignored. The *Course* is read; but the italic type is skipped over.

Saussure could hardly have had this kind of influence if there had not been elements in his work to support such radical readings. But for the uncommitted reader, it is not easy to pick out these elements in a simple reading of the *Course*. In the more radical accounts of his work, on the other hand, these elements are already deeply embedded in later assumptions and arguments of a political or anti-metaphysical kind and are hard to pick out from them. Perhaps the clearest and fairest account of these elements is given in the later parts of a very short book by Jonathan Culler (1976) – Saussure as a Fontana Modern Master. Despite its brevity, this book gives an adequate account of some of Saussure's linguistics and does not omit the linguistic examples. But it takes the later, French view of Saussure's general significance, and the following account is partly based on pp. 70–117 of this work.

Like all accounts of Saussure's radicalism, Culler's begins with his theory of meaning. Many thinkers, including distinguished ones like Heidegger, have attached particular importance to etymology as a guide to some essential original meaning of the words we employ. Later changes in meaning can be seen as accretions which can, if necessary, be stripped away. This position is difficult for the historical linguist to maintain, since in time both the form of a word and its meaning will change; it becomes, in effect a new entity.

Saussure had rejected the view that there was some common essential meaning for some whole historical series of forms, which could thus be known as different successive versions of 'the same word'. He recognized that both sound and meaning change; that the relationship between sound and meaning is arbitrary; that both the perceived sound and the perceived meaning are constituted by patterns of opposition – in the one case among sounds, in the other case among ideas. Neither in the case of the signifier – the word we pronounce – nor in the case of the signified – the concept that we attach to it – do we have an individual item standing by itself. Each derives its very identity from the way it stands within a total system.

Methodologically, this is a point of great importance; but it is a point that belongs to pure linguistics as an autonomous field of study. What happens when you view it in terms of the new structuralist philosophy of the subject? We can approach this in terms of either of two metaphors. If we see the mind as a kind of container, we can say that the Saussurean structures of language are now placed **inside the mind**, along with the structural codes that define society. If we see the mind as a point of view on the world, we will say that it **enters into** a symbolic world constructed from these codes. It was the second metaphor Lévi-Strauss and Lacan tended to use.

On either view the codes are only to a small extent the products of the experience of the subject concerned. In large part they existed before the subject acquired them; Saussure did not invent the French language, or Durkheim French society. And they structure the experience that the subject is capable of having. I must be acquainted with the structure of the French language to recognize remarks in French and I must be acquainted with the structure of social institutions like marriage to recognize a marriage when I encounter one.

According to Culler, in his significance for the human sciences Saussure can be compared with his exact contemporaries, Freud and Durkheim, founding fathers of modern psychology and sociology respectively. What he finds central to the approach of all three thinkers is something that many of us would associate more with a philosopher like Husserl: they all place the 'subject' – that is, the self, the 'I', that which thinks, perceives and speaks – at the centre of their analytical domain. And then, says Culler, quoting Derrida anachronistically and I think slightly altering his meaning, they 'deconstruct' it. That is, they explain meanings in terms of systems of convention that escape the subject's conscious grasp. The subject, or self, is broken down into its constituents which turn out to be interpersonal systems of conventions. The self is dissolved as its functions are attributed to a variety of systems which operate through it.

> In short, sociology, linguistics, and psychoanalytic psychology are possible only when one takes the meanings which are attached to and which differentiate objects and actions in society as a primary reality, as facts to be explained. And since meanings are a social product, explanation must be carried out in social terms. It is as if Saussure, Freud and Durkheim

had asked 'what makes individual experience possible? what enables men to operate with meaningful objects and actions? what enables them to communicate and act meaningfully? And the answer they postulate is social institutions which, though formed by human activities, are the conditions of experience. To understand human experience one must study the social norms that make it possible.

(Culler 1976, p. 72)

This approach Culler contrasts with the empiricist positivism descending from Hume, which recognized essentially two sorts of reality: an objective physical reality of objects and events, and an individual subjective perception of reality. Society for Hume was not the former, and so must be a mere resultant of the latter; perhaps even a collective fiction. Culler also contrasts it with the Hegelian idealism for which everything is a mere expression of Mind as it evolves.

Saussure, Freud and Durkheim are thus brought together as philosophers, or perhaps as a single philosopher, analysing the nature of human experience, rather than as scientists, offering extensive factual information and theoretical explanation. Culler scouts the notion that any of them is engaged in causal explanation, though both Freud and Durkheim said that they were (Freud 1915–17; Durkheim 1895). By a remarkable – though already by the late 1950s a characteristically French – feat of assimilation he has managed to bring together three very different concepts: the notion of structure, the notion of collective representations or norms, and the notion of the unconscious.

Structural explanation relates actions to a system of norms – the rules of a language, the collective representations of a society, the mechanisms of a psychical economy – and the concept of the unconscious is a way of explaining how these systems have explanatory force. It is a way of explaining how they can be simultaneously unknown yet effectively present. If a description of a linguistic system counts as an analysis of a language it is because the system is something not immediately given to consciousness yet deemed to be always present, always at work in the behaviour it structures and makes possible. (Ibid., p. 76)

At this point Culler makes a quite stunning claim, which shows just how radical this re-reading of Saussure is. Saussure, he says, provides better evidence for the existence of the unconscious than Freud does!

Though the concept of the unconscious as such arises in the work of Freud, it is essential to the type of explanation which a whole range of modern disciplines seeks to offer, and would certainly have been developed even without Freud's aid. In fact, one could argue that it is in linguistics that the concept emerges in its clearest and most irrefutable form. The unconscious is the concept which enables one to explain an indubitable fact: that I know a language (in the sense that I can produce and understand new utterances, tell whether a sequence is in fact a sentence of my language, etc.) yet I do not know what I know. I know a language, yet I need a linguist to explain to me precisely what it is that I know. The concept of the unconscious connects and makes sense of these two facts and opens a space of exploration. Linguistics, like psychology and a sociology of collective representations, will explain my actions by setting out in detail the implicit knowledge which I myself have not brought to consciousness. (Ibid., p. 76)

There seems to be an element of verbal magic here, in which theories of very different kinds are being united by a mere labelling process. The rules of a language, the norms of a society and the mechanisms of a psychical economy are not made more alike by calling them 'systems of norms'. The Freudian concept of the unconscious as the repressed – clearly to be differentiated from the merely preconscious or unobserved – is quite different from the linguist's notion of having an implicit knowledge of grammar or his notion of 'the other item of a paradigm that we don't happen to be using at this moment'. All these are different from Durkheim's 'collective consciousness'. It is very difficult to bring these three founding fathers together without ignoring all that is distinctive and interesting in their respective subjects. You have to leave the linguistic detail out of linguistics, the social statistics – among other things – out of sociology, and the analytic situation and procedure out of psychoanalysis.

Bringing together Saussure, Freud and Durkheim in this way may seem strange; it becomes much more plausible if we consider certain major intellectual traditions that flow from each of these three thinkers. Each of these traditions, though important, has the status of a 'minority report', as it were, within its own discipline.

The main tradition descending from Saussure is, as we have seen, the modern science of linguistics; the minority report, which astonishes most linguists, sees him as a philosopher concerned, within the broad framework of semiology, with the nature of subjective experience, the delineation of our concepts and the unconscious foundations of consciousness.

The main tradition that descends from Freud is that of orthodox psychoanalysis, though there are innumerable sectarian differences. The minority report is that of Jacques Lacan, who mocked at the objectifying scientism of orthodox Freudians and claimed that the unconscious is structured like a language – because, in fact, it is an effect of language. And although what Lacan meant by language seems utterly different from anything a linguist like Saussure could have meant, he did (in his maddeningly allusive and incomprehensible way) often refer to Saussure as if Saussure were responsible for his conceptions. As a young American Ph.D said solemnly to me once: 'It's all in Saussure you know.'

The main intellectual tradition that descends from Durkheim is that of the sciences of sociology and anthropology. A major figure within these – who perhaps no anthropologist can ignore, though very few seem to accept him altogether – is Lévi-Strauss, who already in the 1940s had accepted linguistics as an example of method and in the 1960s had come to define anthropology as a branch of semiology. One can hardly see him as occupying a minority position within French anthropology; but he does within anthropology as a whole.

If we take semiology – nowadays rechristened semiotics – Lacanian psychoanalysis and Lévi-Straussian anthropology as the central traditions – there are some arguments for doing so and the French avant-garde of the early 1960s were very eager to do so – it no longer looks eccentric to bring together Saussure, Freud and Durkheim; on this interpretation it is natural. One even begins to see the possibility of some kind of intellectual synthesis between these fields, like that by the British writers Coward and Ellis, described later: though they, like most radicals, substitute Marx – in the reading due to Louis Althusser – for Durkheim. Such a synthesis seemed very possible in the final days of structuralism; it was indeed what all the fashionable fuss was about. And there is no reason in principle even to sneer at the fashion; it is right to be intellectually excited when a unification on such a scale appears to be in the offing, even if you only have a dim notion of what it is all about. Saussure still gets much of the credit for this grand and never quite achieved unification.

To sum up: the central philosophical problem to which all these thinkers are supposed to contribute is that of the nature of the self, the mind or the knowing subject. The contribution that the tradition of semiological structuralism makes to this problem is this: it represents the mind, or subject, as a set of interlocking codes rather than as a unitary entity. These codes form the unconscious foundation for consciousness. On this view, it is inaccurate to say that I know my own language. At the time I began to learn it, I had an incompletely developed self; really, the 'I' that now is, is partly constituted by the language I know and think with; and the rest of me is presumably constituted by other codes. To put it in a rather flowery way 'I am constituted by that of which I am unconscious; I don't speak; language and other codes speak through me. I speak from where I am not.'

The subject, on this view, is thus 'decentred' – no longer occupies the central position given it by the subjectivist philosophical tradition. My own immediate experience, far from being the unarguable ground of scientific truth, as Husserl thought it was and as literary critics always think it is, is processed through the codes made part of me through my culture. It is even possible to relate this, in an illuminating way, to the Marxist concept of ideology. Ideology, for Althusser, is something much more than a false system of ideas, manufactured in capitalist society to confuse the proletariat in its perception of its own class interests. It is rather the very element in which we experience the world, and in which we live. It can be equated with the Lacanian realm of the symbolic, or Lévi-Straussian culture; or Durkheimian collective consciousness; and no society – even after the revolution – could possibly exist without it.

Such a view may not sound particularly Marxist; but it does enable one to offer some interesting solutions to historical problems in Marxist theoretical terms. Capitalist society, for example, requires for its perpetuation an endless supply of apparently free human subjects, to make apparently free and spontaneous decisions, as they take their part in capitalism's free markets. These 'subjects' however do not come into existence spontaneously; they are formed from the prevailing symbolic codes (only, as a Marxist materialist, Althusser prefers to speak of 'practices') by roughly the process that Lacan describes. Althusser thus joins the long procession of those who have produced a synthesis of Marx and Freud. But these practices are the ideology of society; and, according to the later Althusser, capitalist states actually have state ideological apparatuses, like schools, to produce them; and hence to produce these 'subjects'.

Whether or not this is true, or even Marxist, is uncertain; it certainly forms an interesting excuse for Marxists to concentrate their revolutionary efforts on altering the curriculum in schools and colleges. Richard Harland (1987) has found a revealing name for this and all the other late and post-structuralisms, with their inherently idealist tendencies. He calls them '*Superstructuralism*'.

2.5   Is structuralism science?

If you look closely at the four major figures of this phase it is possible to see that the influence of Saussure is rather different for each of them. Lévi-Strauss took his Saussure from Jakobson; took it very seriously; and made a serious attempt to devise a new methodology and a new set of models for anthropology, adapting those of linguistics. Roland Barthes, who I will consider in detail in the next chapter, wrote a reasonable elementary popularization called *Elements of Semiology*, and adapted what he took to be the methods of linguistics to his own rather quirky investigations of, for example, the language of fashion. Lacan borrowed a little terminology – sign, signifier and so on – and used it for his own purposes in an essentially Freudian context. He is much more deeply influenced by Hegel and by Heidegger than by Saussure. Althusser appears to have had little or no interest in language, though the linguistic model influenced other people, like Lacan, who influenced him; he is probably one of those who believed in Lacan's Saussure.

The extent to which work of this third phase can be assimilated to science is a matter for argument. Lévi-Strauss is a dominating figure in anthropology and particularly in mythological analysis; yet very few empirical anthropologists seem to agree with him; as we have seen, in some ways his later work is carefully insulated from any possible empirical refutation; and as I have said, at times he presents his studies of mythology as if they are themselves mythological. Lacan spent much of his career in violent altercation with the psychoanalytic profession, which saw him as trying to make psychoanalysis unscientific. (As I have suggested, many academic psychologists would regard this as a task accomplished long ago by Freud.)

Althusser and Barthes are both later figures; they wrote in the 1960s, in the very last period when the scientific dream still held its magic. Althusser made the most enormous fuss about the scientificity of the work of Marx, which he thought not a part of natural science, but a new continent in its own right, equal in importance to natural science as a whole. Barthes began his work trying to build a science of semiology – as he said, 'in a dream of scientificity' – and ended by repudiating the scientific goal. But even at the beginning, his work had strong political overtones; as Jonathan Culler points out (*Structuralist Poetics*, 1975), it was never a neutral science, seeking positive knowledge for its own sake and offering explanatory theories for their own sake.

It is, however, an interesting point that however personal, quirky and unscientific was the work of the individuals in this third phase of structuralism, and however confused was the public perception of it, the underlying structuralist model was still capable of the hardest of hard-science interpretations. Forget Lévi-Strauss and Lacan; replace Saussure and Barthes by some follower of Chomsky with access to a computer; bring in the cognitive scientists and the neurophysiologists. We can now talk about the structural codes that constitute the mind as computer programs running on the brain, considered as a computer.

We can now say that human experience is a resultant of three causal factors: the physical world we live in, including our own and other physical human bodies; the firmware in our brains – that is, our instinctual drives, considered as built-in programs for our bodies to interact with their environment; and the software – programs representing such entities as the grammar of our language or our knowledge of our society.

Notice that language and society, on this model, will exist only in terms of such programs. Their existence will, in that sense, be wholly mental. Yet it will be entirely objective; it will be a matter of fact whether one program is running or another; as it is a matter of fact whether I speak English or French. Furthermore, it will be possible to conduct objective scientific research into such matters of fact; though since all such research is conducted by hypothetico-deductive method, it will not supply **certain** knowledge; the human robot investigating the programs running on its own brain can never work out for certain what they are, though it can be immediately aware what experience they provide it with. Human robots will be caught up in the same harmless paradoxes of self-reference as human beings are caught up in. I see no reason why they should not have, if they are complicated enough, social practices, history and art.

I am myself a vulgar materialist and a hard-line materialist and I think the theory I have just sketched is very probably true. But I am not proposing to defend it against any of the obvious philosophical attacks at this point. What concerns me is the question: why didn't the structuralists go on to develop this promising line of research in detail? Why do we proceed instead to the sophistries of post-structuralism, which are designed if anything to hide us from material realities and prevent us arriving at any reductive theories – that is to say, at any theories which provide explanations of any serious kind? Why is our next move into a discourse of bullying facetiousness and metaphysical triviality without end? (This is what I take post-structuralism to be.) Could it be – I think there is evidence that it could – that some at least of the structuralists could see the mechanistic outcome of their research strategy and were appalled by it? They saw the desert ahead; and rather than move clear-eyed into that, they preferred to surround themselves with fog.

3   THE COLLAPSE OF STRUCTURALISM

3.1   *The change of style*

Structuralism collapsed in 1967: and this was the manner of it. Some of the most prominent figures began to distance themselves from the structuralist paradigm; to treat it as if it wasn't – and perhaps never had been – a serious model; or as if their attitude to it had been gravely misunderstood. The tone and attitude of new structuralist writing rapidly changed. Some of the most exciting work in this tradition, whatever discipline it might nominally be in, became increasingly difficult to place in relation to ordinary academic studies in the same discipline. There might be a certain overlap of material: between ordinary logic and semiotics, for example, or between ordinary anthropology and the structuralist variety. But the differences in objectives and objectivity were such that it came to seem rather beside the point to make the sort of comparisons that one had made earlier on – to say, for example, that Anglo-American structural anthropology is much more firmly based in field-work than the structuralist variety, or English Marxist historians are more concerned with exact historical detail than Althusserian Marxists are.

In effect a radical change in cognitive style had occurred. Academic disciplines like logic, linguistics, anthropology, political philosophy and so forth compare with the new thought rather as a team of sober accountants compare with a drunken artist. They are not fraudulent – you can trust them with your money. But they will never be fashionable; and they certainly don't have the same careless speculative verbal creativity. From the point of view of an insider – a contributor to *Tel Quel*, for example – the new movement was truly a gay science; not content with revolutionizing human thought, it sparkled with verbal wit as well. 'Post-structuralism' – as it came to be called – was a party.

3.2   *The Play of Lacan*

Some of the roots of this cognitive style can be found in earlier work. It is possible to call Lacan in aid here. This is not because Lacan is irrationalist, or does not believe in large-scale systems of thought like Freudian theory or science, or, like Foucault, does not seem to care about the question of whether psychosis exists and talks merely about the way it has been classified and treated. On the contrary Lacan, like Althusser, continued to insist on the scientificity of his own work – though his conception of science was a rather individual one – deep into the later period when science had come under most attack.

There are however three elements in Lacan that influenced post-structuralist thought. The first of these was his hostility to the unitary Freudian ego, seen as an element necessary for dealing with a social reality to which it is necessary to adjust. We have seen that there is a shift in his work to the notion of a 'subject' which is a field of tensions rather than a unit, and which in some ways is no more than a construct out of the 'subject's' discourses. This idea was incorporated, in a simplified form, in Althusser's theory and so gained wide influence among 'structuralist' Marxists. But it can be used to cast doubt, not only on the existence of the integral self, but on the existence of any univocal reality for it to react to. Lacan himself always retained the concept of the real; in the form of the unsymbolizable, the impossible. But ordinary realism – the kind that says there really are tables, chairs and other people, and the ego exists partly to handle that reality – is harder to find.

The second element was his insistence on the priority of the signifier in language. For the analyst this view can be justified as an instruction to look at the analysand's discourse and not neglect features like word-play and puns. For the theorist it seems to be a way both of claiming to be materialist, and of claiming that the very possibility of meaning something with ordinary signifiers depends on our relation to certain master signifiers, like the phallus; which seems to play a role in this system rather like that of an archetype in Jung's system. But it could be taken as supporting a radical rethinking of the Saussurean theory of language, in which the meanings of verbal expressions are supposed to be constructed out of oppositions of sounds. This theory is linguistic nonsense and, like a Foucauldian madman, it won't work. But it still haunts post-structuralist writing like a psychosis, bringing confusion wherever it comes. I call it the insistence on the phoneme.

The third element, and perhaps the most influential of all, was his characteristic mode of exposition; the darting allusiveness, the puzzling rhetoric, the incessant word-play:

> It is somewhat striking that a dimension that is felt as that of Something-else in so many of the experiences that men undergo, not at all without thinking about them, rather while thinking about them, but without thinking they are thinking, and like Telemachus thinking of the expense (pensant de la dépense), should never have been thought to the extent of

being congruently said by those whom the idea of thought assures of thinking. . . . There is no longer any way, therefore, of reducing this Elsewhere to the imaginary form of a nostalgia, a lost or future paradise; what one finds is the paradise of the child's loves where, baudelaire de Dieu!, something's going on, I can tell you.

(Lacan 1966, pp. 192–3)

Lacan has more justification than his imitators for his use of word-play and puns. He is writing, much of the time, about the unconscious, which according to Freud and much of the clinical evidence, puns all the time. And he has his theory of the priority of the signifier, which I think mistaken (the point is discussed in chapters 3, 6, 7) but which he held on what seemed good grounds and which justifies a great deal of word-play. Whatever the reason, the pun intended as argument runs like a virus through post-structuralism. Even Althusser, who belongs to the earlier, system-building stage of theory, thinks that it in some way supports his arguments to make puns about 'subjects' being 'subjected'; and English followers duly copy. Derrida thinks it does something for his anti-metaphysics to combine the ideas of differing and deferring in the single word '*différance*'; and the whole world has copied.

3.3 The argument of Derrida

This fourth stage of the structuralist tradition is often called 'post-structuralism', and sometimes supposed to be a natural development out of structuralist principles. But it is in fact no longer structuralist in any real sense, though it retains some unexamined and miscomprehended tags from the structuralist period – for example, the principle that language is a system of oppositions with no positive terms and that if it is treated otherwise, that is because metaphysics has crept in. The main thing that is new about this phase is that the central intention to produce large-scale formal systems in the human sciences has been given up: is seen, indeed, as an aggressive and oppressive intention and one that ought to be subverted. This is a change so radical that it must be described as the collapse of structuralism rather than as a development of it. This collapse was hidden for a time by the habit of writing very long books that looked as if they presented systems, though in fact they only undermined them: *Of Grammatology, S/Z, Anti-Oedipus.*

Why did structuralism collapse? I am tempted to say that it died rather abruptly in 1967, killed by a single bad argument from Jacques Derrida. I suppose that this is a melodramatic way to put the case; better perhaps to say that in 1966 a leader of intellectual fashion like Roland Barthes could present himself unequivocally as a structuralist, engaged in a co-operative and constructive research activity; by 1968 it was difficult to do this without looking naïve. (Though naïve, or constructive structuralism actually continued, as in the work of writers like Gérard Genette, throughout the 1970s.) Derrida wasn't the only influence here, and of course Derrida has more arguments than one to his credit – I discussed one about Lévi-Strauss in my last section. But far the most important argument – it is mentioned constantly and quite uncritically, in popular expositions of literary theory and even in some of the secondary philosophical literature – is the one about the metaphysical implications of the supposed phonocentrism of de Saussure.

This argument is presented in *Of Grammatology* – a book about an imaginary science of grammatology, presumably intended to satirize semiology. It says in effect that Saussure, who had been taken as offering a structuralist alternative to the metaphysics of presence exhibited in philosophers like Husserl and Heidegger, himself exhibits the same metaphysics. It is a bad argument, because it is based on false claims about the sense in which Saussure privileged speech over writing; and it relies on the historicity of an entirely mythical tradition of phonocentrism. (I have tried to tease out this difficult question in chapters 1 and 5, and I cannot summarize it here.)

Why should Derrida's arguments have had such a dramatic effect? In a more exact discipline – mathematics, for example – one can have a proof that some line of enquiry is actually impossible. Gödel's theorem is an obvious example. Thereafter anyone in the discipline who pursues such an enquiry is clearly a fool, who doesn't understand his business. In such a case, the direction of a whole discipline can be swung round by the discovery of a single theorem. But structuralist semiology is not such an exact discipline as that; Derrida's deconstructive arguments seem very woolly by comparison with Gödel's theorem, or Russell's set theory paradox. (See for these any standard text in logic or foundations of mathematics – e.g. Curry 1963; Kneebone 1963.)

I think myself Derrida probably does have a valid set of arguments, which he calls deconstructive and I think are a species of *reductio ad absurdum*, that are sufficient not merely to shake phenomenology (which is what he appears to want to do) but to demolish it. So to the extent that the new improved Saussure (unlike the original one) was a phenomenologist, the new improved structuralist semiotics came to seem an implausible project. Before Derrida, sophisticated people intended to produce a formalized theory of human culture; after Derrida, sophisticated people just knew you couldn't.

Anyone acquainted with the history of formal logic in the early twentieth century will be unsurprised by this conclusion. Since it is not even possible to produce a system of mathematical logic that is at once consistent and complete, it is clearly absurd to attempt to produce a formal theory of culture that shall have these properties. It will necessarily be defeated by the paradoxes of self-reference. That does not stop one formalizing limited domains of culture – the grammar of a language, for example. But any theory that aimed at totalization would be impossible in principle.

3.4 Power and Foucault

I am now going to retract part of the last five paragraphs, or at least qualify them half out of existence; not because they are wrong, but because they are absurdly schematic. They privilege Derrida's influence and ignore that of Foucault – wouldn't that make him furious? – not to mention that of Althusser and Lacan; and any of these may seem more important if you stand in a slightly different place. More abstractly, they privilege a purely philosophical argument over influences from the history of ideas and from social and psychological theory.

Most of all, they ignore the *Zeitgeist*: the social and political changes that were going on – the last stages of the reign of De Gaulle, the imminent student revolution: with student revolutionaries darting about the place, saying scornfully to Althusserians: 'Structures don't take to the streets!' and beginning to see the social sciences – with some reason – as devices used by the American government to justify putting Vietnamese peasants in what looked very like concentration camps (Chomsky and Herman 1979); just as Marxism in its Stalinist form had begun to look like a machine for building concentration camps (Solzhenitsyn, *passim*). Against this we had the dream that the imagination should take power: I can remember a time when I did not think this was barmy. The fading dream of liberation from a 'scientific rationality' that has taken on oppressive forms has, I think, fuelled post-structuralism for twenty years now, while the world in general has gone conservative. It explains the appeal of some of the work now to be considered.

117

Foucault is a historian of ideas with a difference. His own title for the subject he professed was 'The History of Systems of Thought'; and that title captures one aspect of his work: the attempt to show, in books like *The Order of Things*, 1966 (in French, more revealingly called *Words and Things*) the way in which common sets of assumptions about the classification of the phenomena of the world may underlie very different academic subjects and violently opposed positions in the same subjects, in a given period. Such a set of assumptions is called the, or an, episteme; the quest for such epistemes might be called, in terms of the title of another book, *The Archaeology of Knowledge*, 1969. This all sounds systematic enough and might seem to place him in the last constructive phase of structuralism. This indeed is how many early readers read his work.

Yet, in another sense, few writers are as hostile to system as this historian of systems of thought. He can be seen as the exact antithesis of Louis Althusser, who was at one time his teacher. Althusser believed that Marx had opened up the great continent of historical science, making an epistemological break with all earlier historiography. Foucault rejected not only Marxism but any form of systematic historical science. Althusser was a philosopher for whom history was a matter of grand structures; it is a matter of opinion whether he knew any historical detail at all; and on his own principles, it hardly seemed to matter. To this day, Althusserian history tends to soar above the empirical world and remain quite untestable; there are English Marxist historians of the older generation who spit at his name. Foucault's historical erudition is staggering and he is never short of particular facts; in some ways he reads like an English Marxist historian. But his treatment of the empirical evidence he produces is cavalier, anecdotal, impressionistic and illustrative in a way that theirs is not; and he retains a habit of breaking out into speculative philosophical rhetoric.

What I mean by philosophical rhetoric can be illustrated by the following sentence from *Discipline and Punish* (p. 23), setting out one of the objectives of that work:

> Instead of treating the history of penal law and the history of the human sciences as two separate series whose overlapping appears to have had, on one or the other, or perhaps on both, a disturbing or useful effect, according to one's point of view, see whether there is or not some common matrix or whether they do not both derive from a single process of 'epistemologico-juridical' formation; in short, make the technology of power the very principle both of the humanisation of the penal system and of the knowledge of man. (Foucault 1975)

This sentence suggests a whole series of claims about epistemology which would be very difficult to defend by explicit philosophical arguments. But Foucault does not offer any such arguments; instead, he tells his history as a set of illustrative stories. The concept of 'power-knowledge' seems to become a central epistemological and metaphysical principle in Foucault's later work; but it is not defended philosophically as such – such a defence would of course lead to yet another idealist philosophical system. Foucault's closest philosophical affiliation is with Nietzsche; and he has in a slighter way the same ability to overset one's normal systematic assumptions about the world, without replacing them by other systematic assumptions.

Foucault's main political contribution was to write histories of the treatment of madness, of the clinic, of the punishment of crime, from the point of view of what society has done to those it classified as mad, or sick, or criminal; while carefully not considering substantive questions about the nature of madness, illness or criminality. (I mean by substantive questions such questions as whether schizophrenia is a disease with a physical basis.) The tendency of such history is of course to suggest that these categories are purely social constructs, and to portray the mad, the ill and the criminal as victims of their warders and doctors – and, more generally, of the rest of us. It is this fundamental sympathy with the victim that makes Foucault a man of the left; though it is the left of a rainbow coalition – of all those groups, however different, which society finds deviant – rather than of a monolithic proletariat.

3.5 Post-structuralism and rationality

Such an attack, carried out with Foucault's persistence over such a range of subjects – his last, unfinished work was on sexuality – undermines the concept of normality itself. Even his early work on madness quite deliberately undermined the normative concept of reason; and it became a classic of the anti-psychiatry movement. If one wishes to do so, one can bring such work as this together with Derrida's purely philosophical attacks upon those aspects of the ubiquitous metaphysics of presence that he calls logocentrism and I would call rationality, to produce the beginnings of a genuinely anti-rationalist position – or at least a position which 'questions narrow notions of rationality' or 'presents rationality as something historically constructed', or makes rationality an effect of power, or in some other way shakes our notions of what is rational without necessarily putting anything in their place. It is such a position that provides one of the intellectual meanings (as opposed to stylistic meanings) of the journalistic term 'post-structuralism'.

It is possible to give a very moderate and reasonable description of this position. One informal account I have heard goes as follows: 'We have to have the grand general accounts of the world.' (Marxism, Freudian theory . . . and natural science, presumably.) 'But look at the small details of such an account, or the gaps and suppressions' (the political suppressions Foucault is concerned with, the logical gaps Derrida claims to find), 'and you will be compelled to construct a quite different story to accommodate them.' The line here – which is compatible with the work of both Derrida and Foucault – is one of suspicion for all grand syntheses, though it does not exactly amount to rejection of them. One would work on the texts that set out these grand narratives, and look for the gaps and suppressions in them.

If 'post-structuralism' had been no more than this it would never have become notorious. It would have been a grey monument to scholarly caution and altogether lacked the air of aggressive intellectual paradox – even revolutionary vigour – that seemed to be its mark. But it was much more than this; much more, even, than this plus Lacanian word-play. There is also idea-play. Derrida, for example never contents himself with producing arguments against the positions he wishes to question. Instead, he writes texts that enact the problems of those positions. This can produce crazy-looking violations of decorum. When John Searle rests an argument on certain conventions of language, Derrida replies with a text that violates just those conventions – to the point of misspelling Searle's name as SARL (Derrida 1977b). This technique is the concrete poetry of philosophy.

Post-structuralism is not a very good name for the whole body of thought we are now discussing. It applies to one or two of our writers, but not to most of them. Roland Barthes could fairly be called a post-structuralist; there was a time when he was an acknowledged structuralist and a later time when he had developed beyond it, under the influence of Derrida, Kristeva and others. Lévi-Strauss was also an acknowledged structuralist and indeed was sometimes supposed to have invented the term; but he never abandoned his allegiance to this model, however much he might have modified his scientific hopes for it.

Lacan was never, in the narrow sense, a structuralist; he was a Freudian, who attempted to bring Freud into the age first of Heidegger, then Lévi-Strauss and Saussure. Derrida is a post-phenomenologist; he was never any kind of structuralist, though he did play a central part in bringing French structuralism to an end and has invented a new mystique of Writing that has partly replaced it as literary-theoretic cult. Neither Althusser nor Foucault were ever structuralists in the narrow sense; the linguistic model on which that sort of structuralism is based has little relevance to history, except as a generalized exhortation to synchronic studies; and Althusser's structural Marxism was a form of historical structuralism, if anything. This point is sometimes obscured by the fact that much modern discourse theory descends from Althusser; but 'discourse' is a woolly notion, part of the point of which is to avoid doing linguistics. Foucault also is not post-structuralist; he is post-Marxist and Nietzschean. Deleuze and Guattari, the authors of the *Anti-Oedipus*, that strange work which appears to argue that we would be better off as schizophrenic collections of unintegrated desires than as Oedipalized members of society, are Nietzschean and post-Lacanian. Julia Kristeva, in some ways the archetypal post-structuralist, with her new form of semiotics whose content was to be solely the questioning of itself (*Semeiotike*, 1969, full version), was I think too young to have a structuralist period at all; though she helped persuade Roland Barthes to abandon his.

It is very unfortunate that structuralism and post-structuralism were imported into England and America in this final phase, and never properly distinguished: they are utterly different in character and demand quite different responses. I would hold that structuralism was a distinguished and important research strategy, which is in many ways continuous with some of the most promising modern scientific research in linguistics and artificial intelligence; on that ground it ought to be useful in developing objective theories of literature. But it was based on an inadequate linguistic model and suffered from what I have called 'logical poverty'; on that ground, it would have needed radical development and revision. The various post-structuralisms, on the other hand, seem to me to be anti-metaphysical soap-bubbles with political slogans written upon them; the only reason for supposing them to be a suitable basis for literary theory is that they share many of the characteristics of literature, including that of being fiction. This point is developed in the next two chapters, on Barthes and Derrida.

BOOKS

Lévi-Strauss: Leach, E. 1970 *Lévi-Strauss*
              Lévi-Strauss 1958, 1976 *Structural Anthropology*
Lacan: Benvenuto, B. and Kennedy, R. 1986 *The Works of Jacques Lacan*
Saussure: Culler, J. 1976 *Saussure*
Althusser: Elliot, G. 1987 *The Detour of Theory*
              Althusser 1984 *Essays on Ideology*
Derrida: Norris, C. 1987 *Derrida*
Foucault: Sheridan, A. 1980 *Foucault: The Will to Truth*
             Foucault 1984 *The Foucault Reader*
Kristeva: Kristeva 1986 *The Kristeva Reader*

FURTHER READING

Anthropology & Lévi-Strauss: Clarke 1981, Durkheim 1895, Dyson-Hudson 1970, Harris, M passim, Leach 1970, Lévi-Strauss passim, Moore, Tim 1969, Raglan 1936, 1940, Shalvey 1975, Tylor 1871, 1881.

Psychoanalytic Alternatives: Boss 1963, Casseguet-Smirgel and Grunberger 1976, Cooper 1967, Deleuze and Guattari 1972, Freud, Anna 1936, Freud, Sigmund passim, Hillman 1983, Koestenbaum 1978, Laplanche and Pontalis 1973, Malcolm 1982, 1984, Piaget passim.

Hegel: Kojève 1979.

Psychoanalysis and Lacan: Clement 1981, Jameson 1977, Johnson 1977, Lacan 1953-5, 1966, and passim, Lemaire 1970, McCabe 1981, Muller and Richardson 1982, Ragland-Sullivan 1986, Schneiderman 1983, Sédat 1981, Smith and Kerrigan 1983, Turkle 1979, Wilden 1972, 1986.

Structuralism and Saussure: Culler 1975, 1976, de George and de George 1972, Hawkes 1977, Kurzweil 1980.

Marxism and Althusser: Althusser passim, Althusser and Balibar 1968, Benton 1984, Dowling 1984, Elliott 1987, MacDonell 1986, Macherey 1966, Pateman 1983, Pécheux 1975.

History of Ideas and Foucault: Foucault passim, Hoy 1986, Schacht 1983 (for Nietzsche).

Post-structuralism: Bogue 1989, Culler 1981, 1983, Deleuze and Guattari 1972, 1980, Derrida passim, Harland 1987, Kristeva passim, Lecercle 1985, Sturrock 1979, Tallis 1988. See also chapters 4, 5, 7.

Cognitive Psychology and Artificial Intelligence: Blakemore and Greenfield 1987, Bloomfield 1987, Searle 1984.

General: Culler 1975, Hawkes 1977, Merquior 1986, Scruton 1985, Soper 1986, Tallis 1988.

For titles and publishers see main bibliography.

CHAPTER FOUR

The Trajectory of Roland Barthes

The Path into Structuralism and Out Again to Belles-Lettres

SUMMARY

The trajectory of Roland Barthes displays how a French literary critic, originally occupied in introducing avant-garde writers like Brecht and Robbe-Grillet, and in commenting sardonically on the 'myths' of the bourgeoisie, moved into semiological structuralism and by the early 1960s turned himself into a kind of scientist – influencing a whole discipline of later semiologists, whom he himself came to view with misgivings. After about 1967, under the influence of Derrida and Kristeva, he turned from constructing structuralist theories to subverting them (*S/Z*, 1970); moved back to the literary fragment and the personal voice; constructed an erotics of the text (*The Pleasure of the Text*, 1973) and elsewhere a textual mysticism to which analytical theory seems inappropriate (*From Work to Text*, 1971): within this mystique, Text is like Hegel's **Spirit**: only the text can know itself. This textual mysticism has greatly influenced post-structuralism.

1   FROM LEFTIST CRITIC TO WRITERLY SCIENTIST: AN INTRODUCTION

The most important thing about Roland Barthes was his trajectory: that is, his own developmental path, and the way he moved from one set of influences to another. This is not to deny that he had considerable importance as a critic, particularly in the work he did to secure the recognition of the *nouveau roman* and of Brecht; nor that he had some significance as a writer, as an intellectual belletrist or manufacturer of conceits, as a left-wing cultural critic and journalist; and as a pioneer of the study of popular culture in France. But his main significance was clearly as a representative and pioneer, phase by phase and point by point, of the cultural fashion for semiological structuralism in French intellectual life in general and French literary culture in particular. By studying his career one can see what it was that particular form of structuralism replaced; what it originally seemed to offer; how it developed and then subverted itself; and how it was finally abandoned. At every stage in this process Barthes managed to keep ahead of, and to set, the intellectual fashion; and his reward is that he now stands as its best representative. Barthes was rather proud of his trajectory, and sets it out clearly in a chart in his alphabetic autobiographical notebook *Roland Barthes by Roland Barthes* (Barthes 1975 p. 195). I reproduce this below.

Intertext	Genre	Works
(Gide)		(desire to write)
Sartre Marx Brecht	social mythology	*Writing Degree Zero* Writings on theatre *Mythologies*
Saussure	semiology	*Elements of Semiology* *Système de la Mode*
Sollers, Kristeva Derrida, Lacan	textuality	*S/Z* Sade,Fourier,Loyola *L'Empire des Signes*
(Nietzsche)	morality	*The Pleasure of the Text Roland Barthes by Roland Barthes*

As will be seen, we can divide Barthes' work into four major phases. The first phase is the pre-structuralist one – that of *Writing Degree Zero* (1953); of the earlier essays in *Critical Essays* (1964), including four good essays on Brecht and three on Robbe-Grillet; and of *Mythologies* (1957). (I won't here discuss the books *Michelet* or *On Racine*.)

This phase could perhaps be called 'Roland Barthes in the Age of Sartre'; there were other influences upon him, like Brecht and Robbe-Grillet; but there was no other overshadow. Barthes was born in 1915; he was ten years younger than Sartre, and like him a leftist literary intellectual, slightly hostile to the French academic system and vocally hostile to the bourgeoisie. Sartre, however, was something more than this. He was the acknowledged leader of the dominant philosophical school in Paris: existentialism. Barthes, in the early 1950s, had nothing like that behind him; only a set of unsystematic insights into the artificiality of bourgeois culture; and otherwise, only the generalized non-party Marxism and unorthodox psychoanalysis readily available in Paris. There was, therefore, no chance of the unreconstructed Barthes replacing Sartre as the arbiter of French intellectual fashion. Not till the 1960s was Sartre toppled from his throne; and it took the whole structuralist junta to do this: Lévi-Strauss, Lacan, Barthes, Althusser, Foucault and Derrida, misrecognized as a government in the realm of the imaginary.

But this rivalry partly explains why, in Barthes' pre-structuralist work of the 1950s the major theoretical text is *Writing Degree Zero* (1953). In this Barthes offers an argument, sparked off by the existence of the late modernist *nouveau roman* and directed essentially against Sartre's polemic *What is Literature* (1948), which favoured politically 'committed' writing. But Barthes presents his argument not as simple polemic, but in an arcane style more resembling that of Sartre's major philosophical work, *Being and Nothingness*. No other work by Barthes of this period is anything like as difficult: the critical essays are clear and straightforward, and *Mythologies* can be described as popular journalism.

The influence of Brecht and of the new novel was to be a permanent one. From the beginning to the end of his career, Barthes was hostile to ordinary bourgeois realism in art, and in favour of the kind of art that announces, or even celebrates, its own artifice. Brecht is the major theorist of this approach in the theatre; though the later Barthes became much less didactic than Brecht. Barthes' treatment of cultural stereotypes, in his *Mythologies*, was of a piece with his treatment of art. For him each new example of a cultural stereotype, or **myth**, as he confusingly calls it, is another way in which the bourgeoisie make their own ideological view of the world seem no more than a natural fact; and Barthes sets himself to undermine these stereotypes by mockery.

The lightweight magazine skits and general *randonnées* of *Mythologies* – still by far the most widely read of Barthes' works since they are so easy to read (and in some ways the best written, since the least pretentious) – were given a theoretical underpinning in the last essay, *Myth Today*. This offers to place the essays within a theory of semiology and ideology, so comprehensive that it will even include *Writing Degree Zero* as 'a mythology of literature'. A less ambitious view of the Barthes of this period would be that he is an amusing critic of the alleged unconscious assumptions of the bourgeoisie. His *Mythologies* essays always seem slightly surprised by the weight of semiological significance they are later deemed to have.

Barthes' second phase is the explicitly structuralist and semiological one. In this phase his major political objective was in no way changed. He still thought that a particular kind of class culture – bourgeois ideology – was **naturalized** by the myths, representations, images, or **signs** people used. He still intended to make his own political contribution by denaturalizing them. But he came to dream of doing this on an industrial scale by developing a science of the sign – Saussure's imagined science of semiology, no less, pursued by the structuralist methods developed from the work of Saussure and Jakobson by such thinkers as Lévi-Strauss. To this end he read and assimilated not only the thinkers named, but works by contemporary linguists, French, English and American: Martinet, Benveniste, Halliday, Z. S. Harris, Emmon Bach.

'Myth Today' can be seen as an introduction to this phase of work, and is still the most widely read manifesto for it. The formal aspects of semiology are however presented much more clearly, and in a far more comprehensive way, in *Elements of Semiology* (1964), an elementary handbook of Saussurean ideas for the semiologist to use. This has the virtues of a good textbook; if Barthes was sometimes obscure, it wasn't because he couldn't write clearly. To this phase also belong some of the later essays from *Critical Essays*; and some first produced in English in the useful collection by Stephen Heath, *Image, Music, Text* (Barthes 1977), including perhaps the clearest statement of the high structuralist programme that Barthes ever made – the article 'Introduction to the Structuralist Analysis of Narrative', first published in his own journal *Communications* (8, 1966). The most laborious work of this period (1957-63) is a full-scale study of the language of fashion, *The Fashion System*, based on a 'corpus' of examples in approved linguistic fashion. Barthes later described his attitude in this period in a biting phrase: 'a dream of scientificity'.

In the third, post-structuralist phase, that dream evaporated: not just for Barthes, but for everybody. One turning point may have been the international symposium at Johns Hopkins in 1966 in which all Paris came to Baltimore. Barthes came, now just a little unsatisfied with linguistics, but delivering a paper which, under a jokey title 'To Write – an Intransitive Verb?', seems to offer a fairly orthodox structuralism. But among the distinguished names present were two other, ominous ones: Jacques Lacan, and Jacques Derrida; and what they offered was something very different: bewildering, rambling critiques of the very idea of semiological structuralism. Lacan's paper was called: 'Of Structure as an Inmixing of an Otherness Prerequisite to Any Subject Whatever'. Derrida's was called 'Structure, Sign, and Play in the Discourse of the Human Sciences'.

Between 1966 and, say, 1968 Barthes assimilated the new critiques, which seemed to make the old structuralist self-confidence seem naïve. And in 1968 something else happened, which made the old politics look naïve: a student revolution which managed to coincide with a strike of ten million workers that nearly led to the toppling of the Gaullist regime. From 1968–9 he gave an extended seminar on a single Balzac short story; originally intended, no doubt, as a practical exercise in structuralist theory. What came out, in the new circumstances, was a strange and difficult extended commentary on 561 fragments of text, along with 93 divagations incorporating sometimes Barthesian versions of Lacanian or Derridean ideas, and sometimes damn silly conceits: this is the book *S/Z*, where Barthes is at once advancing and subverting structuralist theories, and often seems to be parodying the scientific enterprise that he earlier espoused. Barthes calls his work of this period 'textual analysis'. A popular journalistic name was **post-structuralist.**

To this phase also belong some of the critical articles of the late 1960s and 1970s, also represented in *Image, Music, Text.* This phase leads imperceptibly to works such as *The Pleasure of the Text, The Empire of Signs, A Lover's Discourse,* and the fragmented biography and personal photograph album, *Barthes by Barthes*: a final phase, which is a highly personal form of belles-lettres-ism, in which not only the early 'scientific' pretensions vanish, but so does the leftism, and the political animus against the bourgeoisie.

Each one of these four phases reflects, and is reflected by, a cultural movement in French intellectual society; though Barthes seems to have anticipated the general rightward swing in that society by some years. By reading Barthes – at least in the first three of his phases – one can feel a whole intellectual climate as it changes. Moreover, despite the intellectual dandyism that eventually comes to dominate his work – the tendency, that is, to use ideas and paradoxes as display pieces with little concern for their truth – he is for some things a reliable authority. You cannot learn linguistics from him; but *Elements of Semiology* represents what a whole generation in Paris supposed semiology to be; and what, therefore, for the time and place, it actually was.

And even the intellectual dandyism, though intensely personal, is very symptomatic of its period. Here are two examples from Barthes' own comments upon the chart reproduced above. They offer a characteristically Parisian flavour of exhibitionist rhetoric. Barthes in fact uses the word 'Intertext' to label writers who have influenced him. But Barthes won't have it that these are influences: 'The intertext is not necessarily a field of influence; rather it is a music of figures, metaphors, thought-words; it is the signifier as **siren**;' And he uses the word 'morality' to cover his interests in his last period − but that is a long way from any ordinary morality: '**morality** should be understood as the precise opposite of ethics (it is the thinking of the body in a state of language)'; One thing is sure. Any future reader looking at these words will be able to date and place Barthes precisely to a particular state of Parisian excitement in the late 1960s and early 1970s; which shows his representative quality.

2 THE REPLY TO SARTRE: *WRITING DEGREE ZERO*

2.1 *The concept of 'Writing'*

Writing Degree Zero is a pre-structuralist work; it is influenced, obviously, by the new novel, in particular by Robbe-Grillet (though it refers also to Camus, Queneau and others); and it could be seen as a rather heavyweight theoretical rethinking of the whole of French literature in order to make way for the new novel. So far as it is directed against anyone, it is directed against Sartre; but that would be true of any critical enterprise of 1953, including Sartre's. The work Barthes had in mind, as Susan Sontag points out in her preface to the Lavers and Smith translation, is Sartre's *What is Literature?* (1948).

Barthes' approach is one that a linguist or an analytical philosopher (as opposed to a phenomenological one) would find uncongenial: profound theoretical distinctions are drawn − e.g. between language, style, and writing − on an intuitive basis, and revealing at this stage a fairly complete ignorance of the relevant science, linguistics. Thus for Barthes a language is not a structured abstract object, of the kind

Saussure proposed. It is, at least for a writer, a human horizon which provides, more or less at the edge of perception, a certain familiarity. Its value is negative; to say Camus and Queneau speak the same language is simply to point out all the other languages, archaic and futuristic, that they **don't** speak. (Barthes 1953, 1972, p. 10.)

These are bewildering claims. They become less bewildering when one remembers that the word 'horizon' comes from Husserl's phenomenology. We are not looking at a language as an objective phenomenon, as a linguist would; we are looking at it from the point of view of subjective experience, as providing a background against which we experience and understand things. Once we have grasped this subjective and metaphorical approach, it is easier to understand Barthes' account of style. Style is a germinative phenomenon, the transmutation of an *Humeur* (a mood? a body-fluid?). Speech has a horizontal structure, but style is vertical; it dives into the most private recollections. It is never anything but metaphor, here defined oddly enough as an equation between the literary intention and the fleshly structure of the author. It is necessary to remember, adds Barthes in a parenthesis, that structure is the deposit of a duration.

The last point is still very bewildering. One is inclined to ask: Why must this be remembered? Is it true? Does it mean anything? In fact, however, Barthes is merely working up to develop a third category, in which he is really interested, **writing**. Between a language and a style, says Barthes, there is room for another formal reality: *l'écriture.* Within any literary form, there is a general choice of tone, of ethos, and this is where the writer commits himself, and shows himself as an individual. A language and a style are the natural product of Time and of the person as a biological entity; but the formal identity of the writer is truly established only outside these; where the written continuum becomes a total sign, the choice of a human attitude, the affirmation of a certain Good. It commits the writer to communicate a state of happiness or malaise, and links the form of his utterance, which is at the same time normal and singular, to the vast story of other people. So while a language and a style are blind forces, a mode of writing is an act of historical solidarity (pp. 13–14).

We have seen that Barthes' analytical method, so far as one can give it a philosophical name, is a phenomenological one: that is to say, he is making distinctions that seem to him to correspond to essential features of experience, and expressing them by any metaphor or other rhetorical means that seems to convey them. This is a method of analysis that was, I suppose, philosophically legitimized by the vogue of existentialism. It might also be described as impressionistic. For objective linguistics, I am not sure that anything useful can be got out of it; the distinctions are arbitrary and empty. But, of course, objective linguistics is not everything.

It is almost as if Barthes is merely resolved to go one better than Sartre by replacing Sartre's simple two-way distinction between language and style by a subtler three-way distinction between language, style and mode-of-writing (*écriture*). For some intuitive critical purposes this may be a valuable distinction: Sontag compliments Barthes on his subtlety.

The category of *l'écriture*, best translated as Writing with a capital letter, was to have a great future in post-structuralist thought; Derrida took it up – or had it independently from Husserl – as one of his cardinal metaphysical/anti-metaphysical concepts, and it took on many of the attributes of God (Derrida 1967b). It is not actually clear that Derrida's sense of the word is the same as that of Barthes, because it is not clear what Derrida's sense is. But Derrida's sense probably includes Barthes' sense; it includes almost everything else.

Barthes is, however, doing much more than engage in a game of technical one-upmanship with Sartre; he is making a substantive anti-Sartrean point. Sartre thought a prose-writer or critic ought to be committed, to reveal and to change the world. (Sartre 1948, pp. 11–12). This often means being committed in the old-fashioned sense of being on one political side or another. This choice provides the content of the writing, and is the first and substantive choice; a choice of style or manner is secondary, and almost automatic.

The cost of this position, if the critic in question is on the political left, ought to be a certain lack of sympathy with modernist and experimental literature, which has a revolutionary style or manner of writing as its most obvious distinctive feature, and which is bound to appear élitist and perhaps reactionary. If you are on the side of the proletariat, how can you possibly approve, as Sartre and most serious modern critics do, of literary works that the proletariat cannot hope to understand, and which are addressed to distinctly unproletarian sensibilities, classes and tastes? And why should you disapprove of works which are both accessible to the meanest education and on the correct political side – socialist realist novels? All politically committed critics face this problem.

Barthes' solution is not original with him – I think in essence it comes from Brecht, who found this one of the central problems for his own work, as a socialist but modernist playwright; and the ideas behind it go back to the period of Russian formalism. It has become the standard solution of contemporary left-wing criticism: the view

131

that a revolution in politics requires a revolution of form. Barthes'
contribution is to emphasize the linguistic aspects of this view. For
Barthes, true commitment lies in the mode of writing a writer adopts.
His book offers a brief, and highly abstract, description of the
significance of the modes of writing available in literary history,
culminating, of course, in the 'writing degree zero' of the *nouveau
roman*. (I must say I am out of sympathy with this very literary notion
of commitment. My sympathies here are with Sartre; the suspicion is
that Barthes' position is one that replaces actual by symbolic
commitment, and leads in the end to no commitment; and indeed,
that is where it did lead in the end.)

Writing Degree Zero, once one gets into it, turns out to have a less
wide reference than the abstraction of the language would seem to
indicate. Barthes talks about literature in general, as if he had the
whole literature of the world in mind; but it soon appears that the
world writes in French. Thus the whole future of modern poetry is
said to be contained in the distortion to which Victor Hugo tried to
subject the alexandrine, since this is of all metres the most
interrelational; and what is attempted is to get rid of the idea of
connections and substitute an explosion of words. The word shines
out before a series of empty relationships; grammar loses its purpose, it
becomes prosody and is merely an inflexion which lasts only to present
the Word. Connections are not suppressed; but they are a parody of
themselves, a void necessary for the density of the Word to rise out of
a magic vacuum, like a sound and a sign without bottom, like 'fury
and mystery'. In classical speech, on the other hand, 'connections lead
the word on. . .' (p. 46).

It is not always obvious precisely what Barthes **means** in this, or
the preceding, or most other passages of *Le degré zéro de l'ecriture*; but it
is fairly obvious what he is doing. He is, in this style that
communicates as much by metaphor and evocation as by formal
argument, providing a reinterpretation of the accepted map of French
classical, romantic and modern poetry. The truth of his judgements is a
matter for other French literary critics; only they can say whether
Barthes' metaphors capture the right feeling. It is questionable whether
this material has any status at all, outside French literature, as general
literary theory; though it might offer impressionistic data for one; and
one could argue that the development of English eighteenth-century,
romantic and modern poetry presents at least a similar case.

2.2   *The development of modes of writing*

Barthes' account of the development and break-up of bourgeois modes of writing is even more quirkily French. He has three parallel stories to tell. One of them – and this is really the master narrative – is a Marxist history of the development of class society. The key events are the three revolutions – 1789, when the bourgeoisie made a revolution in the name of everybody, including the proletariat; 1848, when the interests of the bourgeoisie decisively separated from those of the proletariat; and the coming revolution, when the proletariat will make its revolution against the bourgeoisie. The second story is about changes in ideology. The third is about changes in language. Barthes' problem is that these narratives do not actually match particularly well; but he wants to imply that there are strong causal connections.

Thus he suggests that the sixteenth and the beginning of the seventeenth centuries have a large number of literary languages, because men are still trying to get to know nature, rather than giving expression to the essence of man. Thus the encyclopedic writing of Rabelais, and the previous writing of Corneille have in common a language where ornament is a method of investigating the surface of the world. Until 1650, French literature hadn't gone beyond a problematic of language, and was therefore still unaware of the possibility of modes of writing. For, says Barthes, 'as long as a tongue is still uncertain about its very structure, an ethics of language is impossible. . .' (pp. 55–6).

If we were British; or if, like the Barthes of a decade later, we had assimilated some linguistics, we would be bound to ask what basis there was for these vast mandarin generalizations. They seem (to make an equally mandarin judgement) to be a peculiar vice of late French culture, equally present in Althusser, Foucault and Kristeva for example. What does it mean to say that a tongue is still uncertain about its very structure? That the French Academy hasn't pronounced yet? What is an ethics of language? And what **evidence** does it take to establish that an ethics of language is impossible as long as a tongue is uncertain about its very structure? Merely to ask these questions shows up the emptiness of the argument. But the Barthes of that period had no difficulty in continuing to generalize.

What the classical grammarians did, he says, was to create a timeless reason which seemed to work through the language. They thus relieved the French from any linguistic problem. This purified language became a mode of writing (i.e. a way of writing that has a value attached to it), and one which was given as universal. 'There was one and only one mode of writing, both instrumental and ornamental, at the disposition of French society during the whole period when bourgeois ideology conquered and triumphed. Instrumental, since form was supposed to be at the disposal of content . . . This classical writing is, needless to say, a class writing.' (p. 57).

Barthes thus confidently stitches together his three narratives. Even to a foreign commentator, counter-examples occur (like the French revolutionaries); but Barthes has a ready way with these: sure, bourgeois writers also faced problems of form, but these did not give rise to different modes of writing; they gave rise to different **rhetorics**. With a single persuasive definition – with one new term, in fact – Barthes abolishes contrary evidence; and continues with this grand historical narrative.

The French revolution changed nothing in bourgeois writing (made it more excitable, perhaps, but those were exciting times). Writing remained much the same instrument from Laclos to Stendhal (Hugo perhaps excepted); but in the 1850s came the demographic expansion in Europe, the birth of modern capitalism, and the scission of French society into three mutually hostile classes. No longer could bourgeois ideology be presented as universal; the tragic predicament peculiar to literature was born; and modes of writing began to multiply.

Thus we have the craftsman's mode, the code of literary labour founded by Flaubert; which represents the bourgeois Necessity which characterizes Emma Bovary and makes her situation tragic; and at the same time in its precise handling of verbal tenses, etc., makes them perform the function of **signs** of literature, in an art drawing attention to its own artificiality, and appealing to 'a sixth, purely literary sense, the private property of producers and consumers of literature' (p. 65).

Then we have the Naturalist mode (Barthes cherished a lifelong hatred of it) of Maupassant, Zola and Daudet. Naturalism, says Barthes scornfully, merely combines the formal signs of Literature (*passé simple*, indirect speech, the rhythm of written language) and the formal signs of realism (incongruous snippets of popular speech, strong language or dialect words, etc.). No mode of writing was more artificial than this. This artificiality was a failure of theory as well as style: 'there is, in the Naturalist aesthetic, a convention of the real, just as there is a fabrication in its writing'. Lowering the subject doesn't make the form unobtrusive. 'Neutral writing' (the writing degree zero of the title) 'is a late phenomenon to be invented only much later than Realism by authors like Camus, less under the impulse of an aesthetics of escape than in search of a writing which might at last achieve innocence' (p. 67).

I have said that at this stage Barthes, though obsessed by language and capable of writing down insightful, but wild and metaphorical generalizations about it, knew no linguistics. In this he was in no way different from most other literary critics and theorists – Dr Leavis, for example. It was, however, Barthes' peculiar distinction, that he noticed his own deficiencies in this area, and went on to put them right. It was eleven years later that he published the little text-book *Elements of Semiology*, which shows considerable understanding of Saussure and others. This was of course in the hey-day of interest in language in France; but it was partly due to Barthes that that hey-day had come about. Barthes should not be condemned for talking some nonsense about language – all literary critics do that; he should be praised for trying to go on and talk sense. And even his nonsense seems to me to contain important insights.

3   THE MYTHOGRAPHER OF THE BOURGEOISIE

3.1 *Mythologies*

The central insight of Barthes' *Mythologies* is explained clearly enough in the preface of 1957:

> The starting point of these reflections was usually a feeling of impatience
> at the sight of the 'naturalness' with which newspapers, art and
> common-sense constantly dress up a reality which, even though it is the
> one we live in, is undoubtedly determined by history. In short, in the
> account given of our contemporary circumstances, I resented seeing
> Nature and History confused at every turn, and I wanted to track down,
> in the decorative display of **what-goes-without-saying**, the ideological
> abuse which, in my view, is hidden there.
>   Right from the start, the notion of myth seemed to me to explain these
> examples of the falsely obvious . . . (p. 11)

The polemical stance of *Mythologies* is thus a very simple one. Barthes will take up, month by month, striking examples of popular cultural phenomena – a 'wrestling match, an elaborate dish, a plastics exhibition' – and say to his readers, in effect: 'You think this is natural? Nonsense; it is a bourgeois myth!' The bluntness and repetitiveness of this polemic is redeemed only by the lightness of the writing.

To turn from *Writing Degree Zero* to almost any article from the *Mythologies* collection is more like changing one's writer than changing one's book. Nobody ever called the *Mythologies* arcane. They are little articlets, full of delicate mockery, at their best when they are shortest, and justified by being funny. What fun, for example, to learn in 'The Iconography of the Abbé Pierre' that his holiness is established by him having a zero degree of haircut. Or – sticking with hair for the moment – in 'The Romans in Films', about the way in which, in a film version of 'Julius Caesar', we deduce the Romanness of the characters from their hair-styles. Yet this little essay is perhaps the simplest statement anywhere of Barthes' opposition to the naturalization of cultural symbols. It is no wonder that the short English *Mythologies* of 1972 is perhaps the commonest undergraduate set text in Barthes' work.

To examine these essays for inadequacies of argument would be to break butterflies on a wheel. On the other hand, to put them forward as part of a serious semiological system – as Barthes does in his essay, 'Myth Today', – is rather like asking butterflies to work a treadmill; an operation for which they distinctly lack the weight. And this highlights something which was to remain the most serious weakness of Barthes' later, and very complex theoretical work, particularly *S/Z* – the fact that he couldn't really tell the difference between an argument and a conceit. In *Mythologies*, however, this deficiency doesn't in the least matter. One is not being argued out of one's bourgeois assumptions; but in Voltairean tradition, laughed out of them.

In looking at the collection – there are two English volumes: *Mythologies* (1972), and *The Eiffel Tower and Other Mythologies* (1979) – I find it best to consider the essays in their own right as light polemical writing; and to consider 'Myth Today' partly as a later attempt to recuperate them for semiology, and partly as a fragment of the personal biography of a self-conscious semiologist.

Two of the best examples of essays as effective polemic come from the *Eiffel Tower* volume. One is 'Bichon and the Blacks': an attack on a *Paris-Match* story of two young photographers who 'courageously' took their young baby with them on an assignment in cannibal country. Barthes has no difficulty in exposing the popular stereotypes about cannibals that underlie such a presentation; and contrasting them with the scrupulous ethnographic work of a Marcel Mauss or a Lévi-Strauss. And the general title 'Mythologies' here seems wholly justified; what Barthes is exposing is indeed a colonialist myth. The second is 'A Sympathetic Worker': a competent exposure of the mystificatory politics of Elia Kazan's film, 'On the Waterfront', by means of a neat comparison with the way Brecht would have handled the same theme; Kazan makes us love and admire the 'good worker', while Brecht would have made us reflect on his stupidity.

In both these cases Barthes' polemical strength is that he has something better to offer than the 'myth' he is attacking. But in many essays – including most of the more entertaining ones – this is not the case. Take his account of 'Writers on Holiday', where the writer, presented by the newspapers as 'working on holiday' is 'a false worker, and a false holidaymaker as well'. Much of this is great fun; but to conclude that 'The good-natured image of "the writer on holiday" is therefore no more than one of these cunning mystifications which the establishment practices the better to enslave its writers' is really rather steep. Only paranoia could believe this; the true mystification is that of Barthes, who is ignoring an important non-symbolic reality – that writers generally enjoy their work, and proles don't. In this case Barthes has no better way to offer for presenting writers to people who don't read them.

A more justified paranoia emerges in Barthes' account of 'Blind and Dumb Criticism'. It is interesting to find that French reviewers of the 1950s sound so like English critics of the same period, and were just as anti-philosophical and anti-intellectual. One can only agree with Barthes. But his position would be more convincing if Marxist criticism and French philosophical criticism were not often bullying or mystificatory. Barthes has the habit of assuming that the other side simply doesn't have a case.

This habit makes him less convincing even in areas like politics, where nobody expects fairness, and even to those who might be initially sympathetic to his position. Political bias is not in itself a literary fault; it is no bar to the enjoyment of George Orwell or of Evelyn Waugh. But a writer who makes the same wholly predictable political point in essay after essay becomes monotonous and even shrill. Consider, for example, Barthes' handling of 'The Blue-Blood Cruise'. I have no interest in royalty myself, and know hardly anybody who has. But what one chiefly notices is that for Barthes, royalty – like the bourgeoisie – cannot win, whatever they may choose to do.

Barthes has a serious political point to make; in the close of the essay, he speaks of the young Juan of Spain, sent to the rescue of Spanish Fascism. But the political force of the essay is weakened by its obvious bias; we feel sure that the Barthes of this phase would have found something to object to in the recent King Juan, who saved

Spanish democracy from a right-wing army coup. There is a point in saying that all kings are bad, especially the good ones; but it's not an effective point of view from which to write this kind of article.

However, the weakest moments in Barthes – still speaking of his essays as polemic rather than entertainment – come when he seems to have lost interest in any non-semiological reality altogether. Thus in 'Soap-Powders and Detergents' he treats as a matter entirely symbolic and risible the claim that chlorinated products 'kill' the dirt while washing powders remove it. But this claim is true! Disinfectants kill germs; detergents stop dirt sticking to things. It seems hard for these facts to be described as a myth. Talking of 'Toys', Barthes sees it as a great proof of their bourgeois status that they are reduced copies of human objects: but what else should they look like? And he sentimentalizes over the disappearance of wooden toys, since wood is 'a familiar and poetic substance', which 'does not wound or break down' – as if he had never heard of splinters.

On a more serious level, the same weaknesses afflict his ingenious account of the trial of the peasant Dominici, which he sees, on account of the hypotheses the judges made about Dominici's intentions, as a triumph of the psychology of the bourgeois novel. What is disturbing is that Barthes shows no interest in the question of whether Dominici actually murdered anybody or not, or what sort of evidence ought to count in such a case, or what you should do with murderers. Semiology here ceases to be amusing.

3.2   The theory of myth today

As I have said, 'Myth Today' differs from all the other essays in the book in that it offers not a particular example of a Barthesian myth, but a general semiological theory of them. The first point of this theory is that 'myth is a type of speech' – that is to say, presumably, that particular 'myths' which Barthes discusses belong to *parole* rather than *langue*. This applies, according to Barthes, whether the myth is realized in language or in some other medium – say a photograph. What makes one of these items of speech a myth is not so much its meaning, as the way in which it is used to convey certain types of general concept. These concepts seem to be the ones like 'French imperiality' that function as part of bourgeois ideology.

Barthes considers myth from three points of view: the producer, (say, a journalist); the mythologist (an analyst/semioclast like Barthes himself) and the consumer (the ordinary reader). The journalist or photographer might want to convey the concept of French imperiality, and come up with an example: the image of a negro soldier happily saluting the French flag. The analyst will distinguish between the meaning of the image – the negro soldier saluting – and its form as signifier of French imperiality; he will see the image as an alibi of French imperialism. The ordinary reader, however, will respond in neither of these ways. He will treat the image as the very embodiment of French imperiality, which will be experienced through, or embodied in, this image.

Two things are obvious about this theory. First, its close dependence upon the thought of Brecht – Barthes' ordinary reader here is like Brecht's ordinary spectator of bourgeois drama, who loses himself in the spectacle on stage, while his analyst/semioclast is like the intelligent spectator who stands back and thinks about the meaning of the spectacle. Second, its loose dependence on the thought of Lévi-Strauss, which is doubtless what accounts for the choice of the term 'myth'. What we have here is an example of what Lévi-Strauss calls 'the logic of the concrete', in which people actually think about the world in terms of these myths. (When they think of the French empire, they think of a happy, smiling negro soldier.)

It is obvious that there is a relationship between this theory of **mythology** and the Marxist theory of **ideology**. Barthes distinguishes them in terms of their relationship to history. Mythology, so far as it is a formal science, is part of Saussure's putative science, **semiology**, which studies the relationship of signifier to signified; so far as it is a historical science, it is part of ideology; 'it studies ideas-in-form'. Presumably it is in the historical part of the science of mythology that we explain, in terms of the class struggle, why we have the myths that we do have.

This is all very neat; but it leaves one asking just how formal is the formal science. Barthes makes an honest attempt to answer this question. He offers another example of mythology, where the 'myth' is apparently non-political: the case where a Latin phrase, from one of Aesop's fables, meaning 'My name is Lion', is used, not as part of the story, but as a grammatical example. According to Barthes, what this has in common with the other example is that we have a phrase, fairly rich in meaning, used merely as a signifier for a general concept (here a grammatical concept rather than a political one). In both cases there is a kind of impoverishment of meaning as we move from the meaning of the linguistic or photographic example used to the general concept it embodies, signifies or stands for.

This is not terribly convincing. The use of a phrase as an example of grammar may be formally comparable to the use of one as an example of French imperialism, but it feels entirely different; there are surely no readers – except a few grammarians – who will feel that the phrase naturally embodies grammaticality, and thus consume it as a myth. Nor is there any obvious sense in which we can call grammar ideology. Barthes makes the tentative suggestion that a lion, could it speak, might feel diminished by being used as a grammatical example; but I doubt if it would be grateful for the services of a mythologist to liberate it from this political oppression.

At the purely formal semiological level of analysis all we have is the phenomenon of a hierarchy of signs. A group of elements in a picture or the words of a phrase like 'French negro soldier saluting the flag' make up the signifier of a concept (the signified) 'French-negro-saluting-the-flag'. Signifier and signified together form a sign. But this sign itself can act as the signifier for a higher level signified: French imperiality. And the new signifier and signified together form a higher level sign: 'French negro saluting the flag as example of beneficence of French empire'. It is this higher level sign which, when absorbed unreflectingly, Barthes calls a 'myth'.

But although this particular 'myth' is a highly political one, it derives its political character entirely from its content. Its formal structure is neutral; it simply happens to be the character of signifying systems, in any conceivable society, that signs on one level of discourse can act as signifiers for another level. If that were not the case language would not work, and human beings would be unable to think.

What this points to is a general weakness in Barthes' approach: in his assumption that a formal science of semiology can be of some use for political purposes, or, as he puts it in his 1970 preface: 'No semiology without **semioclasm**'. Semiology as a formal science is entirely neutral between semioclasm – breaking up signs you don't like – **semiogony** and **semi-underpinning**. The category of 'myth', which Barthes needs and uses for political purposes, cannot be a purely formal one; somehow, it needs to have its politics built in.

For me, the question that hovers over the whole book is this: is it really true that only the Right uses myth, in Barthes' sense, to naturalize what are in fact aspects of bourgeois culture; and that there are no corresponding left-wing myths? Barthes thinks so: he thinks it is a special property of bourgeois society to make its practices culturally invisible by pretending that they are universal and natural. **Naturalization** of culture is thus something specifically bourgeois, and denaturalization is a left-wing protest.

There are two answers to this. It is probably true that the bourgeoisie are the first class to talk of universal human rights and, connected with them, a universal human nature. But bourgeois society, if that is what we have now, is certainly not the first to regard its own practices as entirely natural, or to make them culturally invisible. Most societies do; whether those practices involve human sacrifice, cannibalism or the *baccalauréat*. One might say that it is the natural state of affairs to be ethnocentric. Nor is the discovery that the existing order is not a natural fact necessarily going to lead to a left-wing change; it might lead to a reactionary one.

The strength of Barthes' comments throughout *Mythologies* is supposed to be that they put in question what we have been taking as natural. But Barthes, like many critics on the Left who have followed him, doesn't make this into an open question. He simply presupposes that everything of importance is cultural, instead. And Barthes himself admits that this sometimes leads him to ignore the constraints of material reality: to ignore the fact that the Citroen DS19 was actually a car.

And as Barthes also recognized, the criticism of every commonplace truth as being a myth cuts off the mythologist himself from the felt experience of his own community. His only relation to what interests most of his readers is to be sarcastic about it. Barthes put this point quite bluntly – if grandiosely – in the first preface to *Mythologies*: 'What I claim is to live to the full the contradictions of my time, which may well make sarcasm the condition of truth.'

3.3 The psychodynamics of Barthesian fantasy

There is a point more personal than this that also has to be made. It is clear that Barthes' major ambition is to be not just a theoretician, but a writer; but as a writer there is something strangely barricaded about him, as if he is not in touch with his own deeper experiences, or is anxious to construct rhetorical defences against them. He would regard this as a very bourgeois criticism; as a critic, he is nearly as hostile to the concept of psychological depth as he is to that of realism. But consider the very first of his *Mythologies*, on 'The World of Wrestling'. It isn't really political. I suspect the true value of this piece is in what it **doesn't** quite say – that Barthes is erotically excited by the cruelty of a wrestling match, as indeed are the spectators; all-in wrestling is a sado-masochistic spectacle. Barthes' brilliant account of this is not so much an excuse for dwelling on the scene as a demonstration of the power of rhetorical analysis for rising above the emotion.

Barthes seems to have spent much of his writing life putting up delicate Japanese screens in front of his personality; and I am half afraid to develop this point any further. But the erotic theme is an important one in his work – one critic describes him as a 'Professor of Desire'. He sometimes professed it by psychoanalytic methods, as in the study of castration symbolism in Balzac, discussed later on. This is commonplace enough. An approach much more original in Barthes is to relate the erotic, the sadistic, or the perverse to rhetoric and language. In *Sade/Fourier/Loyola* (1971), the work of de Sade is studied as an exercise in repetitive rhetoric. In *The Pleasure of the Text* (1973), language itself becomes an erotic object. There is much mention of the perverse, and a famous distinction is drawn between *plaisir* and *jouissance* – pleasure and orgasmic bliss. This major theme of Barthes' writing had hardly begun to develop in *Mythologies* (1957); but it was, in my view, to play an important negative role in the next, scientifically oriented phase of his work.

4   THE DREAM OF SCIENTIFICITY: SEMIOLOGY AND STRUCTURALISM

4.1 *Masochism and the fashion system*

In the trajectory of Roland Barthes the period from 1957 to about 1968 is the great age of semiological structuralism. Not everybody regards this as time well spent. It is sometimes suggested that Barthes should be treated as a writer – even, as a modernist writer – and his science of semiology should be seen as a mere theatrical gesture. Surely this would be patronizing, and wrong? This work was a major undertaking into which he poured all his efforts for several years; it provided him with many insights which many workers in the field continue to take seriously. It is a kind of science, even if it isn't exactly philosophy.

It is marked by two movements, both of them rather negative. The first is the drive toward systematicity. There is some reason to think that this was a movement against Barthes' own nature. Up to that point he had been a master in the most unsystematic of forms – the monthly journalistic essay. At the end of his career – only partly for theoretical reasons – he was writing books constructed of paragraphs arranged in alphabetical or random order. In this middle period, however, he went for system, order and organizing logic; and attempted to place his insights into the significance of fashion, or the structure of narratives, within large-scale impersonal and theoretical systems, just like science.

If you are not actually one of nature's scientists, there is a certain masochism in this; this is not a metaphor; I am speaking literally about the type of unconscious fantasy that could, on certain assumptions about psychoanalytic theory, be taken to motivate such enterprises. And if your main gift is for essayistic insights, systematic forms spread the insights rather thin. But there is a temperament which actually likes systematization; and cares little for politics. It is people of this stamp who have built much of the vast edifice of modern semiotics – see, for example, the 1,237 pages of Chatman, Eco and Klinkenburg, the proceedings of the first conference of the International Association for Semiotic Studies (1974), published under the apt title: *A Semiotic Landscape/Panorama Sémiotique*.

This is the field that came to see Barthes as one of its modern founders; but the interesting thing is, from a personal point of view, that this is the kind of book, these are the kinds of people, that came to frighten Roland Barthes. As he put it in his autobiography: '. . . the goal of a semiological science is replaced by the (often very grim) science of the semiologists; hence, one must sever oneself from that . . .' (*Barthes by Barthes*, 1975, p. 71). Why should he have seen these semiologists, and their science, as grim?

The second negative movement is the withdrawal from politics. The motto of *Mythologies* was 'No semiology without semioclasm'; the motive was to expose and attack the presumed ideology of the bourgeoisie. This critical spirit rather evaporates when we get to *The Fashion System* and *Elements of Semiology*; and it leaves them dry. Some bite returns by the time of *S/Z*, mainly because of Barthes' hatred of realism. But an attack on the bourgeoisie that is confined to the conventions of the realist novel is a fairly limited one; though it has done great service to a whole generation of leftist critics in France and England who trace a part of their lineage to Barthes. It may be true, as Jonathan Culler (1975) suggests, that semiology was never intended to be a value-neutral science. But it had many of the features of a neutral science, in this, its Barthesian period; and to this day much of semiotics is pursued in precisely this value-neutral spirit. It would probably be valueless as science if it were not; but there are sensibilities for whom value-neutrality kills.

Barthes' major empirical work, *The Fashion System*, is actually a study of linguistic descriptions of fashions, taken from two years of issues of two fashion magazines – *Elle* and *Le Jardin des Modes*. Very little of his empirical material appears in the published work. Most of it is a discussion of methodology; and Barthes' methodological conclusions are far more conveniently summarized in *Elements of Semiology* (1964). So *The Fashion System* is not very widely read.

Barthes has to distinguish between two semiotic levels – that of the linguistic descriptions, which he calls the 'Rhetorical System', and that of the implied underlying system of fashion itself, which he calls the 'Vestimentary Code'. The vestimentary code is one in which the replacement of one significant minimal unit of costume – 'vesteme' – by another will change the meaning of the costume. The rhetorical system is concerned with the writing up of fashion, and with the ideology of fashion. There is a rhetoric of the signifier – fashion writing – which gives us a poetics of clothing; and a rhetoric of the signified – ideology – which gives us the world of fashion.

This is not the place – and indeed I am not sure what is the place – to deal with the technicalities of Barthes' vestimentary code, which are like those of an old-style descriptive grammar of a language. Most of these complexities arise, however, because of the grammarian's desire to cover every case in his material. The principles are fairly simple. In analysing a fashionable item we have the Object itself – e.g. a blouse – and the Variant that makes it fashionable – e.g. a large collar; the latter we may analyse into the Variant itself – being large rather than small – and the Support for that variant, namely the collar. We thus analyse the written item 'a blouse with a large collar' as a matrix O (V.S.) in the vestimentary code. The phrase 'high waists for gowns' would come out as (V.S.) O. (The order of the symbols is purely linguistic and doesn't affect the vestimentary code.)

Take a more complicated case:

> She likes studying and surprise parties, Pascal, Mozart, and cool jazz. She wears flat heels, collects little scarves, and adores her big brother's plain sweaters and those bouffant, rustling petticoats.

Here the vestimentary code is represented simply by the phrases:

> flat heels, little scarf, plain sweater, bouffant petticoat

each of which can be analysed V SO (variant – e.g. 'flat' followed by support object 'heels'. The whole group can then be put together to form a single implicit Object in the vestimentary code: the Outfit.These four items then act as the supports of a single variant that makes that outfit fashionable. So we produce a complex matrix:

flat   heels,   little   scarf,   plain   sweater,   bouffant   petticoat

$$\underbrace{\text{V} \qquad \text{SO}}\quad \underbrace{\text{V} \qquad \text{SO}}\quad \underbrace{\text{V} \qquad \text{SO}}\quad \underbrace{\text{V} \qquad \text{SO}}$$

$$\underbrace{\text{S1} \qquad \text{V} \qquad \text{S2} \qquad \text{V} \qquad \text{S3} \qquad \text{V} \qquad \text{S4}}$$

$$\text{O}$$

This diagram will greatly appeal to those who like to see studies of semiotic codes on the model of phrase-structure trees. On Barthes' own principles, however, it is misleading; since the order of the elements in the matrix is not supposed to count in the vestimentary code. (Order here adjusted for English.)

Barthes also considers the rhetorical system, in which the writing of fashion signifies the ideology of fashion. Here, certain purely verbal features of the second sentence – 'little', 'big brother's', 'rustling' – signify a 'mythological' order of fashion, in a kind of poetics of clothing. The first sentence: 'She likes studying and surprise parties' describes the world which this fashion is supposed to signify. The forms of the sentences rhetorically signify 'the way in which the magazine represents itself and represents the equivalence between clothing and the world, i.e., fashion'. Barthes devotes a whole chapter to each of these three – poetics of clothing, world of fashion, reason of fashion – and in these chapters some of his literary critical instincts, and even his political instincts, occasionally stir.

I am afraid I am rather misrepresenting *The Fashion System* in this brief summary, mainly because I am picking out all the thrilling bits. It is in fact a work of nearly unbearable tedium; and this point should not go unnoticed. Barthes has the reputation of a witty and graceful writer; and he sometimes has wit and grace. What he doesn't have is the ability to make a theoretical system interesting as a whole. This raises the question of why he tried.

There is an obvious suggestion here within a psychoanalytic framework of theory; it is speculative, but no more speculative than the work of Lacan, and much less than that of, say, Deleuze and Guattari. This is that the search for very abstract and formal systems in the humanities is, at the level of unconscious phantasy, masochistic. This is a suggestion that throws a good deal of light on the possible unconscious motivation behind the development of structuralist systems, at least in the French period, when these systems were meant to account for the structure of the human subject, and the workings of human desire. Structuralism, to the extent that it is conceived of as a net to bind desire, is a masochistic fantasy: literally, a bondage fantasy. So far as it is a net to bind other minds or bodies, it is a sadistic fantasy. (Althusserian theories of ideology have this sadistic feel about them, and the delight Althusserians used to have in pronouncing themselves 'theoretically anti-humanist' had a definitely sadistic quality – one could feel their joy in going about rooting out cowering humanists.)

To say this, incidentally, is not in any way to discredit structuralism as a theoretical system. On most versions of Freudian theory, all human beings are working out one infantile fantasy or another in everything they do. And an abstract theory may well be true, even if it is sadistic or masochistic in its appeal; we determine its truth, not by psychoanalysing the user, but by examining the evidence for the theory. Nor am I suggesting that structuralist theories of language are any more sado-masochistic than generative ones, or indeed than mathematical theories in physics. One wouldn't suggest that a mathematical physicist is employing formal methods for masochistic reasons; but there is an important difference in his case; the theory works. Barthes' fashion system is a good imitation of a formal theory, but it doesn't actually do anything: so one is encouraged to ask the question: where did the **desire** for such a theory come from. And questions about the origins of desire may legitimately be answered on a psychoanalytic basis.

One might extend this argument one step further. It does not discredit post-structuralism to suggest that it offers a phantasied release from structuralist sado-masochistic bondage. It seems to be this that gives the *Anti-Oedipus* of Deleuze and Guattari its appeal; but a happier feeling of release and play is present in Barthes' late work *The Pleasure of the Text* (1973) and encoded in such central technical terms as *jouissance* (orgasmic release, bliss). This seems (still working on the same assumptions) to have been Barthes' psychic reward for his adventurous escape from his structuralist phase.

4.2   Philosophical logic and semiological structures

To return to 1964: *Elements of Semiology* is a simple handbook of Saussurean ideas that might be useful for the aspirant semiologist. I have already discussed most of these. There are two general points worth commenting on, that arise both in this book and *The Language of Fashion*. The first is that Barthes has some major logical problems, which arise directly from the logical poverty of the Saussurean model he is using. The only sign-relation Saussure recognizes is the arbitrary relationship of signifier and signified to form a sign. In the analysis of something logically quite complicated like the language of fashion magazines, we are actually dealing with many different kinds of meaning relationship between linguistic expressions, non-linguistic signifying units, and non-linguistic non-signifying items. Barthes has to map all of these onto sign-relationship – sometimes by claiming that a whole sign at one level acts as a signifier at a higher level.

Obviously, he does not always succeed in this reduction. What is needed is a theory that admits the full complexity of meaning-relationships – a theory that will, for example, distinguish between (1) the function of phonemes in distinguishing between one word and another; (2) the Saussurean sign-relation between a word and a concept; (3) the Fregean distinction between sense and reference; (4) standard philosophical distinctions between assertion, implication, presupposition, etc. and (5) a host of others. One can't map all these onto the Saussurean sign. Barthes is acutely aware of most of them, but lacks, and cannot himself construct, an adequate formal theory.

The second point is that Barthes does not accept the Saussurean view that linguistics is merely a part of a broader science of semiology. He feels that the presence of language is always necessary for the delimitation of complex ideas. So it is more likely that semiology would be absorbed into a kind of trans-linguistics than the other way around. This is a very important idea, which hasn't perhaps yet had its full development in semiotics. (I would guess myself that basic cognitive structures and linguistic structures are essentially separate; but that complex concepts can only be formed with the aid of some language or artificial symbol system. See chapter 6.)

Despite these problems, there were several years to go before Barthes moved decisively beyond the structuralist model in semiology. Indeed perhaps the clearest statement of that model occurs in a paper, 'Introduction to the Structural Analysis of Narratives', published in his own journal *Communications* in 1966. This is available in English in Barthes (1977; 1982). I shall call it *ISAN*.

ISAN is an attempt to lay out a research strategy for the analysis of narrative structure, using the model of linguistics as a guide. A narrative is to be treated as a vast sentence. As Barthes puts it: 'A narrative is a long sentence, just as every constative sentence is in a way the rough outline of a short narrative'. A narrative is built up in a way closely resembling the phrase-structure diagram of a sentence, from basic units called 'functions' – there are two types of these, the cardinal, or nuclear narrative functions, around which narrative structures are built, and the fillers or 'catalysers' which fill up the space between. This is an obvious, but reasonably workable analogy to natural-language syntax; something like it has already been put on computers, to persuade those beasts to write little stories.

There is also a kind of semantics – units may act as 'indices' of global properties of the narrative, or as 'informants' giving us, e.g. realistic details which give the narrative apparent authenticity. In a later part of the paper, Barthes adopts a different notion of semantics, in which units at a lower level – forms – are integrated into units at a higher level – meanings. This is actually inconsistent with the Saussurean conception of the sign and shows the effects of some of Barthes' other reading in linguistics; he quotes Benveniste; in the English tradition this conception is Firthian. In terms of most other traditions it involves a confusion between syntax and semantics. Barthes is obviously trawling very widely for useful ideas; but lacks the philosophical sophistication, and the inwardness with linguistics, needed to clarify them and take up a clearly thought out theoretical position of his own. But no other critic is better.

There is a discussion of the analysis of 'characters' in structuralist terms – i.e., as agents within narrative structures rather than as imitation persons; a discussion of what or who is the 'subject' of a narrative; of the relation (or, as far as structuralist analysis is concerned, the complete lack of relation) between the narrator implied by the text of the narrative, and any actual person who may have written it. Finally, there is a brief discussion of the system of the narrative; the extent to which sequences of actions are distorted, expanded, etc. for literary effects like suspense; and the usual Barthesian rejection of the notion of 'realism' in narrative. These are all brief treatments of familiar philosophical problems.

4.3 The structuralist and the textualist hypotheses

The final judgement on Barthesian structuralism, as on all structuralism of this period, must be that it was programmatic. It represented not a complete theory, but a rational programme for research; and a programme which has not yet been fulfilled. The obvious next move – which was not what actually happened – would have been to modernize the linguistic model employed and try to rethink the nature of literary study in a comprehensive way. This was actually done, not by a French, but by an American scholar, Jonathan Culler, in a book called *Structuralist Poetics* (1975). I have mentioned it already (see chapter 2); but must now expand.

Generative linguistics represents a language by a set of formal rules which specify all and only the well-formed expressions of that language, and are taken to represent the **linguistic competence** of a native speaker – that is, his capacity to produce and to recognize the expressions of the language. Culler suggested that literary theory should study **literary competence** – a putative system of rules, acquired by competent readers of literature in the course of their reading, which are what enable them to read and respond to works of literature.

Culler's analogy is a brilliant one, and it looks at first as if the insight underlying it simply must be true. Given that readers do learn how to read new works by reading old ones, how else can they proceed but by deducing general rules from the works they have read? A moment's consideration will show, however, that there is another way open. Readers might simply remember the works they read earlier, and when they read new ones, make direct comparisons with the old. We know (or at least, despite connectionist theory, we can be pretty sure) that in language, it doesn't usually work that way; between the utterances a speaker has heard, and those he produces, stands an abstract competence, probably expressible in a system of rules, which enables him to project the first set into the second. The fundamental **structuralist** hypothesis, then, in the sophisticated form given to it by Culler, is that this is true for literature as well.

But literature is not language; people don't spontaneously and unconsciously construct new works of literature which are understood equally spontaneously and unconsciously. Nor is there any natural way to draw a distinction between the synchronic and the diachronic – as T.S. Eliot points out, all the classics we have read are simultaneously present as possible models for comparison. Most important of all, when we read or write a new work, we are not limited in our use of earlier reading, to formal features already abstracted from the old works and reduced to a rule. We may go back to the actual works we have already read, and relate a new work to features of the old works we have never before noticed.

The new text thus operates partly by direct comparison with a whole series of earlier texts, without the intervention of any system of formal rules. We might call this the **textualist** hypothesis, in opposition to the structuralist one already mentioned. Barthes himself speaks of **textuality** as the guiding idea in his next phase of work; and the textualist hypothesis – in the form of a claim that each text is traversed by numberless other texts – is an important part of the concept of textuality.

So long as we continue to think in rational and reductive terms about the reading process, it seems certain that either the structuralist, or the textualist hypothesis or both must be true. For we certainly do need to have knowledge of literature (conscious or unconscious) in order to read it; and either we have that knowledge in the form of abstract principles or in the form of concrete examples. Probably both; when we meet in a book some angry and imposed-upon old man, we probably call both upon an abstract stereotype of such a man, which may or may not be derived mainly from literature, and on reminiscences of *King Lear* and *Le Père Goriot* if these cultural references are available to us.

The interesting cognitive questions here are of course to what extent each of these hypotheses is true; and how they each work. How far, in our response, do we rely on formalizable abstract principles, and how far on what Lévi-Strauss would call 'the logic of the concrete'? What are the abstract principles? How are our reminiscences of works we have read stored, and how do they come into play?

In his treatment of the structuralist hypothesis, Culler does not in fact instantiate the notion of literary competence in the only way possible – by producing a sketch of a formal grammar of some fragment of literature. His book is rather a sophisticated discussion of the possibility of a theory of literary competence than a contribution to that theory. But it may well be that to move directly from linguistic to literary competence is to make too big a jump. Probably we need to postulate a series of competences – on top of linguistic competence, various types of intellectual competence and rhetorical competence. Literary competence would fit on top of these, and be a later and more sophisticated acquisition. For in order to be able to read literature, you need more than a basic linguistic ability. You need lots of information about the world, and many true or false beliefs. You need to be able to think (draw inferences, that is), have conversations, and handle figures of speech.

Curiously enough, the best basis for a view of a complete theory of literature on these lines might be the pattern of mediaeval higher education. In this, Grammar is something fairly basic; it corresponds to the acquisition of linguistic competence (in Latin, of course). Logic is the study of valid patterns of inference. Rhetoric is the study of figures of speech. The study of literary kinds is something that fits on top of all these disciplines and presupposes them. Mediaeval and renaissance writers took it for granted that an educated man would draw on all these disciplines both when he wrote literature and when he read it.

It is still possible that theoretical developments of this kind will come to dominate modern higher education in the arts. Linguistics is only one of the major social and behavioural sciences that might contribute here. Modern logic, modern cognitive psychology, some of modern sociology and some aspects of modern semiotics offer a far more sophisticated basis for such work than the Middle Ages had. There are already numerous degree courses in such subjects as Communication Studies which I used to believe were the wave of the future.

But the interesting thing to note for our present purposes is that this line of development, in Barthes – toward a full and in principle complete theory of literary competence – is precisely what did not happen. It was not merely because it proved infeasible – impossible to achieve with the resources available to him. And it was not because he wholly adopted the alternative, textualist hypothesis. In *S/Z*, where he is supposed to be concerned with textuality, Barthes works with abstract, interpretive codes, not merely cross-references to other literary works.

On the contrary, this line was rejected, by Barthes and many of his colleagues, in principle; on grounds that were partly philosophical, partly political, and partly, no doubt, unconscious phantasy. Derrida argued against it – or, at least, arguments of his directed against certain supposed metaphysical assumptions of this research programme were used against the research programme as a whole. Julia Kristeva argued against it, and strongly influenced Barthes, though it is difficult for a foreign linguist to see quite why – her grasp of linguistics seeming to be much less secure than Barthes' own. (Consider the article, 'The Ethics of Linguistics', in which she argues a **moral** case against transformational grammar!)

In his book, Culler considers and rejects many of these arguments;

and at a rational level, there is no doubt that he is in the right. But that is not the way that history went. For this was one of the great dividing moments in intellectual history, when the very concept of a rational research strategy was abandoned, and replaced by an in my view irrationalist protest against that research strategy.

This is what we sometimes think of as the replacement of 'structuralism' by 'post-structuralism'. So powerful was this intellectual movement, that in the end it swept away Culler himself, and he has become remarkably apologetic about his own original proposal. Culler's *On Deconstruction* (Introduction and chapter 1) is one of the few rational and persuasive accounts of why Culler's *Structuralist Poetics* will not quite do. And Culler is still often abused, on philosophical or political grounds, for that very rationality. Movements of this kind, of course, require historical and sociological explanations, not merely intellectual or personal ones; not for the first or last time, Barthes was a symptom.

5   *S/Z* AND THE GAME OF POST-STRUCTURALIST SELF- SUBVERSION

5.1   *Separating structuralism from post-structuralism*

'Post-structuralism' is not a coherent theoretical position, even in the very limited sense in which structuralism was, in its final French period. Structuralism at least had conscious adherents, who knew precisely what they were practising and gave it that name. Lévi-Strauss spent months acquainting himself with linguistics, and years considering how best to adapt the linguistic model to anthropology. Barthes did much the same in literary and cultural criticism. Both of them often called themselves structuralists. 'Post-structuralism' on the other hand was not a position anybody claimed to hold. It was a name the newspapers gave to what certain famous structuralists started to do, after they had ceased to take the structuralist model seriously; and what other people did, who had never been structuralists at all. Barthes himself called his later approach 'textual' analysis. All the same, Barthes had once been a card-carrying structuralist and now clearly no longer was; to that extent the word 'post-structuralist' has at least a logical justification.

One can separate structuralism from post-structuralism very easily, by looking at two of Barthes' works only four years apart in time. The two works are *ISAN*, the 'Introduction to the Structural Analysis of Narratives', (1966) – which I have just been discussing, and his much more famous book, *S/Z*. This appeared in 1970, and was based on his own seminars during 1968–9. It is an extended analysis of the Balzac novella *Sarrasine*.

ISAN is an honest old-fashioned structuralist work. It lays out a plausible, if not entirely feasible research strategy for the analysis of narrative structure, using linguistics as a guide. The style is relatively clear, as Barthes' theoretical work goes; it positively invites us to read critically in the hope of understanding what Barthes is at, and perhaps of applying his methods ourselves. Moreover, the enterprise being undertaken is clearly a collective one. There are respectful references to the work of other scholars – Todorov, Greimas, Genette – who have made alternative decisions about particular technical points. We are, in fact, in the world of rational scholarship, or science.

S/Z is an altogether different affair. The difference comes out in the very first few pages of the two works. Both of them are, as it happens, about the same topic: the vast number of narratives to be handled. In *ISAN* this is treated soberly as a methodological difficulty which makes it impossible to proceed by simple induction and necessary to form a theory – there is an apposite reference here to contemporary discussions in transformational grammar. The treatment in *S/Z* is a very different matter. It begins with a joke about a Buddhist and a bean. It continues with an obscure and dismissive travesty of anything any theorist of narrative, **including Barthes himself**, had ever proposed to do: 'we shall . . . extract from each tale its model, then out of these models we shall make a great narrative structure, which we shall reapply (for verification) to any one narrative: a task as exhausting (ninety-nine percent perspiration as the saying goes)⋆ as it is ultimately undesirable, for the text thereby loses its difference.'

In this passage, post-structuralism starts as it means to go on; with self-conscious and obscure in-jokes at the expense of those benighted souls who ever took structuralism seriously – or of course at writers like Gerard Genette or a whole tradition of non-ironic semioticians not considered here, who were to carry the taxonomic approach to narrative on into the next decades.

⋆ (<Science avec patience, Le Supplice est sûr>)

5.2 The readerly, the writerly and the five narrative codes

If, however, you look at the main content of this most complex book, it looks quite forbiddingly scientific in character. Barthes examines a short story by Balzac, by postulating five **codes** which interact with each unit of the story in turn, to produce a complex meaning. These codes are: the proairetic, concerned with the successive actions that make a narrative, which Barthes labels **ACT**; the hermeneutic, concerned with questions or enigmas (what has happened, who is this, etc.) which Barthes labels **HER**; the symbolic, concerning matters like the great antithesis between garden and salon, life and death, etc., with which the story opens, which Barthes labels **SYM**; the connotational, in which signifiers (here called 'semes') represent general categories like femininity, and which Barthes marks **SEM**; and finally the referential code, often mistaken as referring to an external reality outside the text, but which Barthes describes as referring to various codes of cultural commonplaces, and labels **REF**.

It will be seen that it would be quite difficult to make a tidy logical classification that would clearly distinguish between these codes; Barthes gives no evidence whatever for them, and the book reads as if he simply made them up in the first day or so of his seminar. They are a triumph, or disaster, of *ad hoc*cery.

These codes are applied as appropriate to successive units – set up by Barthes on an arbitrary basis – of text. Some of these units, or **lexias** are a paragraph long; some only a word or two. Barthes proceeds systematically till he has examined all **five-hundred-and-sixty-one** lexias in the story. One's first impression is of an inference-machine, eating its way steadily through the story and grinding out meanings. Now and then the machine stops, for one of the **ninety-three** theoretical essays on some aspect of narrativity, or of the reading or the analytical process.

At a second look, the scientificity of the book evaporates. To begin with, the exact status of the codes is very unclear, and Barthes' style is not calculated to reduce the unclarity. It is in fact an oracular and joky style, designed I think to mystify the question of what status Barthes' theoretical claims actually have. (One feels that it is somehow empiricist and vulgar even to press the question.)

However, the following logical possibilities seem to be available:

(1) Barthes may be postulating that the codes he describes are part of the structure of the mind of any reader of Balzac, and account for the reading he will in fact produce. This would be an

empirical hypothesis about readers, and would be falsified, for any particular reader, if he were to produce a different reading from the one Barthes predicts. This would be objective research into semiological science.

(2) Barthes may think that these are codes that the bourgeois reader has learned; they produce his bourgeois reading and make it appear natural and spontaneous. If Barthes can produce another reading, and show that this is as natural as the bourgeois one, it will undermine yet another bourgeois myth – this time, the myth of the 'naturalness' of realist writing. This would be a continuation of the propagandist work Barthes was doing in *Mythologies*.

(3) Or Barthes may think of his codes as independent of the consciousness of any reader, and as forming a mechanical inference producer which enables the critic to grind out new interpretations. Some of these might even be interesting in their own right. On this view, the codes would not in any way be refuted if the interpretations of the text that they gave were ones that no reader had thought of. Indeed, why bother with the codes if you could think of the interpretation for yourself?

In *S/Z*, Barthes hovers between all these positions, and some others, in a way that is very confusing to the reader, and may represent equal confusion in himself. But he doesn't do this by accident. At the time he wrote *S/Z*, Barthes had come under the influence of philosophers like Derrida and Kristeva, for whom the very notion of a systematic and consistent 'theory of reading' would be highly suspect.

Their philosophy casts doubt on the existence of any realm of meaning – any transcendental signified – beyond, and independent of, the text itself; or of a single and univocal meaning for that text. If ever a text is seen as embodying a whole abstract system of meaning, Derrida will seize upon some little detail of it, and show that that has implications that subvert the whole system. No system is fully coherent and closed; and it is the vice of **logocentrism** that makes us want such systems. Derrida writes as if, for him, meaning is created endlessly anew by the energy of writing itself; or is a kind of fluid stuff that disseminates itself all over the place, leaking from text to text.

This philosophical position (of which I have here offered not so much a sketch, as a cartoon – see chapter 5 for a critique of a tiny bit of it) heavily influences Barthes, in the introduction to *S/Z*. He makes a distinction, at first between two types of text, then, more

155

fundamentally, between two types of reading, which is related to Derridean concepts. The classic text – i.e., the realist text – is **readable**, or **readerly**. We try to move from the text to a single, coherent meaning system. The modernist text – or perhaps just a modernist practice of reading which Barthes is advocating – is **writable**, or **writerly**. We can get a rich harvest of meanings – not necessarily consistent with each other – out of it.

In the light of this, *S/Z* has two purposes – a practical purpose and a theoretical one – which are properly classed as **post–structuralist** rather than structuralist. The practical purpose is to read a classic realist text – that of a Balzac short story – as if it were a writerly modernist one, with endless diverging meanings. The theoretical purpose is not to exemplify, but to undermine and subvert the mechanistic structuralism that might make us propose set codes for the production of meaning.

5.3   The problem of arguing with S/Z

The joky 'subversiveness' of a book like *S/Z* presents peculiar difficulties to anyone who wants to argue with it. One is constantly in danger of looking humourless; of taking seriously something that is not intended to be taken seriously. This is a danger that must be faced: only by assuming that the book is a theoretical work and solemnly arguing one's way through some of it can one justify the later judgement that it is more like literature than theory.

I am going to consider three aspects of *S/Z*: its method of analysis of narrative; its account of the narrator's story; and one reasonably typical example of the interpolated essays on the nature of narrative. I begin by repeating some points from an earlier paper (Jackson 1982) about the method of analysis of narrative, which differs in obvious ways, for the worse, from the method recommended in 'Introduction to the Structural Analysis of Narratives' (*ISAN*).

Barthes refuses to look at the overall structure of the text; instead, he divides it into 561 arbitrary units, or lexias, and checks each against the five codes. He also intersperses his analyses of lexias with general discussions of narrative theory. This gives the book an air of being at once systematic, theoretical and immensely rich. But the system, the theories and the riches are not related to each other.

The only theory that this particular systematic structure would be appropriate to test, would be the absurd one that a fictional narrative consists of a linear series of lexias, each communicating according to one or more of the five codes; and that the 5 × 561 squares of the matrix thus produced specify the total meaning of the narrative. But Barthes does not believe this, as is clear from incidental remarks in *S/Z* itself. Moreover it is clear from *ISAN* that he is perfectly aware that many structures of a narrative cannot be mapped onto a linear sequence of elements. One needs complex tree-structures and fugal interweaving of narrative themes. Barthes' device in *S/Z* of numbering narrative themes when they reappear is quite inadequate to represent these structures. Once again we find that *S/Z* neither supports nor subverts any theory which any serious structuralist **including Barthes himself** ever held.

Nor does this matter much, as the theories are not offered in testable form anyway. They are bright ideas; one is in the company of McLuhan rather than Chomsky. There are also rich insights, and others less impressive – the book seems to contain every single thing that had occurred to Barthes and his pupils, about this one short story, in a two-year seminar – but these are not organized in any way. (Barthes prides himself on this, and I imagine his followers would regard it as terroristic even to try.) And the simple linear way in which the book is organized, following the narrative of *Sarrasine*, prevents any higher organization from arising.

It is clear that Barthes did not make his book systematic because he was systematically testing a theory. He made it systematic because, at this stage of his career, he liked the rhetorical effect of systematicity. At earlier and later stages, he liked other effects: a scientificity arid to the point of being castrating in *The Fashion System* and *Elements of Semiology*, and in his later work, an erotics of the text which, in its continuous willed production of fantasy objects, becomes (in ironic quotes) masturbatory. To the extent that this is true, it supports the judgement that *S/Z* is a literary, or at least rhetorical rather than a theoretical work.

5.4 Barthes rewriting the story

Barthes' elaborate procedures have some highly productive effects, which his commentators celebrate; and some grimly reductive effects, which they tend to pass by. I will try to keep a balance here by putting these effects side by side. Barthes manages to produce a highly productive reading of Balzac's castration symbolism. There is no doubt that Balzac consciously put this in; Barthes' method shows it proliferating all over the place in unexpected ways; and readings like this are a foreseen, and valuable product of the method. The unforeseen effect is to hide, both from Barthes and his followers, a gross, crude and oversimplifying misreading – in effect, a replacement of the story by Barthes' castration complex. I don't mean by this that Barthes has added new subtleties and Freudianisms that a reactionary critic might question. I mean that he has offered a crude account of the story that doesn't fit the text, and ignores what Balzac wrote.

Barthes says that the narrator in *Sarrasine* offers his mistress a contract of prostitution: a night of love for a story. She agrees; but the story turns out to be about castration; repelled by this, she breaks her contract with him. But none of this happens in Balzac's story. No such contract is made, and therefore none can be broken; and the lady's motive for not proceeding with her love affair is not the one Barthes ascribes to her.

Balzac shows the narrator having reached a certain stage in a love affair; he is permitted to take his mistress to a party. He wishes to be admitted to the next stage, when he will be permitted to attend her in private, at her home. He uses the promise of the story to achieve this. When he tells the story he hopes, of course, to end in the lady's bed; but he hopes it in the sense in which any lover does; he hopes to impress her sufficiently for her to accept him as a lover. Unfortunately, the story that he tells carries with it a moral, that one is all too likely to be deceived in love; the object of love is likely to be unworthy, as Zambinella was, appearing to be a woman, while in fact being a *castrato*. The lady takes this point, and decides to play safe and stick to Christian virtue.

That is Balzac's story – the one in the actual text. It is obviously better than Barthes' story. For one thing, it *is* just plausible. Why did Barthes substitute his own story for the original? He may, of course, have simply not noticed what the text said; though he did spend two years reading it. In that case one is entitled to suggest that his critical method is like an elaborate suit of armour that is too heavy to fight in. Alternatively, he may have wished to substitute a crude story for one that seemed to him over-refined; presumably as part of a fight against bourgeois standards. But this is no more than an oppositional gesture. It is no more than cocking a snook.

Any real opposition to the standards Balzac is embodying would have to start by recognizing what they are. (After all, Marx and Engels did!) To refuse to read the story (while pretending one has read it more carefully than anybody else in the history of criticism) is to engage in a fantasy of opposition to bourgeois standards; in which, I am afraid, Barthes has had a substantial readership accompanying him.

5.5   Argument in S/Z: conceits as criticism

I now turn to one of the interpolated divagations on general narrative theory. It comes from p. 135 of the English edition of S/Z, p. 141 of the French. (LVIII, L'Intérêt de l'histoire).

> Sarrasine is free to heed or reject the unknown man's warning. This alternative freedom is structural: it marks each term of a sequence and ensures the story's progress in 'rebounds' ('*rebondissements*'). No less structurally, however, Sarrasine is not free to reject the Italian's warning; if he were to heed it and to refrain from pursuing his adventure, there would be no story. In other words, *Sarrasine is forced by the discourse* to keep his rendezvous with La Zambinella: the character's freedom is dominated by the discourse's instinct for preservation.

How are we to take this? We might start by trying to take it seriously. Is it true? Is the free will of a character in a story affected by the fact that the outcome of the story is predetermined?

Freedom − here, freedom of the will − is a property that can be predicated only of real people. Of characters in fiction we can only say that they are, or are not, **represented** as having free will. Margaret Thatcher has free will. Clytemnestra is represented as having it. If we say Clytemnestra has free will in the story it will be taken to mean that the story shows her as having it. If we say Clytemnestra actually has free will, and mean it, it will entail that we are thinking not of the character in the play, but of a real human being.

Now if we are thinking of a real Clytemnestra, nothing in a later story about her can affect what she did or what she was. If we are thinking of a fiction in a play by Aeschylus, the fact that the end of her story is predetermined has no bearing on whether Aeschylus represents her as having free will. He can say either: 'she chose freely to murder her husband' − thus making her free choice the cause of the end of the story − or: 'fate determined it − she could not choose but murder him' − thus making the predetermined end cause her choice.

There is thus no conceivable situation in which the fact that the story has a predetermined end can affect the question of the heroine's freedom of will. If she is a person, she can have it, whatever the story says; if she is a fiction, she can only be represented as having it, whatever the story says.

Barthes' argument is therefore an absurdity, based on an equivocation; it is an interesting question, which as usual with Barthes one cannot settle simply from his style, how far he was aware of this. But this still leaves open the question: 'How are **we** to take this argument, now it has been shown to be silly?

The first thing to consider is what Barthes uses it for. He does not use it as an essential part of a large-scale overarching theory. No such theory is to be found in *S/Z*: that is one of the surprising things about the book, given its vast scale and formidably technical appearance. Instead (within a section the size of a short essay, about one-third the length of one of his *Mythologies* articles) he builds on it a series of similar arguments, each as absurd as the last, ending in a triple pun on the word *interest*.

> The game is an economic one: it is to the story's interest that Sarrasine ignore the stranger's dissuasion; he must *at all costs* keep the duenna's rendezvous . . . to ensure the very survival of the anecdote . . . to protect an article of merchandise (the narrative) which has not yet been put on the reading market: the story's 'interest' is the 'interest' of its producer (or its consumer) . . .

Where have we met this kind of argumentation before? The obvious place is Elizabethan and Jacobean poetry and drama. Shakespeare's clowns do it all the time; but that is intended to be funny. A love poem, however, can have a very similar series of arguments in it; we call them conceits. We attend to them half-seriously, for the pleasure they give. There are many indications in *S/Z* – and still more in later works like *The Pleasure of the Text* – that Barthes would be happy for his work to be read in this way.

Does it work? There are **ninety-three** of these cleverly silly little essaylets in *S/Z*. It is an awful lot of disbelief to suspend. My own reactions don't include pleasure. I remember, instead, indignation, despair, hopelessness and, more than anything else, tedium.

5.6 Post-structuralism as rhetoric and comedy

The analysis of section LVIII makes one important point, however, which I think can be generalized. When we examine a section of post-structuralist argument carefully, and with close attention, we often – not always – find that it is a series of quasi-jokes. It would be going too far to say that this was true of all the material in *S/Z*. But it would not be going too far to say that the book as a whole contains not, or not mainly, a series of arguments intended to produce conviction because they are valid, but a set of figures of speech, intended to dazzle through their rhetorical effect.

This point, I think, applies quite generally. At least it applies to every major post-structuralist figure whose work I have read; and where it does not apply, the figure is not a major one, but usually a minor expositor like me trying to make sense of the field. Thus my generalization applies to Barthes, in his late stage, to Lacan, to Foucault, to Derrida and to Kristeva; it does not apply to Culler, to Eagleton or to Norris, though sometimes they let through into English material which they have been unable altogether to reduce to rationality.

At times one is inclined to think that post-structuralism is not just a succession of little jokes; it is the technique of the one great big joke, hidden in solemn academic wrappings. The great big joke is to reverse (without being too serious about it) some central assumption of philosophy or science; and see what it leads to. Here are three examples. First, the *Anti-Oedipus*, of Deleuze and Guattari. This is the anti-Lacanian book, mentioned in the last chapter, that reverses the Freudian proposition that the passage through the Oedipus complex is the entry into culture and humanity. Better for us all, it says, not to pass through; we should all remain schizophrenic desiring-machines and wouldn't that be nice. Second, a widespread recent view of epistemology. It's really a branch of narrative theory! This implies, I think, that there are all sorts of ways of changing the plot; it's another ingenious way of arguing for relativism. I am not denying there have been some interesting insights on these lines: for example, Misia Landau's account of prehistory as epic narrative (Lewin 1987, pp. 31–46). But as epistemology?

Or perhaps the best example: de Saussure, in the lectures which provided the foundation for modern linguistics (a serious undertaking, if ever there was one) suggested that there was actually a logical space for a broader science of signs, semiology, of which linguistics would be merely a part. Much of the structuralist tradition has consisted of speculative contributions to such a science. One major post-structuralist work, highly respected by all, consists of speculations about the possible implications of a science called **grammatology** which, if it could be constructed, would be based on the proposition that writing came, or comes, before speech. As one philosopher friend of mine remarked: grammatology **must** be a joke. I am not dismissing this book – there is an extensive serious discussion of it in the next chapter. But I am pointing out an important rhetorical quality of the field, whose significance has not been widely enough considered. There is a discussion of it in Pêcheux (1975), in which he speculates on the cause of his own facetiousness.

Again, it would be going too far to say that the post-structuralists are merely joking. If they were joking, their work would be funnier. It would not be going too far, however, to say that they are presenting figures of rhetoric, of which jokes are merely one variety, as a substitute for argument, and instead of argument. In this respect, Barthes in *S/Z* is typical of the movement beyond structuralism, and not in the least eccentric. And curiously enough, there is a general defence for this approach, which has the character of an argument.

This argument runs as follows: philosophers in the past (and, by extension, literary theorists, psychologists, et al.) have pretended to produce cogent abstract arguments, put in words for convenience, but not limited in validity by the language in which they are clothed. But this is to neglect the constitutive part played by metaphor and other figures in the arguments themselves. (Consider, for example, the effect of the word 'clothed' on the apparent validity of the argument expressed by the first sentence of this paragraph.) One may well accept this argument – as I do – without quite seeing that it follows that the very concept of a literal statement is a delusion, or that rhetoric should replace logic throughout the human sciences.

A true post-structuralist has no such reservations. I have repeatedly found myself attacked for making the obvious point that there are profound elements of irrationalism in post-structuralist thought. What is wrong, I am told, is my mechanistic equation of rationality with a narrow scientific model of the world, which is ethnocentric into the bargain. To this, the only possible reply is a case-by-case one: this is one of the cases: there is no conceivable society and no conceivable period of history in which the argument Barthes put forward is valid. That is to say, in no society which has a conception of fiction and of free will can these words be true; and they are certainly not true in modern French: '*Sarrasine est contraint par le discours* d'aller au rendezvous de la Zambinella: la liberté du personnage est dominée par l'instinct du conservation du discours' (Barthes, *S/Z*, 1970, p. 141).

On the other hand, in any society with a tradition of verbal play the words make a very fair conceit, or intellectual joke: it is not I who am being humourless or narrow in suggesting that this is how they should be taken here. And a very quick trawl through post–structuralist writings will find numerous parallels. How about the suggestion that language is fascist because grammars are hierarchical? (see chapter 3, this book). Try believing that without going mad!

6   THE BEGINNINGS OF TEXTUAL MYSTICISM

6.1   *The text as slime-mould*

But for all the jokes, there is now a project going on which seems to me profoundly irrational, in that it is directed against the kind of detailed theory-based analytical understanding of the text that structuralism promised, and toward a mystique of the text. I find this present already in Barthes' article of 1971, 'From Work to Text'. This is a profoundly anti-structuralist article, and that is ironic, for for many Anglo-American readers, it is articles like this that provided their first conception of what structuralism was! But the gospel is a relativist one, and an anti-analytical one:

> Just as Einsteinian science demands that **the relativity of the frames of reference** be included in the object studied, so the combined action of Marxism, Freudianism, and structuralism demands, in literature, the relativisation of the relations of writer, reader and observer (critic). Over against the traditional notion of the **work**, there is now the requirement of a new object, obtained by the sliding or overturning of former categories. That object is the **Text**.

The new object is an almost unbelievably deliquescent one. It slides about all over the place. It is a 'fragment of substance'; it is a 'methodological field'; it is experienced 'only in an activity of production'; it is constituted by 'its subversive force in respect to the old classifications'. (Kristeva, the arch-metaphysical-subverter, must have been talking very persuasively at about this time.) The text is, in short, anything whatever that Barthes likes to say it is, and never mind whether that thing is consistent with all the other things: as he says himself, he is not producing arguments, but metaphors. It works up to a splendidly revealing climax:

> These few propositions, inevitably, do not constitute the articulations of a Theory of the Text and this is not simply the result of the failings of the person here presenting them (who in many respects has anyway done no more than pick up what is being developed round about him). It stems from the fact that a Theory of the Text cannot be satisfied by a meta-linguistic exposition: the destruction of meta-language, or at least (since it may be necessary provisionally to resort to meta-language) its calling into doubt, is part of the theory itself: the discourse on the Text should itself be nothing other than text, research, textual activity, since the Text is that **social** space which leaves no language safe, outside, nor any subject of the enunciation in position as judge, master, analyst, confessor, decoder. The theory of the Text can coincide only with the practice of writing.
>
> (Barthes, 'From Work to Text', in Harari 1979)

What we have now is full-scale textual mysticism. The very possibility of textual analysis has now been firmly blocked. Of course in practice it can still be done, but there cannot be any principles on which it is done; and what will be produced is just more text. In the name of structuralism, what we have just seen is the death of structuralism. In fact it is something more than that. It is the death of theory as an independent enterprise, and the capture of the ground that it occupied by literature. It is also – if we take with absolute seriousness what Barthes says – the emergence of a new type of religious mysticism.

I had better unpack this point. When one first considers the opposition between the structuralist approach to literature of *ISAN*, and the textualist approach here, the metaphor that occurs is a biological one. The narrative, for *ISAN*, is an arthropod. It has joints and limbs. The text, on the other hand, is a slime-mould. It can slide in anywhere and has no structure one can talk about. But in fact the case is worse than this. The naturalist can, after all, describe a real slime-mould just as easily as he can describe a spider. But by hypothesis the critic cannot describe this literary slime-mould at all; only the slime-mould can describe itself. I think we have met this thing before: this unstructured thing that contains the whole world and can recognize itself; and can even give it its correct German name: it is called *Geist*.

In short what I am saying is that **text**, once it is given the properties above, becomes a disguised version of **mind**: and that a large proportion of the post-structuralist analysis that has gone on since this paper was written, and in its spirit, has been a recycling of the history of idealist philosophy, under the cover of textual analysis.

The influence of this on textual analysis as an activity seems to me to have been mixed, and mostly bad. One sees a tendency to reverse the mechanistic scientism of the structuralists into a woolly philosophical relativism; to replace traditional terms of philosophy by words like discourse, signifier and text; and to replace potentially finite problems in literary theory – such as, to what extent is a particular literary work (on a particular reading) intelligible in terms of internalized rules, and to what extent in terms of allusion to other specific texts – by invocations of the infinite indeterminacy of reading and of allusion. In short, instead of analysing works of literature, one divinizes, and makes a mystique of something called the Text.

6.2   Barthes as guru and in his own write

Poor Roland Barthes, in the last stages of his career, had the task of keeping up with thinking of this kind. Sometimes he even had to write introductions to collections of it, and make it sound like intellectual enquiry. Here is an example of the way he coped:

> The Text: let us make no mistake about either this singular or this capital letter; when we say **the Text**, it is not in order to divinise it, to make it the deity of a new mystique, but to denote a mass, a field requiring a partitive and not a numerative expression: all that can be said of a work is that there is Text in it. In other words, by passing from text to the Text, we must change numeration: on the one side, the Text is not a computable object, it is a methodological field in which are pursued, according to a movement more 'Einsteinian' than 'Newtonian', the statement and the speech-act, the matter commented on (the *commenté*) and the matter commenting (the *commentant*) . . .
> ('Research: the Young'; from *Communications*, 1972; in Barthes 1984)

It is interesting to see how smoothly Barthes moves from denying mystique into mystification: 'all that can be said of a work is that there is Text in it'. All! Structuralist ambitions have now been left far behind: 'the text is not a computable object, it is a methodological field . . .' and the references to Einstein and Newton are strictly decorative. (It is interesting to see how often Einstein appears, on the basis of a misunderstanding of the word 'relativity', as the patron of an anti-scientific reaction. It is a reaction just as fetishistic, in its own way, as the cult of 'Einstein's Brain' which Barthes had mocked in *Mythologies*.) It is to this that Barthesian semiology has come by the 1970s, and although Barthes is to blame, it is Kristeva and Derrida who gave him his alibis.

It is of course still possible to find flatteringly impressive descriptions of what Barthes is doing, or representing, or theorizing, in the later period. 'From *The Pleasure of the Text* to the *Barthes*', writes Steven Ungar, 'the cleaving of consciousness into contiguous entities of self and body provides the working model for Barthes' transition from science to art, a move which he justifies in the cause of eros' (Ungar 1983, p. 65). And with reference to *Barthes*, he refers to Stephen Heath's argument (*Vertige du déplacement*) 'that metaphor acts primarily as a force to open the text and displace fixed meaning and reference'. Those who take the post-structuralist project seriously will find this an interesting thing to want to do. Those who, like me, think that displacing fixed meanings and reference is a fantasied sexual liberation, or a displacement activity which occurs when political revolution turns out to be impossible or undesirable will probably take a different view.

I think that in his own writing, with characteristic ingenuity, Barthes used the new theory in a rather different way, to help him jettison unwanted theoretical burdens. Barthes' concern in this period seems to be no longer with founding a science or establishing an academic reputation, but with being, or becoming, a writer. Perhaps that had always been his deeper intention; but now it comes out in a negative intellectual way, as well as a positive stylistic one. After about 1970, he does not cease to have new thoughts – for example, about the pleasure principle, or about the importance of the body – but he does stop being, in any serious sense, a thinker. The thoughts are arranged in fragments, in no systematic order, for a kind of intellectual browsing. The fragments of his autobiography, *Barthes by Barthes*, are bound in at the back of a family photograph album. The form here is partly given by the series the book appears in; but it expresses the effective intention: to present not a system, but a set of intellectual aperçus, chosen at the writer's pleasure. The reader's pleasure doesn't come into it very much, though there is evidence that some readers have been given pleasure by these books, even if I have not.

Barthes described this phase of his development in an interview (January 1977) for *Le Nouvel Observateur* (in Barthes 1981).

> 'When it's a *writing* commission, things work fairly well . . . on the other hand, when the request is for a dissertation, when I have to discuss a certain subject, for example, then things run into trouble . . .'

> 'I'm moving closer and closer to the fragment – I enjoy its savour, and I believe in its theoretical importance. To the point, by the way, that I'm starting to have trouble writing texts of a certain length and continuity . . .'

> 'There are themes. The image-repertoire, for example. The indirect. *Doxa*. Also the theme of anti-hysteria, even if it has evolved only recently. But I repeat that they are themes.'

> '*Do you mean that they are not philosophical 'concepts'?*

> 'No. They are concepts. But they are metaphor-concepts, functioning like metaphors. And if what Nietzsche says is true, if concepts do have, as he says, a metaphorical origin, then it's at that origin that I situate myself. And so my concepts don't have that rigor usually conferred by philosophers.'

It is not to the point of this book, and it would be quite inappropriate – indeed, impossible – for me to judge Barthes as a modern experimental French writer. My perception of him through an imperfect ear for the nuances of French style is that he is often whimsical, empty and silly; he would need considerable literary virtues to overcome such a start, and I don't see what they are. However, on my principles (though not perhaps on his) my view of him as a writer is quite irrelevant to my view of the truth, importance, or influence of his ideas, all of which come from other people anyway; though he sometimes makes them seem fresh and new. The only point in mentioning the literary question is that there is a possible line of argument to the effect that you cannot legitimately extract the ideas from the texts, or perhaps *the Text*. In that case, literary criticism becomes the only discipline that can bite; and it is worth reminding oneself that a literary judgement on Barthes might be a very adverse one.

Those who admire Barthes as a writer or post-structuralist 'thinker' are sometimes ready to throw the more systematic material overboard, as of little real interest. I must confess that I would think much worse of Barthes if I thought of him solely as a writer, than I do, thinking of him as the distinguished intellectual middleman who popularized structuralism and semiology.

BOOKS

Barthes, Roland 1982 *Selected Writings* (Ed. Susan Sontag). Now probably the best cheap collection of the more accessible writings.
Barthes, Roland 1974 *S/Z* (trans Richard Miller). Barthes moves from structuralism to post-structuralism.
Lavers, Annette 1982 *Roland Barthes: Structuralism and After*

FURTHER READING

Barthes: Barthes passim, Heath 1974, Lavers 1982, Macksey and Donato 1970, Thody 1977, Ungar 1983, Wiseman 1989.
Structuralism and Semiology: Chatman, Eco and Klinkenburg 1979, Eco 1976, Guiraud 1971, Hayakawa 1939, Korzybski 1933,

Macksey and Donato 1970, Sebeok 1975, Winner and Umiker-Sebeok 1979, Wuthnow, Hunter, Bergeson and Kurzweil 1984.

For titles and publishers see main bibliography.

CHAPTER FIVE

Textual Metaphysics and the Anti-foundation Myths of Derrida

From the Deconstruction of Phenomenology to a New 'New Criticism'

SUMMARY

Jacques Derrida, probably the most important of the 'post-structuralists', is a philosophical commentator: he produces texts exposing the alleged hidden metaphysical underpinnings of other texts. He began by subverting from within the philosophical tradition of Husserl and Heidegger; then tried to do the same for structuralism, which for him is based on the same metaphysics of presence he finds everywhere. His technical non-concepts – differance, trace, etc. – are meant to smash up our metaphysics, and not offer a new one. No full treatment of Derrida or deconstructive criticism is attempted here; but it is argued that his critique of Saussure is based on a myth about the Western philosophical tradition – that of **phonocentrism** – imposed on Saussure by misrepresentation; and that the deconstructive school of criticism influenced by his work and popular in America is actually a romantic textual metaphysics.

1 THE MYTHS OF PHONOCENTRISM AND ARCHE-WRITING

I am not, in this chapter, going to conduct a general attack on Derrida as a philosopher, and make a critical survey of post-Derridean criticism. That would be outside the scope of this book, and an enormous undertaking, quite beyond my powers. I shall confine myself to discussing in detail only two of what, in an old-fashioned terminology he would probably reject, might be called Derrida's philosophical claims. The first is the existence of something called 'phonocentrism'; I shall argue that it doesn't exist. The second is the ontological priority of something called Writing or Arche-writing – I shall argue that this is an incoherent notion.

At a more general level I shall make a suggestion about the character of Derrida's philosophical work which is by no means dismissive, and may seem obvious: that it is metaphysics. And I shall make a suggestion about the general character of deconstructive criticism: that it is not the argus-eyed and rigorous analytical method of its own self-image, but a form of textual idealism, or, to be more precise, of romantic textual mysticism.

2 THE NEED FOR METAPHYSICS AND THE ADVANTAGES OF LOGOCENTRISM

It is not the least of Derrida's achievements that he has turned a leading school of literary critics into amateur metaphysicians. This is because it is a part of his method to uncover the hidden metaphysical assumptions in apparently innocent texts. It is not the least of my embarrassments that, in order to argue against him, I shall have to explain what I take metaphysics to be.

Metaphysics is the study of the general nature of the world and of the first principles of philosophy. It examines both the basic assumptions behind common-sense views of the world, and those behind systematic empirical forms of investigation, like the natural and the social sciences; and it often does this by examining the most general categories in terms of which we find ourselves trying to describe the world. Consider, for example, the metaphysical category of 'existence'. I hold that rocks, tables, people and institutions like the Prudential Assurance Company exist, while clepts, chairdogs, elves and the monarchy of Narnia do not exist. That is merely a common-sense belief, with which most people would agree; though it might, of course be wrong. I also hold that whether these things exist or not is a matter largely independent of my own thoughts about them, or of any description I could give of them; they would still exist, or not, if I were dead, and some of them would exist if everybody was dead. This is a metaphysical position, which I call common-sense realism. One might contrast this with the view that what common sense regards as real objects out there are actually constructs; properties of human culture, which would vanish if that did.

I hold also that electrons, genes and strangeness probably exist, and that phonemes, the id, social classes and superstrings may; while phlogiston, caloric and anti-gravity almost certainly do not. These are merely scientific beliefs. I hold them within the metaphysical belief that the existence of these entities is substantially independent of my scientific beliefs about them. I call this position scientific realism, in contrast to an idealist position holding that electrons are mere theoretical constructs: a view which I reject because I don't see how mere theoretical constructs could draw real pictures on a television screen. (A more careful analysis, facing up to the 'Copenhagen interpretation' of quantum theory, is in *The Dematerialisation of Karl Marx*.) I hold that one can modify common-sense realism, to incorporate scientific realism; and this combined view is again a metaphysical theory.

One might well ask about the status of this category 'existence': is it a mere word used in discourse, or a category of logic, or what? It is the business of metaphysics to examine such questions, and to discuss the philosophical principles on which we should proceed to answer them: linguistic analysis, axiomatic system-building, analysis of intuitions or whatever.

All Western metaphysics descends from Aristotle; indeed, the word 'metaphysics' is merely the name of the book that happens to come after physics in his collected works. Aristotle himself called the subject matter of this book 'First Philosophy', which is a much better name. First philosophy has three parts. The first is the theory of being, that is, of what ultimately exists, what aspects of the world are ultimately real. The second is concerned with a hierarchy of values in being. What is the best, or the highest, or the most real being, the Being in terms of which other beings have their being? The third is concerned with the first principles of philosophical method. Aristotle's book is actually a collection of works, and it contains a curious mixture: a philosophical lexicon, defining notions like being, substance, quantity and quality, etc.; critiques of Platonism; a quick outline of fourteen standard metaphysical problems; a theory of the four types of causation, and so forth. Some of this is first philosophy in the sense of being an elementary philosophical primer; some in the sense of being very profound, and philosophically primary: basic to all other philosophical questions.

171

Metaphysics has retained this philosophically mixed character ever since, and as a result it is possible to have elementary text-books on the subject which hardly overlap in subject matter. I found a striking example of this recently when making a comparison between D. M. Mackinnon (1974), *The Problem of Metaphysics*; and Bruce Aune (1986), *Metaphysics: the Elements*. Professor Mackinnon holds a chair in divinity. He begins with Plato, and moves rapidly to Kant. By chapter 6 he is talking about parables; by chapters 10 and 11, miracles, irony and tragedy. Professor Aune moves straight from Aristotle to Bertrand Russell; much of his work is clearly a philosophical accommodation with modern science; neither God nor literature plays a significant role.

Neither work has an entry in the index for Heidegger! This is a salutary reminder for those of us who, working in literary theory, tend to identify the question of being with Heidegger's work. We need to remind ourselves that Derrida's tacit assumption, that the whole history of philosophy culminates in Husserl and Heidegger, is highly partisan; Karl Popper may have more to offer literary theory than Heidegger does; he has certainly had more to offer linguistics.

Metaphysics, then, if it is any one thing, is the study of the ultimate principles governing all being and all philosophical enquiry. It is the most general study that it is possible to undertake, and all other studies – including natural sciences like physics, and political, ethical and aesthetic theories – must fit into it and be compatible with its principles; or at least, formulable within its categories. This seems a strong claim. It means that if we want to know about the origins and construction of the universe, it is all right to read Professor Hawking; but we shall not know how to understand his work, or whether to believe it, until we have placed it within the categories of our metaphysics. For all that it covers the whole universe, and the smallest and largest things in it, physics remains a 'regional science', or specialist discipline. But metaphysics covers everything.

So metaphysics claims a kind of *de jure* priority over all empirical disciplines. Against this, there have been claims that what it actually offers is nothing more than a set of empty categories derived from those very disciplines. Thus, one suggestion that has been made is that the categories of metaphysics, such as 'being' or 'existence', are derived from the structure of language. Benveniste suggested (and he was not the first) that the categories of Aristotle's metaphysics were derived from the structure of Greek. The metaphysical derives from the empirical. In 'The Supplement of Copula' (Derrida 1982) Derrida offers a vigorous critique of Benveniste's position:

. . . none of the concepts used by Benveniste would have seen the light of day – neither linguistics as a science, nor the very notion of language – without this little 'document' on the categories. Philosophy is not only before linguistics in the way that one can be faced with a new science, outlook, or object; it is also before linguistics in the sense of preceding, providing it with its concepts, for better or worse. (p. 188)

Whether this is true or not, it shows Derrida as, in a certain sense, a defender of the logical priority of metaphysics.

Does metaphysics put any real limitation upon the content of the specialist disciplines? This depends on whether it has any sources of knowledge of its own. It has sometimes been claimed that there are metaphysical first principles which determine, in some detail, what kind of world this can possibly be, and what we can know about it. The determination of these has logical priority over, say, the work of a physicist; and any theories he produces have to wait to be ratified until the metaphysician is in a position to pass them. The metaphysician knows what makes physics possible.

Against this view, it could be maintained that the specialist disciplines – biology, linguistics, anthropology, etc. – contain all the knowledge there is to be had. If so, metaphysics is vacuous; or perhaps it is simply the requirement that the specialist disciplines shall be internally consistent, consistent with observation and practical tests, and consistent with each other. Even this weak requirement is not actually negligible; and it may be the rational core of what Derrida calls logocentrism. 'Logocentrism' and 'the metaphysics of presence' are central concepts of Derrida's own philosophy; he identifies them jointly as 'the exigent, powerful, systematic, and irrepressible desire' for a transcendental signified which will 'place a reassuring end to the reference from sign to sign' (Derrida 1967c, p. 49). But what achieves such an end in science, as opposed, perhaps, to religious faith, is consistency with the evidence and self-consistency. And what corresponds, in science, to the 'transcendental signified' is the concept of the hypothetical entity, or process, or structure, which the scientist postulates in order to explain the facts – the electron, for example, or the superstring.

As a matter of fact, at any given time in history there are likely to be major inconsistencies both within and between specialist disciplines, when they postulate hypothetical entities that cannot coexist. In the nineteenth century geology required a lifetime for the earth orders of magnitude greater than physicists could allow for the lifetime of the sun; it would have taken much longer to lay down the sedimentary rocks than for the sun to cool down. This anomaly was not cleared up until the discovery of nuclear interactions in the twentieth century which explained what really fuelled the sun. At the present time there are fundamental incompatibilities within physics between quantum and relativity theory. Clearing up such inconsistencies is one motive for theoretical research.

If logocentrism covers the exigent, powerful, systematic and irrepressible desire that beliefs about hypothetical entities should be explicit and consistent with each other and observation, then it is to the logocentric metaphysics of scientists that we owe the whole body of modern science, so far as it is consistent. Logocentric metaphysics sets a goal for science: it asks scientists to produce a rational and consistent account of the world that fits all the evidence. It sets a goal for mathematics and logic: it asks mathematicians to produce a rational and consistent account of the set of all possible worlds.

If this is so, calls to break out of logocentrism may be expressions of a hostility to rationality, consistency, evidence, science and mathematics. They may not be hostility to metaphysics as such. To say this, incidentally, is not to accuse Derrida himself of hostility to natural science or mathematics; after 1962 he has shown little philosophical interest in them. But he appeals to those who are hostile to them; or, as we shall see, to those who wish to transcend them. It is an interesting question to ask why literary critics should have decided that logocentric metaphysics is an evil, if it is responsible for the achievements of natural science and maths; and one obvious suggestion is that the developed discourse of science and mathematics makes literary critics feel inferior.

It is possible to develop very elaborate metaphysical systems by taking a few abstract categories and manipulating them. Hegel did this in his *Logic*, which is not really logic, but a system of metaphysics. Thus he took a category very close to the one above – 'being/ nothing' – and argued that it was intelligible only in terms of a category that necessarily implied both aspects of it: he called this 'becoming'. McTaggart called it 'transition to being determinate'; a notion which may be compared with Derrida's concept of 'trace'.

Derrida presents himself rhetorically as an anti-metaphysician; but he reasons in exactly the same way as a metaphysician (e.g. Derrida 1962; 1967a,b). He detects within the phenomenological framework a master category which governs everything that the phenomenologist supposes to exist: presence. This is a difficult concept precisely because of its extreme generality: it covers presence to the sight, presence in the mind, self-consciousness (the presence to himself of somebody thinking) and many other things. Derrida gives a partial list of various historical meanings for it in *Of Grammatology* (1967c, p. 12). An example of presence, as I understand it, would be my perception of the word-processor screen I am looking at now. I might want to erect a whole philosophy on the fact that that screen is present to my sight now; or that I am thinking some thought now.

But the category of presence cannot operate without a category of non-presence; what is there now is intelligible only in terms of what is excluded now, and of what was, or will be, there in the past or future. If we want a single master category to cover both it will be a category of difference, in space and in time: in fact it will be in terms of such a category, of difference/deferral, that we construct the experience of space and of time. And we won't be able to think about the category itself – named by Derrida *différance* – since we construct everything else out of it (Derrida 1962; 1967a,b,c). More generally, one might say, there is a fundamental limitation on our ability to give a systematic account of the ultimate underlying elements, assumptions or whatever out of which we are trying to give a systematic account of the world. Ultimate foundations of a system cannot be placed within the system. (This is a loose paraphrase: see Gasché (1985) for a careful account.)

I am keeping quite close to Derrida here; but at the same time I am a long distance away. What I am leaving out is his technique of detailed textual commentary, which is his whole technique – he rarely states a theory without reference to other people's books, as Husserl and Heidegger do all the time – and his numerous explanations of why he is not doing metaphysics; and why '*différance*' is not a metaphysical concept but neither a word nor a concept, a non-concept that is there just to jam one's metaphysics up. I do not believe these protestations. I think Derrida is a metaphysician: but a special kind of metaphysician who proceeds exclusively by exposing or inventing the metaphysical assumptions in other people's texts.

Given the definition above, it seems to be logically impossible to say anything intended to be true that does not fall somewhere within the enclosure of metaphysics. Playful uses of language, which make no assertions, can possibly escape. But even 'Shall I compare thee to a summer's day?' has presuppositions about the existence of time, and of persons, and of the existence of objects, with properties which allow them to be compared with one another. However, with playful or poetic uses of language there is no obligation to keep our presuppositions, or even our assertions, consistent with each other. Literature thus seems to give us access to a broader range of worlds (illusory worlds) than literal and assertoric uses of language can deal with; and this can feel like a kind of liberation. Indeed, it is a metaphorical liberation, being a liberation from the metaphysics of consistency.

Derrida often tries to undermine such distinctions as that between playful and serious uses of language; or between the literal and assertoric, on the one hand, and the metaphorical, rhetorical and fictional on the other. In doing this he offers a rhetoric of liberation from an enclosure of metaphysics. This is the ground of his appeal. Given that the liberation concerned is from the requirements of objectivity and consistency, it is not surprising that the appeal has been greatest to literary theorists and least to physical scientists and analytical philosophers. Some of his arguments seem to have escaped from the original metaphysical contexts in which they made sense, and become dogmas of other people's criticism that I very much doubt he would himself believe. One of these is that there is actually no difference between literal and metaphorical uses of language. I shall show in the next chapter that if you really believe this you will be unable to write a useful English dictionary; let alone criticize a poem.

3   DECONSTRUCTING PHENOMENOLOGY

Phenomenology is a philosophical method designed to provide secure foundations for knowledge – or perhaps, for our understanding of the meaning of our knowledge – or even for our understanding of the meaning of our being in the world – without resting upon metaphysical assumptions. It is common to a whole school of philosophers, but its chief exponent was Edmund Husserl. It seems to rest upon the claim – which is surely itself a metaphysical assumption, though it is supposed not to be – that one can offer a presupposition-free description of experience, or being, or of the world as it is lived in. The claim is not of course that our everyday descriptions of phenomena are free of such presuppositions; but rather that we can by reflection free ourselves of them, and turn to the phenomena themselves. Various techniques are proposed by which this can be done; some have the character of rigorous argument, and some resemble techniques of meditation, or even psychotherapy. It is not an accident that there is strong Catholic interest in Husserliana, or that phenomenology has influenced psychoanalysts, both Lacanian and otherwise (Husserl, *passim*; Farber 1966; Kockelmans 1967; Koestenbaum 1978).

The idea seems to be that a descriptive approach to the essential structure of experience, or of being, or of the world, will not need to use pre-existing categories such as subject and object; it will, rather, offer the data out of which such philosophical categories are constructed. Thus, experience is given as intentional; that is to say, consciousness is always consciousness of something; I, for example am conscious of a table, and the table is an object for me. Our world is in all cases given with an objective and a subjective pole, and we can turn our attention to the objects, or, by reflection, to the subjectivity that experiences them. The two poles of being are strongly interdependent; one might say that objects only exist as objects for some subject; and subjects only in relation to their objects. For this philosophy it would appear – though the point is denied – that the concept of unexperienced being – the being of a stone on an uninhabited world, say – makes no sense; and commonplace scientific concepts, like that of the evolution of consciousness, become densely puzzling.

To the extent that this approach is a valid method of philosophical enquiry at all (as opposed to a private technique for meditation) it seems to me to be a radicalized version of Cartesian doubt; it rests on the assumption that whatever else we deny, we cannot deny the contents of consciousness, simply regarded as contents of consciousness. The question is, in what way do we make these contents available for research into the essential nature of the world and the foundations of our knowledge? Here is a rather oversimplified account, which I think applies to certain periods of Husserl's work. The first stage – the phenomenological reduction – is to bracket, or set aside, the question of the objective existence outside consciousness of the phenomenon being investigated. The second stage is to step back from my own actual empirical consciousness of the phenomenon and view it from the standpoint of a 'transcendental' subjectivity; a pure observer, empty of content or character except for any characteristics which are necessary characteristics of subjectivity as such. This new 'I' will now be able to observe the empirical self's consciousness of the phenomenon.

I return to the example of my word processor, whose screen I am looking at now. It is possible that this word processor doesn't exist; and it is possible that I don't exist; but what is given for transcendental subjectivity as a phenomenon and cannot be denied is my empirical consciousness looking at a screen. It will be seen that I have lost rather little in detail by the double reduction I have performed. Everything that was available before to my observation is available to me now, as content of consciousness, with what is called apodictic certainty. Phenomenology is therefore a very rich philosophy. Scientific hypotheses are rather narrow and over-simplified in comparison with the data they explain; but phenomenology gives us back the whole world, though only in the form of knowledge or human meaning.

But the point, of course, is not to reflect the whole world, but to arrive at essential truths about it, with apodictic certainty. In order to do this we might actually have to use our imagination: imaginatively vary the phenomenon being considered, to find out what was essential to it, and what we could not vary without destroying it. What kind of truth can be discovered in this way? Here is one such truth:

> The essence of consciousness, in which I live as my own self, is the so-called intentionality. Consciousness is always consciousness of something. (Husserl 1967, Paris Lectures, trans. Koestenbaum, pp. 12–13).

There are several obvious criticisms of this approach; the one that impresses me was made by Heidegger (*Being and Time*, 1962, p. 98). The concept of knowledge – as the relationship of a pure consciousness to its objects – is too abstract. We are forgetting the way human beings are. Human Being is being-in-the-world; and it is this that must be explored in detail by philosophy. Thus, using a hammer to put in a nail is as much a part of human activity as thinking about the hammer; it is even, or at least involves, a perfectly valid way of being aware of the hammer, as something ready to hand for the job. Heidegger gives this way of being aware the special technical name of '*umsicht*' – literally, 'looking around'. It is not the same as thinking about the hammer as a thing. We think about the hammer as an entity in its own right only when the job goes wrong!

This kind of approach, with its potential fidelity to the concrete detail of life, offers an even richer account of human experience than Husserl does, though it cannot pretend to offer apodictic certainty. Indeed, it offers many of the qualities of the novel; for there is now no limit to the kinds of human experience and action that one can write about, and call philosophy. Sartre, Heidegger's successor at a distance, actually wrote novels. Back in Oxford in 1954, if you asked about this exciting new philosophy, existentialism, you would be told: 'They aren't philosophers. They write novels.'

A more standard criticism of any approach in this school would be based on the nature of language. It is not possible for any philosopher of this – in my view – subjectivist kind to convey any of his results without putting them into language; and language is essentially a collective phenomenon. The process of putting Husserlian insights into a comprehensible language forces them back into the common existing concepts and, it is suggested, removes the certainty they possess in their subjective and prelinguistic state. I am not convinced by this, or any version I have seen of the 'no private language' argument. Husserl clearly expects everyone to do his own phenomenological research. Language doesn't have to convey all the fine detail of private experience in the first instance; only set people going on the right lines. We can later extend language by a process of successive approximation, to establish in the common public realm experiences which were originally private and unformulated but common to many people. If we cannot do this, how does art criticism, or wine buffery, ever get off the ground?

The Derridean critique of phenomenology goes much deeper than this, though it also involves the concept of language. It turns precisely on the role of language, or signs, in making permanent, public objects out of private phenomena; and it begins, curiously enough, with an analysis of the origin of geometry.

Throughout his life, and in all the changes of his theory, Husserl was concerned with the status of mathematical objects: numbers, geometrical theorems, and so forth. The problem with these is that they appear to be purely subjective, in the sense that they are constructed wholly in thought, and empirical observations do not affect them in any way except as illustrations. But in another sense they are wholly objective. Nothing about the thinker can affect the truth of the thought that two and two is four. Pythagoras may have discovered the theorem that bears his name; but neither he, nor anyone who has since followed it through, has had the power to **make** it valid or invalid. It just **is** valid.

In an early book, *The Philosophy of Arithmetic*, Husserl leaned too far to the position that mathematics was subjective; and was gently demolished in a review by Frege. Thereafter, he accepted the objectivity of the objects of mathematics; but spent his life wondering how they could have been constituted as such, when their initial construction came about subjectively:

> . . . how does the intrapsychically constituted structure arrive at an intersubjective being of its own as an ideal object which, as "geometrical" is anything but a real psychic object, even though it has arisen psychically?
> (Edmund Husserl 1936, 'The Origins of Geometry': in Derrida 1982)

In this late fragment, 'The Origin of Geometry', Husserl gave an answer in terms of language and of writing. A geometrical theorem comes into existence as something self-evident to the geometer; it can be reactivated in its self-evidence on later occasions, but remains intra-psychic – i.e. exists only within a single person's mind – even though repeatable. It becomes intersubjective because language makes it possible for a second person to grasp – that is, reactivate as self-evident – a proof originated by the first; it becomes objective when writing makes it possible for the same self-evidence to be reawakened, many years later, when perhaps the original individuals are dead.

Husserl goes on to represent geometry as the very type of human or spiritual achievements that are built up and handed on in a tradition: such tradition forms the essential history of man. The implication of this is quite stunning. It is that the objective human world – that is, the world containing all those ideal objects constituted by human culture, including not only such entities as works of literature but all the ideal objects of mathematics – is created in or by writing; or perhaps that the possibility of ideal objectivity is created by the possibility of writing things down. (This view is not confined to Husserl: Popper has a rather similar view about his 'world 3' – the world of hypotheses, arguments, etc. that is neither material nor purely subjective. Popper 1972; 1974.)

The importance of this fragment to Derrida's work is obviously very great indeed. It enables us to see what is otherwise quite puzzling: why Derrida attached philosophical importance to writing, and came to see it as something that constitutes a world. In his *Edmund Husserl's Origin of Geometry: an Introduction* (1962) and in other work on Husserl – in particular *Speech and Phenomena* (1967a) which is a study of Husserl's theory of the sign – Derrida came to make a fundamental distinction of a philosophical nature between speech and writing as **metaphysical** categories: a category of speech in which the sign seems to have the immediate presence of human intentions in it, versus a category of writing in which the sign is detached from the intentions of any particular sign user. Derrida came, indeed, to write the history of philosophy in terms of the relative philosophical priority given to these two. Throughout the history of Western thought, according to Derrida, there has been a repression of writing in favour of speech; and the reason for this is that speech is taken to give transparent access to immediately self-evident experience; while writing is something detached from immediate experience, and its meaning is not guaranteed by the presence of the speaker.

There are several criticisms to be made of this; the main problem is what order to put them in. I think the most basic objection is to the fundamental Husserlian claim that mathematics is constituted as objective by writing, or even by the abstract possibility of writing. There are three features of mathematics for which every theory of it must account. The most important of them is its internal validity. The second is that some parts of it are self-evident, at least to suitably qualified people. The third is that it applies to the real, physical and social world. What Husserl must do is to explain the first feature – internal validity – and the third – physical applicability – on the basis of the second – self-evidence. And I do not see how he can possibly do this.

Let me return to the word processor. This is a machine that depends on the application of a mathematical theory. When it reformats a paragraph, what it is really doing is calculating how to arrange the words and what spaces to insert. The mathematics is valid, in the sense of following the correct rules; if it weren't, the program would not work properly. The mathematics of this program is simple, and within my capacity; if I were to examine it carefully enough, I would find it self-evident. The program makes a physical machine work reliably to do the job it is designed for. On Husserl's principles, the firm ground here is self-evidence; and objective validity is something that arises because we can put things in writing. But this simply will not do. I can put anything in writing, but only if I follow the objectively correct rules (which I have to discover) will I produce a part of the unique valid system that is mathematics; and I can do that in some cases without writing. Finally, no explanation whatever is offered for the fact that the machine works! Even Husserl doesn't suggest that physical machines work because of the invention of writing.

Jacques Derrida is the most subtle critic of Husserl who has ever lived; I would not dream of arguing with him on that subject. But his work remains within the problematic of Husserl: he deconstructs from within. In the end, the privilege accorded to immediate, uncontradictable experience has gone; that is all part of the metaphysics of presence. The privileged position of voice has gone (though I am not sure it was ever quite as prominent in Husserl as Derrida suggests). But writing remains – modified, for its new position, and by some new arguments, but with very much the same world-creating function that Husserl gave to it. And as far as I can see, nothing whatever has been done to make it capable of creating the ideal-mathematical or the physical world: it is no better than Husserl's version at that.

It seems to me that this is a fundamental weakness, not simply in

Husserl or Derrida, but in the nineteenth-century idealist, the phenomenological and the existential traditions of philosophy. Once accept the ontological priority of the subject – or of experienced being (like the experience of understanding a theorem) – over unexperienced being (like the theorem itself, or the system of which it forms part, or some physical machine like the brain in which it might be incorporated) – and there is no dialectic by which you can wriggle out into the real physical world again. Is there an alternative position? Well, there was one proposed during the High Structuralist period; and I want to repropose it, even though it requires, in the sense given above, a logocentric metaphysics. I think we can regard mathematics as the study of the infinite set of all possible structures; science as the investigation of which of them are real; and subjectivity as a side-effect of objective structures. It was probably this objectivist vision that drove structuralism when it was at its height. Notoriously, it is Derrida more than anyone who is responsible for undermining this vision.

4 MISREADING SAUSSURE

The greatest philosophical achievement of Jacques Derrida is supposed to have been to show that the same ubiquitous metaphysics, the metaphysics of presence, that underlies phenomenology and existential philosophy, also underlies structuralism; and thus to undermine the scientific pretensions of structuralism. For this purpose the founding text of structuralism, Saussure's *Cours de Linguistique Générale*, was analysed and what is usually taken as its most 'scientific' aspect – the phonology – was subjected to particular scrutiny. A critical step here was to show the existence of a metaphysical tradition of phonocentrism, alongside of or united with logocentrism, and governing all Western thought.

Phonocentrism means something much stronger than the commonplace observation that some people, at some time – Romantic poets, Hebrew prophets, for example – have thought that an inner voice gives contact with God; just as others have thought that an inner light gives such contact, and others that it is to be found in sacred books, or rituals, or dances, or peculiar physical exercises. Phonocentrism means the universal metaphysical privileging of speech over writing as the authentic vehicle of meaning and truth; it is supposed to dominate the entire conceptual tradition of the West, and to be present even in our use of alphabetic writing. Derrida convicts

Saussure of phonocentrism, and attempts to show from Saussure's own text that a kind of writing – an 'arche-writing' is presupposed by both speech and writing. (This kind of reversal is known as 'deconstruction'.)

Derrida has to face two problems here – a philosophical problem in mapping the phenomenological conception of the sign on to the linguist's conception; and a historical one. The philosophical problem is that while it is true that Saussure's 'sign' is a combination of . sound-image and concept-about-the-world, Saussure, with his fundamental principle of the arbitrariness of the sign, explicitly denies that the meaning is inherent in, or in any sense constituted by, the sound. Moreover, the sign for Saussure belongs to *langue*; it is a part of a pre-existing social store of sound-image/concept combinations and it doesn't represent any intention or idea in any subjectivity until it is used in *parole*. Husserl, however, doesn't have a concept of *langue* – few philosophers did – and seems to think of writing and speech alike as processes in some subjectivity. Finally, both sound-image and concept are for Saussure determined by purely conventional systems of oppositions with other signs; and not the same system of oppositions either; the principle later known as double articulation is already clear enough in the text. There is hardly any logical space for inserting **presence** into this theory. Really, Saussure's signs are intended to do a different job from Husserl's; something like helping us to write grammars of Modern French; they have to be forcibly conscripted into the philosophy of the subject.

The historical problem that Derrida has to face – and his followers often magnificently ignore – is that there is no evidence whatever that phonocentrism in this strong sense exists, or ever has existed. What the historical record shows is that in civilizations – at least since Ancient Egypt, from which we have an eloquent document about the wonderful privileges of being a scribe – writing, that is, ordinary, empirical, worldly, everyday writing, has been privileged in every possible way over speech. In every possible way: books have always been thought of as more authoritative than speeches, even to the point of having magic powers; literate people have had political privileges over illiterate ones, even to the point of escaping with a penance when their fellow men were hanged. Compared with the mass of evidence against phonocentrism, there is not much for it. Voice has never been systematically privileged over writing; the case is, rather, that a few important thinkers have protested at the privileging of writing over speech. Derrida trawls through the whole of intellectual history and picks up such items as Plato grumbling that you can't ask questions of a book. (This is a slightly unfair summary, but much less unfair than Derrida's account.)

What makes the point even more striking is that logocentrism and phallocentrism certainly do exist. If logocentrism means the desire to talk consistently about, and act on consistent assumptions about, the real world – i.e. rationality – then it is surely true that the whole of Western thought has evolved under the partial control of this metaphysical category. And a very good thing too; the alternative is irrationality. And if you believe in any version of Freudian theory, phallocentrism is a condition of being socialized; the only alternative is to be a schizophrenic, and only Deleuze and Guattari are in favour of that. But there is no evidence for phonocentrism; it has to be manufactured, by applying deconstructive arguments to Saussure, to an essay by Lévi-Strauss which says that writing is a device for political dominance, and to an essay by Rousseau, *On the Origin of Languages*, which takes no very decisive stand either way.

The crucial text in which these arguments are set out is a very curious one; it is called *Of Grammatology* and, as I have already said, it appears by title to be a satire on proposals for a science of semiology: a vast book on a pseudo-science of marks to mock the efforts of those who thought they were working on a real science of signs. But most of the arguments in *Of Grammatology* are serious enough, once one has adjusted to the phenomenological perspective Derrida takes for granted as the only possible philosophy.

The method known as 'deconstruction' is particularly powerful within this framework. Phenomenological and existential accounts of the world are often heavily descriptive and metaphorical and rely on this for much of their force. It is characteristic of the deconstructive method to pick out ways in which the presuppositions of an argument undermine the argument; or in which rhetorical procedures, which are essential to the presentation of some doctrine, undermine the doctrine. It will be seen that this is a looser version of the standard argument form called *reductio ad absurdum*, in which a theory is refuted by drawing self-contradictory conclusions from it. I personally think that deconstruction is valid only when it does entail a *reductio*; and it often does, when the argument is phenomenological and metaphysical. But deconstruction is never very convincing when it is applied to science or engineering. Expositions of these are full of dead metaphors inconsistent with current theory, and nobody cares much. The atomic theory wasn't refuted when somebody split the atom, even though 'atom' means 'unsplittable'.

The three texts considered in *Of Grammatology* are of rather different kinds. The Rousseau is a speculative philosophical essay comparable to the Husserl essay mentioned earlier. It is safe to say that Rousseau knew no more about the origin of languages than did Husserl about the origin of geometry. Deconstruction as a method bites very well on speculative philosophy of this kind. And the Lévi-Strauss is more political polemic than anthropology. The Saussure text, however, is a very different matter. It is a series of university lectures giving an elementary introduction to a science about which a great deal is already known. It contains an immense amount of factual detail. Its philosophy consists largely of a set of methodological proposals for reconstituting and developing that science – proposals which had been very successfully followed out by the time Derrida was writing. We have here the basic ingredients of the metaphysician's nightmare: that his philosophy will come to contradict the findings of an established science on some matter of fact. And – although he is careful to say that he is not questioning the right of a scientist, on the empirical level, to say what he needs to say – this in the end, in my view, is exactly what Derrida does.

What Derrida is entitled to do, by his method, is to consider the categorial foundations of the proposed science of linguistics in order to establish what metaphysical commitments they involve. There are several of these he might look at. There is, for example, the definition of the sign as an arbitrary pair of signifier and signified. There is the sharp distinction between language, as a collection of signs, and speaking or writing as the use of them. There is the distinction between the synchronic study of a language as a system, and the diachronic study of its history. There is even the division within the synchronic study of language between the syntagmatic and the associative axes of connection. Each of these technical concepts has a genuine metaphysical dimension which would repay analysis. But rather than any of these, Derrida picked out for stress the one major distinction that is not part of the founding apparatus of linguistics as a science, being as familiar to laymen, or philosophers, as to linguists: the distinction between speaking and writing.

The reason that he thought this distinction of importance presumably lies in the world-constituting functions that speech and writing, under very different and philosophically essentialist definitions, have in phenomenology. They have no particular philosophical significance in linguistics; linguistics as a science, set up on the basis of the categorial distinctions above, is interested not in the putative world-creating functions of speaking or writing, and not even in the relative proximity of the signs used in them to the intentions of a putative speaker/writer – for the linguistics of *langue* is not concerned with intentions at all – but in the internal grammatical and other structures that speech and writing have. For this purpose linguists can study either speech, or writing, or both; nothing in the categorial constitution of the science raises speech above writing in the way that *langue* is raised above *parole*. But linguists do have a lot to say about the relation between the two; and one of the things they have to say is that the spoken language is the primary object of study in linguistics, writing being a merely derivative and secondary form.

Their basis for saying this is a factual one. Languages have been spoken for perhaps a quarter of a million years (that is my guess based on physical evidence – an analysis of the evolution of the vocal tract, Lieberman 1975); but writing has been around for only a few thousand. Most languages don't have writing systems. Even where they do, people always learn the spoken language first, and sometimes don't learn to write at all. Like everyone else who has taught linguistics, I have made these points to my first-year students. Saussure made them at great length and with vigour; and every incautious word was paraded by Derrida as solid evidence for phonocentrism. For if one thing seemed certain to Derrida, it was that Saussure couldn't be getting that excited about a matter of fact. 'The tone counts,' he said. Everyone knows people get excited only over metaphysics.

If you put the text of Saussure back into its original context you can see a rather better reason to get excited. Saussure is giving a course of lectures to students of philology. Philologists are people who study old texts in order to describe the history of languages. A very substantial part of their work is describing sound changes. The laws governing sound changes apply to the spoken language. But the evidence the philologist is considering exists in written texts. He is therefore under constant temptation to identify the language he is studying with the written form, and this will lead him to make mistakes in his scientific work. Many professors do get excited about things that cause their students to make mistakes, and go on about them at great length in lectures. As I said earlier, people in factual sciences do get excited about facts.

Derrida's distortion of Saussure's original intentions is very great here, and I think quite inexcusable. It amounts to a big lie, which is believed because no one can imagine why it should have been told. Why should anyone say that Saussure is a philosopher with a metaphysical prejudice against writing if it is not true? To this day, linguists who have read Saussure find themselves hopelessly explaining the facts of the case to incredulous literary critics, who have not read

Saussure and can't believe that an important philosopher should have told such whoppers about him. And nonsensical lies about Saussure are routinely written into literature syllabuses and philosophy syllabuses.

Derrida's next move is to show how Saussure subverts his own position by privileging writing above speech. Saussure does this, according to Derrida, when he explains what phonemes are. The phoneme is supposed to be the fundamental linguistic unit, and the letter of the alphabet is merely a representation of it. Yet when Saussure wants to make the concept of the phoneme understood, he explains it in terms of letters of the alphabet. Does this not undermine the priority of speech? I think this must be one of the worst arguments Derrida puts forward. The phoneme is supposed to be a more fundamental unit than the letter, not a more familiar one. When you are explaining things, you explain unfamiliar things in terms of familiar ones: atoms in terms of billiard balls, for example, not billiard balls in terms of atoms. But that doesn't stop billiard balls being made of atoms. The reason that the letters of the alphabet are not a bad model for the phoneme is that the invention of the alphabet was a partial discovery of the phonemic structure of language. But language would still have a phonemic structure even if no human being had ever discovered the fact, and even if no alphabet had ever been invented. The existence of phonemic structure is a condition for the invention of alphabetic writing; but the existence of alphabetic writing is not a condition for the existence of phonemic structure, though it certainly helps people to become conscious that language has such a structure.

Let us be clear about the probable history of the phoneme and something rather different, the concept of the phoneme. Human language differs from other animal call systems, we might say, in being doubly articulated, at morphemic and phonemic levels; and this probably developed during the Neanderthal period, from half a million to fifty thousand years ago. Writing systems based on these two forms of articulation – ideographic systems on the one hand, and syllabic and phonemic systems on the other – were developed in the period of early civilizations, from six to two millennia ago. Phoneme theory – the developed concept of the phoneme – developed out of the work of Saussure and others in the twentieth century; but it has its roots in thousands of years of grammatical study and has no doubt been influenced by the existence of alphabets. On the other hand, if the phoneme itself exists at all – that is, if language has a phonemic structure – it exists independently of the alphabetic signs that represent it.

When a clever philosopher puts forward a really bad argument, it is worth examining his possible reasons for mistake: they may reveal the problems of an entire philosophical framework. Why should Derrida, and his very sophisticated followers like Rodolphe Gasché quoted below, suppose that Saussure has undermined the scientific status of the phoneme by explaining it in terms of letters of the alphabet? It derives, I think, from considering linguistics as a phenomenological study in Husserl's sense. Because the data of linguistics are indeed entities present to consciousness, it is supposed that the fundamental structures of linguistics must be structures – transcendental ones, perhaps? – uncovered by phenomenological enquiry. Just as the fundamental structures of geometry, for Husserl, become objective structures only through the agency of writing, so the fundamental structures of phonology become objective only through the agency of a kind of writing – here embodied in the alphabet.

But in fact the linguist's method of analysing the distribution of phonemes is not at all the same as a phenomenological analysis, and it rests on a quite different metaphysical assumption: namely, that the underlying structures of language exist objectively, and independently of the phenomenological facts which they serve to explain. Jakobson and Halle begin their little book *Fundamentals of Language* (1956) with an introduction at a New York party: 'Mr Ditter' says the host. He might have said Bitter, Chitter, Sitter, Kitter, etc.; and each of these words would have been instantly recognised as a distinct name within the language spoken. The postulation that there is a set of phonemes, /b/, /ch/, /s/, /k/, etc., is a hypothesis intended to explain this fact, and is logically independent of the existence of any writing system that might represent those phonemes. The metaphysical assumption here is that the language spoken can have an objective underlying structure of which the speakers are not necessarily conscious at all, but which explains what they are conscious of, and what they can say. This is closely parallel to the metaphysical assumptions behind physics.

Jakobson's feature theory – that the contrast between /b/ and /d/, for example, is an effect of a distinctive feature of pronunciation, namely closing the vocal tract at one end rather than in the middle – is a further hypothesis intended to explain the behaviour of phonemes. Both phonemes and distinctive features are hypothetical entities meant to explain a contingent feature of consciousness and human activity – the ability to recognize and produce linguistic expressions. But phonemes are only partially accessible to consciousness, and features are not directly accessible at all; they are physiological and acoustic entities. Closing the vocal tract at one end rather than in the middle produces rather deeper resonances. This makes it possible to tell phonemes like /b/ apart from phonemes like /d/ when we hear them. Again the metaphysical assumption is that these physiological and acoustic properties are independent of consciousness, though they help to explain some of the contents of consciousness.

Philologists use written texts as evidence, but form hypotheses about changes in the sound system of a language over perhaps thousands of years. The underlying assumption is that it is possible for languages to have existed over long periods of time, in which every generation has acquired a sound-system by hearing the preceding generation talk; and has been enabled to talk recognizably by having acquired that sound-system. The metaphysical assumption again is of the possibility of the objective existence of languages in the past, independently of our enquiries into them. The assumptions that philologists make about the derivative relation of the written form of the language to the spoken form, and about the problems of making inferences from surviving texts to past languages, are not metaphysical but empirical; and they are based on a good deal of empirical evidence.

Derrida finally proposes a new sort of writing – arche-writing – from which both the phonological and the graphological elements in some sense derive. This is admittedly not part of linguistics; it has no function within linguistics. And it is not to be thought of as having some site of its own. It is, rather, another of these non-concepts, like *différance*, trace, hinge, etc., designed to jam up our metaphysics; yet it communicates, in a way entirely mysterious, with 'the vulgar concept of writing' and there is no doubt it will play a central role in the non-science of grammatology when that comes not to be written.

It is very difficult to comment on this from a linguist's point of view; what it seems to be is a metaphysical transcription of the fact that *parole* – that is, either speaking or writing a language – is dependent on *langue* – that is, on the structure of the language. But why should the structure of a language – the system of German irregular verbs, for example – be described as writing, or arche-writing, or be supposed to connect with the vulgar concept of writing more than it does with the vulgar concept of speaking? I suppose one might draw vaguely on the artificial-intelligence metaphor again, and say that the structure of the language must in some sense be written on the brain.

There is, I think, only one way of rescuing the arche-writing hypothesis into some sort of sense. One might say that it belongs to a phenomenological history of twentieth-century linguistic theory rather than to a phenomenological history of language. The claim would then have to be put as follows: that it wouldn't be possible to understand such a concept as that of the phoneme unless we already had at least an archetypal notion of writing. This is not an easily testable claim, since modern linguistics, like other modern sciences, developed in a society that had been literate for thousands of years. The Jakobson and Halle example quoted earlier suggests that it is false, since it suggests a way of explaining phoneme theory without assuming a literate audience.

What is clear, however, is that a poverty-stricken notion of arche-writing like this – amounting to no more than a tacit expectation that language has some structural units that can be represented by signs – will not do the rhetorical job for which Derrida needs his concept of Writing. Much of the evidence for phonocentrism – if there is to be evidence for phonocentrism – must apply to the ordinary sense of writing, and make reference to social institutions within which people are, or are not, prejudiced against it. Furthermore, Writing in one sense Derrida needs – the sense of *Writing and Difference* – seems to cover the whole field of human creativity. The notion of the Text plays much the same part in the later work of Derrida and the critics who have followed him. These larger metaphysical metaphors obviously resist analysis of the kind I have pursued so far.

After this, it will seem surprising that there are some writers, like Christopher Norris, who see *Of Grammatology* as one of Derrida's 'rigorous' works. Where is the rigour? To some extent it is in the eye of the beholder. Here, for example, is an account of the argument I have just summarized by a philosopher who holds that deconstruction 'reveals, to even a superficial examination, a well-ordered procedure, a step-by-step type of argumentation based on an acute awareness of level-distinctions, a marked thoroughness and regularity' (Rodolphe Gasché 1985); and adds that:

> The inconsistencies characteristic of the level of philosophical
> argumentation can best be illustrated by the discrepancies in philosophical
> texts between the philosopher's explicit declaration of what he wishes to
> argue and how he argues in fact – for instance, between Saussure's
> declaration that writing must be condemned and his simultaneous
> assignment of writing to a predominant, even constitutive role when
> determining the structure of speech. Or when Plato argues in writing that
> writing must be reprehended. (Ibid.)

But as we have seen, the 'discrepancies' are here invented by Derrida and do not exist in Saussure. Saussure did not 'condemn' writing for metaphysical reasons, and he did not assign it a constitutive role when determining the structure of speech. The only explanation I can find for this kind of judgement is that the philosophers concerned simply do not read the texts that Derrida is deconstructing. Perhaps they are in too much of a hurry to rush on to the really thrilling bits where the non-concepts come, and where we get accounts of the world that are meant to be only a hair's breadth away from metaphysics without ever falling into it. For me, this kind of thing fulfils one traditional definition of metaphysics as news from nowhere. It seems entirely vacuous.

In the meantime, however, something rather important hasn't been done. Derrida has not provided a rigorous argument, or any sort of argument, that undermines the scientificity of linguistics, or shows that it has the same metaphysical bases as phenomenology. If high structuralism wasn't pursued after Derrida, it wasn't because he had provided an argument that undermined it. It was because people didn't want to pursue it. What they wanted were the self-undermining aporias of post-structuralism; and to believe that Derrida has provided rigorous arguments to justify them: his mythical role has been that of provider of rigorous arguments to justify what is in fact a variety of textual mysticism. Meanwhile, the man himself went on to a new phase in which he began, more and more, to enact his arguments and positions rather than present them. This is the philosopher as modernist writer, poising himself to write in the non-existent space between rationality and irrationality; it is to this phase that works like *Glas* and *The Post-Card* belong.

5   ENACTING PHILOSOPHY

Despite my own scepticism, I once found myself in the bizarre position of having to defend Derrida against the objections of an analytical philosopher. My colleague's argument was simple: Derrida wasn't a philosopher at all, since he didn't, in the text under discussion – Derrida 1977b *Limited Inc abc* – present any arguments. My reply had to be that in that text the arguments were there all right, even if Derrida wasn't stating them: he was enacting them. The philosophical exchange in *Limited Inc* was with John Searle, doyen of speech-act philosophy; and Searle had argued that there are rules for the normal, serious use of language. In reply Derrida was, laboriously and at great length, violating all those rules. The result is to split the philosophical world into two camps: those who say that by doing this Derrida is ceasing to use language normally and seriously and therefore ceasing to be a philosopher; and those who say that he is undermining, and showing the philosophical inadequacy of, the concepts of normality and seriousness.

One might say that Derrida could perfectly well have raised his questions in abstract terms, keeping enactment in its usual place as part of the odd philosophical example. I used to recommend to my students of semantics (in a joint linguistics degree) a series of classic articles that opened these issues: Frege, 'On Sense and Reference'; Russell, 'On Denoting'; Strawson, 'On Referring'; and Searle's little book on *Speech Acts* theory. If we make Derrida follow straight on from that lot, it is a bit like having a man come into an academic conference and symbolically saw the legs off the table. A fine joke and a liberating experience? Possibly. But what if he does it very, very slowly, and with intense pedantry, with a nail file?

Why should Derrida have to enact his arguments rather than presenting them? Well, if his argument is intended to undermine certain conventions of discourse, there would be a kind of practical absurdity in presenting it in accordance with those conventions, and therefore strengthening them. It is impossible to present, say, a rational argument against rationality without falling into a practical self-contradiction. In a sense the most serious thing you can do is to don cap and bells, and stand upside down on your hands, balancing a pair of flatfish on your feet. Or, in this case, since he is actually doing something slightly more subtle than argue against rationality, to misspell Searle's name as 'SARL'.

It is relevant here to consider Derrida's early review (1967b) of Foucault's *Madness and Civilisation*, in which he questioned the very possibility of presenting unreason from the point of view of the mad. By violating a convention and yet communicating, Derrida shows that that particular convention is not a logical prerequisite for communication; though one might argue that the existence of that convention is a logical prerequisite for violating it, and it is the violation of the convention that is here doing the communicating. Derrida would presumably regard this as an example of the way we are all trapped in logocentrism in the end.

My sympathies are not with Derrida here. I think that there is, and must be for human survival, a normal serious register of language use, which is the one you use to buy the groceries or deal with a traffic accident; and don't see why that shouldn't be the language of philosophy. I think there are also playful or non-serious uses of language; and they appear in literature though not only there. It is in literature too that we expect to find philosophical problems – and not only philosophical problems: moral problems, social problems, religious problems, general intellectual problems – acted out in play. So it is not surprising that the general drift of Derrida's work has been towards literature: and towards blurring the line between philosophy and literature; and his influence has been to create a school of literary critics who also wish to blur that line.

Why should one object to this? We are moving here towards matters of taste rather than of reasoning; so I will shift to a more personal voice. I don't object in principle. The blend of philosophy and literature is hardly new: Plato is both. I fell in love with James Joyce and with Bertrand Russell in the same year, when I was sixteen; and still liked teaching both of them twice as many years later. What is then wrong with a fresh treatment of the paradoxes of set-inclusion and self-reference, of language use and language mention, using all the techniques that literary modernism can devise to enact all the problems that philosophy of language has discussed? Only, I think, the immense tedium of books as long as *Ulysses*; as difficult to follow as *Principia Mathematica*; and having a content certainly no more substantial than 'On Denoting'.

The problem, in short, is that enactment, in Derrida, takes a long time, is very obscure, and seems to say very little in proportion to the time it takes. Analytic statement, in Frege, in Russell, in Strawson and in Searle, says more, in less time, and with crystal clarity. But this is not a necessity of the literary form of expression. Few philosophers could be shorter or more epigrammatic than Nietzsche.

And yet, in a sense, all this misses the essential point. Why would people read him if he were as I say? People read a philosopher if he manages, by whatever method he chooses to employ, to involve them in his central question. So what is Derrida's central question? When I first read him I found myself remarking: 'The metaphysics of presence plays the same part in the work of Jacques Derrida as does sin in some seventeenth century divine. Constantly detected, repented of, and banished, it as constantly reappears in undreamed-of forms' (Jackson 1982). I was wrong to think of it as sin: at that time, I assumed that Derrida was hostile to **presence**. But I had the theological structure exactly right. One knows what Derrida's question is if one asks oneself: Whose presence is missing? Who left that trace? Who made the *différance*? Who did the writing? Perhaps it should be What rather than Who; I don't see any evidence that Derrida is concerned with a personal God. But a negative theology is exactly what I do see.

6   THE DIASPORA OF 'THEORY'

It was in the 1960s that structuralism began to be imported in appreciable quantities into what in many ways was a different critical continent: Anglo-America; structuralism and post-structuralism travelled in the same cargoes, and have ever since remained inextricably mixed up together.

Or to translate the metaphor: the work of all five of our major figures, and later others like Kristeva, was discussed at the same academic conferences, and ideas of the 1950s, 1960s and 1970s freely, and often very confusingly, combined. The resultant mash of theory was in Britain seen in conflict with Eliotic and Leavisite conservative orthodoxies, and was heavily political in flavour; to this day it counts as a major victory for left-wing politics if you succeed in changing the university curriculum – firing the canon, it is called – and these are the only victories the left has had, for as long as anyone can remember. In America the new theory was largely in conflict and synthesis with New Critical positions, and my impression is that it was slightly less political.

One of the most important of the conferences was that held at Johns Hopkins University in October 1966, and briefly mentioned in the last chapter: it was called grandly *The Languages of Criticism and the Sciences of Man: The Structuralist Controversy* (Macksey and Donato 1970). All Paris moved to Baltimore for this one; Lucien Goldmann, Roland Barthes, Jean Hyppolite, Jacques Lacan, Jacques Derrida and others all on the same platform. It is hard to overestimate its importance: this was the conference at which de Man met Derrida. Moreover, this seminar inaugurated a two-year programme of seminars and colloquia. In economic terms, this can fairly be described as the large-scale, well-funded import programme that my first metaphor implied. Nor was Baltimore the only American port to be active in the decades to follow.

The name given to this confused mass of ideas has varied a great deal. At first it was called 'structuralist' thought. The term 'post-structuralism' emerged along with others as the extreme inappropriateness of the name 'structuralism' for work influenced by, for example, Derrida became more apparent. Clear definitions of these positions were not achieved and not much sought. As Macksey and Donato put it:

> By focusing attention on the structuralist phenomenon, the organisers
> were not seeking to promote a manifesto nor even to arrive at a fixed and
> unambiguous definition of structuralism itself. To many observers there
> seemed already to be too many manifestos, while satisfactory definitions of
> such polymorphic activities, or cultural events, are generally only achieved
> after the principals are safely dead. The danger was clearly that of
> deforming a method or a family of methods into a doctrine.
>
> (Macksey and Donato 1970, p. ix)

I am sure there is some truth in this; I am aware that my own concern with getting it clear what structuralism and post-structuralism are is closely connected with my hope that they will both be recognized as dead. But the danger here foreseen was not the only one. There was also the greater danger of never getting it clear what these theories were, what claims they made, whether they were compatible with each other, and whether they were true. I certainly think it is a pity nobody noticed that structuralism proper, in the sense of the productive literary–theoretical programme which had flourished since 1928, had just died. But the various post-structuralisms were due to flourish exceedingly.

More recently the names given to this body of ideas have included 'literary theory' (which marks the fact that it is the literature departments that have been most enthusiastic about psychoanalysts like Lacan and philosophers like Derrida); or 'textual theory'; or even, with what might seem breathtaking arrogance, simply 'theory'. This last practice reminds one of the character who appeared on a satirical TV programme billed simply as 'an expert'. Not an expert on anything in particular, but just a general-purpose expert. Literature departments have of course always been full of experts of this kind; and not from personal arrogance; it is a necessary platform for launching certain types of general cultural criticism; and that criticism is itself culturally necessary. As we have seen, the correct name for anything general enough to be called simply 'theory' is metaphysics; and Danto has recognised this in a recent article (Danto 1989). Theory is the current metaphysics of cultural and literary criticism.

There are no universally held principles or total summations of 'theory'; but it has a recognizable identity arising out of the tradition from which it came. People originally took their own elements from the great gurus, and made their own syntheses. One took ideas from the big five; criticized and reinterpreted (or frankly rewrote) thinkers of earlier phases in the light of these; formed new syntheses of Saussure (as a philosopher), Marx and Freud with a philosophical tradition running (as one would expect) through Husserl and Heidegger, but also including a new major philosopher of a very different kind: Nietzsche. There are many doctoral theses on this pattern.

Some syntheses are mainly political. An influential one in England (though it is delphically obscure) has been that of R. Coward and J. Ellis, *Language and Materialism* (1977). This was adopted as a theoretical framework by Catherine Belsey for her book *Critical Practice* (1980), and its ideas are present in a number of other books and articles. Coward and Ellis take their structuralism from Saussure – in the radically reinterpreted version – and combine it with a semiology taken from Barthes, a Marxism from Althusser, and a psychology from Lacan, here seen through Althusser's eyes. This involves several theoretical elisions. It is discussed in chapter 7. Positions like this remain influential, though Foucault is much more important than Althusser nowadays. Lacan remains important, particularly for feminists who like the challenge of making him non-sexist.

This synthesis is not the only one, and perhaps is not typical. The United States is far more important nowadays than Britain and France put together in the world production of theory; this is one of the areas in which it is least likely to be overtaken by Japan. And few American theorists are, like Jameson, Marxist. What they are defies short summary; even the Yale Mafia cannot be reduced to a single deconstructionist model. But what I chiefly notice is the influence of Jacques Derrida in a powerful mystique of Writing; and some of the most persuasive special pleading ever published, to convince a sympathetic academic world of just how impossibly difficult it is ever to read a text.

7   THE METAPHYSICS OF THE TEXT

It is no part of my intention, in this last short section of a rather long chapter, to attack the modern critical practice of two continents. Instead, I shall confine myself to offering one criticism of one school of theory: American literary deconstruction. This is a school which has the rather contradictory public image of (1) being rigorously, even frighteningly philosophical, in its basis, and yet (2) consisting in practice of obviously wild interpretations and random wordplay. Its self-image is rather different from that: its practitioners see it as the most rigorous possible mode of rhetorical analysis, ever vigilant against metaphysical seductions (Hartman 1989; Hillis Miller 1989). I shall argue that it is neither of these. It is not a rigorous development of Derrida's philosophy; it is only sometimes wild interpretation and random wordplay; but it is, in my view, in its central inspiration, an idealist metaphysics of the text.

One might summarize the public image of deconstruction as follows. It begins with the negative proposition that there is no definitive unitary meaning to a text, for an analytical process like that of the old New Critics to find. There is instead an endless process of dissemination of meaning, and subversion of familiar meaning. To capture (or liberate) this, the text is treated as a pre-text for further writing; in which all the resources of modernism – in particular, Joycean wordplay – may be used to enact the critic's meaning. This school is thus as freely impressionistic in its approach to criticism as the school of Walter Pater, though the tone is different.

There appear to be no philosophical arguments in Derrida's early work that provide a philosophical foundation for the positions of such a school (see Harrison 1983 for a cogent argument). Some philosophers have therefore argued that the whole school is based, as it were, on a gigantic misunderstanding; that the philosophical positions in, say, *Dissemination* have been wildly over-generalized. But this seems implausible in view of the close personal associations of Derrida with some of the most prominent critics of the school; and the seamless way in which his own work fits, along with those of his followers, in an anthology like Hartman's *Deconstruction and Criticism* (1979a). If he misunderstands the bearings of his own theories, who shall correct him?

Perhaps the most important thing to say about the critics of this school is that they were very good before they ever became deconstructionist; and what they were good at was close reading. Deconstruction as a method didn't add to this skill in any way at all; on the contrary, deconstruction was so acceptable because it is essentially a method of close reading and the Americans were already skilled at that (de Man 1986, interview with Rosso). In America, this school probably ought to be called 'post-new-criticism'; it differs from New Criticism in its controlling ideology, and in admitting certain methods which that would have rejected. Derrida's approach has contributed to this school in at least two rather different ways, which are perhaps best illustrated by the work of Paul de Man, and that of Geoffrey Hartman.

What de Man has taken from Derrida is the deconstructive method. Derrida used this to show how the rhetoric of a philosophical argument undermines the argument itself. De Man does much the same for literature; and he comes to see literature and criticism alike as virtually defined by their self-undermining quality. The continuity of this with New Criticism is perhaps shown most clearly in the opening chapter of de Man (1979a), *Allegories of Reading*; a work which started out as a historical study of Nietzsche and Rousseau, and ended up as a theory of reading. De Man begins by acknowledging that 'the spirit of the times is not blowing in the direction of formalism and intrinsic criticism'; people want to move to the external, referential and public aspects of texts. After all, 'from a technical point of view, very little has happened in American criticism since the innovative works of New Criticism'.

Fortunately, however, the French cavalry was at hand. In literary semiology a New Formalism was available which provided far more to research into than anybody had thought possible: as well as offering philosophical tensions between, for example, grammar and rhetoric which are, literally, undecidable. We can therefore happily postpone – indefinitely – the move into the world outside the text. (In 1989 Hartman and Hillis Miller were still fighting this fight.) I find myself greatly admiring the care of de Man's analysis, and valuing the way in which he refuses, like some structuralists, to collapse the rhetorical to the grammatical level of analysis. I am less happy with the actual rhetoric employed – see chapter 2 for some doubts about the use of Jakobsonian metaphor and metonymy. But when I find the social theories of Rousseau turned into questions of reading and 'the political destiny of man structured like and derived from a linguistic model' I still, after some years, find it difficult to believe.

De Man was a distinguished critic who had important things to say about Nietzsche and Rousseau. And there is in a sense nothing wrong in the habit of interpreting every work of literature as an allegory of the process of reading it. Indeed, in the last chapter of this book I argue that all critical interpretation works by taking a work of literature as an allegory of the main interests of the critic. That is what interpretation means. But a critic whose central interest is in the problems of reading is very likely to fetishize reading and its problems. In its solemnity and religious tone, as much as in its insoluble metaphysical paradoxes, the final sentence of de Man's first chapter inaugurates what is properly described as a period of textual mysticism in American Theory:

> Literature as well as criticism – the difference between them being delusive – is condemned (or privileged) to be forever the most rigorous and, consequently, the most unreliable language in terms of which man names and transforms himself.   (de Man 1979a).

It would be possible to provide a rational paraphrase of this sentence, resolving its paradoxes; but in an important sense this would miss the point the sentence is making. De Man is claiming a superior status for the language of literature or criticism, with its paradoxes, ironies and self-deconstructions, to that of the language of philosophy or science. It is in that precise sense that we can see him as inaugurating the work of an **irrationalist** critical school.

De Man, however, doesn't show anything like the rhetorical self-display of, say, Hartman (1981), in which a commentary on Derrida's late work *Glas* is offered very much in the style and spirit of *Glas*. What Hartman does, in *Saving the Text: Literature, Derrida, Philosophy* (1981), is to copy the external properties of the later Derrida work – the incessant wordplay, for example; and comment on *Glas* in as near the style of Glas as he can manage:

> Derridadaism? The illustrious fish, suspended in page or picture, is surely an exmonument or erection, a J(e)(u) "angled with meditation", strangled by the graphic energies that overflow the mirror surface of this doubled and caesuraed page.
>   (Hartman 1981, p. 33. This is actually a comment on a picture by
>   Adami including part of Derrida's signature.)

I am suggesting that this school of theory is an irrationalist one, and I had better explain what I mean by that; it is not simply a crude term of abuse. In my usage, a rational theory, of literature or anything else, is one that makes a consistent set of claims about the world, supported by valid arguments based on sufficient evidence. An irrational theory, on the other hand, is one that makes inconsistent claims, or supports them by invalid arguments, or is not based on evidence. An irrationalist philosophy is one that is in favour of irrational theories, and against rational ones. Derrida himself is a philosopher who very carefully treads the line separating rationality and irrationalism. It is possible to interpret his work as a set of *reductio ad absurdum* arguments directed at particular philosophical claims; or sometimes as a dramatic allegorical enactment of textual problems which undermine those claims. But it is also possible to take him as attacking the whole set of metaphysical ideas that define rationality: the very idea of making claims about the world; the idea of consistency; the idea of validity; the idea of normal conventions; the idea of evidence.

Both perceptions are I think correct; which explains the very different ways in which serious philosophers have taken him. It might be useful to have different names for the two Derridas: perhaps, following Hartman, Derrida and Derridada. It is Derridada who is the model for both sides of the American deconstructive school. De Man is in one sense the most rigorous critic of that school: his detailed textual analyses are as niggling as those of Derrida himself. But his general position is the irrationalist one that literature is the most rigorous language for describing man because it is the most unreliable language. Hartman, on the other hand, produces not grand metaphysical paradoxes, but baroque language play. Neither is aiming at consistency, validity of argument, etc.

Other critics find non-Derridean ways of being irrationalist. Harold Bloom (1979), seeing the whole tradition of poetry as a series of Freudian patricides of a poetic father, seems to find deconstruction the only school extreme enough to be worth arguing with. He doesn't want to talk to moderates; and when some of his critics ask him to clarify his position, retorts that for them, "clarity" is mainly a trope for philosophical reductiveness, or for a dreary literal-mindedness that belies any deep concern for poetry or criticism'. (I hereby identify myself with these philosophically reductive, drearily literal-minded critics; I wouldn't want the deep concern with literature that leads one to mystify it.) Bloom's next step, naturally, is the Kabbalah. Stanley Fish currently seems to believe that there is no such thing as valid argument or evidence, but only persuasion: the thumbscrew school of criticism.

I believe that there is a deep irrationality in positions such as these; but textual metaphysics as such belongs to the deconstructionists. What is the connection of this with Derrida? I believe the true connection between the philosophical and the critical work lies in what might be called the latent negative metaphysics in Derrida's texts. In exposing, or inventing, 'logocentrism', 'phonocentrism' and other features of the 'metaphysical enclosure' within which all Western thought is supposed to have taken place, Derrida has implicitly outlined a metaphysics outside this enclosure: a metaphysics in which texts produce worlds. In this metaphysics, a generalized textuality becomes a master metaphor for the whole of human life; and the dissemination of meaning through this world of text becomes a metaphor for all human experience.

We can see this textual metaphysics quite clearly stated, and related to deconstruction, in J. Hillis Miller (1979, pp. 231-32).

> The place we inhabit, wherever we are, is always this inbetween zone, place of host and parasite, neither inside nor outside. It is a region of the *Unheimlich*, beyond any formalism, which reforms itself wherever we are, if we know where we are. This 'place' is where we are, in whatever text, in the most inclusive sense of the word, we happen to be living. This may be made to appear, however, only by an extreme interpretation of that text, going as far as one can with the terms the work provides. To this form of interpretation, which is interpretation as such, one name given at the moment is 'deconstruction'.

It is this metaphysics which provides the basis for a kind of textual mystification in which it is impossible to extract theories from the texts in which they are stated, and test them against the world; since within this framework there is no world sufficiently outside the text. This would be plausible as a general world view only in a world in which natural science and technology did not exist, and we manipulated things by verbal magic. In the universe of the technologically blind, the literary theorist would be king; which is one reason for believing that all this mystical theory is an elaborate way of escaping from the discourse of the sciences and not explaining anything.

Am I being paranoid here and attributing a kind of mystical megalomania to a set of hard-working critics who are just doing their jobs producing good criticism, and have no ambition to textualize the universe? Well, I have found one critic who makes perfectly explicit claims: Danto (1989), mentioned already in the Introduction. Danto argues, with close attention to some important papers in biology, that the content of science changes perpetually, while the criterion for a beautiful scientific theory is always the same. And – by some leaps of argument that Danto himself characterizes as involving seven- and fourteen-league boots – criticism, in its capacity as the theory of the text, is what can tell us what beautiful science is. Textual criticism is in fact the paradigm human science. 'We had always been taught,' Danto concludes, 'that the last should be first. But who would have suspected metaphysics of becoming once more the queen of the sciences?'

BOOKS

Norris, C. 1987 *Derrida*
Derrida, Jacques 1981 *Positions*. Brief, and for Derrida, accessible.

Derrida 1967a,b,c (see bibliography) are the tryptych that founded Derrida's reputation: comments in chapters 3 and 5; they need considerable philosophical background in Husserl and Heidegger particularly; they are very difficult, but not as impossible as Lacan.

Gasché, Rodolphe 1985 'Infrastructures and Systematicity'. Perhaps the best article on Derridan anti-metaphysics.

FURTHER READING

Metaphysics, Philosophy of Science, etc: Aristotle 330 BC, Aune 1986, Bachelard 1934, Danto 1989, Esposito 1980, Hawking 1988, Kant 1790, Lakatos 1978a,b, Lewin 1987, McKinnon 1974, Mahaffy and Bernard 1889, Margolis 1986, Popper passim, Scruton 1982, Strawson 1966, Walsh 1963.

Logic and the Foundations of Mathematics: Curry 1963, Derrida 1962, Frege 1952, Hilbert and Ackerman 1950, Kneebone 1963, Prior 1962, Quine passim, Russell 1967, Tarski 1944, Tymienecka 1965.

Origins of Language: Lieberman passim, Stam 1976,

Analytical Philosophy and Epistemology: Ayer 1956, de Gelder 1982, Feigl and Sellars 1949, Flew 1956, Frege 1892, Linsky 1952, Russell 1905, Searle 1969, Strawson 1950, 1967, Wittgenstein 1922, 1953.

Hegel: Findlay 1958, 1963, Hegel passim, McTaggart 1910, Royce 1919, Soll 1969, Taylor 1975.

Phenomenology, Existentialism and related approaches: Biemel 1977, Caws 1979, Farber 1966, 1967, Heidegger passim, Husserl passim, Ingarden 1960, Iser 1976, Jaspers 1935, Kockelmans 1967, Kwant 1966, Mays and Brown 1972, Sartre passim, Seung 1982, Spanos 1976, Steiner 1978, Warnock 1970, Waterhouse 1981.

Post-structuralism and Derrida: Culler 1981, 1983, Derrida passim, Descombes 1979, Dews 1987, Gasché 1985, Harrison 1983, Laruelle 1986, Norris passim, Sallis 1987, Searle 1977, Tallis 1988, Ulmer 1985.

Post-structuralism, De Man etc: Bloom 1979, Brenkman 1977, Felman 1977a, b, 1980, Brooks and Felman 1985, Cohen 1989, Danto 1989, de Man passim, Fish 1989, Harari 1979, Hartman G passim, Lentricchia 1980, Miller J Hillis 1979, 1989, Ray 1984, Said

1983, Scholes 1985, Selden 1985, Spanos, Bove and O'Hara 1982, White 1989.

For titles and publishers see main bibliography.

CHAPTER SIX

How Far Do We Construct the World in Language?

Modern Linguistics versus the Myth of de Saussure

SUMMARY

In the aftermath of post-structuralism, Anglo-American literary theory of the 1970s and 1980s, if its comments on language are taken literally, often assumes various forms of linguistic idealism: it argues that reality, or our reality, is constructed in language or discourse; and these theories are attributed to Saussure. It can be shown by comparison with Saussure's text that most of these claims he did not believe; and by arguments from modern linguistics that those he did believe are not true. I argue that all forms of linguistic idealism are false: the material and social worlds are not constructed in language and there is no evidence that language determines the concepts we can develop. There are, however, exciting possibilities in the study of the way in which language influences human thought, provided this study is carried out by way of coherent and empirically testable hypotheses in linguistics and cognitive psychology. For example, it is probably true that the syntactic mechanisms of language have a special part to play in building up complex concepts; and that the structure of metaphors in the dictionary reveals, though it does not constrain, the underlying structures of thought. But in investigating this, there is as much interest to be found, from a technical point of view, in how we ask for a cup of coffee to be passed as in all the linguistic meditations of Heidegger (chapter 1), or in the greatest poetry.

1   LINGUISTIC IDEALISM AND ITS DISCONTENTS

We have seen that a good deal of modern literary theory is actually an alternative metaphysics. In the 1970s and the 1980s, Anglo-American literary theory came to be dominated by a new linguistic metaphysics; by forms of **linguistic or discursive idealism** that would do more credit to a witch-doctor than to a linguistic scientist: that is to say, by claims that **reality, or at least our reality, is created, or controlled, or at least structured, either by language or in discourse**. To make the claims more astonishing, it was supposed that the structure of the language or discourse which has these magic powers is a very simple one: it is a structure of pure differences, at the level both of meaning and of sound. To give ancestry to this family of claims, the linguistics of Ferdinand de Saussure has been rewritten to make him into an idealist philosopher of language; and positions have been assigned to him, and are routinely taught in the English departments, which are the diametric opposite of what he actually held. I document some of these positions in chapter 7.

In this chapter I am going to do two things. The less important is the historical job of showing that Saussure himself didn't believe most of this. The more important is the strictly contemporary argument that all of these claims – from the strongest, that language or discourse or texts actually create reality and meaning, to the weakest, that language or discourse merely structure our experience of reality – are false. **Linguistic and discursive idealism are untrue**.

One claim that can be sustained, in my view, is that some of the metaphors in the language offer evidence of underlying conceptual frameworks that do indeed structure our experience of the world. Another is that the grammatical features of natural languages that make it possible to represent complex concepts play some part in the actual temporal construction of those concepts: I speculate briefly on how this might work. Even these weak properties of language, however, require it to have an immensely complex structure: certainly not a structure of pure differences. To discuss these points, I call upon some ideas from modern linguistics; though no attempt is made to provide a comprehensive review, or even a balanced introduction to this rich subject.

2 SAUSSURE'S ACTUAL PHILOSOPHY: SCIENTIFIC REALISM

I am going to show first that Saussure himself did not believe in the referential interpretation of 'Saussure's philosophy': that the world – even the world of abstract objects of a highly theoretical character – is created or constructed in language. On the contrary, like most working scientists, he believed in the real existence of the world he was investigating, and the independence of that particular world from any linguistic description he might give of it, or from the vagaries of different language-vocabularies. What makes this point more startling is that the particular aspect of the world he was working on was language itself; and the particular features of the world that he thought he had discovered and solidly established were his own categories of *langue* and *parole*. In short he adopted – and in my view was right to adopt – the logocentric metaphysics of scientific realism. This is stated clearly in the *Course in General Linguistics*.

> Note that I have defined things rather than words; these definitions are not endangered by certain ambiguous words that do not have identical meanings in different languages. For instance, German '*Sprache*' means both 'language' and 'speech'; '*Rede*' almost corresponds to 'speaking' but adds the special connotation of 'discourse'. Latin '*sermo*' designates both 'speech' and 'speaking' while '*lingua*' means 'language', etc. No word corresponds exactly to any of the notions specified above [that is, to the technical senses of '*langage*', '*langue*' and '*parole*' – LAJ]; that is why all definitions of words are made in vain; starting from words in defining things is a bad procedure.' (Ferdinand de Saussure, 1916b, p. 14)

> 'Il est à remarquer que nous avons défini des choses et non des mots; les distinctions établies n'ont donc rien à redouter de certains termes ambigus qui ne se recouvrent pas d'une langue à l'autre. Ainsi en allemand '*Sprache*' veut dire '*langue*' et '*langage*'; '*Rede*' correspond à peu près à '*parole*', mais y ajoute le sens spécial de '*discours*'. En latin '*sermo*' signifie plutôt '*langage*' et '*parole*', tandis que 'lingua' désigne la langue, et ainsi de suite. Aucun mot ne correspond exactement à l'une des notions précisées plus haut; c'est pourquoi toute définition faite à propos d'un mot est vaine; c'est une mauvaise méthode que de partir des mots pour définir les choses.'

> (Ferdinand de Saussure, 1916a, p.31)

This is a remarkable passage. If the common interpretation of Saussure were true – that is, that he was a linguistic idealist who believed that the world is constructed in language – it would make no sense. Even in the sympathetic surroundings of de Mauro's standard 1973 edition of the *Cours* (Saussure 1916a), it provokes an indignant footnote two pages long beginning: 'Cette déclaration a une odeur positiviste . . .' But Saussure appears to have been a philosophical realist, who believed in the real existence of things, independently of any linguistic descriptions that might be given of them; and this applied even to complex theoretical entities like his own *langue* and *parole*. It is a pity this point is not more widely known.

(See chapter 8 for an attempt to defend a realist – not positivist – point of view in literary theory.)

Saussure's referential fundamentalism was so much at odds with the needs of the 1970s that considerable efforts were made to reinterpret his text in order to lessen it. By going back to original sources it is possible to construct a much more complex text for the *Cours* (Saussure 1967, ed. Engler). This gives considerable freedom to reconstruct Saussure's arguments in line with modern needs, and some commentators have used it. Saussure's earlier philological works have proved rather intractable, and have not been revived. But the greatest discovery for these purposes was of the unpublished work he did on hidden anagrams in Latin poetry. This has been held to show that he was, at heart, convinced of some very modern theses – e.g. of the priority of the signifier – and he has been severely criticized for his timidity in not publishing this work.

Paul de Man gives a relatively balanced account of this episode in a couple of paragraphs of his article, *Hypogram and Inscription*, on Michael Riffaterre (de Man 1986). He speaks of 'Saussure's conviction, or strong hunch, that Latin poetry was structured by the coded dispersal (or dissemination) of an underlying word or proper name throughout the lines of verse . . . '. This hypothesis is

> potentially disruptive to the highest degree; one knows that Saussure himself backed away from it and had abandoned his investigations by the time he started to deliver the lectures that lead to the *Cours de linguistique générale*. The potential drama of this most private and inconspicuous revolutions (including its assumed suppression by its discoverer, as if Columbus had decided to keep his discovery of the New World to himself) has acquired a certain mythological quality among contemporary theoreticians. For Saussure's caution supports the assumption of a terror glimpsed. As is well known, he claims to have interrupted his enquiries partly because he could find no historical evidence for the existence of the elaborate codes he had constructed, but principally because he could not prove whether the structures were random, the outcome of mere probability, or determined by the codification of a semiosis. (pp. 36–37)

What is extraordinary about these comments is the assumption that Saussure's claims are untrue; a mere cloak for some kind of metaphysical terror. Far the most plausible view of the situation is that they were true; and Saussure's behaviour was (on normal scientific assumptions) rational enough throughout, though obsessively thorough (140 notebooks filled!). He had a hunch that some Latin poetry was based on anagrams. There is nothing particularly implausible about that. He looked for historical evidence that this was so, and couldn't find any. He looked for probabilistic evidence, and couldn't find any. So he dropped the hypothesis, as unprovable.

Saussure was thus not satisfied with constructing elaborate codes of interpretation, however productive these might be. As a philosophical realist and a working scientist he wanted to know if they were true; that is, if they corresponded to the historical facts. This position was so incomprehensible to the *Tel Quel* generation of post-structural idealists that they imagined he must be actuated by fear. And de Man is not that far removed from the *Tel Quel* assumptions.

The real question for us today is not why Saussure felt as he did, but why the *Tel Quel* group and De Man felt as they did.

3 FRENCH SHEEP: THE DIVISION OF THE CONCEPTUAL FIELD BY SIGNIFIERS

But surely Saussure at least believed in the conceptual interpretation of 'Saussure's philosophy'? He believed, that is, that our **concepts** of the world are constructed in language? Here the evidence is equivocal. There is of course a weak sense in which everybody agrees that our concepts of the world are so constructed. We get a great deal of information about the world through the medium of language; it comes to us in a linguistically structured form and a pre-existing vocabulary; when we formulate our own ideas, we do so in language. It is common ground that language influences thought; you don't need to be a Saussurean to believe that.

Saussure's special contribution – the supposed 'radical' element in his thought – was to extend the model of the phoneme to the level of vocabulary items: to suggest that word-meanings, like the differences between phonemes, are simply a matter of differences or oppositions between available words. There are no concepts independent of language for words to signify; language cuts up a vague conceptual field into separate concepts. What does this mean?

It really involves two claims, which are logically distinct and need separate treatment. One claim is a **psychological** one. It is that, apart from the effects of our language, our thoughts form only a vague conceptual field; this is cut up into precise concepts by the signifiers of the particular language we speak. I will deal with this claim first. The other claim is a **formal linguistic** one. It is that a language system is a system of pure differences at the level of word-meaning. Words are like phonemes as far as signification goes. I will deal with this in the next section.

The basis of both Saussure's claims is a general empirical truth about languages, of which any comparative linguist rapidly becomes aware. There are, in general, no one-to-one translations between languages. A word in one language will translate, in different contexts, into two or three different words in another. Saussure gives an example which has become quite famous, and which I shall use several times in this book, along with some of my own. English makes the distinction between sheep and mutton. French gets along with the single word 'mouton'. It follows, according to Saussure, that neither of the English words can have the same linguistic value as the single French one, even if they have the same signification.

> Le français 'mouton' peut avoir la même signification que l'anglais 'sheep', mais non la même valeur, et cela pour plusieurs raisons, en particulier parce qu'en parlant d'une pièce de viande apprêtée et servie sur la table, l'anglais dit *mutton* et non *sheep*. La différence de valeur entre *sheep* et *mouton* tient à ce que le premier à côté de lui un seconde terme, ce qui n'est pas le cas pour le mot français.   (Saussure 1916a, p.160)

We may well grant this point to Saussure as an analytical truth. The term 'value' is one that he has imported from economics especially to refer to the 'exchange value' that a word derives from its place in the system of the language as a whole. He has a perfect right to use his own technical terminology in this way.

But what does 'have the same signification' mean? This is not simply a point of translation (Baskin translates as 'signification'; Harris translates as 'meaning'). We must treat the question in a Saussurean way and ask: 'What distinction is Saussure making here?' Is he making the claim:

The French word 'mouton' may represent the same *concept* as the English word 'sheep' but cannot have the same *linguistic value*.

This claim is true; but it amounts only to a technical observation within linguistics about the usage of Saussure's own term 'linguistic value'. Or is he claiming:

The French word 'mouton' may refer to the same *animal* as the English word 'sheep' but cannot convey the same *concept*.

It will be seen that it is the latter claim that is needed as the foundation for 'Saussurean philosophy'; but is it remotely credible? Is it true that the French concept of a sheep is different from the English one, in precisely the sense suggested by the difference in the French and English vocabulary systems? To put the point simply, is it true that the French cannot tell the difference between sheep and mutton, since they have only one word for both?

This sounds like a silly joke; and indeed it is funny. But it is not a joke at all; it is a valid *reductio ad absurdum* argument against an absurd claim. We need to ask ourselves, with plenty of examples in mind, what it **means** to say that our concepts are structured by our language. Here is one example; one child asks another: 'Have you any brothers or sisters?' Does the child have to acquire the learned word 'sibling' before having a concept of 'brothers or sisters'? Why is the word 'sibling' a valid word for a single concept and the phrase 'brothers or sisters' not?

Here is an example that brings out the problem even more clearly. There is supposed to be an Eskimo dialect – I haven't verified this, but people are always talking about it – which has fifty-three different words for different types of snow. (Lakoff says twenty-two – he doesn't actually know either. It's an old chestnut, though the theoretical point being made is an important one.) The point is that my English gets along with two: snow and slush. Again the value of the words, in Saussure's technical sense of 'value', cannot possibly be the same in the two languages. However, the interesting question is, am I, with my miserable two words distinguishing snow and slush, going to be conceptually limited compared with the Eskimos, who can instantaneously distinguish between hard-packed snow suitable for building igloos and soft, powdery stuff with no structural strength, because they have a different word for each? Am I going to be unable to form these subtle concepts?

The answer is, that not only am I perfectly able to form these concepts, but I just have formed them. Language is extensible. If I don't have a single word for a concept I can make up a phrase; if I use the concept often enough to need it I can coin a word. The availability of an existing word makes things easier and quicker; but that is all. This is not, by itself, proof that the psychological version of Saussureanism – that language determines the classification of concepts – is false; it does show that the doctrine needs careful formulation and some evidence in its favour if it is to be taken seriously.

Before we try to provide these, we might ask why it is the Eskimos who have fifty-three words for snow. It is presumably no accident;

they also have a good many different kinds of snow that, in their culture, they regularly need to distinguish between. Intuitively it would be quite surprising if the Hottentots had fifty-three different words for snow, imposing a subtle conceptual classification on a substance none of them had ever seen. But the thesis of the priority of language in imposing conceptual classifications would lead us to expect precisely such phenomena as this.

We might sum up the argument as follows. Whether we think that concepts are determined by language will depend on how we define concepts; but some definitions are more plausible than others. If a concept is defined as an intra-linguistic affair, as the linguistic value of a word, let us say, then it is an analytic truth that our concepts are structured by our language. But in that case, we shall have no way of explaining the fact that language, by way of our concepts, can relate to the external world and to our own experience.

If on the other hand we mean to include under concepts the various ways in which we intellectually organize and classify for practical purposes both the objects of the external world and our own experiences, then the thesis that these are simply side-effects of the oppositional structure of our language becomes extremely difficult to maintain. We shall have to take seriously the proposition that the French do not notice when a sheep is dead; and that the reason for this is that their language does not make this distinction for them. We shall predict that they will have to learn English in order to cook mutton dishes.

My own view is that Saussure was uneasily conscious of these potentially absurd consequences of his theory; and for this reason he imported the term 'value' into linguistics to refer to whatever it was about meaning that was determined by the oppositional structure of language. Hence also he uses the term 'signification' which has no defined meaning in his system, rather than 'signified' (*signifié*), which has already been defined as the concept which a signifier cuts out of the general conceptual mass.

But elsewhere, when he is dealing with a less concrete example, he is much less cautious in what he says. Thus, a page later, commenting on the diagram joining the signifier 'juger' to the signified 'to judge', Saussure claims that a concept like that of judging is not pre-given and independent of the sign; it is rather a value determined only by its relations with other similar (linguistic) values, and that without these its signification would not exist:

On voit dès lors l'interprétation réelle du schéma du signe. Ainsi

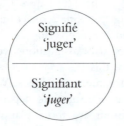

veut dire qu'en français un concept 'juger' est uni à l'image acoustique *juger*, en un mot il symbolise la signification; mais il est bien entendu que ce concept n'a rien d'initial, qu'il n'est qu'une valeur déterminée par ces rapports avec d'autres valeurs similaires, et que sans elles la signification n'existerait pas. (Saussure 1916a, p.162)

It is on statements like this that we can build a 'Saussurean philosophy'; and indeed the claim that the French and English concepts of judging are wholly dependent on the network of semantic oppositions to be found in each language is less easy to reduce to manifest absurdity than the claim that their concepts of sheep and mutton are. But the logical arguments against this position are exactly the same. Do we really want to say that nothing in our concept of a social or intellectual practice like judging is due to direct experience of that practice; that no differences in French and English conceptions on this topic derive directly from the fact that the two legal systems are entirely different; that everything is down to structural oppositions in the dictionary?

And is it really true that Saussure held to this extreme philosophical position? This is how he goes on from the point just quoted:

When I say simply that a word signifies something, when I hold to the association of an acoustic image with a concept, I perform an operation which can to a certain degree be exact and give an idea of the reality; but in no way do I express the linguistic fact in its essence and in its fullness.

Quand j'affirme simplement qu'un mot signifie quelque chose, quand je m'en tiens à l'association de l'image acoustique avec un concept, je fais une opération qui peut dans une certaine mesure être exacte et donner une idée de la réalité; mais en aucun cas je n'exprime le fait linguistique dans son essence et dans son ampleur. (Saussure 1916a, p.162)

It is certainly possible to read this as expressing an alternative 'Saussurean philosophy' of meaning. But it is also possible to read it as doing what the whole of the rest of the book does; namely, marking out a domain for scientific linguistics, and marking off this domain from that of other disciplines like those of philosophy and psychology. On this view the work of the linguist is to look at the systems of opposition and contrast in the vocabulary and grammar of natural languages. This – 'expressing the linguistic fact in its essence and in its fullness' – is a very big job, and no one but a linguist will be likely to do it. When doing this, he should not assume that there is a set of preformed universal concepts that words or grammatical items have to stand for. He should work out what concepts are being expressed from the language itself.

Viewed in this light – as methodological advice for linguists – Saussure's work, as always, is valuable. And for the very long period when Saussure was still regarded as a scientific innovator, that is how his work was viewed. The case changed only when a new improved Saussure, forty years after his death, had to compete with Jean-Paul Sartre for intellectual hegemony in France. It then became a positive advantage to have available a metaphysic quite as paradoxically counter-intuitive as anything in *Being and Nothingness*; and Saussure's semantic theory was interpreted as providing this.

4   THE LOGICAL POVERTY OF THE STRUCTURALIST MODEL OF LANGUAGE

Unfortunately, this doesn't quite let Saussure off the hook. Even if we abandon the idealist linguistic ontology that has been falsely attributed to him; even if we reject, as none of his, the conceptual linguistic determinism in which he may or may not have believed; even if we correctly limit his philosophical concern to proposing a new methodology for a technical linguistic science, and a possible model for a more general, but still empirical and technical science of signs: we still have to ask just how valid Saussure's principles are for that science. We have to ask if Saussure's theory will work, in the sense of providing descriptions, explanations, and even predictions within its own particular sphere.

The answer, in the main, is yes. For thirty to forty years Saussurean principles were at the heart of progressive research in linguistics, until the structuralist model was superseded by the generative one. You cannot ask more of a theoretical framework than that. But there are certain fundamental weak points to the theory as well – features that not only didn't work, but couldn't possibly work, and left masses of phenomena in want of an explanation. Consideration of these points will show that the structuralist model is essentially too weak to handle certain types of data. This is what I call **the poverty of structuralism**. Some of these points have been raised already; some are discussed in later chapters. In this section I want to consider just three problems.

The first is Saussure's basic theory of meaning as the product of pure oppositions among signs. It is a very important theory; most of modern radical structuralism (that is, the thinking consciously based on the so-called 'radical elements' in Saussure) takes off from it. But it cannot possibly work; and I give a simple demonstration of this in section 4.1.

The second is the problem of constructing whole sentences which are grammatical and make sense. With it goes much of the problem of the normal creative possibilities of language; of how it is possible routinely to express new thoughts while keeping within an existing structure. Saussure, notoriously, abandoned this problem to *parole*. Old-fashioned grammars handled it much better, on an intuitive basis; and generative grammar handled some of it formally.

The third is the problem of the linguistic basis on which sentences can be related to their context, whether this is a text or a situation, and pick up meaning from that. A theory of this kind is presupposed by most of the philosophical arguments about texts, and by all arguments about the meaning of literary texts. No literary critic, one might think, should be without one. Yet such a theory is far beyond the capacity of the structuralist model, however modified, emended and expanded. Indeed, it is beyond linguistics at the present time. One might say with some grimness that we are still in the stage of arguing which bit of the theory should be contributed by which pseudo-science: sociolinguistics, psycholinguistics, pragmatics, discourse theory (is there such a thing as discourse theory?) or even the philosophy of language. As a piece of self-indulgence (which none the less I take fairly seriously) I contribute my own mite to this argument at the end of the chapter.

The attitude of radical structuralists to these serious problems has been a very strange one. It is clear that Saussure's theory fails because it is too simple to handle the phenomena. But (under the influence of some of the subtlest and most difficult thinkers in the world) many radical structuralists have reacted by simplifying the Saussurean model even more. Saussure's theory of meaning won't work; so they have kept it. They have dropped the notion of the sign as signifier–signified pair, and kept only the signifier. Some of them have even committed the un-Saussurean howler of arguing that meaning arises out of the oppositions between phonemes. With all this technical over-simplification, they have often kept the philosophical claims I rejected in the last section. In the end, in some sub-Lacanian writings, one has a picture of a human subject and its correlative world brought simultaneously into existence through the operation of a chain of phonemes: never did so much come out of so little, nor with so little theoretical plausibility. (See chapter 7, section 3.)

4.1 The collapse of Saussure's theory of meaning as pure difference

The theory of meaning as pure difference has now to be considered as a pure linguistic theory. Our question is: can a linguist actually describe the semantics of a natural language like English on the basis of such a theory? Can he write a satisfactory dictionary, for example? It turns out that he can't.

The problem is that difference semantics, despite Saussure's conjecture, won't allow one to describe the meaning of even the simplest words in a language. I mean by that that it is logically impossible to describe the meaning, say, of a simple kinship term like 'aunt' within the framework of a theory of semantics with a single primitive operator that merely represents the fact that there is a difference between one signifier and another. Since there is a very simple informal proof of this, I will present it straight away.

Consider the English word 'aunt'. One principal meaning of this word is given by the phrase 'sister of parent' or the equivalent longer phrase 'sister of father or mother'; and any description of the semantics of English – any dictionary, say – that does not represent this meaning will be descriptively inadequate. But the only thing that it is possible to represent within a pure difference semantics is the difference between one sign and another. Suppose we represent the single difference-operator by an English phrase like 'different-from-' or just 'not-'. Then our representation of the meaning of 'aunt' will be:

> not-father, not-mother, not-sister, not-brother . . . not-man,
> not-woman . . . not-boy, not-girl . . . not-panther,
> not-elephant . . . not-motor-cycle, not-bus, not-aeroplane . . .
> not-planet, not-electron . . . not-hypothesis, not-value . . .

and so on, through the entire vocabulary of the language. That is how a difference semantics will represent the meaning of every word in the language, the difference between the dictionary entries for each word being only that a word cannot appear, with the 'not-' operator, in its own dictionary entry.

Now not only is such a theory preposterously clumsy; not only would it render it quite impossible for anybody ever to learn a language, since the memory-load would be too great; worse, it is actually logically impossible to represent the meanings of the word 'aunt', or of hundreds of other equally simple words. One cannot, in such a system, represent the sense 'sister-of-parent' at all, since it contains 'of'. One cannot represent the logical relation 'or' in the phrase 'father or mother'. But if one cannot represent the meaning of the word 'aunt' one certainly cannot represent the meaning of more complex words like 'Marxist' or 'metaphysician'.

We are dealing with a logical impossibility here; and though I can't go into the argument here, it is possible to show that we need a fairly large number of semantic primitives, of several different logical kinds – for example elementary logical relations like 'or', basic semantic oppositions like *physical substance* versus *abstraction*, and so forth – for a dictionary to be writable, or for a language with these properties to work.

We might note too that this logical impossibility carries over from the theory of language to any possible theory of discourse. If our discourse is composed of meaningless signifiers, whose sole signification is their difference from other signifiers, it is logically impossible that the play of differences will ever throw up the meaning of the word 'aunt'. If we assume that there are the signifiers 'sister', 'brother', and 'or', but all we know about them is that they are different from each other, then the verbal sequence 'sister or brother' in our discourse will not convey the meaning – sister or brother – that it does in English. It will convey not-brother not-and not-sister, which is useful; but then it will also convey not-dragon not-computer not-Kwame-Nkrumah, which is not so useful.

The full force of this argument is not always grasped by literary critics. I have met the reaction: 'that may be true, but I still find the opposition principle useful in analysing advertising' – or Proust. The answer to this is that literary criticism and analysis normally make opportunistic use of theories, whether or not they are adequate on their own ground; but users tacitly monitor the application of each theory to avoid producing absurd consequences. Hence a *reductio ad absurdum* argument like the one above, where it is shown that on a particular theory of meaning the phrase 'sister or brother' means, *inter alia*, 'not-dragon not-computer not-Kwame-Nkrumah', is seen as a mere sarcasm, meriting only the reply: 'I would never say anything as silly as that.' But if the theory of meaning were a serious one, an absurd consequence would have to be eliminated by the theory itself, not left to the intelligence of the user of the theory. If your interest is in theories for their own sake, then the correct response to the reduction of a theory to absurdity is to abandon or modify the theory.

The reason for this is that theories of meaning, in late structuralism and in generative grammar alike, have a very ambitious role. They are meant to give the ground or basis on which linguistic meaning, reasoning in language, and most forms of thinking arise. They shouldn't need supplementation by the intelligence of the user, because they are part of an attempt to **explain** the intelligence of the user. They are not bases in the sense of an idealist metaphysics; but they do have a role in empirical psycholinguistic theory.

Under these circumstances, it is very surprising to meet with people who still talk about meanings 'arising from a play of differences', since it is easy to see that if even simple meanings like that of the word 'aunt' cannot so arise, complex and interesting meanings would be quite out of the question. I wonder whether the proponents of this position are resting on a misunderstanding of an argument by Jacques Derrida, directed against Husserl's theory of the sign. Husserl's theory is said to rest on a metaphysics of presence: meaning as immediately present in subjective experience. Derrida is arguing, against this, that there is an element of difference, delay, non-immediacy even in signs that carry apparently self-evident meaning. Within phenomenological philosophy he is no doubt correct; but it is a far cry from this negative metaphysics to offering pure differences as the basis of a theory of linguistic meaning.

There is a brief discussion of this issue, in the context of Artificial Intelligence work, in Colomb and Turner 1989. They comment:

> This compositional view even underlies the efforts of those who would explode Saussurean notions of meaning. The thrill of deconstructing Saussurean grammars (see Derrida 1966,67) depends upon the observation that, if meaning is a matter of differential contrasts within a system, then nothing in the relational system can prevent indefinite slippage of meaning. The mistake in this reasoning lies in the premise, not the conclusion. Only a simple compositional view of meaning can bring us deconstruction's 'vertiginous possibilities of referential aberration' (de Man 1979). (Colomb and Turner, in Cohen 1989, pp. 389–90)

It will be noted that Colomb and Turner go further than I do; they are arguing against the whole compositional model of meaning, and I merely demonstrated the inadequacy of a sub-type of compositional model, that which includes **only** the relation of simple opposition. I think myself that some compositional theory is an essential sub-system in an overall theory of linguistic meaning: that is, at some point one has to represent the meaning of the word 'boy' as 'male, human, immature', and 'girl' as 'female, human, immature'. But other semantic representations will also be necessary to interact with these. Speakers of English, for example, know that petrol and diesel engines are engines that burn petrol or diesel fuel; while a fire engine is a vehicle containing equipment for putting fires out. But in what form do they store this knowledge? The representations in the mental lexicon that we use to think with may well partly resemble practical dictionary entries like those of the *NED*: having complex explanatory sentences encoding knowledge of the world, and possibly even example sentences in which the word is used. They will also have to include standard metaphorical senses; but that is something worth a section on its own.

Saussurean semantics offers the simplest example of what I have called '**logical poverty**' in a structuralist theory. Even if some compositional model of meaning is adequate, the theory of meaning as pure difference, however elaborated, has too few logical kinds of semantic element to allow it to describe adequately the complex ways in which sentences actually mean things. If language were like that we couldn't use it to say anything about the world; and we couldn't supplement a theory of this kind by bringing in social and psychological theories, since the semantics of pure difference offers no way of hooking language into such theories.

5   THE REALITY OF METAPHOR AND THE STRUCTURE OF OUR WORLD

Some very odd things are said, in post-Saussurean work, about the role of metaphor in language. Sometimes, the simple Jakobsonian account is given, with its opposition between metaphor as movement along the paradigmatic axis of language and metonymy as movement along the syntagmatic axis. This view can hardly survive the change from Saussure's chain and choice model of syntax to a later one in which sentences are structured like trees, and trees mapped on to other trees by transformations. Sometimes it is suggested that metaphor is primary, and is in some rather mysterious way the origin of language itself. This seems to be a metaphysical theory about origins, based on some real cognitive properties of metaphor that we shall shortly consider. Sometimes it is suggested that there is no distinction between metaphoric and literal senses of words. This is definitely wrong, and would make it impossible to write dictionaries.

It seems clear that active metaphor formation is a process that transcends any particular language. New metaphor – like its long-winded literary cousin, allegory – can always be translated from one language to another. Indeed, active metaphor formation may transcend language altogether. I seem to remember seeing the Marx brothers turn an imbroglio in an opera house into a rugby match with no word spoken. I suspect that, as Aristotle thought, the fundamental process of metaphor is merely the general conceptual process of finding an illuminating analogy between one thing and another; as such it may indeed be at the heart of thinking, though there seems to be no special reason why it should be at the heart of language.

What is important for language is **dead** metaphor. An enormous proportion of the words in any language bear one or more derived senses which are no more than habitual and well-known metaphors. One learns these dead metaphors when one learns the language; and one isn't competent in the language unless one knows them. Here is an example of a family of dead metaphors:

    the boy kicked the ball (literal meaning)
    the kick of a gun
    the runner kicked for home
    living for kicks
    he kicked the drug habit
    let's kick the idea around for a bit
    he kicked the bucket

All but one of these sentences – the literal one – involve a suppressed comparison which gives it a peculiar rhetorical force – different in each case, since the rhetorical force depends on the substance of the suppressed comparison. Thus, 'living for kicks' means living for violent, self-destructive pleasures – pleasures that, in their violent and sensational and destructive nature, are rather like being kicked. 'Kicking the idea around' means discussing it in a playful way, without any formal order of debate – like kicking a football around in the park. (See Jackson 1971 for further discussion.)

Any adequate dictionary will have to mark the metaphorical senses of words and explain them, or it will fail to describe the knowledge of the native speaker, or to provide adequate information for the foreign learner. How deep the explanation should be is a matter for debate. Most speakers do not know consciously what the suppressed term of comparison is in a dead metaphor; but they seem to know unconsciously, or at least to recognize it as soon as it is pointed out.

Two things follow from this account of dead metaphor. The first is that it makes no sense to argue that there is 'no difference' between metaphorical and other senses of words, or that metaphorical senses are primary: you can't write a dictionary of English on either basis. And if you can't do something elementary like writing a dictionary of English, you certainly can't do something sophisticated like explaining how a poem works. The second is that in yet another way Saussure's account of meaning as a matter of pure oppositions is inadequate. There is no way I can see in which one can map metaphorical meanings on to any form of compositional theory.

The interesting thing about the colloquial metaphor 'let's kick the idea around a bit' is that it is not a metaphor of violence, but one of play; the feeling-tone is controlled not by the superficial linguistic properties of the text, but by the underlying comparison. (There is violence present, of course, but it is subordinated to play.) This suggests that what is crucial even to stylistic effect is a set of essentially logical or conceptual processes which are seen through the language, rather than the language itself.

Consider now a metaphorical description of a more committed style of argument: 'I attacked his position.' Here argument is being conceived as war, and thought or ideas as the territory being fought over. It is clear from the very large number of similar metaphors – I won the argument, Your claims are indefensible, His criticisms were right on target, etc. – that we have here something more than a casual comparison: we have one of the fundamental conceptual structures, in terms of which we actually understand what thinking and argument are. The argument-is-war metaphor is one way in which the abstract concept of an argument is meaningful to the user. For Lakoff and Johnson (1980), from whose book the last examples come, most of the human conceptual system is metaphorical in nature in this way. Dead metaphors are, in the title of their book, *Metaphors We Live By*.

The deeper metaphor, that thought is a territory, is perhaps more important conceptually speaking than the one built on top of it, that argument is a war over that territory. As physically embodied organisms, we can be presumed to understand directly and preconceptually the relationship between our own bodies and the territory we walk over; we understand thought by an analogical extension of the notion of territory (and of other systems of metaphor based ultimately on bodily experience). I am simplifying slightly here; Lakoff (1987, p. 283) actually proposes that there are certain **image-schemas**, themselves derived from bodily experience, in terms of which we form concepts of abstract entities and relationships. Thus conceptual categories in general are understood in terms of image-schemas of **containers**; hierarchical structure is understood in terms of **part-whole** schemas and of **up–down** schemas. All these abstract schemas are based on bodily experience and are given preconceptually, and presumably are equally given in every human society.

Thinking, for the cognitive science of Lakoff and Johnson, maps the world into a space of bodily experience: it isn't a matter of having some abstract symbol system representing an objective world independent of the organism. We find, in the words of Mark Johnson, *The Body in the Mind: the Bodily Basis of Reason and Imagination*. The conceptual system is thus grounded in biology: specifically, in the natural structure of a perceptual and preconceptual system which not only provides fundamental image-schemas of the kind mentioned, but also settles what type of object we naturally recognize in our environment, and treat as the prototype for later, more general conceptual categories.

Thus we are set up by nature to come to recognize such middle-level features of the environment as trees and dogs and people. Recognizing either more specific and detailed categories – e.g. a particular breed of dog, like an Airedale terrier – or more abstract and general categories – e.g. the category 'solid' or 'fluid' – is a matter for complex learning built on top of earlier and simpler concepts. We build idealized cognitive models of the world in terms of these middle-level concepts. To reach more specific or more general concepts we develop further the cognitive models that are based on our initial categories. Lakoff suggests that the level of generality of the categories we find easy to learn corresponds roughly to that of the biological species rather than the genus or the variety, but I don't think this can be literally true: much must depend on the level of classification needed in our daily experience. (Since my parents kept Airedales when I was a child, for me the Airedale terrier is the prototype dog; it is what I mean by dog; all other dogs are variants on it, and there is almost an element of metaphor in calling a greyhound a dog! To think of an Airedale as an Airedale terrier, i.e. as a specimen of a sub-class of dog where the main class includes equally Airedales, greyhounds, Irish wolfhounds and small yappy things is a recognizably more complex act than to think of it just as a dog.)

On this theory, the process of category formation is given by nature; but it is developed in culture; and some of it seems to be represented and stored in set phrases of the language. Thus it is part of our understanding of time, in certain cultures but not others, that time is a resource, just like physical resources: we can waste time, or lose time. Some cultures could not make any sense of such a phrase, but for us it is so natural a way of expression that we are no longer conscious of it as a metaphor. Moreover, it is a metaphor that social pressures in a capitalist society may well extend. Lakoff quotes the sinister case of an article which argues that an employee who wastes time – takes too long a coffee-break, for example – is actually stealing time. It would take only one small section of a parliamentary bill to turn that from a metaphor into a real offence, punishable, presumably, by a prison term. Time as a resource with a price would then be no mere rhetorical metaphor, but a socially constructed reality.

If this theory is correct – and I have mentioned only a few salient points here, with very little supporting evidence – what are the implications for our central question in this chapter, the relation of language to thought, experience and reality? Lakoff argues that the theory casts doubt on any general objective realism, but retains a certain basic realism: that is, there is a real world that we are biologically equipped to respond to, but concepts like time-as-a-resource are cultural constructs. Lakoff's own name for his philosophical position is **experientialism**. I would accept the position that human beings live, ultimately, in a space whose dimensions are given by their own biology; and that complex concepts are constructs within this space. But I would say this is an empirical truth within a realist philosophical framework; after all, Lakoff's biology and psychology are empirical sciences, not phenomenological frameworks.

What is clear, however, is that there is no case for saying that the conceptual systems embodied in the fundamental metaphors in which we think are mere byproducts of language. The concept of argument-as-war is not an assemblage of metaphorical phrases, but one of many general conceptions that organize the way we think and behave, when we are arguing or thinking about argument. It is, however, a concept that is stored and represented in the language in many set phrases; and no doubt a part of our induction into the culture comes through learning these phrases when we learn the language. Moreover, the existence of these set phrases makes certain patterns of thought easy and quick.

Thus, it is not that the existence of the phrases 'attack his position', 'defend my position' makes us conduct argument as war; but they certainly facilitate thinking about argument in that way; and they are good linguistic evidence that we do think in that way. But they do not tell the whole story. Consider such non-warlike metaphors as 'Let's look at all the evidence and try to find the truth,' or the phrase I have myself just employed: 'They do not tell the whole story.' Probably every language contains the full range of unconsciously metaphorical expression that is required, to perform the cognitive tasks that the culture requires of it. If we are looking for ultimate causal factors, to answer the question 'why those cognitive tasks and not others?' I would still look to Marxist and Freudian explanations – and ultimately to Darwinian explanations in terms of survival and of sexual selection.

6   THE CONSTRUCTION OF COMPLEX CONCEPTS IN LANGUAGE

If Saussure's theory of language is inadequate at the semantic level, we might ask ourselves – by way of setting up a benchmark – what kinds of theory would be adequate. It is not the purpose of this section, or even of this book, to propose such a theory; merely to set out one or two of the significant problems of meaning – like the problem just discussed, of the cognitive significance of metaphor – with which it needs to deal.

The most important property of human language is not, I think, that it communicates ideas, but that it encodes them. To say that is not to say that the ideas could exist separately, in some unencoded form. They can, however, usually be transferred from one encoding to another, by translation or by paraphrase. Thus to take the example which is readiest to hand, the fundamental ideas on language of Ferdinand de Saussure exist in French, in versions of his original lectures, and in English, in distinct versions by Baskin and Harris; Jonathan Culler has explained them in his book in the Fontana series, and I have explained them in different words in section 2 of chapter 1. No doubt we all disagree in detail; but the very fact that these are all versions of each other shows that concepts have some degree of independence of the words in which they are put.

Although our concepts must in some sense be independent of the way they are expressed, since translation and paraphrase are to some extent possible, it seems reasonable to assume that complex concepts could not be constructed without the support of some language. The question of interest, then, is what formal properties of natural languages make it possible to construct complex concepts in them. It is clear that the possibilities of building up concepts by word coinage, original metaphor and rule-breaking are very slight. What other linguistic mechanisms are possible?

An obvious example of a concept that is built up, in the mind of anybody who ever does come to grasp it, largely by verbal explanation, is 'the British economy'. Most newspaper readers, or followers of broadcast news programmes, have a fair notion of what is meant by this, and can respond in some way to the news that it is doing well or badly, or suffers from some disease like rigidity or has had a boost from the discovery of new sources of oil. These features of the economy have their direct impact, in innumerable ways, on our lives; we really feel them when we start to make more money or alternatively lose a job. But there is no way in which we could understand this concept simply from experience without verbal explanations.

What a linguistic theory ought to be able to do is explain how that whole vast set of verbal explanations can assign a meaning – an underlying representation of a complex concept – to the phrase 'the British economy'. To the best of my knowledge and belief, no linguistic theory at present available can do this, and linguists don't typically set it as one of the goals of linguistic theory to do this. One might say that it is the business of a separate, quasi-philosophical theory of Pragmatics (e.g. Levinson 1983), the empirical status of which is rather unclear. Or one might gesture vaguely at cognitive psychology as a science concerned with matters like this; but actually psychology is helpless in this unless there is a linguistic theory *in situ*. What a psychological theory ought to do is to explain by what universal psychological mechanisms a linguistic theory of this kind (if it were available) would work. Again to the best of my knowledge and belief, no adequate psychological theory is available.

6.1 Rules of syntax and computer models

A great advance towards understanding the construction of complex concepts in linguistic terms was made about 1957 when Chomsky revived the interest of linguists in syntax – that is to say, in the rules of construction of languages, which appear to be, to a limited extent, independent of the meanings of the words we use. Chomsky wasn't thinking specially of computers when he wrote *Syntactic Structures* (1957), but his work has been influential in computer science. If you put a set of the rules of construction of a language, and its vocabulary, in a computer program, the machine will be able to produce an indefinite number of well-constructed sentences, each of which will seem to a reader to express a complex idea, though of course the computer has had no such idea. This may suggest part of what is going on in the brain when we think or speak; though it doesn't come near to providing a working model of linguistic performance and isn't intended to.

Thus the computer on which I am writing this is also running a miniature grammar of a fragment of English, and has just made up these sentences:

    a man that passed away became a director of the polytechnic
    a frantic girl compromised a rock-star
    the clerk-of-the-court answered for the desperate husband

All of them are grammatical and intelligible and convey a clear idea to me (though not to the computer). The program is thus simulating some parts of human knowledge of language.

It is possible that we can go a step further by providing some model of the meanings of words, broken down into semantic features or primitive units of several kinds. These units might include logical relations like 'and' or 'or', semantic features based on the physical nature of human beings and the powers of classification they are born with, like the oppositions between animate objects and inanimate, and semantic features based on cultural experience. One might also provide accounts of how such features may be combined, in accordance with the structure of sentences provided by the rules of construction, to provide complex representations of meaning. Such extensions may make it possible to simulate other, more sophisticated language abilities, such as making up and recognizing some valid logical arguments.

A good deal of interesting discussion of this kind took place in the 1960s in America and even Britain, while the French structuralists were still wasting their time with the obsolete structuralist model of language; how it has been extended, modified or replaced by quite different logical models in recent years is something I won't consider here. One model of language – 1965 'classical' transformational grammar – had a set of basic phrase structure rules that generated grammatical structures into which lexical items (the underlying forms of words) were then inserted. This operation produced what were technically known as '**deep structures**'. There was a deep structure for every sentence of the language; deep structures were assigned a meaning by semantic rules, and a pronunciation by transformations and phonological rules.

This, incidentally, is the only way that the term 'deep structure' should be used except as a conscious metaphor. It doesn't mean any old underlying idea, or deep meaning, or what have you. Not every form of generative grammar uses deep structures: the generative semantics of the late 1960s and early 1970s, for example, had underlying logical representations of meaning instead. Technical concepts like this should really be stamped with the name of the manufacturer and the date – thus: 'Deep structure (Chomsky 1965)'. This is not because of the law of property but because otherwise it is a fair bet that metaphors based on the concept will be ill-considered.

Linguists would regard most of the models I have mentioned as obsolete now; but it is fair to say that no model of a pre-generative kind is worth considering seriously. Merely by their existence, and by the features of language they manage to explain (like embedded clauses, question–and–answer relationships, etc.), they show up the weaknesses of the simpler structuralist model. In particular they explain our ability to make up new sentences according to regular principles of construction, that express complex and novel ideas which are nevertheless transparent and comprehensible to speaker and hearer. Any possible cognitive theory will have to handle this problem in some way. We are not talking here of advanced philosophical thinking or specialized uses of language like poetry. Once you realize what is going on, cognitively speaking, there is almost infinite complexity in asking for a cup of coffee.

6.2 Complex ideas in simple situations

Here is an example of the way we can build up a complex concept in a sentence or so, and casually refer to it, for quite immediate and practical reasons:

> Pass my coffee over, will you?
> Which is it?
> The one with coffee spilt in the saucer, with a soggy cigarette end in it, making a horrible mess.
> Oh, **that** one.

That's it.
Here it is.

This is a very simple dialogue, but it works in an extremely complicated way, and to describe just how it works, we have to call upon some quite elaborate machinery from linguistics, psychology and philosophy. Furthermore, not all the machinery needed is yet developed within these subjects. The most important feature of the dialogue is that the third remark builds up a representation of a complex and unique concept, from standard semantic elements of the language which are shared by both speakers:

> The cup of coffee with coffee spilt in the saucer, with a soggy cigarette
> end in it, making a horrible mess.

Any speaker of English can build up this concept, by hearing or reading the sentence that expresses it. The first linguistic theory to provide anything like an adequate account of how the grammar of English forces the dictionary meanings of the words to combine into one complex meaning was a theory I have mentioned already: Chomsky's transformational-generative grammar of 1965 combined with Katz–Postal semantic marker theory of 1963. (In a broad sense, this only gave an algebraic formalization to grammarians' intuitions that were millennia old. But successful formalization is, as Lacan used to insist, a crucial step in science: Lacan himself never achieved it.)

We now have to move from a linguistic to a philosophical description of what is happening in this little dialogue. By using this sentence, the speaker succeeds, in the context of this particular situation, in **referring** to a unique real object, the cup of coffee. This is a **speech act.** He also succeeds in providing his hearer with a concept which enables him to **identify** the same object – identifying is a non-verbal process including physically looking for it! The hearer indicates that he has made the identification concerned by making an elliptical **reference** to it; the original speaker confirms this **reference**. The hearer then uses the concept as a guide to action (passing the cup); at the same time he describes his action. In this description he uses the word 'it' to **refer** to the cup.

In my view, what linguistics and psychology between them have to explain is the fact that a dialogue of this kind functions as described. No accounts of language (like the structuralist one) or of human psychology (like the behaviourist one) which are too simple to be compatible with such workings are worth considering. Further, any valid philosophy of language must also be compatible with such an account as this. This rules out theories that suggest we can't actually refer to real objects like cups of coffee; or that we can't form concepts of them that can be tested in action against the corresponding reality; or that when a complex concept is formed by verbal construction, the corresponding object must be a mere verbal construct. The coffee here is real enough, even if I construct its concept verbally. (Though it does add another twist to the complexity of the situation if one remembers that the whole situation is fiction – I made the dialogue up!)

There is something logically rather interesting that happens at the end of this dialogue. The last remark, 'Here it is,' refers to the cup of coffee already mentioned. In this case, the reference is to a real object, which one of the participants to the conversation has in his hand. But reference back is possible to quite abstract objects which are not physically present and could not be: one could talk of 'my disappointment at not being able to solve the *Times* crossword' and then refer to that disappointment as 'it' in a later part of the conversation. What on earth is happening now?

I personally think that such references back as this are made by assigning the complex concept earlier developed as the temporary meaning of the word 'it'. And I think that this fact should be reflected in any linguistic, psychological or philosophical analysis of the problem of reference back (known usually as 'anaphora'). We need to recognize, in fact, that **the structure of our language is designed to enable us to build up complex concepts and to recall them in simple linguistic forms**. This is in my view the central point of human language; communication is secondary. Human language is an intelligence amplifier. We need of course to state explicitly the rules of language and of language use which enable us to do this; and this has not yet been done.

I have said nothing so far about complex social interactions, implicit intentions of the speakers, or the kind of subtlety a literary critic would pick up – for example the irony signalled in 'Oh, **that** one.' This might imply something very complicated indeed. Here is a possible paraphrase: 'I acknowledge that you intended me to grasp your self-deprecating implication that you are a repulsively sluttish person to whom I am none-the-less or possibly for-that-reason unshakeably committed and acknowledge further the irony that guarantees this is not a total account of the situation between us'!

Effects of this last kind cannot in my view be handled by linguistics; and this is not a defect in linguistics. Indeed, I am not sure that they are part of rule-governed behaviour in any straightforward way. Rather, they seem to be inferences, based on **opportunistic** behaviour within a framework of **rule-governed** behaviour. I suspect that linguistics, and other rule-oriented sciences, can study only the rule-oriented framework. It would be quite something if we could even give a reasonable account of complex concept construction; expressive human interaction is way beyond the horizon of possible science for the moment. And literary theory, of course, has to handle matters more complex even than this.

It would, however, be a great mistake to suppose that the existence of complex phenomena of this kind casts doubt on the adequacy of formal linguistic and logical treatments of simpler phenomena. On the contrary, opportunistic uses of language and inferences from them are built upon, and presuppose, regular rule-governed uses. No treatment of them can be satisfactory that is not based on either a formal or an informal treatment of regular elements like syntax and vocabulary. As speakers, we have to know these to use language expressively; as analysts, we have to have theories of these before we can make *ad hoc* analyses of opportunistic uses of language.

In this section I have been making some strong assumptions about the nature and purpose of theories of language, and of philosophy of language, and indeed, of philosophy in general. Roughly speaking, I am assuming that the point of scientific theories of language is to explain facts; the point of philosophy of language is to clarify the scope and limits of linguistic science; I am seeing philosophy itself as the under-labourer of the sciences. Much philosophy – for example the whole tradition of Frege, Russell, Strawson, Searle and Grice – lends itself to this use. Some – that of Husserl, for example, despite his ambition to provide apodictically certain foundations for the sciences – does not. The philosophies of Heidegger and Derrida emphatically do not; and it is only fair to say, neither does the second philosophy of Wittgenstein. The two types of philosophy are perhaps incommensurable. Only a partisan could summarize the famous non-confrontation between Derrida and SARL (in which SARL assumed the very point Derrida was questioning, and Derrida played the fool to show that not all discourse is cooperative) as a philosophical victory for Derrida. (Discussed in Introduction and chapter 5: refs Derrida 1977a, b; Searle 1977).

6.3 Building the context into linguistic meaning

Chomsky paid particular attention to the role of what are called recursive rules in his theories. Recursive rules effectively embed sentences inside other sentences, and so build up complex sentences. Thus you can take almost any noun phrase, and add a relative clause to it; and continue with this process indefinitely. Here is a familiar example of a complex sentence:

> **This is the man that beat the dog that chased the cat that caught the rat that spoilt the malt that was kept in the house that Jack built.**

This sentence conveys a complex idea, but is quite transparent even to a young speaker of English. What is more impressive, perhaps, is that even the young hearer knows what rat we are talking about – yet it is a very complex rat. How complex it is we can see by extracting it from its sentence and putting it in a noun phrase of its own:

> **the rat that the cat that the dog that the man beat chased caught that spoilt the malt that was kept in the house that Jack built.**

This complicated structure truly represents the complexity of the idea of the rat we are talking about, because it represents correctly the hierarchical nature of the qualifications applied to the rat: it is the rat that the cat caught, but the cat in question is the one the dog chased, and the dog we are talking about is the one the man beat. But (because the structure is what is called 'self-embedded') the sentence is getting extremely difficult to follow, even for adults who can see it in print.

Suppose we now try the same trick with Jack – who, we say, is the boy

> **that built the house that the malt that the rat that the cat that the dog that the man beat chased caught spoilt was kept in.**

Again we are correctly representing the complexity of the concept, in the sense that we are correctly representing the hierarchy of qualifying clauses. But the description is quite incomprehensible; it simply isn't possible for the brain to process a linguistic expression of this kind of complex structure. Yet we clearly do need to handle concepts that are far more complex than this, without losing track of qualifying clauses that are far more remote than any represented here. So how do we do it? Like many questions about common activities, this has an obvious answer, covering over great complexities.

We use a sequence of expressions, in which the later ones refer back to the earlier:

> **The man beat the dog that chased the cat that caught the rat that spoilt the malt that was kept in the house that Jack built. This is Jack.**

It is clear that somewhere in our account of language, or else of the use of language, we must explain the way that the second word 'Jack' refers back to the first, and takes on the complex meaning built up in the preceding sentence. It does this in a quite transparent way, even for young children; so we are probably dealing with a fundamental property of language, not a special intellectual feat.

Our theory really ought to handle other examples of reference back as well. We can refer back by pronouns. If we simply add the sentence

He was furious!

we know it refers to Jack. If we had deleted the earlier sentence 'This is Jack' then the pronoun 'he' would refer to the man who beat the dog. If we added the sentence

The malt was quite unusable.

it would refer, not to any old malt, but to the particular malt which our rat had spoiled in such complicated circumstances. So definite noun phrases can refer back as well; and so can other forms.

We can see that there is absolutely no limit to the sequence of connected sentences we might employ to build up more and more complicated ideas. Think, for example, of the complexity of the meaning of the name Dorothea by the time we have reached the middle of *Middlemarch*. If we tried to encapsulate our knowledge in one complex linguistic unit, a deeply embedded sentence, it would be far too complex to understand. (Our brains can unravel only clauses embedded less than about seven deep and have difficulty well before that.) Yet we read the book for fun and understand much of it. The reason is of course that the concept has been spread out over a long sequence of sentences.

What I am saying is that the language has available two sorts of grammatical machinery. One sort (the recursive phrase structure rules described by Chomsky in 1965) make it possible to build up representations of immensely complex concepts, which take the form of the underlying structure of immensely complex sentences. The second sort (which I used to put among the transformational rules) make it possible to turn the very complex underlying structures into simple linear sequences of fairly simple sentences, which thus become linear representations of these complex ideas.

What is the psychological status of these very complex ideas I am talking about? They are definitely psychologically real, in the sense that we can manipulate them, communicate them, and so forth. But they equally definitely do not exist as representations in or on the brain. It is the simple linear representations that exist. What does it mean to say you know the character of Dorothea in *Middlemarch*, or that you understand the meaning of the phrase 'the British economy' after reading an article on it? Not, assuredly, that you actually have in your head a full sentential representation of one of these ideas in all its complexity; but that you have a sufficient memory of some linear representation of the idea in many successive sentences to go back over and reconstruct any particular aspect of the idea you need.

In short, complex ideas are meanings of virtual sentence structures, not real ones; and these in turn are transformed into linear sequences of sentences which can actually be spoken, or written, or represented in the brain. Such sequences of sentences have a curious independence of any one individual subjectivity. They can, for example, exist as a dialogue. I have given the example of a conversation which builds up a complex idea of a cup of coffee. Such a conversation requires two people; the words wouldn't make sense on one pair of lips.

There is a final point to make, which is at once utterly commonplace, and much stranger still. Part of the meaning of a sentence can be derived, not from another sentence, but from the physical and social context in which the sentence is uttered. One points and says 'Please . . . ' and the utterance is equivalent, in its context, to 'Please pass the coffee over there.' How does this work? There are all sorts of explanations, and levels of explanation, that one might try; but I think it is connected with the phenomena already referred to. The complex idea is the meaning of a virtual linguistic form (roughly, the underlying form of 'Please pass me the coffee that is over there'). And that virtual linguistic form is represented, in this situation, partly by the utterance of the real English expression 'Please' and partly by the contextual situation, experienced in common by both participants, of there **being** a coffee over there.

It is in this sense, and only in this sense, that the physical and social world becomes impregnated with language; that we come to live in a linguistic world; that at times the world we live in can make linguistic statements, or at least, can fill out the gaps in the linguistic statements we make. But it is far from being the case that this casts any doubt on the reality of the world. Why is it that context of situation can sometimes stand in for a linguistic statement? The fundamental reason is that linguistic statements can sometimes be true accounts of contexts of situation. It is because there can actually be a cup of coffee over there, and a person to pass it, that the word 'Please . . . ' in the appropriate context can mean 'Please pass the cup of coffee that is over there.'

I have deliberately chosen trivial examples for my account of the relation between complex concepts and the texts, and non-linguistic contexts, in which they are built up and manipulated. But that does not mean that the properties of language that make this possible are trivial ones. On the contrary, I would rate them as the most important properties human language has, at least from an evolutionary point of view, because they multiply the effective intelligence of *homo sapiens*. Apes, dogs and hens have concepts of their surroundings, in the sense of mental representations that can be a guide to action. But only human beings can form the very complex concepts represented in part by linear sequences of sentences and in part by contexts of situation. In a sense, this ability is more important than the communicative function of language. Before complex ideas can be communicated, they must first of all be formed; by representing them partly in words, and partly in an indicated situation.

So I return at last to that messy cup of coffee; the reader will remember it. It is:

> The one with coffee spilt in the saucer, with a soggy cigarette end in it, making a horrible mess.

On my view, this single noun phrase is semantically equivalent to the whole of the following indigestible sequence of noun phrases and sentences.

> A cup of coffee. The cup of coffee has a saucer. Coffee is spilt in the saucer of the cup of coffee. A cigarette end is in the coffee that is spilt in the saucer of the cup of coffee. The cigarette end that is in the coffee that is spilt in the saucer of the cup of coffee is soggy. The soggy cigarette end that is in the coffee that is spilt in the saucer of the cup of coffee makes a horrible mess.

Chomsky's formulations of 1957 and 1965 handle recursive rules, and the embedding of one sentence inside another, in slightly different ways; my example suggests a slightly different way again; and all of them are different from, and inconsistent with, Chomsky's work of the 1980s. I would myself have liked, in 1965, to extend the whole principle so that any phrase making anaphoric reference is counted as incorporating the whole structure of the earlier phrase that it refers back to. This means that the word 'it' in my dialogue has an underlying representation on the lines of: '(The) cup of coffee that I asked you to pass me.'

If you apply this theory consistently you get what I once called a 'transformational theory of context'. The principle of this is that where the nth sentence in a passage of prose contains an anaphoric reference to the mth sentence, it has an underlying representation that actually **contains** the underlying representation of the mth sentence. If the sentence stands by itself, but it is possible to work out the content of some earlier sentence from the context of situation, then it is permissible to **insert** the underlying structure of that sentence in that of the sentence actually present; and thus create anaphoric reference.

This theory explains why we can use definite articles and pronouns to refer back in passages of prose, and also why we can use them to refer to particular objects in particular concrete situations. But it leads to fearful complexity in underlying representations, and few linguists have liked it; though I still think it true. But it is less well adapted to current models in generative grammar, or to Lakoff–Johnson cognitive linguistics, than to the theories of the 1960s; it seemed to me to go very well with the generative semantics of about 1970.

I raise these problems in this book mainly to show the kinds of question which it is possible to discuss in terms of linguistic theory, and which cannot even be raised in Saussurean linguistics. None the less, as I have pointed out, modern formal linguistics is quite powerless to explain the effects literary critics can pick up from a text. This makes it particularly ironic that, in the 1960s, critics like Roland Barthes were solemnly going to Saussurean linguistics for a model for a new scientific literary criticism; and it goes a little way towards explaining why some of them so rapidly became disillusioned and switched to the deliberately jokey, anti-scientific approaches we sometimes associate with the label post-structuralism. (There is an interesting self-critical discussion of the role of facetiousness in theory in Pêcheux 1975 (trans. 1982). Pêcheux is an example of the scholar poised uneasily between linguistics and Althusserian discourse theory half-recognizing that, by the standards of each, the other just won't do.)

Nothing in this chapter, however, will appease the kind of person who finds this whole approach to language profoundly wrong, because it somehow doesn't explain what makes language language, or meaning meaningful. The Heideggerian, the Lacanian, the Derridean, will find in what I have written nothing but an elaborate and philosophically trivial missing of the point (the point being a metaphysical and hermeneutical, not a scientific one); and all I can hope to persuade them is that the historical Saussure missed their point as completely as I. They have, as consolation, an imaginary Saussure that they themselves invented. There is, I think, no scientific argument about language that could possibly be put forward that would be allowed to impact upon the modern anti-metaphysicians: they would see themselves as working in a different field; I think myself it is the Elysian field of textual idealism.

BOOKS

de Saussure, Ferdinand 1916a,b,c *Cours de Linguistique Générale*. See appendix for versions and translations.
Lyons, J. 1981 *Language, Meaning, and Context*
Garnham, A. 1985 *Psycholinguistics: Central Topics*
Lakoff, G. and Johnson, M. 1980 *Metaphors We Live By*
These are elementary introductions to a wide range of linguistically sensible approaches to the problems of language, meaning, context, concept formation, and the underlying structure of our concepts, as evidenced by the metaphors we use.
Grinder, John T. and Elgin, Susan Hayden 1973 *Guide to Transformational Grammar.* Even very advanced students of literary theory need to be careful when trying to grasp linguistics by reading Chomsky's, or anyone else's, discursive writings. Doing linguistics is rather like doing applied mathematics: you have to write actual rules, and perform manipulative algebraic exercises to account for linguistic data in terms of these rules. It is quite unlike the work of, say, Lacan, where algebraic formulae have a purely pictorial sense and can't be calculated with. Hence my inclusion of a basic class text of the period, with exercises.

FURTHER READING

Linguistics and Saussure: Gadet 1986, Saussure 1916a,b,c, Saussure 1967, Harris R 1987, Wells 1947.
Linguistics and Syntax: Chomsky passim, Fodor and Katz 1964, Grinder and Elgin 1973, Harris Z 1947, Radford 1981.
Linguistics and Semantics: Colomb and Turner 1989, Fodor 1980, Katz and Fodor 1963, Levinson 1983, Sperber and Wilson 1986, Steinberg and Jakobovitz 1971.

Cognitive and Psycholinguistics: Garnham 1985, Halle and Bresnan 1978, Lakoff and Johnson 1980, Lakoff 1987.

Logic and Language: Austin 1962a,b, Carnap 1937, Cresswell 1973, McCawley 1981, Parkinson 1968, Reichenbach 1947, Staal 1965.

Other Views of Language: Coward and Ellis 1977, Korzybski 1933, Pécheux 1975, Silverman and Torode 1980, Skinner 1957, Whorf 1956. See also chapters 2 and 7.

For titles and publishers see main bibliography.

CHAPTER SEVEN

Linguistic Idealism and the Critics of the 1970s

Bennett, Kristeva, Coward and Ellis, and the Revolution of the Word

SUMMARY

Three examples are given of typical critical theory of the 1970s that exhibits the features described in chapter 6: Tony Bennett's use of Saussure for a kind of Marxist linguistic idealism; Julia Kristeva's account of 'the semiological discovery' and her preference for Heidegger and Mallarmé over scientific linguistics; and Coward and Ellis's attempt to produce a Saussurean–Althusserian–Lacanian synthesis of all kinds of post-structuralist thought in the interests of producing a 'revolutionary subject' – truly a revolution of the word. These theorists are here criticized from a linguistic, rather than a Marxist or psychoanalytic point of view; the general arguments of chapter 6 are supplemented by detailed comments on particular passages.

1 TONY BENNETT AND 'SAUSSURE'S PHILOSOPHY'

Many modern critics have adopted a form of linguistic idealism, based on a misrepresentation of Saussure; in this chapter I give my examples from three sources who I think are representative: the post-Althusserian, Tony Bennett; Julia Kristeva, in her role as prophet honoured in yet another country, explaining **the semiotic discovery** to the English in 1973; and the writers of probably the most influential English textbook on *Language and Materialism*, Rosalind Coward and John Ellis. Nothing in what follows is intended as personal criticism of these writers, who seem to me valuable. Even when they are talking nonsense it is representative nonsense, and often comes direct from original masters like Lacan. And I am not attempting to give an account of their work as a whole; only the 'Saussurean' elements of it, in work of the 1970s.

Tony Bennett is a Marxist theorist strongly influenced by Althusser. But, like many of this school, he attributes his philosophy – which I personally think derives from Althusser's idealist theory of science – to Saussure. Bennett (1979) is a major source for the school of Marxists who break with the distinguished tradition of Marxist aesthetics, and claim that Marxists should analyse texts without using the category of 'literature'; and it is interesting to see how he gets this doctrine from Saussure. In his book *Formalism and Marxism*, he adopts a conceptual linguistic idealism that confuses sense and reference:

> Baldly summarised, Saussure's central perception was that language signifies reality by bestowing a particular, linguistically structured form of conceptual organisation upon it. What the signifiers of language – the sound structures of speech and the notations by which these are represented in writing – signify, Saussure argued, are not real things or real relationships but the concepts of things, the concepts of relationships, each signifier deriving its meaning from its relationship to other signifiers within the system of relationships mapped out by language itself.

Bennett is clearly correct up to this point: Saussure's signified is a concept; it is not a real object to be referred to. But there is something rather mysterious about this notion of 'signifying' reality. It seems to fall somewhere between referring to things and conveying ideas; and this is shortly going to lead to a blur in the argument:

> 'The "objects" of which language speaks are not "real objects" external to language, but "conceptual objects" located entirely within language.'

At this point Bennett falls into confusion. To 'speak of' an object is to refer to it; and it is not language which speaks of objects, but people, using language. That is to say, reference is a speech act; in Saussure's terms, it is part of *parole*. It is perfectly possible to speak of real television sets; I know people who do it all the time. Any philosophy of language which denies the possibility of a speaker ever referring to real objects has something seriously wrong with it.

Of course, in use the phrase 'television set' does not only refer to an object; it also conveys, constructs or presents a concept – that of a device for receiving pictorial signals transmitted from afar. There are two logically distinct relationships here, usually referred to by the Fregean labels 'reference' and 'sense', which cannot be amalgamated by speaking of 'conceptual objects'. What sort of 'conceptual object', I ask, is a television set; and how does it differ from the real television set on the one hand and the concept of a television set on the other?

> The word "ox", according to Saussure's famous example, signifies not a real ox, but the concept of an ox; and it is able to do so by virtue of the relationships of similarity and difference which define its position in relation to the other signifiers comprising modern English.

This too is perfectly true. For Saussure, to signify means to be connected to, or to convey, a concept; it does not mean, to refer to an object.

> There is no intrinsic connection between the real ox and the word "ox" by virtue of which the meaning of the latter is produced. The relationship between the signifier and signified is arbitrary: that is, it is a matter of convention.

Bennett now falls back into the same confusion between referent and concept. What Saussure said was arbitrary was the relationship between the concept of an ox and the sound pattern /oks/. He said nothing about there being any relationship, arbitrary or otherwise, between the sound pattern /oks/ and an actual animal. Normally, relations between sound patterns and objects occur in referring expressions, and are mediated by concepts. That is to say, when we speak of 'the ox over there' the referring expression conveys a complex idea which partially determines what we can use it to refer to. The only time when there is a direct relationship between a sound pattern and an actual animal is when you give it a proper name – and even then, the sound pattern is often mediated by a concept; you might call the animal 'Curly', referring to it by a property of its hair.

Bennett is now, as a materialist, seriously alarmed at his position; so he tries to qualify it:

> This is not to deny that there exists a real world external to the signifying mantle which language casts upon it. But it is to maintain that our knowledge or appropriation of that world is always mediated through and influenced by the organising structure which language inevitably places between it and ourselves. Oxen exist. No one is denying that. But the concept of an 'ox' as a particular type of domesticated quadruped belonging to the bovine species – a concept through which, in our culture, we appropriate the 'real ox' – exists solely as part of a system of meaning that is produced and defined by the functioning of the word 'ox' within language.
>
> (Bennett 1979, pp.4–5; passages quoted run continuously)

239

What is wrong with the last sentence is the word 'solely'. If it were replaced by the word 'partly' the whole paragraph would be true. As it stands, it would be possible from this word to deduce many things about the life of Bennett and his associates in the editorial we. They are not farmers or butchers. They have nothing whatever to do with the vast socio-economic process by which, in our culture, we appropriate the 'real ox', and which is the real source of the concept. Nor do they have any interest in this process – which means that they are not, in Marx's sense, materialists. One can go further. They do not drink oxtail soup. Or at least, if they do, they do it when they are unconscious and do not allow it to form any part of their solely linguistic concept of the animal that has the tail. If they ever walk in the country they do so in blindfolds. They only meet oxen in poems.

I repeat that I have no animus against Bennett; I regard him as an exceptionally clear writer and thinker in a tradition stuffed with muddled ones. But he is a linguistic idealist – if an uneasy one. He is preparing the ground for an argument from language and concepts to reality – specifically from the vicissitudes of the word 'literature' to the nature of the thing to which it does or doesn't refer. This is characteristic of the later development of the followers of Althusser; for of course it is an Althusserian position that Bennett is adopting here, not a Saussurean one.

It is worth briefly uncovering the Althusserian argument that underlies the confused Saussurean one. Althusser held that a science like physics or Marxism is constituted by a theoretical break from 'commonsense' or ideological conceptions of its subject matter; and a new science constructs its own new objects of knowledge, which can only be investigated by the methods of that science. Chemicals are only accessible to study by the methods of the chemist; and classes or modes of production only by the methods of the Marxist. You can't, as empiricists think, check the new knowledge-objects directly against corresponding real objects. There is no appeal to immediate experience, which is embedded in ideology.

There is an analogy here for Marxists working on literature – including particularly the Althusserians who, at the time Bennett was writing, still believed that literature existed, and offered a form of cognitive appropriation of reality. They too needed to make a theoretical break from commonsense and bourgeois ideology. They too needed to recognize that literature, as an object of study, should be seen as something constructed by the literary theorists, and accessible for study by their methods alone. Here too there is no way of comparing this object with some corresponding real object, existing prior to theory. There is no appeal to immediate experience, which is even more obviously embedded in ideology in the case of literature than it is in the case of economics or chemistry (cf. Eagleton 1976).

Bennett is so impressed by the Althusserian account of science, that he attributes it to Saussure; he quotes (p.47) one remark from Saussure, 'far from it being the object that antedates the viewpoint, it would seem that it is the viewpoint that creates the object', as Saussure's general account of science. It is in fact Saussure's lament that linguistics seems, so far, unlike other sciences; and it is part of an argument toward the conclusion that *langue* is a self-contained whole, a principle of classification, and a natural order; in fact, the firm ground on which we can put both feet, and have a real science. (Saussure 1916b, pp.8–9).

It is fairly obvious in natural science that Althusser's extreme anti-empiricism will not work; effectively, it makes the whole material world an artefact of unchecked scientific discourse; and this is discursive idealism not materialism. But the same is true of literature; to make culture an artefact of cultural analysts is just as idealist, however material the labours of these people may be. Yet, following Bennett, a number of critics have adopted this position; though the Althusserian argument for it has usually been dropped, now that Althusser is out of fashion, and replaced by the 'Saussurean' one. This makes little difference since, as we have seen, the 'Saussurean' argument is merely Althusser's argument projected onto Saussure. For the left, Saussure haunts literary theory in the form of Althusser's ghost.

2   JULIA KRISTEVA AND 'THE SEMIOTIC DISCOVERY'

2.1   *The vision of semiotics*

Saussure's most famous project was that for a great science of signs in general – semiology, or nowadays, semiotics – which would be modelled on linguistics, but of which linguistics should be only one part. What linguistics provided for semiotics was the model of a system in which meaning arises out of rules, internal relationships and internal structural oppositions. What semiotics provided for linguistics was the broad theoretical picture within which the science of language proper makes a kind of general human sense. This is still how many semioticians think of the relationship between the two subjects.

But there are ways in which de Saussure's vision differed sharply from that of some of his present-day followers. He clearly thought of semiotics as a limited and scientific discipline, even if a very broad one. It was to be like linguistics writ very large. It would study the life of signs in society, and not merely spoken and written language. But it does not seem to have been intended to replace the study of society, or of general human behaviour, and provide a complete substitute for psychology and sociology. And, while it obviously had philosophical implications, it does not seem to have been intended as a general philosophical system.

Part of the history of semiotics in the modern period has been a steady increase in the magnitude of the claims made for it, and a change in the nature of those claims. From being a strategy for scientific research, semiology has changed (in the hands of some of its advocates, not all) to being a general philosophical position about the nature of man; or about his lack of it, until semiotic codes build him one, or build her another. And at the same time there is a certain decline in interest in the more scientific side of the operation; and even a decline in grasp of the details of the basic linguistic model on which everything was originally founded.

Thus Saussure and the structuralist tradition which followed him made a major contribution to phonology; Derrida (1967c), with some justification, attacked the way phonology was always being offered as a guarantee of the scientificity of the semiotic project. But some modern semioticians give the impression that they learnt their phonology from Derrida! The whole of semiotics is built on an analogy between other domains of behaviour and either the complex internal structures that human language displays, or the complex functions that it performs. But as the claims for semiotics have enlarged, so, sometimes, the interest in offering a detailed factual description, either of these structures or of these functions, has diminished. And, as I said earlier, some of the most confused passages of structuralist and semiotic analysis occur when it is not clear, even to the writer, which analogy – the structural or the functional – is being claimed.

Here is an example from Julia Kristeva, which is by no means the worst I could have found. I have quoted the whole of the first paragraph of her article: 'The System and the Speaking Subject' (first published *Times Literary Supplement* 12 Oct. 1973, reprinted Sebeok 1975; Kristeva 1986). There is nothing omitted; but I have inserted my own comments at what I think are the points of confusion.

No one can combine as well as Julia Kristeva the most grandiose ideas, genuinely profound critiques of received opinion, and elementary mistakes of a kind that would fail a first-year student. To be fair to her it is necessary to respond on all levels at once. I have therefore included comments from other scholars on the substance of the claim she and others have made, as well as nit-picking of my own on the details of her presentation of it.

> However great the diversity, the irregularity, the disparity even of current research in semiotics, it is possible to speak of a specifically semiotic discovery. What semiotics has discovered in studying 'ideologies' (myths, rituals, moral codes, arts etc.) as sign systems is that the law governing, or, if one prefers, the major constraint affecting any social practice lies in the fact that it signifies; i.e. that it is articulated like a language. Every social practice, as well as being the object of external (economic, political, etc.) determinants, is also determined by a set of signifying rules, by virtue of the fact that there is present an order of language; that this language has double articulation (signifier/signified); that this duality stands in arbitrary relation to the referent and that all social functioning is marked by the split between referent and symbolic and by the shift from signified to signifier coextensive with it.

Kristeva here begins by actually defining the function of signifying as the property of being articulated like a language. She thus builds the confusion between signifying function and phonological, syntactic and even, as we shall see, semantic structures into her account of the basic discovery of semiotics. (This combination of exciting ideas with technical confusion is typical of Kristeva's work, and indeed of late structuralist and post-structuralist work in general and accounts for much of its flavour.)

She then makes an important distinction between the external determinants of cultural systems and their language-like internal properties; but she immediately adds to this a second, technical error about language itself: that double articulation is the difference between signifier and signified. Unfortunately, this is not what it means. The term 'double articulation' is used in linguistics to refer to the fact that the oppositions between phonemes like /b/ and /g/ are distinct from the semantic oppositions between words like 'boy' and 'girl'. To say that 'double articulation' refers to the difference between signifier and signified is a howler. Double articulation, incidentally, is not a property of all signifying systems; it is one of the special features of human language.

To this double misunderstanding, Kristeva now adds a third: 'that this duality stands in arbitrary relation to the referent'. If this is a

243

reference to de Saussure, it is another howler; what Saussure said was arbitrary was the relationship between signifier and signified within language, not that between the signifier–signified pair and the object in the non-linguistic world to which the sign refers. In Saussurean terms, as I have said, the question of the referent would arise only when a language (*langue*) is used in speaking or writing (in *parole*). This third error leads directly to linguistic idealism.

The final generalization is typical of Kristeva, and of French high structuralism, in its megalomaniac scope ('all social functioning is marked by'); and its substitution of Lévi-Straussian or Lacanian concepts for linguistic ones ('by the split between referent and symbolic and by the shift from signified to signifier coextensive with it'). I will deal with the supposed shift from signified to signifier when I look at Lacan's influence, in my comments on the Coward and Ellis passage discussed later on.

To be fair to Kristeva, she is a model of clarity by comparison with many well-respected expositors of structuralism; and the distinctions she is drawing – between the external determination and general social function of an ideology, which is what Marxists talk about, and its internal structure and internal way of functioning, which is what semioticians describe – are valid and important. But so is the distinction that she fails to draw, between a resemblance to the syntactic and phonological structure of language, which in principle could be possessed even by non-signifying objects; and a resemblance to its signifying function, which in principle could be possessed even by objects bearing no structural resemblance whatever to human language – like cathedrals or paintings, for example.

Of course, once you have made the distinction between structure and signifying function, it emerges that there are real problems on the borderline. Logically, the really difficult bit is the distinction, relationship, or identity between semantic structures – like that of the word 'aunt' which in some sense contains the concepts 'sister', 'parent' and 'of' – and signifying relationships, whereby the word 'aunt' signifies 'someone who is the sister of a parent'. But such a problem cannot even be made clear until the basic distinction between the structure of a language and its various functions has been made.

I believe that this point is not simply pedantry; it would be essential to get distinctions like this clear, if ever we wanted semiological structuralism to work as an explanatory theory, as opposed to merely being gestured at in a rhetorical way. The problem with most structuralist exposition is not its magniloquence but its vagueness. By pointing in a cloudy way to linguistic analogies, it hides from us the hard logical work that is needed to make clear just what analogies are supposed to hold, and how exactly they do hold.

2.2 Institutional success and intellectual bankruptcy

All the same, Kristeva might be right about the broad picture. There might have been a major 'semiotic discovery' even if she is not describing it correctly in detail. In the absence of alternative testimony, most people will assume that that is the case. So I quote the views of two scholars in the hard linguistics camp; they are commenting not on Kristeva herself, but on the same range of work that she is describing:

> The recent history of semiotics has been one of simultaneous institutional success and intellectual bankruptcy. On the one hand, there are now departments, institutes, associations, congresses, and journals of semiotics. On the other, semiotics has failed to live up to its promises; indeed, its foundations have been severely undermined. This is not to deny that many semioticians have done valuable empirical work. However, it does not follow that the semiotic framework has been productive, let alone theoretically sound; merely that it has not been entirely sterilising, or that it has not been strictly adhered to in practice.

> Saussure expected that 'the laws discovered by semiology will be applicable to linguistics, and the latter will circumscribe a well-defined area within the mass of anthropological facts' (1974: 16). What actually happened was that for the few decades in which structuralist linguistics flourished, the semiotic program was taken seriously and spelled out in more detail. Linguists such as Hjelmslev (1928; 1959) and Kenneth Pike (1967) developed ambitious terminological schemes as tools for carrying it out. However, no semiotic law of any significance was ever discovered, let alone applied to linguistics. . . As the structure of language became better understood, its *sui generis* nature became more and more striking. The assumption that all systems of signs should have similar structural properties became more and more untenable. Without this assumption, however, the semiotic programme makes little sense.

> . . . valiant attempts were made by anthropologists such as Lévi-Strauss or literary theorists such as Barthes to approach cultural or artistic symbolism in semiotic terms. In the course of these attempts, they certainly shed new light on the phenomena, and drew attention to many interesting regularities; but they never came near to discovering an underlying code in the strict sense; that is, a system of signal–message pairs, which would explain how myths and literary works succeed in communicating more than their linguistic meaning, and how rites and customs succeed in communicating at all.
>
> (Sperber and Wilson 1986, pp.7–8)

These are damning judgements. 'No semiotic law of any significance was ever discovered'. 'the semiotic programme makes little sense'; 'never came near to discovering an underlying code in the strict sense'? The curious thing is that it is not clear that Kristeva would disagree with any of them. On the contrary, she would I think deny that semioticians were looking for semiotic coding in this strict sense at all. She would go further. She would add that linguists ought not to be looking for it. In *The Ethics of Linguistics* (Kristeva 1980) she argues that linguists are 'wardens of repression and rationalisers of the social contract in its most solid substratum (discourse)'. This is because they write formal grammatical rules to describe simple constructions of French or English:

> . . . formulating the problem of linguistic ethics means, above all, compelling linguistics to change its object of study. . . . this would establish poetic language as the object of linguistics' attention in its pursuit of truth in language . . . I shall then be talking about something other than language – a practice for which any particular language is the margin . . . what is implied is that language, and thus sociability, are defined by boundaries admitting of upheaval, dissolution, and transformation. Situating our discourse near such boundaries might enable us to endow it with a current ethical impact. In short, the ethics of a linguistic discourse may be gauged in proportion to the poetry it presupposes.
>
> A most eminent modern linguist believed that, in the last hundred years, there had been only two significant linguists in France: Mallarmé and Artaud. As to Heidegger, he retains currency, in spite of everything, because of his attentiveness to language and 'poetic language' as an opening up of beings . . .   (Kristeva 1980, pp.24–5)

Linguistics has thus become not the model for semiotics, but the anti-model. It is to Mallarmé, to Artaud and to Heidegger's romantic intuitions about language that we should look, not to Chomsky's formalism. These particular positions are Kristeva's own. She is, however, wholly representative of 'post-structuralist' thought when she argues – on epistemological, on ethical, on political grounds – that the point is not to look for laws and principles, formal or otherwise, but to keep on questioning them. I doubt whether Sperber and Wilson would be impressed by a defence on these lines, or would count her as a colleague in their own enterprise.

They too find the linguistics model, the code model, an inadequate one on which to found an account of the whole of communication, cognition and culture. But, being competent linguists – that is, actually knowing some of the relevant facts about language – they do not respond to the inadequacy of the linguistics model for the description of non-linguistic phenomena by throwing away the linguistics model for the purpose of describing languages. What they do is to offer supplementary principles – principles of inference, Gricean principles of conversational implicature, their own technically defined principle, which gives the title to their book, *Relevance*. It is these which will handle the more complicated phenomena – working up to the beginnings of poetry on p. 236.

I am drawing attention as much to a difference in cognitive style as to conclusions. Sperber and Wilson want to explain the simple things first, and work up to the complex ones. They hope that it will cast some light on the poetic functions of language if they can explain, as their example 107, the metaphor (which they describe as 'marginally more creative' than their examples 1–106):

Robert is a bulldozer.

Kristeva wants to start with Mallarmé, Artaud and Heidegger; she thinks it is these who give us a real understanding of language. But it is not clear that she wants to explain anything in the limiting mechanistic sense which Sperber and Wilson would give to the notion of explanation.

Here is the Sperber and Wilson (1986, p. 236) account of poetic metaphor:

In general, the wider the range of potential implicatures and the greater the hearer's responsibility for constructing them, the more poetic the effect, the more creative the metaphor. A good creative metaphor is precisely one in which a variety of contextual effects can be retained and understood as weakly implicated by the speaker. In the richest and most successful cases, the hearer can go beyond just exploring the immediate context and the entries for concepts involved in it, accessing a wider area of knowledge, adding metaphors of his own as interpretations of possible developments he is not ready to go into, and getting more and more very weak implicatures, with suggestions for still further processing. The result is a quite complex picture, for which the hearer has to take a large part of the responsibility, but the discovery of which has been triggered by the writer. The surprise or beauty of a successful creative metaphor lies in this condensation, in the fact that a single expression which has itself been loosely used will determine a very wide range of acceptable weak implicatures.

Sperber and Wilson move immediately to Flaubert; one may indeed feel that their theorizing has an affinity with Flaubert, and Kristeva's with Mallarmé. But that would be to miss the point; Sperber and Wilson's account is just as good at explaining how language works in modernist texts as in nineteenth-century realist ones. Kristeva is for the most part explaining nothing. She is, rather, evoking attitudes by means of rhetoric; and it is her attitudes that are closer to literary modernism than theirs. Post-structuralists don't explain modernist texts; but they often produce them.

It's a steady slog, is science, and you don't get much credit for it till you're dead; but I daresay Sperber and Wilson would rather be themselves than Kristeva; and she rather than they. My point is that there is a world of difference in fundamental attitudes, in goals, between the intellectual model of the painstaking scientist who wishes to build up true theories about complicated phenomena like signification, or poetic metaphor, and that of the intellectual revolutionary who wishes to engage in an endless and brilliant questioning of the sign (Kristeva 1969, *Semeiotike*).

This kind of revolution strikes me as idealist for precisely the reasons that Marx gave for finding the left–Hegelians idealist: it makes revolutions in the head and supposes reality will conform. Sperber and Wilson seem to me to be in the right both on the general issue of the intellectual success of semiotics, and on the more specific issue of how poetry works. And the slightly 'computerate' quality of their writing – thinking is referred to as 'processing' – is one that I personally find very attractive. In an obvious sense it is they who are the true heirs of de Saussure, and are contributing to the science of semiotics whose existence they doubt.

3   A GRAND SYNTHESIS: LANGUAGE AND MATERIALISM

3.1   *Collapsing linguistics into discourse theory*

Judged by institutional standards, the Coward and Ellis textbook of 1977, *Language and Materialism*, must be one of the most intellectually important ever produced in Britain. I think I must have seen it on the syllabuses of twenty institutions; though the difficulty of the style will have put most students off. Intellectually, too, the book is impressive; merely to have put together Saussure, Lévi-Strauss, Barthesian semiology, Althusserian Marxism and Lacanian psychoanalysis, and constructed a single system out of them, in English in 1977, was a considerable achievement.

The main merit of this book is to transmit into English some of the major positions of Julia Kristeva and the Tel Quel group. In particular the authors' understanding of linguistics seems to come very much from Kristeva; though there is also a direct influence from Lacan. Unfortunately Lacan is of all the major French thinkers the one who most deeply misunderstands or misrepresents linguistics. It is from him as much as anybody that there comes that 'turn to the signifier' of which Kristeva speaks; and any representation of his position extracted from the context of psychoanalysis and made into general linguistics is likely to take a very crass form: if you take his account literally meaning has to be built up out of phonemes attached to a phallus.

The aim of the book is to produce a materialist theory of language. 'Materialist' in this context has a political sense. It means Marxist materialism: that is, the materialism of material practices. This is to be distinguished from metaphysical materialism, which, I suppose, would be the simple recognition of matter as the basic stuff of the universe, without drawing any conclusion for human practice, and mechanical materialism, which, I suppose, would be the view that human beings are machines themselves, and part of a mechanical system, and so can't act to change the system.

Dialectical materialism has always been supposed to show man both as a part of the material world and as an active agent in changing it; but it has never been clear how these can be reconciled. Coward and Ellis think that a materialist theory of language can do the trick. In order to do this, they adopt a broad definition of language which includes everything done in language as an aspect of language itself. 'Because all the practices that make up a social totality take place in language, it becomes possible to consider language as the place where the social individual is constructed. In other words, man can be seen as language, as the intersection of the social, historical, and individual' (Coward and Ellis 1977, p.1).

Coward and Ellis seem to believe that if they can give, drawing on Lacan's language-oriented psychoanalysis, a 'materialist' account of how the human subject is **produced**, it will solve the philosophical problem of how, within a materialist framework, such a subject can possibly be said to act. They derive this conviction from Althusser, but it is not at all easy to share; unless indeed one holds that the whole concept of human action is an illusion, and the only question of interest is how that illusion comes about. In short, they don't really address the philosophical problem, but only a minor technical one: what part does language play in constituting the self, or 'subject'.

The central technical problem Coward and Ellis have in this project is the same one Lacan had in his: language as seen by the linguists will not serve them very well, whether for philosophical, psychoanalytic or political purposes. They therefore find it necessary to go through the theory of language, abandoning all the awkward bits that would get in the way of their project. Fortunately, they do not know enough linguistics to be aware of the evidence against each of the steps that they take. In this way they can radicalize Saussure, or, to be more precise, they can dismantle his theory and replace it with a much simpler one. This is a 'discourse' or 'signifier theory'.

Their first step is to collapse three entirely different two-way distinctions – *langue/parole*, synchrony/diachrony, syntagm/paradigm – into two 'dominant modes of analysis':

> One mode analyses the structural form at any one moment, the substitutions that are possible within it, the analysis of a particular state of langue. This is analysis of the paradigm, synchronic analysis of that which exists at a certain moment or during a definite epoch. The second form of analysis is that of the actual combinations that are generated, the signifying chains that are produced, the analysis of parole. This is the analysis of the syntagm, the diachronic analysis of that which unfolds through the passing of time. (Coward and Ellis 1977, p. 14)

This is of course a three way howler. The first distinction here, between *langue* and *parole*, is the logical one between a language – say, English – of any period whatever, and speeches or writings in that language. The second, between synchrony and diachrony, is a distinction between two ways of studying *langue*. You can write a grammar of modern English or Old English: those will be synchronic studies of *langue*. Or you can write a historical study of the development from Old English to Modern English. That will be a diachronic study.

The third distinction, between paradigm and syntagm, is a distinction drawn **within** the synchronic study of *langue*. In English there are paradigmatic choices of verb, noun, grammatical form, or whatever – like 'I' and 'you' and 'he' or 'am' and 'are' and 'is'. There are syntagmatic chains like 'I am', 'you are', 'he is'. Each is equally synchronic ! That is, the synchronic state of a language is defined by a number of syntagmatic and a number of paradigmatic relationships.

There is no special grouping of syntagm, diachrony and *parole* on the one hand, and paradigm, synchrony and *langue* on the other. What has misled Coward and Ellis here is that one group seems to have a time factor attached and the other group doesn't. But they are not thinking concretely enough about language to realize the difference in the time factors involved. A synchronic state of language might last, I suppose, about twenty-five years; that is, one generation of speakers; though the rate of change does vary quite a bit. A diachronic study might cover the changes in the course of two hundred years, or a thousand.

A man's *parole* presumably lasts his life long; but an individual speech or conversation, which is what one would normally consider, will take a period measured in minutes; a very long bit of *parole*, like a book, might take weeks to read. *Langue*, of course, is timeless; strictly speaking, therefore, so are both syntagm and paradigm, since they are merely aspects of *langue*. But if you are speaking a language, most syntagms will take less than a second to say. Time means something very different in such different-sized chunks; and there is no way one can identify the history of a language, a person speaking in that language, and a single construction he uses, and call them all a chain of signifiers.

Nevertheless, this is what Coward and Ellis seem to have in mind, as it is a necessity for the next step they take. Having collapsed six terms into two, they feel that the distinction between the two is still too rigid, and obscures the process of producing meaning. Saussure's

> . . . rigid division of language into synchronic structure and diachronic change obscures his fundamental discovery that the establishment of signification by a process of difference is not static, but is a constant process of articulation of new signifieds by the signifying chain . . . it is the signifying chain which produces the chain of signifieds. Language, then, becomes a ceaseless productivity. (Coward and Ellis 1977, p. 22)

They refer to this as a radical rethinking of Saussure's dichotomies, and they are right: in linguistic terms, the concept of the signifying chain means nothing. Is it *langue* or *parole*? A principle of structural organization or any expression of a language? Or what? They say that the idea came from looking at avant-garde texts and the discourse of the unconscious.

3.2 The discourse of the unconscious

We also might have a look at the discourse of the unconscious, in Lacan's version, which Coward and Ellis give later in the book, and offer as the final sophisticated version of their theory. Lacan largely drops the signified, and has chains of signifiers only.

> The units of the signifier are submitted to the double condition:

> (1) of reducing to its distinctive features, that is, to phonemes. [Presumably Lacan and Coward and Ellis don't realize that distinctive features aren't phonemes.] These do not have a fixed or static status, but are part of the synchronic system by which sounds are distinguished from one

another in a given language. The letter is therefore seen as the essentially localised structure of the signifier.

(2) that the units combine according to a closed order; from this Lacan is led to posit the necessity for a topological substratum which he calls the signifying chain. (Coward and Ellis 1977, p. 97)

And where does the meaning come in all this? What makes a signifier signify? Coward and Ellis offer a direct quote from Lacan here, which has all his characteristic verve and clarity: 'It is in the chain of the signifier that meaning insists, but none of its elements "consists" in the meaning of which it is at that moment capable' (p. 97). The signified slides about under the signifying chain and is held to it not at every point but by occasional upholstery buttons – this is Lacan's phrase. On my reading of Lacan, the signified may actually be another signifying chain, only in the unconscious rather than the conscious.

The signifying chain has astonishing powers for something with such a simple structure. It is responsible for both the conscious and the unconscious mind, for the construction of the subject, and for meaning generally. I am not sure what its relationship is to the objective world, because it is difficult to find the objective world in Lacan's company; he has only three ontological categories: the imaginary, the symbolic and the real, and the real is the unsymbolized, the impossible.

I pause here to make the obvious point (though some Lacanians would deny it) that we have now moved out of the realm of linguistic science altogether, and are dealing with vivid metaphors of the analytic situation. The phrase 'the signified slides about under the signifying chain' corresponds, I take it, to the fact that the patient under analysis says a series of things; there is a quite different series in the unconscious; and there is only the occasional connection (upholstery button) holding them together. Good advice for analysts, of course; but there is no way this can be seen as a general theory of meaning. Nor is it obvious that most Lacanians would want it to be.

Coward and Ellis believe that their new theory has eliminated all the traces of Saussure's idealism, and is satisfactorily materialist. In fact, something rather different has happened. Saussure's theory attributed a complex structure to language, but very small powers; and took for granted the existence of an objective world, to which language could be made to refer, and in which it was used by people whose minds were partly clarified and formed by language, but not wholly constructed by it. The new theory gives language a much simpler structure, but powers to construct a world rather than merely refer to it, and construct minds rather than be used by them. Such a theory resembles traditional idealist theories in which the world was constructed in the mind. If the theory is merely that the productivity of the signifying chain constructs an inner world, a subject, this is not idealist, though it is (given that the signifying chain is merely a chain of phonemes with a quite mysterious relationshp to a master signifier, the image of the phallus) highly implausible. If it is that it constructs the objective world, then we have a theory that is both idealist and a form of verbal magic.

What Coward and Ellis want to argue, I think, and could reasonably argue, is that thinking does not go on independently of words and other signs, but is conducted by putting together chains of the signifying parts (the sound-images) of these signs. What they fail to note is that this is in no way inconsistent with the view that these signs are part of a language; indeed, the materialist theory of thinking requires such an assumption if it is to work. Nor is there any difficulty in admitting such an assumption into a materialist view of the world; one only has to assume that the *langue* in question is stored in physical form in the brain of the speaker, as a computer program is in a computer. The irony is, that Coward and Ellis would probably regard this as a mechanical form of materialism, and reject it in the name of the Marxist kind.

BOOKS

Eagleton, Terry 1976 *Criticism and Ideology*
Hawkes, Terence 1977 *Structuralism and Semiotics*
Coward, Rosalind and **Ellis, John** 1977 *Language and Materialism: Developments in Semiology and the Theory of the Subject*
Bennett, Tony 1979 *Formalism and Marxism*
Belsey, Catherine 1980 *Critical Practice*
Widdowson, Peter (ed.) 1982 *Rereading English*
Eagleton, Terry 1983 *Literary Theory: an Introduction.*
These books represent a critical school which could reasonably be titled 'modern British orthodoxy'; their work is taught on all the theory courses including mine. For reasons which escape me its members often see themselves as rebels confronting a powerful establishment. All except Eagleton (1976) and Coward and Ellis are fairly easy to read.

Sperber, Dan and **Wilson, Deirdre** 1986 *Relevance*
Kristeva, Julia 1986 (ed. **Toril Moi**) *The Kristeva Reader*.
It is an interesting exercise to try and get the Sperber and Wilson book into the same head as Kristeva's articles on Linguistics, Semiotics, Textuality: science and non-science together. See text of chapter for the contrast between these projects.

For further reading see booklist to chapter 6.

CHAPTER EIGHT

Towards a Realist Theory of Literature

Natural and Social Science, Objective Literary History and Functional Literary Values

SUMMARY

Recent theory often generalises its critical discourses – feminist, anti-racist, anti-imperialist, anti-capitalist, anti-metaphysical etc. – into anti-epistemological claims: e.g. that 'truth' is something produced in relations of power, or that meaning is a product of interpretation. This can form the basis of broad philosophical attacks on the concepts of impersonal rationality, objectivity and truth. Thus post-modernists appear to reject the very notion of having general theories. In literary study a certain relativism is now taken for granted, and the notion that there might be objective phenomena to be explained seems strange, and even oppressive. This chapter does not confront post-modernism as such, nor argues against the discourses listed above. But it does attack relativism.

This chapter takes as central to literary theory the problem of explaining why millions of people attach almost exactly the same meaning to a text: every reader of Ian Fleming thinking the James Bond books are spy stories, not text-books of electrochemistry, for example. It takes as marginal – though not non-existent or unimportant – the various uncertainties of interpretation, the variety of evaluative judgements, and the infinite range of ways in which other texts can be read into the one under consideration. It argues for an approach to literary theory that is constructive and explanatory – and in that sense 'scientific' – and less concerned with the antimetaphysics of indeterminacy. It sets that approach in a realist philosophical framework. It argues that certain relativist positions – such as that meaning is always a product of interpretation, never its basis – are incoherent; and it briefly outlines some possibilities for objective theories of structure, meaning, and even, within certain limits, value.

1 THE BANKRUPTCY OF SUBJECTIVIST PHILOSOPHY

Most of this book so far has had a destructive intention. I have tried to give a fair account of several of the theories which have led us to current critical discourse, and which still underlie it; but I have made it clear that I think them largely mistaken. That is not to say that the grand theoretical enterprise itself was a mistake. The great merit of French theory (whatever one thinks of its conclusions) has been to put on the agenda of cultural studies certain philosophical questions concerning the nature of reality, of knowledge and of representation; and certain fundamental questions of social science concerning the nature of society, of mind and of language. It would have been hard to get these questions taken seriously, in, say, Anglo-American literary criticism of the 1950s; it is strange that we needed a French student revolution to do it.

The problem is that the answers to these questions have been given within the framework of a broadly subjective philosophical tradition, in a period of revolutionary romanticism. This philosophical tradition was, as Lévi-Strauss stated and Piaget (1965) complained, hostile to empirical enquiry (see chapter 3). As a result, literary theory, instead of becoming a branch of empirical enquiry looking to a range of social sciences for its explanatory theories, has tended to become an idealist textual metaphysics, one of whose main concerns is to ward off reductive empirical theories and stress the endless openness of interpretation. Empirical studies of literature, language, psychology and society, though they flourish, have no clear place in literary theory when oriented by such a philosophy. Meanwhile historical, sociological and psychoanalytical literary theories have remained stuck in the revolutionary romanticism of the 1960s, despite the steady triumph of the Right in national politics throughout the West, and now, Eastern Europe. Theorists still dream of revolutionary changes in the forms of rationality itself; which gives a feeling of immense power; though in practical politics they get no more than occasional triumphs on the syllabus committees.

In this new environment, the prospects for an objective and empirical theory of literature seem poor: poorer than they were in the 1950s. Indeed, in some ways, the pursuit of such a theory now feels naïve. The very possibility of a general theory of literature seems to have been undermined by the post-structuralist phase of the French revolution. We draw, from the undeniable premise that no theory can determine its own conditions of application, the false conclusion that all general cultural theories are self-undermining. We feel – even if we don't accept the specific position of a Foucault or a Derrida – that no theory that does not have their self-reflexive, self-questioning quality can be other than crude; as if all theory aspired to the condition of Kristeva's semanalysis (Kristeva 1969b): to have absolutely no content except the questioning of itself.

And in one important respect my first paragraph was misleading: it ignored the hostility to science which permeates current thinking. I spoke of the 'sciences' of society, mind and language. I meant empirical sociology, psychology and linguistics, for all of which literature is in principle a legitimate object of investigation. But what critic currently refers to these sciences at all, when there is the alternative of Foucault, Lacan and the mythical Saussure? To us, conditioned by the French experience, it seems as if the very concept of an objective social science is a crude philosophical absurdity. From the height of our privileged discourse, we look down on such absurdities; indeed, some of us think that even the natural sciences do no more than construct ideal entities like electrons by main force of social consensus; and I have even heard a paper arguing that scientific progress is a consequence of the rhetorical structure prescribed by learned bodies for scientific papers. In this intellectual environment, to base a putative literary theory even partially on scientific models is a perilous enterprise.

But what is wrong is the intellectual environment. This is what we need to dismantle; and the best person to help might be the arch-textualist himself, Jacques Derrida; if we recognize the way in which his substantive arguments can be used to go diametrically against the tendencies of his own work.

Derrida belongs to the last stages of what might be called the continental version of the linguistic revolution in philosophy. The linguistic revolution (to give a simple, oversimplified story) was a move from the nineteenth-century interest in ideas and in the grounds of knowledge, to the twentieth-century interest in language and in forms of representation; one trajectory within it is given by the names of Russell and Wittgenstein; a quite independent one by those of Husserl and Derrida.

257

This revolution has been as important in its way as the earlier one, which we might associate with Descartes, in which (to give another simple story) philosophy abandoned its interest in the objective world to the natural sciences, and began to base its metaphysics on a sceptical enquiry into the grounds of knowledge.

What I am suggesting is that post-structuralism offers us evidence of the bankruptcy of this whole philosophical project, and grounds for reversing both revolutions and moving back into the objective world again. To say this is to accord it very considerable significance as a philosophical position; though the significance is exactly opposite to the kind usually accorded it.

There are many things that Derrida is reputed to have shown that he has not shown, and that could not possibly be shown. In particular he has shown nothing whatever about the relationship between writing and speech. (The empirical relationship, I mean – what other is there?) But what I think he has shown, again and again, is that any foundational enquiry undertaken within the framework of existentialism or phenomenology can eventually be subjected to deconstruction, and shown to rest upon a metaphysics of presence, or an ontotheology. Such enquiries are never presuppositionless, as they sometimes claim to be; they never destroy or avoid metaphysics, as they sometimes claim to do. I suggest that the implications of these arguments are clear. There is something wrong with the entire philosophical framework. We should, therefore, abandon that framework. It is pointless to turn a whole critical and philosophical industry over to the manufacture of further aporias. We should treat these as *reductio ad absurdum* arguments directed against the fundamental premises of the philosophy that produces them, and abandon that philosophy.

We may need to abandon something broader than that. The intertwined traditions of phenomenology and existentialism both operate within a framework of enquiry that might be called hermeneutic. Hermeneutics (Waterhouse 1981, pp. 5–11; Seung 1982) is a philosophical tradition extending back to the exegesis of the Bible and classical texts, and articulated by Schleiermacher and Wilhelm Dilthey into a general methodology for the human or cultural sciences. These subjects are supposed to be quite unlike the natural sciences; to understand them, we have in each case to enter into a closed circle of cultural meanings. A book – or even a simple sentence – has to have its meaning in terms of categories we already understand; and any new things we say will be constructed in terms of these categories.

In this framework, the categories of meaning in a particular culture may evolve historically; but they are based ultimately on the inner experiences of the human beings concerned, and they also form those experiences. If we live in that culture, we will have direct access to meanings within it. If the culture is alien to us, we have to enter into it with an intuitive leap, based upon categories evolved from our own experience of life; but there is no understanding without entering into the hermeneutic circle. How could there be an external and objective treatment of such meanings?

The attraction of this position is obvious: it closely corresponds to experiences we all have. But its defects are very great. It creates a gulf between any two cultures that seems to be crossable only by a leap of analytically inexplicable faith. And it creates a Chinese wall between our subjective and our objective understanding of the world that seems to be logically impossible to cross at all. It is true that however far the sciences advance, they can never possibly replace our human understanding. But it is not true that they can never interact with it or modify it. Scientific understanding and humane culture are constantly modifying each other: consider the advance of medicine and our attitude to diseases. And millions of people find themselves comparing different forms of cultural understanding, and rejecting one in favour of another, often on objective grounds, such as the ability of a particular culture to feed its members, cure diseases or win wars. The hermeneutic approach, if made precise and general, always seems to me to lead to a cultural relativism, and to viewing objective reality as something of a cultural irrelevance.

2   THE CASE FOR OBJECTIVE AND SUBJECTIVE REALISM

It is for these reasons that I would propose to construct cultural theory so far as possible within a framework of objective and subjective realism. **Realism** is not a popular philosophical position currently, though I think it is a true one. Systematic philosophical defences of realism in general from very different political points of view are to be found in Popper (1972 and *passim*) and Bhaskar (1986). But the language of linguistic or discursive idealism is far more common among literary critics and theorists. And it is often taken for granted that to postulate the objective existence of works of literature, or of the meaning of a text, or of the value of a text, however qualified, is to make an elementary philosophical mistake. These things must exist, the assumption goes, only as ideal or discursive constructs, or as the projections of the reader. I propose to contest that assumption.

Philosophical realism is quite different from literary realism. This point ought to be too elementary to be worth making, but it is in fact necessary; for they have sometimes been confused in theories of the type discussed in chapter 7, and epistemological conclusions – conclusions about the theory of knowledge – have been drawn on the basis of studies of realist and non-realist texts. But philosophical realism is a metaphysical doctrine about the nature of the world, with some secondary implications for our knowledge of the world. It has no obvious connection with literature. Literary realism is a set of conventions applying to a particular art form over a limited historical period: it is a literary movement. Its connections with philosophy are partly contingent, and have to be discovered by historical enquiry.

The realist claim, as I understand and defend it, is that there are, or have been, entities and structures in the world that exist independently of the thoughts we have about them, or of the linguistic descriptions we give of them. Such entities may include not only material objects like mountains, and organisms like dinosaurs, but entities which we have physically made, like tables or word-processors; and complex social entities, like insurance companies. They may also include works of literature, like *Hamlet*, which were originally constructed in words, and in the mind. They may also include purely subjective experiences, like the experience of a performance of *Hamlet*, which is complex and takes a considerable time; and even momentary thoughts and feelings, such as the thought of a single sentence of English, or the experience of uttering it; or even some momentary and quite evanescent feeling, impossible to remember clearly or to put into words.

The argument for the real existence of such entities as these is quite a simple one. It is that we cannot in general, by thinking about them, or redescribing them, or taking any action whatever after the event, make them change significantly or cease to have existed. Faith can't move mountains, unless it motivates large numbers of men to dig, or smaller numbers to use high explosive charges; that is how we know mountains are real. But faith was also notoriously unable to stop people finding fossils of the dinosaurs; which is why we think dinosaurs were probably real; at least, there are real fossils to be accounted for, and the story that the dinosaurs were real is the likeliest account. My mind can't even lay the table, let alone uncreate it; no words of mine can process my word-processor. That is why I think they are real. And all these things we call material.

But nor can my words persuade the Abbey National Building

Society to exist or cease to be. If Shakespeare wrote *Hamlet*, my thoughts cannot unwrite it; if I have uttered an English sentence I cannot un-utter it; and if, in my idiolect, it is grammatically correct, I cannot make it incorrect. If I have the most momentary, the most fleeting feeling, I cannot by anything I do make it the case that I do not have and have not had that feeling. All I can do is forget it; or persuade myself that I have not had it. None of these things are material; but by the only criterion of reality that has ever been available to me, they are as real as physical objects are.

This position may seem obvious: in fact it is obvious. But it is not empty; for it excludes two of the most common accounts given of the status of cultural objects. The first account is the view that I am in some sense a subject who constitutes these objects as objects: they are only objects for me as a subject. This operation of constituting something as an object seems to me quite empty. It is a vacuous philosophical analogue of the real psychological operation of recognizing or misrecognizing something as an object. The principle that objects are only objects for some subject is merely an *a priori* rejection of realism. It is supported only by an *a priori* commitment to a phenomenological framework. But as we have seen, that framework itself always leads to the paradoxes of deconstruction. The second account is that works of literature and other elements of culture are constructed by a process of discourse about them; and this, as I have pointed out, is a version of nineteenth-century idealism in which discourse has replaced ideas.

In both cases, all we have is an *a priori* rejection of the realist claim; and in both cases, if we reject the realist claim for the existence of cultural objects, we are doing so on grounds that ought to force us to reject it for material objects as well. Tables and chairs are no less 'culturally constructed' than works of literature; so, for that matter, are mountains, since only a human observer can pick out where a mountain begins or ends, and human observers have learnt to talk about mountains from the discourses they have heard. But the real physical structure of human artefacts and natural objects alike remains independent of any discourse; and continues to have its physical effects. For example, the existence of a mountain affects the way the rivers run, and hence the tribal water-supply, whether the tribal culture condescends to recognize the existence of the mountain or not.

There is of course an important truth underlying these false accounts. It is true that our experiences of works of literature, and indeed of everything else, depend not only on the intrinsic features of the text or whatever it is, but on the culture we have internalized; and that the culture we have internalized comes from the discourses (in a rather broad, metaphorical sense) in which we have been engaged. In this way, a critical discourse we have read will enter into our own reconstruction of the meaning of a text in front of us; though it will only ever do this through the action of a real physical brain belonging to a real social being in a real society: texts don't read texts and it is a confusing metaphor to say they do. It is nevertheless quite possible to argue that 90 per cent of the meaning of a text (if we could quantify it) is reconstituted during our reading from other discourses: though not 100 per cent, unless we cease to read and begin to hallucinate.

What cannot happen is that the text we read, or our experience of it, should be constituted by some later critical discourse about it. That would be a magical reversal of the arrow of time. However loaded with the effects of past discourse and the potential of future discourse is the experience we are now having, it is a real experience as it happens, and future discourses cannot change that; any more than the discourses of later palaeontologists could change either the objective reality of the dinosaurs, or whatever subjective experience the dinosaurs, in their reptilian way, may once have had. The world is an objective reality, including the subjective parts of it.

The objective and subjective realism that I favour has close relationships with materialism. It seems to me that materialist theses are often difficult to defend at a philosophical level, but can readily be defended as empirical claims within a realist framework. Thus the thesis that mental states are identical with brain states is logically indefensible; there are many predicates that apply to one, and make no sense with the other; and even a simple descriptive adjective like, say, 'overheated' means something quite different when applied to the brain and when applied to the mind. On the other hand, the empirical thesis that every state of mind corresponds to some features of the physical state of the brain is very plausible, and can be stated quite simply on the realist assumption that both brain-states and states of mind exist. So also can the other plausible empirical hypothesis – that ideas reflect, or represent, features of the objective world; they may distort those features greatly, but they do not create them. A further empirical claim would be that the function of ideas is practical; it is to guide the actions of real creatures – human beings – in a real world; so there is some check upon the ideas which it is possible for human beings to have, in that if they are too wildly discordant with reality, the human actions they guide will begin to fail. Notoriously, this check is not so strong that it will rule out all error and illusion.

This is an anti-idealist doctrine. It is very close to traditional materialism, and is compatible with the rational forms of Marxist materialism, such as most of the positions of Marx himself and of Lenin. In particular it does not exclude (though it does not entail) the central claim of historical materialism, that changes in society are the product of conflicts over the control – often the class control – of material resources, rather than of conflicts of ideas; and that ideas about society and culture are usually a consequence rather than a cause of economic arrangements. But it also does not attempt metaphysically to reduce complex social and cultural entities like nations, classes, insurance companies, arts and industries to their material parts, or even to that curious abstraction: 'material practices'. It is a materialism that does not deny that *Hamlet* can be a real object, merely because it is obviously not a material one.

When we speak of *Hamlet* we are not speaking of something abstract, like the meaning of a linguistic description, nor of something purely experiential, like the experience of a particular performance, nor of something purely material, like a particular text of the play; but of something complicated, with both material and immaterial parts: a play that was, in the context of a definite historical series of societies with objective social and cultural structures of their own, written, rehearsed, performed, published, read, commented on, theorized about and even used as a philosophical example. The objective and subjective reality of the play is established by the fact that these things happened. Its being is in these actual circumstances, and it has no being apart from these; which is not to say that it doesn't have a future. To be precise, its objective reality is established by the fact that any of the first five things listed happened. If none of them had happened except the last three, the play would be an imaginary one that I or another had invented.

The difference between this view and what I would consider an idealist view is as follows. The idealist would argue that the play, *Hamlet*, cannot be identical either with a physical text, or with any specific material practice, such as a production of the play. It must therefore be an abstraction from these; and an abstraction is an ideal object formed out of physical texts, material practices and so forth in the mind of some person describing the play. There is, therefore, no determinate play, *Hamlet*, since different persons might form different abstractions. There is, rather, an enormous family of ideal objects, at least one for every person who has even slightly different beliefs about the play; and it is not clear that any belief could be counted as false, since it will be true of its own ideal object; and there is no way of constraining the kinds of abstraction from experience that have given rise to it: even if the belief in question is actually that *Hamlet* is about Richard III.

Many modern critics like such consequences as these, and enjoy the notion of the indeterminate text. But the account is absurd nonetheless; and its absurdity can be seen by drawing the following conclusion: that the very existence of the play, *Hamlet*, on this account, depends on its presence in the mind of its readers; and when the last of these is dead, not only will the play not exist; it will never have existed. The whole argument seems to me to depend on the same mistake on which all idealism rests: the mistake of supposing that epistemology governs ontology; to be is to be known. On that principle, not only *Hamlet* will flash out of existence as soon as the last human being is dead; so also will the entire material world, taking its past with it. For atoms are just as much the mental constructions of physicists, and dinosaurs are just as much the mental constructions of palaeontologists as plays are the mental constructions of critics; and cows, chairs and mountains are the mental constructions of everyman, in any society where these objects are known.

On an objective realist view, a thing can exist without being known; on a subjective realist view, a thought or feeling can exist without the person whose thought or feeling it is being conscious of it – that is, it can be unconscious. As a practical matter, a complex object like *Hamlet*, with objective and subjective aspects, could hardly have come into existence without Shakespeare knowing it, since he had to write it; and that is too complicated an action to be performed unconsciously. But for it to have existed, neither Shakespeare nor anyone else has to keep rewriting it in his head; nor does it have to have been written down by anybody. *Hamlet*, and with it, the contents of human culture, high and low, are objects of history, not products of historians; all we can do in the present is know about them or be ignorant of them; approve of them or disapprove of them; and (the most important relationship) imitate or be influenced by them, or not.

Realism has certain implications for the theory of knowledge: roughly speaking, it increases the importance of the concept of truth, and decreases the importance of subjective certainty (cf. Popper 1972 for an extended discussion of this). It makes it possible for our beliefs to be right or wrong – we can, for example, get the date of the first performance of *Hamlet* right, or we can get it wrong; even if we never know whether we are right or wrong. It reduces the scope and interest of the concept of 'certain knowledge': we cannot have certain knowledge of real entities, except possibly purely logical or mathematical ones; most of our knowledge is conjectural, including our knowledge of the sun, and the room upstairs, and of history, of our own feelings, and of other people, whether we know them by description or are personally acquainted with them. Realism, whether about objective things or subjective thoughts, reduces the philosophical interest of subjective experience. A realist will not deny that we are sometimes aware of some things; but he will deny that what we are aware of is more real than what we are unaware of; he will find no appeal in the phenomenological motto: 'Back to the phenomena themselves'. In this respect he will not hold to a metaphysics of presence; and the Derridean deconstruction of such a metaphysics will not, I think, apply to a realist position.

Objective realism is compatible with the concept of scientific investigation of reality: investigation, that is, by experiment, employing a hypothetico–deductive method to determine which experiments count for what. The assumption here is that there may be real, if as yet unobserved entities and structures to investigate; and that one may be mistaken about entities and structures one at present supposes to exist. On this view, changes in our knowledge are possible; but changes in our knowledge do not change the reality we are apprehending. This principle may not be compatible with certain idealist interpretations of modern physics; a point that has been of concern to Marxist materialists, and is extensively discussed in my second book, *The Dematerialisation of Karl Marx*. On my view, changes in reality itself certainly do occur, in course of time; and human action can sometimes bring them about. But changes in our knowledge only change reality by influencing human action; and they can never change the past.

3   THE POVERTY OF STRUCTURALISM

From this standpoint, structuralism must be thought of as a theory of the structures of the objective world; including, of course, those structures in such parts of the objective world as the human brain, and human societies, that underlie consciousness. We can begin to review some of the more fundamental objections to the whole structural approach from this point of view. Much of this book has been devoted to a criticism of the structuralist movement, and a criticism of a very fundamental kind; I have suggested that every important specific proposal within it – structuralist linguistics, Lacanian psychoanalysis, Althusserian theory of ideology and subjectivity – has suffered from logical poverty: each proposal has been inherently too simple to account even in principle for the kinds of phenomena to which it was addressed.

Despite its sweeping nature, such a criticism, in my hands, is an essentially empirical one. For me, structuralist linguistics won't work, but generative grammar might. Lacanian psychoanalysis won't work (because of its generally unscientific nature, and its inadequate theory of language in particular – see the third book in this sequence, *Making Freud Unscientific* – but a dynamic psychology with a credible relation to modern cognitive theories is not ruled out. Neither Lévi-Strauss's nor Althusser's theories of society will work; but a structural anthropology supporting, and supported by, a materialist economics is not impossible.

But it is possible to make a more far-reaching criticism of this whole approach: a philosophical criticism that suggests that no amount of tinkering with the individual components will save us: that it is logically impossible to account for human experience and human consciousness in this way. It is impossible, so the story runs, if the human sciences are conceived as natural sciences and such concepts as consciousness and value are not surreptitiously smuggled in, that those concepts should ever be constituted or explained within the human sciences.

The clearest version of this argument is perhaps that given by John Searle in his polemic against the concept of artificial intelligence (Searle 1984). Imagine a man inside a room, who processed messages passed to him through the door. And the messages were in Chinese; and the man did not know Chinese. But he operated by consulting a dictionary and mechanically applying some rules of grammar, just as a computer program might. In this case, neither the man, nor the room, could be said to be thinking in Chinese. The force of this argument is a humanist one; however closely you simulate human behaviour, you can never get beyond the syntax of it; the semantics will evade you. However intelligently a computer might answer Searle's interrogatory, he would, I think, deny it consciousness, even if the evidence available from behaviour were sufficient to justify assuming consciousness in a person. But I would not. For me, if enough information could be built in, and built in in the right way, the computer would not merely be simulating a person; it would be a person. Persons are no more than biological computers running those complex programs that we call, collectively, human cultures. And in that sense, the anti-humanists of the 1960s were right; the human subject is no more than an effect of culture.

Yet to believe this – to reject the supposed philosophical distinction between the human and the non-human – is not to think less of the human subject, but more. Its complexity is awesome. The achievements of the human sciences in mapping it are piddling. As a practical matter, not only are we nowhere near simulating a human being; we are nowhere near simulating a cockroach. The value of computer science here is to offer a philosophical analogy: that cultural objects like the English language or *Hamlet* not only resemble formally, but have the same kind of reality as a computer program. Both kinds of object are real. Neither is material. Both can have material embodiments. Neither is identical with its material embodiments. Both can have material effects. Neither is identical with its material effects. Both are involved with human practices. Neither is identical with the practices connected with it.

4   THE STATUS OF A THEORY OF LITERATURE

In this framework, what is the place of a theory of literature? It needs to have philosophical, empirical and formal aspects; and these interact. At a philosophical level, it has to confront a number of problems: for example, the nature of the relationship between cultural representations and reality (signifier theory seems useless for this purpose) and the nature of value judgements. At an empirical level, it needs to provide a testable account of the relationships, both causal and cognitive, between literary works and the languages from which they are made, the minds which create and experience them, and the societies within which writing and reading are practised. The empirical part of a theory of literature must then contain linguistic, psychological and sociological elements. It is important that these should be satisfactory by the ordinary standards of theories in linguistics, psychology and sociology; and on the other hand that the sciences of linguistics, psychology and sociology should not be so logically poor that they can give no account of works of literature. This may indeed be the greatest importance of literary theory, when rationally conceived: that it will act as a final test for the human sciences; if they can account for literature, they can account for everything.

At a formal level, a literary theory has to provide some definition of its objects; that is, it has to say what a work of literature is, and how it differs from a philosophical theory or an egg. This is a distinctly non-trivial question, which may well involve empirical studies in anthropology – to determine how far works of art in general, and works of literature in particular, are cultural universals – and in history, to determine how far art and literature are historically constructed and historically specific. It seems certain that literary theory has a historical dimension. It may be that the formal definition of literature must contain an essential historical element – that what counts as literature is itself determined by historically conditioned social practices, and by historically constructed literary traditions. It is quite certain that literature exists and finds a meaning only within human cultures; and that human cultures are themselves historically constructed. It is also the case that most literary scholarship has always had a historical dimension. That suggests strongly that there is something in literature that demands a historical dimension for literary theory.

In a programmatic sense, such work as this can be, and is being done now. There seems to be no logical, philosophical or principled reason why we cannot have a theory of literature, any more than of society or the mind; and plenty of people are working on all of them. In a detailed sense – the sense in which we speak of physics having theories, or a grammar being a theory of a language, and in which we would expect to be able to base the design of a work of literature upon our theory – the Huxleyan or Orwellian world of programmable writing machines – literary theory is obviously beyond the bounds of possible science, and will be reached only when we get beyond the cockroach stage of computing.

5   OBJECTIVE MEANING AND INTERPRETATION

It is a standard assumption of modern theory that texts have no objective standard meaning; meaning is a product of interpretation and is infinitely variable. I am going to argue the exact opposite of this. The meaning of a work is wholly objective. It depends exclusively on objective factors such as the exact words in the text, the current conventions of reading, and so forth, and is independent of subjectivity. The experience of a work is something that happens in real time, when a subjectivity – a person – grasps or distorts that meaning. Interpretation, on the other hand, is a way in which critics transform a work into an allegory of their own interests. It is opportunistic and subjective, and essentially open-ended and without limits.

There is nothing new about this position. In concrete terms, I am saying that it is an objective truth about *Hamlet* that it is about a Prince of Denmark whose uncle has killed his father; but it is an interpretation to call it a play about the Oedipus complex. Most people took this point for granted until the rise of recent critical theory.

The assumption that meaning is an infinitely variable product of interpretation is nowadays widely but uncritically held; this appears to be a consequence of the fact that most critics spend their time arguing over nuances of interpretation. As I pointed out in the introduction to this book, what a Martian would notice is the extreme uniformity and certainty of meaning. A million readers will read the same spy thriller and every single one of them will suppose it to be a story about spies. Not one will mistake it for a textbook in electrochemistry. But if meaning were a product of interpretation one would expect there to be some critics who argued that *Dr No* was a textbook of electrochemistry, and James Bond was the name of a chemical. A Martian would say that it is a characteristic feature of texts that they have elaborate and determinate meanings attached to them. This is one of the things that distinguishes them from other cultural objects, like bricks and people, which do not.

The publicly available meaning of a text seems to be objectively determined by the particular arrangement of words the text contains; by the language it is written in; by the conventions that determine how it is read; and by the contextual references (to real situations, or to other texts) which it is capable of making at particular times, and in particular contexts of reading. (One example of a 'context of reading' would be consulting the telephone directory; another, reading a poem to oneself for pleasure.)

The text can thus have a public meaning only in a particular society, since only a society can provide conventions of reading and so forth; and these change with time. Individuals in the society, whether they are writers or readers, can manipulate but not override these conventions, since they produce their own readings through them. A text thus has a determinate public meaning, at a particular time, for a particular individual in a particular society, which that individual will have no power to change, even if he is the author of the text. No doubt there will also be scope, in the mind of author and reader alike, for idiosyncratic associations; but these are no part of the public meaning of the text.

The claims made in the last two paragraphs are obvious to the point of banality; and it is not worth arguing with naïve objections to them. What is interesting is that almost every one of them is contested in modern literary theory, sometimes by arguments of great philosophical subtlety and depth. It is beyond the scope of this book to engage in detail with the arguments of the later Derrida or the Yale deconstructionists. But I can point out the principles on which they proceed; and on which it is therefore possible rationally to disagree with them.

A determined relativist might begin where I ended by attacking the concept of an objective distinction between 'idiosyncratic associations' and 'conventions of reading'. In a sense, Modernism itself contained such an attack. *The Waste. Land* was criticized at the time of its publication for depending upon curious private associations of ideas; these have now become part of the institutionalized competence of every student of modern poetry. But one might argue that the very process of drawing such a distinction as this, between the idiosyncratic and the conventional, is a way of constructing, rather than recognizing, a normal world for ourselves. The politically oriented might argue that it is a way of imposing a political cultural order: a bourgeois order perhaps. The metaphysically oriented might argue that it is a way of providing a transcendental signified, a ground of being, perhaps even a godhead. The distinction between the conventional and the idiosyncratic is thus seen, rather strangely, as a metaphysical distinction.

A further attack is possible on the notion which turns up in the literature under several names, and which I have chosen to call the 'context of reading'. It is clear that in any society, the number of possible contexts of reading is infinite; and each one will change the meaning-in-context of what is read. The Derrida–Searle controversy is illuminating here. But the general question is this. Does the fact that the number of possible contexts of reading is infinite, even in one particular society, preclude the possibility of giving an empirical account of such contexts? After all, there is an infinite number of possible sentences in any natural language. Does that mean we can't do linguistics?

As soon as we have asked this question we can see that the metaphysical critique of the claims I made goes much too far. We cannot adopt a metaphysical system – nor, for that matter, a political system – that rules out, as a matter of principle, quite ordinary areas of empirical study. If the consequence of our metaphysics is that we cannot give an account of the difference between a context of reading such as consulting the telephone directory and a context of reading such as reading a poem for pleasure, then there is something wrong with our metaphysics. If the consequence of our metaphysics is that we cannot speak of the difference between the conventions of a love-sonnet and those of an epic poem, then there is something wrong with our metaphysics. And exactly the same is true if we substitute for metaphysics, anti-metaphysics; and sign it with the name of Derrida.

6   THE NATURE OF LITERARY INTERPRETATION

There is in fact something very strange about the whole family of arguments found in post-structuralist literary theory. Grizzled professors, grown grey with explaining works of literature to the young, now claim that they do not know how to read a work of literature. Yet one would make a great mistake if one supposed that they had not learnt, or had forgotten, all the standard conventions of reading which one as a matter of fact has to employ. The case is otherwise; they believe themselves to have found philosophical arguments which in some sense undermine the authority of those conventions. Yet this sense is a Pickwickian one. It is not at all clear that literary conventions ever had the kind of authority that philosophical argument can undermine. The arguments, so far as they are valid, are directed against transcendental claims: that is, claims about the necessary nature of subjectivity. The conventions of literature are arbitrary and historical. Fundamentally, they are historical matters of fact, touching on the empirical nature of past subjectivities. They generate past meanings which are also matters of historical fact.

Since we cannot change the past, the meaning that literature has historically possessed is something fixed, though complex. This seems to be the major object of study for literary scholarship to recover and literary theory to explain. But there is also a perpetual revolt among both writers and readers of literature against a purely historical understanding. Hence the critical claim that the meaning of a work of literature is the meaning that it has for us. It is in the present that literary interpretation and criticism have their own semi-creative roles, respectively in connecting literature with our own present concerns, and in evaluating it for us now.

Literary interpretation and evaluative criticism are extraordinary social practices; but they are as universal as literature itself: they occur in the Bible and Plato. Any coherent literary theory needs to be able to give an account of them. One account we can safely dismiss is that every reading is, and is equally, an interpretation; and no one reading is more authoritative than any other; as if *Wuthering Heights* could legitimately be read as a delicate study in lesbian love, set in fourteenth-century China. This view of interpretation is the lazy-minded person's way of ensuring there is nothing interesting to explain. If I say that *Paradise Lost* is an epic poem about the fall of Man, I am not offering one interpretation among others; I am not even offering a specially privileged interpretation; I am not offering an interpretation at all; I am saying what the poem is and what it is about.

The rebel against historical understanding would reply here: 'No. You are saying what the poem was; and what it was about. I can make it mean something different now.' But that rebel would be wrong. The basis of his claim would be, that since the meaning of every element of the work rests on convention, he has only to change all the conventions, and it will mean something else. But the work is too complicated, and too many of the conventions are unconscious, for this to be psychologically possible.. I cannot, for example, decide that every time I meet the name 'Satan' I shall read it as 'Dorothea' or 'Heathcliff'. I cannot decide to count the number of lines in the poem as fourteen, or to fit them to the rhyming scheme abba abba cdcd ee. These things are impossible; I would not begin to know how to try to do them; and nor would our rebel. Of course I can say anything; but if I say that *Paradise Lost* is a sonnet about Stella's eyes I am not offering a fresh interpretation; I have simply got it wrong; I am probably talking about the wrong poem and the wrong poet.

It is a mark of the confusion that French subjectivist theory has caused that many modern critics suppose they somehow don't need to make the distinction between the meaning of a text and an interpretation of it. Catherine Belsey (1988) in her book on Milton, supposes that the only sense we can give to the notion of the meaning of *Paradise Lost* is some subjective personal intention Milton had: 'an intended meaning which preceded the writing process'. She goes on, quoting Derrida as her sacred text, to castigate readers who want to know that meaning, for their metaphysical yearnings: 'Reading in its conventional understanding and practice has been deeply imbued with a metaphysical desire for meaning as presence, for access to the relegated, supplanted "thought", intention, or idea, which common sense so often locates "behind" the text itself.' Meanings, she adds, are an effect of interpretation, not its origin; and an interpretation 'is not a transcription of anything outside language, but a set of signifiers concerning another set of signifiers' (Belsey 1988).

The odd thing here is that Belsey shows no interest in (though she does not deny the existence of) the objective historical meaning of Milton's texts, as determined by the actual arrangement of words in them, the language they are written in, and the literary conventions that then prevailed. It is this public meaning, which constrains Milton and his readers alike, that is the true opposite of a modern interpretation; not the subjective phantom that Derrida attacks. This is a case − not untypical of post-structuralist writing − where the introduction of sophisticated Derridean theory has simply encouraged the critic to set up a straw man.

The theory of interpretation proposed is equally vacuous. How can one set of signifiers concern another? What does 'concern' mean? Are we talking of reference? Of sense? Of metaphor? Of allegory? Of mental association? If there are only chains of signifiers without any signifieds, all you can really do is lay them side by side and connect them with upholstery buttons. I suspect she is relying on some theory like that of Coward and Ellis, discussed in chapter 7. This theory suffers from logical poverty; it is in this respect quite typical of adaptations of Derrida or Lacan for literary analysis.

We need a better theory of interpretation than this, and can find it outside textual mysticism. Interpretation arises − and becomes an interesting activity, worth theorizing − when by some rhetorical procedure rather more interesting than changing the subject − by some such procedure as allegory, or local metaphor, or so forth − the critic can show a connection between formal features of the work and some present interest of herself and her own contemporaries. Thus the Freudian critic can find very good formal grounds in the text and in psychoanalytic theory for supposing Heathcliff in *Wuthering Heights* to be a phallic symbol; and the Marxist rather less good grounds for making him stand for the proletariat. In both cases the reason for the new interpretation would be that the critic found it more interesting than the meaning the text had for its original writers and readers. (The anti-relativist, anti-Derridean metaphysical assumptions of the last phrase are of course intended, and are, indeed, the whole point − I hope, by now, they have been justified.)

Most discourse about literature is not literary theory, and not even literary scholarship, but is, rather, interpretation and evaluation. It is on this work that post-structuralism has had its greatest influence. Given the opportunistic nature of interpretation (one might say, the essential and principled opportunism of interpretation) it is not surprising that most post-structuralist interpretations of literature bring out the intertextuality, the significant breaks in the textual surface, the paradoxes of self-reference and so forth; in short they make works of literature into allegories of post-structuralism. When was it ever different? Interpretative criticism since Socrates has proceeded by making works of literature into allegories of the interests of the critic; so, for de Man, they have to be allegories of reading.

It is an interesting study to see how Milton has been appropriated, in the course of three centuries, for orthodoxy, for Whiggery, for national liberty against the Napoleonic tyrant, for Victorian high seriousness, for democracy, for Marxism – the 1970s student revolutionary kind – and lastly, by Catherine Belsey, for Derridean textual mysticism. The constant factor is that in every case the critic finds more interest in the preoccupations Milton is being translated into, than in the preoccupations he actually had. Nor is there anything wrong in this; it keeps the texts alive, often in unexpected ways. Thus Derrida's metaphysics does what C. S. Lewis could not do – it turns *Paradise Lost* back into a religious poem; it is astonishing that this should happen at the hands of Belsey, who I thought was a materialist. But here is a quotation from what, despite anything I have said above, is an interesting critical book: '. . . it is exactly this triumphant versatility, this difference within the voice of the poet/prophet, that calls in question the authority of the text and begins the Fall into differance. . . . Milton's poetry continues to be haunted by the problem of voices which query presence even while they construct it' (Belsey 1988, p. 25).

The naturalness with which Derrida's work provides a religious interpretation of *Paradise Lost* brings out the theological character of the former. Indeed, there is no serious doubt about Derrida's piety; as he once remarked: 'Presence is Good. Presence is the Best.'★

★ In response to the question 'What is wrong with presence?' at a conference in Glasgow (University of Strathclyde) 1986, Derrida's answer was that nothing was wrong with presence: he then indicated some of his reasons for deconstructing its metaphysics.

7   THE THEORY OF OBJECTIVE FUNCTIONAL VALUE

The last bastion of defence against the claims of realism is in the question of value. If an objective theory of value means a theory that provides objective reasons for value judgements it appears to be a logical impossibility; you cannot say that *Hamlet* is a good play on the basis of any objective qualities of the text, nor even on the basis of any empirical facts about the number of people who like it. There is no logical absurdity in T. S. Eliot's assertion that *Hamlet* is an artistic failure, despite or even because of the number of people who have admired it for (what Eliot considers to be) the wrong reasons. But there is something mystifying: as C. S. Lewis put it: we need more failures like this. One feels like saying that *Hamlet* can simultaneously be, from one point of view a failure, and from another a rather striking success; and that the two points of view do not invalidate each other. But this is essentially what is meant by saying that judgements of value are purely subjective in character.

Perhaps the most surprising claim I have to make in this chapter is that value judgements should be seen as essentially objective. They are objective judgements, I will argue, not about intrinsic qualities or structures, but about how well certain functions are performed. Complex cultural objects perform many different functions; that is why we can say they are good, and bad, in a complex mixture of ways. It is not a matter of different people making different, but equally valid, judgements about the same object; but of different people, or even the same person, making correct or incorrect judgements about a range of different, and perhaps equally valid, functions. The argument derives from the general principle of objective realism. It seems to be possible to describe the world, on an empirical basis, as containing objective entities and structures; and to find that parts of it have objectively describable **functions**. Thus, a description of an ecosystem will include many functional descriptions which are in no sense a projection of the values of the person describing it.

Now it seems to be the case that, as soon as functional descriptions are available, so is a language of values. That is to say, if we can describe something – whether it is a knife or an elephant's trunk – as having a function, we can also describe it, by comparison with other entities, as being good or bad at that function. Furthermore, such a description is capable of being objectively true or false. We thus have the basis for an objective theory of values, which can apply even to the animal world, and independently of questions of human meaning.

Discussion of the value of a work of art obviously involves socially and historically constructed functions of great complexity; but the logic of value appears to be the same. A knife is good if it cuts well whatever it was designed to cut. But what makes *Hamlet* a good play? The easy part is to say that it performs well whatever functions a play has; the difficult part is to say what those are; or perhaps, what those are, in a particular culture, at a particular period, perhaps even in a particular class, or for a particular group of people. If one could establish the functions of the play, a value judgement would be objective in character: that is, it would be an assessment of how well, compared with other plays, this one performed its function. There might even be several different, equally objective value judgements to be made, according to what the function was: whether it was to provide a certain type of undemanding entertainment (for which purpose *The Mousetrap* might perhaps be superior to *Oedipus Rex*); or to purge the soul with pity and terror.

To make matters more difficult, the proper functions of a play are not uncontested. They are a site of struggle: involving political, moral and religious questions at least; and this struggle may take place inside one's own mind. In any judgement of the value of a work of literature, two types of judgement are being made simultaneously: how well it performs its function, and whether that function ought to be performed. Only to the extent that the two types of judgement can be analytically separated is it possible to distinguish aesthetic from moral, political and religious judgements.

And this separation can be very difficult. It is possible to emerge from a relentlessly successful farce, and feel that one has wasted an evening that could have better been spent at a more serious, if less functionally effective play. Is this a moral or aesthetic judgement? It is also possible to emerge rather dispiritedly from an ineffective serious play, and wish it had been a good farce. In this riot of subjectivity, quite a number of difficult, but objective judgements are being made: about the artistic purpose of the plays concerned, and hence the functions for which they are intended; and about their relative success. Such judgements will always be relative to a particular ideal audience; but that does not stop them being objective. A theory about the objective elements in literary value judgements is going to be very complicated. This chapter is not the place to set out such a theory in all its ramifications. My concern here, as throughout the book, is with arguments that have developed during, or out of, the structuralist episode. But there is no harm in saying that my position is one of objective realism in relation to the existence of works of art, and of a historically qualified, objective functionalism in relation to their value. I hope the meaning of these terms, and the precise claims I am making, have become clear.

8   THE NON-SCIENTIFIC GOAL OF HUMAN UNDERSTANDING

When everything has been said, there is another, less sophisticated type of argument against mechanistic and structural theories in the human sciences. This is that we do not really want humane studies to be sciences. We are not thinking of explanation and prediction when we read a book; we are thinking of understanding. To read a book is not like formulating a scientific theory; it is like talking to a friend. And the general model of humane studies is reading literature rather than doing scientific research, pursuing understanding rather than explanation, mastering a symbolic code in order to communicate rather than employing a theory in order to predict and control natural processes.

It is clear that we cannot reject this view as a false statement of fact about the human world; it is, rather, a deliberate choice of a different goal for our studies of it. Such studies may be very serious – talking to a friend can be very serious – but they do not need to be theoretical. And one possible consequence of recognizing this would be not that we should develop different kinds of theories in the human sciences, but that we should develop no theories; that we should abandon theory-making altogether. This has been, on the whole, the position taken by modern English literary critics. They have chosen to concentrate on providing supremely intelligent readings of particular works, without wishing to theorize about their own methods and procedures. Dr Leavis is often quoted as a typical example of this position; but he was not; he actually produced a theoretical defence for it, in the article 'Literary Criticism and Philosophy', reprinted in *The Common Pursuit* (Leavis 1952). This makes him a major theorist of the anti-theoretical camp.

There is nothing incoherent or indefensible about the anti-theoretical position, provided that all that is claimed is that literary critical activity is not the same as theorizing, and theorizing is not a necessary condition for critical activity. After all, there are plenty of activities we can perform, while being unable to give any serious analysis of them: riding a bicycle, walking across the room and thinking are examples that come to mind. If criticism is defined as, say, public and articulate interpretation of complex works of art, at a level found acceptable by artist and audience, it is a fair prediction that no satisfactory theories of such a complex activity will be available for some time to come. The reasons are the same as those given in chapter 1 for our lack of any serious scientific theory of history. Reading is not the mystically impossible activity that some post-structuralists suppose it to be; but it is, scientifically, too complicated an activity for any theory of it to work at the present time. At the moment we have very little idea of what is going on, in psychological terms, when we ask for a cup of coffee to be passed; or when we understand in its context a simple sentence like: 'The boy kicked the ball.'

APPENDIX

Comparing Translations of de Saussure

There are two translations of de Saussure's *Cours de Linguistique Générale*. The essential differences turn on the translation of a few key words, so I will comment on these.

Wade Baskin translated Saussure in 1959, and was published by McGraw Hill. (My references are to the paperback edition, quoted in bibliography as Saussure 1916b). There is a later edition (Fontana 1974) with a preface by Jonathan Culler. Baskin's translation is in my view clear, fluent (despite some Gallicisms) and easy to read. Roy Harris's translation, 1983, is published by Duckworth. (In bibliography as Saussure 1916c). It is stiffer and less easy to read, but probably more accurate overall. Harris and his publisher are very contemptuous of Baskin – I think unduly so – and accuse him of bad mistranslations. But Harris has these too. Either can be used; but there are (though it sounds paradoxical) major differences of detail. I mean by this that there are differences in the translation of one or two words that add up to major differences in one's assessment of what it was Saussure actually discovered. The last one, about phonemes, is the one that really matters.

The first crucial terms are ***langage, langue, parole***.

Baskin translated *langage* as **speech**, which is wrong. Harris translates it as **language**, which is correct for one sense – the very general sense – of the English word 'language' (see chapter 1 section 2).

Baskin translated *langue* as **language**. This is correct, in another sense of the word 'language' as when you say 'German is a language'. Harris translates it in several different ways: **linguistic structure, language as a structured system, a language as a structured system**. These translations are all correct in context, but the use of multiple translations has one very unfortunate effect – you never learn what Saussure meant by *langue*, since you can't identify repetitions of the word. But this is one of the main motives for reading Saussure!

Baskin translates *parole* as **speaking**. Harris makes it **speech**. Either is acceptable, but both are in one sense misleading: they suggest an opposition to 'writing' which is not here intended. Writing a letter in English and speaking in English on the telephone are both examples of *parole* in the English *langue* (of speech in the English tongue). I slightly prefer Baskin here; he captures the performative quality of *parole*.

Although I don't want to say that the translation of *langue* as 'linguistic structure' is wrong, it must be said that it sounds rather odd. The reason is that the phrase 'linguistic structure' is a precise term whose meaning is given by seventy years in the development of linguistics; while *langue* is an imprecise term, newly coined as a technical term at the beginning of that period. The same objection would apply if one used the translation 'linguistic performance' for *parole*. It is correct, but far too closely associated with Chomsky to be happy as a Saussurean term.

E. Jackson has offered me an illuminating analogy from classical scholarship: there is a phrase in Plato, *to on*, which literally means 'that which is'. Jowett translates it 'absolute being'. In terms of the sophisticated idealism of the nineteenth century, he wasn't wrong; but it does sound very odd, and amounts to reading what should be the commentary into the original text.

The best solution if one is interested in structuralist or semiological applications is not to translate these terms at all. If one is reading or writing on structuralism, one should keep the terms *langage, langue, parole,* which are what most people use and understand. From this point of view, Baskin is better; he often prints the French word alongside his English translation, so that one can learn it.

Harris's oddest decision as a translator concerns the components of the sign. Saussure's words are *signe, signifié, signifiant*. Virtually every English discussion in the whole literature of structuralism follows Baskin in translating these as:

sign, signified, signifier.

These words are now ordinary English technical terms, and it is surely no longer open to a translator of Saussure to change them. Nevertheless, Harris uses:

sign, signification, signal.

Baskin, who provided the standard translations, also helpfully adds the French terms in brackets. Harris does not.

Another term of importance is that for the signifying part of a word: in the French, *image acoustique*. The important point here is that this is not a physical sound, but a psychological representation of one: a sound as recognized by a person, or as present in the mind. Baskin translates it as **sound–image**, which seems fine to me. Harris objects that this suggests a visual image, perhaps even the written form, and makes it **sound–pattern**. I don't much go for this. Baskin seems closer to the French; but then, Harris actually dislikes the French term!

Baskin and Harris do not differ, thank God, about the **diachronic** and the **synchronic**; nor about **syntagmatic** and **associative** relations. However, Harris turns the ordinary English term **syntagm**, which Baskin uses, into **syntagma**. This raises the question: if Saussure had used the opposite notion of 'paradigm', would Harris have turned it into '*paradigma*'?

SAUSSURE LOSES HIS PHONEMES!

I have kept the big news till last. Harris's translation has made a substantial change in the history of ideas; though one that has been discussed from time to time, e.g. by Jakobson. Harris has deprived Saussure of the credit for phoneme theory. Here is his policy decision, stated in the translator's introduction:

> However, a few comments on the problems involved in translating Saussure's technical terminology may be in order here. Some relate to changes in usage since Saussure's day. For example, it would nowadays be misleading to translate *phonème* by phoneme, since in the terminology currently accepted in Anglo-American linguistics the term **phoneme** designates a structural unit, whereas it is clear that for Saussure the term *phonème* designates a unit belonging to *la parole* (whatever his editors may have thought, and in spite of remarks in the *Cours* which – rightly or wrongly – are held to have been influential in establishing the modern theory of phonemes). Similarly, Saussure's *phonologie* does not correspond to what is nowadays termed **phonology**, nor his *phonétique* to **phonetics**.
> (Harris 1987, p.xiv)

This is a disastrous decision by Harris, though one can see what the pressures were. The underlying problem is this. Modern linguistics recognises a distinction between **phonetics** – the study of the actual sounds of speech, either as sound (**acoustic phonetics**) or as movements of the vocal organs (**articulatory** or **physiological**

phonetics) – and on the other hand **phonology** or **phonemics** – the study of the sound patterns and minimal units of sound that are significant in language. For Saussure, this distinction was embryonic. (It took thirty years for full-scale phoneme theory to develop.) He wanted to use the word phonology to apply to what is now called physiological phonetics; but later theorists have not followed him in this.

There is a large section of the *Cours* concerned with what Saussure calls phonology, but modern linguistics calls phonetics. Harris uses translator's licence to make Saussure call it phonetics throughout, **even at the very moment when Saussure is saying that he wants to call it phonology**!

Here is Baskin:

> The physiology of sounds (German *Laut-* or *Sprachsphysiologie*) is often called phonetics (French *phonétique*, German *Phonetik*.) To me, this name seems inappropriate. Instead, I shall use **phonology**.
>
> (Saussure 1916b, p. 33)

And here is Harris:

> The physiology of sounds (German *Lautphysiologie* or *Sprachsphysiologie)* is often called simply 'phonetics' (French *phonétique*, German *Phonetik*, English *phonetics*). But this is inappropriate. We prefer to call it **physiological phonetics**.
>
> (Saussure 1916c, p. 32)

It is of course Baskin who is correct here. Harris is falsifying history, and making Saussure say the opposite of what he actually said. The reason is obvious: he is afraid that his students will be confused by the difference between Saussurean and modern terminology, when they read this part of the *Cours*. But students ought not to be learning physiological phonetics from this book anyway: it is anything from seventy to ninety years out of date. Saussure's work is of use now to only two classes of people: those who want to learn about the history of ideas, in particular the history of linguistics; and those who want to learn about the structuralist tradition. And these people need to know the historical facts: such as the fact that Saussure wanted to call 'phonology' the discipline that we now call 'phonetics'. (Baskin makes this point in a footnote.)

Worse is to follow. I have said that in Saussure the distinction between phonology and phonetics was embryonic. This is particularly so in the substantial Appendix to the Introduction, entitled 'Principles of Phonology' (which Harris, of course, translates as 'Principles of Physiological Phonetics'). The reason is that this section dates from lectures of 1897; Saussure at that stage naturally hadn't developed his later theories. Later in the book, and ten to fifteen years later in his life, Saussure stumbled upon the phoneme principle. Here is Baskin:

> . . . This is even more true of the linguistic signifier, which is not phonic but incorporeal – constituted not by its material substance but by the differences that separate its sound-image from all others.
>
> The foregoing principle is so basic that it applies to all the material elements of language, including phonemes. Every language forms its words on the basis of a system of sonorous elements, each element being a clearly delimited unit and one of a fixed number of units. Phonemes are characterised not, as one might think, by their own positive quality but simply by the fact that they are distinct. Phonemes are above all else opposing, relative, and negative entities.
>
> (Saussure 1916b, pp.118–19)

And here is Harris:

> Considerations of the same order are even more pertinent to linguistic signals. Linguistic signals are not in essence phonetic. They are not physical in any way. They are constituted solely by differences which distinguish one such sound pattern from another.
>
> This fundamental principle applies to every material element used by a language, even the basic speech sounds. Each language constructs its words out of some fixed number of phonetic units, each one clearly distinct from the others. What characterises these units is not, as might be thought, the specific positive properties of each; but simply the fact that they cannot be mistaken for one another. Speech sounds are first and foremost entities which are contrastive, relative, and negative.
>
> (Saussure 1916c, p. 117)

Poor Saussure! He has the word (*phonème*) – correctly translated by Baskin. And he has the precise modern description of the phoneme – even clearer in Harris's version than Baskin's. No wonder five generations of linguists have (in the main) supposed that he discovered it! And now Harris takes it away.

Harris is uneasy about his decision, and offers a puzzled footnote:

> When this passage is compared with the detailed account of speech sounds given earlier (p. [63] ff), it is evident that the published text of the *Cours* lacks any careful and consistently drawn distinction between phonetic and phonological units. The speech sounds discussed on p.[63] ff are clearly language-neutral elements, characterised in physiological terms [**i.e they are phonetic** – LAJ]; whereas the speech sounds discussed here are defined contrastively in the context of particular languages [**i.e. they are phonemes** – LAJ]. Cf. p. 180 fn.   (Saussure 1916c, p.117)

What is really apparent here is a lack of historical understanding. It was precisely the working out of phoneme theory that created the modern distinction between phonetics and phonology/phonemics. To expect that distinction to be fully worked out at the first moment of emergence of the phoneme concept would be quite absurd.

One could say that Harris represents the opposite fault to that characteristically displayed by post-structuralist interpreters of Saussure. They go to all lengths to attribute complex and advanced philosophical principles to Saussure, which in the eyes of a linguist it seems quite impossible that he should ever have entertained.

Harris, on the other hand, seems to me to be depriving him of an interesting and extraordinarily influential concept which I believe he most certainly had – and which is, indeed, one of his major claims to fame.

NOTE ON A COMMENTARY

Professor Harris has also published a valuable commentary on the *Cours*; a scholarly commentary to be read after the original text and not as an introduction to it or a substitute for it. It raises many interesting problems of detailed interpretation of the kind which popular expositions (and my own in chapter 1) tend to gloss over, in the interest of making general sense of Saussure's position. Harris has far more doubts than I both of Saussure's conception of linguistics as a science and of Chomsky's; and he has a tendency to put back on Saussure's desk all the technical problems which took seventy years of later theoretical investigation to uncover. I am afraid I read the commentary too late to make any use of it in the body of this book. It doesn't make me want to change any major point of interpretation; in particular, I would stand by the comments above on Harris's translation. Incidentally, Harris is not here concerned with later, controversial post-structuralist interpretations of Saussure – he seems to have only three passing references to Barthes, one to Derrida, and none to Lacan. (Harris 1987).

Bibliography

Althusser, Louis 1965 (trans. Ben Brewster 1969) *For Marx* (London: Verso)

Althusser, Louis 1970 (trans. Ben Brewster) *Lenin and Philosophy* (London: Verso)

Althusser, Louis 1984 (trans. various) *Essays on Ideology* (London: Verso)

Althusser, Louis and **Balibar, Etienne** 1968 (trans. Brewster 1970) *Reading Capital* (London: Verso)

Aristotle 330 BC ? (trans. John Warrington 1956) *Metaphysics* (London: J. M. Dent & Sons)

Arvon, Henri 1970 (trans. Helen Lane 1973) *Marxist Aesthetics* (Ithaca and London: Cornell University Press)

Aune, Bruce 1986 *Metaphysics: the Elements* (Oxford: Basil Blackwell)

Austin, J. L. 1962a *How to Do Things with Words* (Oxford: OUP)

Austin, J. L. 1962b *Sense and Sensibilia* (Oxford: OUP)

Ayer, A. J. 1956 *The Problem of Knowledge* (London: Penguin)

Bachelard, Gaston 1934 (trans. Arthur Goldhammer 1984) *The New Scientific Spirit* (Boston: Beacon Press)

Bann, S. and **Bowlt, J.E.** (eds.) 1973 *Russian Formalism* (Scottish Academic Press)

Barber, Charles 1964 *The Flux of Language* (London: Allen & Unwin)

Barker, F., Hulme, P., Iverson, M. and **Loxley, D.** 1983 *The Politics of Theory* (Colchester: University of Essex Press)

Barthes, Roland 1953 (trans. Annette Lavers and Colin Smith 1967) *Writing Degree Zero* (New York: Hill & Wang)

Barthes, Roland 1953, 1972 *Le degré zéro de l'écriture* and *Nouveaux essais critiques* (Paris: Editions du Seuil)

Barthes, Roland 1954 (trans. Richard Howard 1987) *Michelet* (Oxford: Basil Blackwell)

Barthes, Roland 1954–6; 1957; 1970; (trans. Annette Lavers 1973) *Mythologies* (London: Granada)

Barthes, Roland 1957 *Mythologies* (Paris: Editions du Seuil)

Barthes, Roland 1964a (trans. Lavers and Smith 1967) *Elements of Semiology* (New York: Hill & Wang)

Barthes, Roland 1964b (trans. Richard Howard 1972) *Critical Essays* (Evanston: Northwestern University Press)

Barthes, Roland 1966 'Introduction to the Structural Analysis of Narratives' in Barthes 1977, 1982a, 1985

Barthes, Roland 1967 *Système de la mode* (Paris: Editions du Seuil)

Barthes, Roland 1970 *S/Z* (Paris: Editions du Seuil)

Barthes, Roland 1970 (trans. Miller 1974) *S/Z* (New York: Hill & Wang)

Barthes, Roland 1971a (trans. Richard Miller 1977) *Sade, Fourier, Loyola* (London: Jonathan Cape)

Barthes, Roland 1971b 'From Work to Text' in Harari 1979

Barthes, Roland 1973 (trans. Miller 1975) *The Pleasure of the Text* (New York: Hill & Wang)

Barthes, Roland 1975 (trans. Richard Howard 1977) *Roland Barthes by Roland Barthes* (New York: Hill & Wang)

Barthes, Roland 1977 (selection of essays by Stephen Heath) *Image, Music, Text* (London: Collins/Fontana)

Barthes, Roland 1979 (trans. Richard Howard) *The Eiffel Tower and other Mythologies* (New York: Hill and Wang)

Barthes, Roland 1980 (trans. Richard Howard 1981) *Camera Lucida* (London: Collins/Fontana)

Barthes, Roland 1981 (trans. Linda Coverdale 1985) *The Grain of The Voice:* Interviews 1962–1980 (London: Jonathan Cape)

Barthes, Roland 1982a (ed. Susan Sontag) *Barthes* Fontana Pocket Readers (London: Collins/Fontana)

Barthes, Roland 1982b (trans. Richard Howard) *Empire of Signs* (London: Jonathan Cape)

Barthes, Roland 1984 (trans. Richard Howard 1986) *The Rustle of Language* (Oxford: Basil Blackwell)

Barthes, Roland 1985 (trans. Richard Howard 1988) *The Semiotic Challenge (L'Aventure Sémiologique)* (Oxford: Basil Blackwell)

Belsey, Catherine 1980 *Critical Practice* (London: Methuen, New Accents)

Belsey, Catherine 1988 *John Milton: Language, Gender, Power* (Oxford: Basil Blackwell)

Bennett, Tony 1979 *Formalism and Marxism* (London: Methuen New Accents)

Benton, Ted 1984 *The Rise and Fall of Structural Marxism* (London: Macmillan)

Benvenuto, Bice and **Kennedy, Roger** 1986 *The Works of Jacques Lacan* (London: Free Association Books)

Bernstein, Basil 1971 *Class, Codes and Control* (2 vols) (London: Routledge & Kegan Paul)

Bhaskar, Roy 1986 *Scientific Realism and Human Emancipation* (London: Verso)

Biemel, Walter 1977 *Martin Heidegger: an Illustrated Study* (London: Routledge & Kegan Paul)

Blackburn, Robin (ed.) 1986 'Alternatives to Capitalism' *New Left Review* 159

Blakemore, Colin and **Greenfield, Susan** 1987 *Mindwaves: Thoughts on Intelligence, Identity, and Consciousness* (Oxford: Basil Blackwell)

Bloom, Harold 1979 'The Breaking of Form' in Hartman 1979a

Bloomfield, Brian P. (ed.) 1987 *The Question of Artificial Intelligence* (London: Croom Helm)

Bloomfield, Leonard 1933 *Language* (London: Allen & Unwin)

Bogue, Ronald 1989 *Deleuze and Guattari* (London: Routledge & Kegan Paul)

Boss, Medard 1963 *Psychoanalysis and Daseinanalysis* (New York: Basic Books)

Brecht, Bertholt 1957 (trans. 1964 John Willett) *Brecht on Theatre: The Development of an Aesthetic* (London: Methuen)

Brenkman, John 1977 'The Other and the One' in Felman 1977a

Brooks, Peter and **Felman, Shoshona** 1985 *The Lesson of Paul de Man*: Yale French Studies 69 (Yale: Yale University Press)

Burgess, Tyrrell 1972 *The Shape of Higher Education* (London: Cornmarket Press)

Burgess, Tyrrell (ed.) 1969–74 *Higher Education Review* (London: Cornmarket Press/Tyrrell Burgess Associates)

Carnap, Rudolf 1937 *The Logical Syntax of Language* (London: Routledge & Kegan Paul)

Caws, Peter 1979 *Sartre* (London: Routledge & Kegan Paul)

Chasseguet-Smirgel, Janine and **Grunberger, Béla** 1976 (trans. 1986 Claire Pajaczkowska) *Freud or Reich: Psychoanalysis and Illusion* (London: Free Association Books)

Chatman, S., Eco, U. and **Klinkenberg, J–M.** (eds.) 1979 *A Semiotic Landscape/Panorama Sémiotique* (The Hague: Mouton)

Chomsky, Noam 1956 'Three Models for the Description of Language' in Luce, Bush and Galanter 1964

Chomsky, Noam 1957 *Syntactic Structures* (The Hague: Mouton)

Chomsky, Noam and **Miller, George** 1958 'Finite State Languages' in Luce, Bush and Galanter 1964

Chomsky, Noam 1964 *Current Issues in Linguistic Theory* (The Hague: Mouton)

Chomsky, Noam 1965 *Aspects of the Theory of Syntax* (Massachusetts: The M.I.T. Press)

Chomsky, Noam 1966a *Cartesian Linguistics* (New York: Harper & Row)

Chomsky, Noam 1966b *Topics in the Theory of Generative Grammar* (The Hague: Mouton)

Chomsky, Noam and **Halle, Morris** 1968 *The Sound Pattern of English* (New York: Harper and Row)

Chomsky, Noam 1968 *Language and Mind* (New York: Harcourt Brace and World, Inc)

Chomsky, Noam 1971 (ed. J. P. B. Allen & Paul van Buren) *Chomsky: Selected Readings* (Oxford: OUP)

Chomsky, Noam 1972 *Studies on Semantics in Generative Grammar* (The Hague: Mouton)

Chomsky, Noam 1976 *Reflections on Language* (London: Temple Smith/Collins/Fontana)

Chomsky, Noam 1979a *Language and Responsibility* (Sussex: Harvester Press)

Chomsky, Noam 1979b *The Washington Connection (The Political Economy of Human Rights I)* (Nottingham: Spokesman)

Chomsky, Noam and **Herman, Edward S.** 1979 *After the Cataclysm (The Political Economy of Human Rights II)* (Nottingham: Spokesman)

Chomsky, Noam 1980 *Rules and Representations* (Oxford: Basil Blackwell)

Chomsky, Noam 1982 *The Generative Enterprise* (Dordrecht: Foris Publications)

Chomsky, Noam 1989 Interview in *Radical Philosophy* **53** Autumn 89.

Clarke, Simon 1981 *The Foundations of Structuralism* (Sussex: Harvester Press)

Clément, Catherine 1981 (trans. A. Goldhammer 1983) *The Lives and Legends of Jacques Lacan* (New York: Columbia University Press)

Cohen, Ralph (ed.) 1989 *Future Literary Theory* (London: Routledge)

Colomb, Gregory G. and **Turner, Mark** 1989 'Computers, Literary Theory, and Theory of Meaning' in Cohen 1989

Cooper, David 1967 *Psychiatry and Anti-Psychiatry* (London: Tavistock Publications)

Copleston, Frederick S. J. 1946 *A History of Philosophy: vol I: Greece and Rome* (New York: Doubleday Image Books)

Copleston, Frederick S. J. 1963 *A History of Philosophy: Vol VII Modern Philosophy II Schopenhauer to Nietzsche* (New York: Doubleday Image Books)

Cornforth, Maurice 1968 *The Open Philosophy and the Open Society* (London: Lawrence & Wishart)

Coward, Rosalind and **Ellis, John** 1977 *Language and Materialism* (London: Routledge & Kegan Paul)

Cresswell, M. J. 1973 *Logics and Languages* (London: Methuen)

Culler, Jonathan 1975 *Structuralist Poetics* (London: Routledge & Kegan Paul)

Culler, Jonathan 1976 *Saussure* (London: Collins/Fontana)

Culler, Jonathan 1981 *The Pursuit of Signs: Semiotics, Literature, Deconstruction* (London: Routledge & Kegan Paul)

Culler, Jonathan 1983 *On Deconstruction* (London: Routledge & Kegan Paul)

Curry, Haskell B. 1963 *Foundations of Mathematical Logic* (New York: McGraw-Hill)

Danto, Arthur C. 1989 'Beautiful Science and the Future of Criticism' in Cohen 1989

Deleuze, Gilles and **Guattari, Felix** 1972 (trans. R. Hurley, Mark Seem, and Helen R. Lane 1977) *Anti-Oedipus* (New York: Richard Seaver Viking)

Deleuze, Gilles and **Guattari, Felix** 1980 *Mille Plateaux* (Paris: Minuit)

Derrida, Jacques 1962, 2nd ed. 1974 (trans. John Leavey 1978) *Husserl's Origin of Geometry: An Introduction* (Sussex: Harvester Press)

Derrida, Jacques 1967a *Speech and Phenomena* (Evanston: Northwestern University Press)

Derrida, Jacques 1967b *Writing and Difference* (London: Routledge & Kegan Paul)

Derrida, Jacques 1967c (trans. Gayatri Spivak 1974) *Of Grammatology* (Baltimore: Johns Hopkins University Press)

Derrida, Jacques 1967d 'Structure, Sign and Play in the Discourse of the Human Sciences' in Macksey and Donato 1970, and in Derrida 1967b

Derrida, Jacques 1972a (trans. B. Johnson 1981) *Dissemination* (Chicago: University of Chicago Press)

Derrida, Jacques 1972b (trans. Alan Bass 1982) *Margins of Philosophy* (Sussex: Harvester Press)

Derrida, Jacques 1972c (trans. Alan Bass 1981) *Positions* (London: The Athlone Press)

Derrida, Jacques 1977a 'Signature Event Context' *Glyph 1* (Baltimore: Johns Hopkins University Press)

Derrida, Jacques 1977b 'Limited Inc abc' Supplement to *Glyph 2* (Baltimore: Johns Hopkins University Press)

Derrida, Jacques 1978 *Spurs: Nietzsche's Styles/Eperons: Les Styles de Nietzsche* (Chicago: Phoenix)

Derrida, Jacques 1979 'Living On – Border Lines' in Hartman 1979a

Derrida, Jacques 1980 (trans. Alan Bass 1987) *The Post Card: from Socrates to Freud and Beyond* (Chicago: University of Chicago Press)

Derrida, Jacques 1984 (trans. Peggy Kamuf 1988) *The Ear of the Other* (Lincoln: University of Nebraska Press)

Derrida, Jacques 1986 *Memoires: for Paul de Man* (New York: Columbia University Press)

Derrida, Jacques 1987 (trans P. Leavey and Richard Rand) *Glas (Lincoln: University of Nebraska Press)*

Descombes, Vincent 1979 (trans. 1980 Scott–Fox and Harding) *Modern French Philosophy* (Cambridge: CUP)

Dews, Peter 1987 *Logics of Disintegration* (London: Verso)

De Gelder, Beatrice (ed.) 1982 *Knowledge and Representation* (London: Routledge & Kegan Paul)

De George, Richard T. and **De George, Fernande M.** 1972 *The Structuralists* (New York: Doubleday Anchor Books)

De Man, Paul 1979a *Allegories of Reading* (Yale: Yale University Press)

De Man, Paul 1979b 'Shelley Disfigured' in Hartman 1979a

De Man, Paul 1983 *Blindness and Insight: Essays in the Rhetoric of Contemporary Criticism* (London: Methuen)

De Man, Paul 1984 *The Rhetoric of Romanticism* (Yale: Yale Univeristy Press)

De Man, Paul 1986 *The Resistance to Theory* (Manchester: Manchester University Press)

Dowling, William C. 1984 *Jameson, Althusser, Marx – an Introduction to the Political Unconscious* (London: Methuen University Paperbacks)

Durkheim, Emile 1895 (trans. Sarah Solovay and John H. Mueller 1938) *The Rules of Sociological Method* (New York: Free Press)

Dyson–Hudson, Neville 1970 'Structure and Infra-Structure in Primitive Society' in Macksey and Donato 1970

Eagleton, Terry 1976 *Criticism and Ideology* (London: Verso)

Eagleton, Terry 1983 *Literary Theory: an Introduction* (Oxford: Basil Blackwell)

Eagleton, Terry 1984 *The Function of Criticism* (London: Verso)

Eagleton, Terry 1986 *Against the Grain* (London: Verso)

Easthope, Antony 1983 *Poetry as Discourse* (London: Methuen, New Accents)

Eco, Umberto 1976 *A Theory of Semiotics* (Bloomington: Indiana University Press)

Eliot, Thomas Stearns 1919 'Tradition and the Individual Talent' in Eliot 1951

Eliot, Thomas Stearns 1944 *Four Quartets* (London: Faber & Faber)

Eliot, Thomas Stearns 1951 *Selected Essays* (London: Faber & Faber)

Elliott, Gregory 1987 *Althusser: the Detour of Theory* (London: Verso)

Elliott, Gregory 1986 'The Odyssey of Paul Hirst' in Robin Blackburn (ed.) *New Left Review* 159 Sep/Oct 1986

Ellis, John 1989 'Doing Something Different' *London Review of Books*, 27 July 1989

Engels, Frederick 1877 (trans. Emile Burns) *On Eugen Duhring's Revolution in Science (Anti-Duhring)* (London: Martin Lawrence)

Engels, Frederick 1878 (trans. Clemens Dutt 1940) *Dialectics of Nature* (London: Lawrence & Wishart)

Engels, Frederick 1884 (trans. Alick West 1972) *The Origin of the Family, Private Property, and the State* (London: Lawrence & Wishart)

Esposito, Joseph L. 1980 *Evolutionary Metaphysics* (Ohio: Ohio University Press)

Eysenck, Hans 1985 *Decline and Fall of the Freudian Empire* (London: Penguin/Viking)

Eysenck, Hans and **Wilson, Glenn** 1973 *The Experimental Study of Freudian Theories* (London: Methuen)

Farber, Marvin 1966 *The Aims of Phenomenology* (New York: Harper Torchbooks)

Farber, Marvin 1967 *Phenomenology and Existence: Toward a Philosophy within Nature* (New York: Harper & Row)

Feigl, Herbert and **Sellars, Wilfred** (eds.) 1949 *Readings in Philosophical Analysis* (New York: Appleton Century Crofts)

Felman, Shoshona (special ed.) 1977a *Literature & Psychoanalysis: the Question of Reading: Otherwise Yale French Studies (55–6)* (Yale: Yale University Press)

Felman, Shoshona 1977b (in Felman 1977a) 'To Open the Question'

Felman, Shoshona (ed.) 1980 *Literature and Psychoanalysis: the question of reading: Otherwise* (Yale: Yale University Press)

Findlay, J. N. 1958 *Hegel – A Re-examination* (London: Allen & Unwin)

Findlay, J. N. 1963 *Language, Mind, and Value* (London: Allen & Unwin)

Fischler, Claude (ed.) 1976 *Arguments 2: Marxisme, révisionnisme, méta-marxisme* (Paris: Union Générale d'Editions)

Fishman, Joshua A. (ed.) 1968 *Readings in the Sociology of Language* (The Hague: Mouton)

Fish, Stanley 1989 *Doing what comes naturally: Change, Rhetoric, etc.* (Oxford: OUP)

Flew, Antony (ed.) 1956 *Essays in Conceptual Analysis* (London: Macmillan)

Fodor, Janet Dean 1980 *Semantics: Theories of Meaning in Generative Grammar* (Cambridge: Harvard University Press)

Fodor, Jerry A. and **Katz, Jerrold J.** 1964 *The Structure of Language: Readings in the Philosophy of Language* (New Jersey: Prentice-Hall)

Foucault, Michel 1961 (trans. 1965 D. Cooper) *Madness and Civilisation* (London: Tavistock Publications)

Foucault, Michel 1963 (trans. A. M. Sheridan 1973) *The Birth of the Clinic* (London: Tavistock Publications)

Foucault, Michel 1966 (trans. 1970) *The Order of Things* (Originally *Les Mots et les Choses)* (London: Tavistock Publications)

Foucault, Michel 1969 (trans. A. M. Sheridan 1972) *The Archaeology of Knowledge* (London: Tavistock Publications)

Foucault, Michel 1975 (trans. Alan Sheridan 1977) *Discipline and Punish* (London: Penguin/Peregrine)

Foucault, Michel 1980 (ed. Colin Gordon) *Power/Knowledge – interviews, etc 1972–77* (Sussex: Harvester Press)

Foucault, Michel 1984 (selection ed. Paul Rabinow) *The Foucault Reader* (London: Penguin/Peregrine)

Frege, Gottlob 1892 'On Sense and Reference' in Frege 1952

Frege, Gottlob 1952 (trans. P. Geach and M. Black) *Philosophical Writings* (Oxford: Basil Blackwell)

Freud, Anna 1936 (trans. Baines 1937) *The Ego and the Mechanisms of Defence* (London: The Hogarth Press)

Freud, Sigmund 1900 (rev. 1908; trans. Brill 1913) *The Interpretation of Dreams* (London: Allen & Unwin)

Freud, Sigmund 1904 (trans. J. Strachey, A. Freud, A. Tyson 1960) *The Psychopathology of Everyday Life* (London: Ernest Benn Ltd)

Freud, Sigmund 1905a *Three Essays on the Theory of Sexuality* (London: The Hogarth Press)

Freud, Sigmund 1905b (trans. J. Strachey 1960) *Jokes and their Relation to the Unconscious* (London: Routledge & Kegan Paul)

Freud, Sigmund 1915–17 (trans. J. Strachey 1963) *Introductory Lectures on Psychoanalysis* (London: The Hogarth Press)

Freud, Sigmund 1933 (trans. W. J. H. Sprott) *New Introductory Lectures on Psychoanalysis* (London: The Hogarth Press)

Gadet, Françoise 1986 (trans. Gregory Elliott 1989) *Saussure and Contemporary Culture* (London: Century Hutchinson)

Galan, F. W. 1985 *Historic Structures: The Prague School Project 1928–1946* (London: Croom Helm)

Garnham, Alan 1985 *Psycholinguistics: Central Topics* (London: Methuen)

Garvin, Paul 1964 *A Prague School Reader on Esthetics, Literary Structure, & Style* (Georgetown: University School of Languages and Linguistics)

Gasché, Rodolphe 1985 'Infrastructures and Systematicity' in Sallis 1987

Geras, Norman 1983 *Marx and Human Nature: Refutation of a Legend* (London: Verso)

Grinder, John T. and **Elgin, Susette Haden** 1973 *Guide to Transformational Grammar: History, Theory, Practice* (New York: Holt Rinehart)

Guiraud, Pierre 1971 *Semiology* (London: Routledge & Kegan Paul)

Halle, Morris and **Bresnan, Joan** 1978 *Linguistic Theory and Psychological Reality* (Massachusetts: The M.I.T. Press)

Halliday, M. A. K., McIntosh, A. and **Strevens, P.** 1964 *The Linguistic Sciences and Language Teaching* (London: Longman)

Harari, Josué V. 1979 *Textual Strategies: Perspectives in Post-Structuralist Criticism* (London: Methuen)

Harland, Richard 1987 *Superstructuralism* (London: Methuen, New Accents)

Harrison, Bernard 1983 'Deconstructing Derrida' in Shaffer, 1983

Harris, Marvin 1968 *The Rise of Anthropological Theory* (New York: T. Y. Crowell)

Harris, Marvin 1975 *Cows, Pigs, Wars and Witches* (London: Collins/Fontana)

Harris, Marvin 1978 *Cannibals and Kings: the Origins of Cultures* (London: Collins)

Harris, Marvin 1980 *Cultural Materialism* (New York: Random House/Vintage Books)

Harris, Roy 1987 *Reading Saussure* (London: Duckworth)

Harris, Zellig S. 1947 *Structural Linguistics* (formerly *Methods in Structural Linguistics*) (Chicago: Phoenix)

Hartman, Geoffrey 1975 *The Fate of Reading* (Chicago: University of Chicago Press)

Hartman, Geoffrey (ed.) 1979a *Deconstruction and Criticism* (London: Routledge & Kegan Paul)

Hartman, Geoffrey 1979b 'Words, Wish, Worth: Wordsworth' in Hartman 1979a

Hartman, Geoffrey 1981 *Saving The Text: Literature/Derrida/Philosophy* (Baltimore: Johns Hopkins University Press)

Hartman, Geoffrey 1989 'The State of the Art of Criticism' in Cohen 1989

Hawkes, Terence 1977 *Structuralism and Semiotics* (London: Methuen, New Accents)

Hawking, Stephen W. 1988 *A Brief History of Time: From the Big Bang to Black Holes* (London: Bantam Press)

Hayakawa, S. I. 1939 *Language in Thought and Action* (London: Allen & Unwin)

Heath, Stephen 1974 *Vertige du déplacement* (Paris: Fayard)

Hegel, G. W. F. 1807, 1831 (trans. Baillie 1910, rev. 1931) *The Phenomenology of Mind* (London: Allen & Unwin)

Hegel, G. W. F. 1812 (trans. Johnston & Struthers 1929) *Science of Logic* (London: Allen & Unwin)

Hegel, G. W. F. 1953 (ed. C. J. Friedrich) *The Philosophy of Hegel* (New York: Random House/Modern Library Editions)

Heidegger, Martin 1926 (trans. 1962 Macqarrie and Robinson) *Being and Time* (Oxford: Basil Blackwell)

Heidegger, Martin 1935 (trans. 1959 Ralph Manheim) An Introduction to Metaphysics (Oxford: OUP)

Heidegger, Martin 1959 (trans. Peter D. Hertz and Joan Stambaugh 1971) *On the Way to Language* (New York: Harper & Row)

Heidegger, Martin 1971 *Poetry, Language, Thought* (New York: Harper & Row)

Hilbert, D. and **Ackerman, W.** 1950 (trans. L. M. Hammond, G. Leckie, and F. Steinhardt, 1928, 1938) *Principles of Mathematical Logic* (New York: Chelsea Publishing Co)

Hillman, James 1983 *Archetypal Psychology: A Brief Account* (Dallas: Spring Publications Inc)

Hjelmslev, Louis 1943 (trans. Francis J. Whitfield 1969) *Prolegomena to a Theory of Language* (Wisconsin: Wisconsin University Press)

Hockett, Charles F. 1958 *A Course in Modern Linguistics* (New York: Macmillan)

Holenstein, Elmar 1976 'Jakobson und Husserl' in Parrett 1976

Hoy, David (ed.) 1986 *Foucault: A Critical Reader* (Oxford: Basil Blackwell)

Humboldt, Wilhelm von 1836 (trans. Peter Heath 1988) *On Language:* (Cambridge: CUP)

Husserl, Edmund 1929 (trans. Churchill 1964) *The Phenomenology of Internal Time Consciousness* (Bloomington: Indiana University Press)

Husserl, Edmund 1950 (trans. Dorion Cairns 1960) *Cartesian Meditations: an Introduction to Phenomenology* (The Hague: Martinus Nijhoff)

Husserl, Edmund 1967 (ed. Peter Koestenbaum) *The Paris Lectures* (The Hague: Martinus Nijhoff)

Husserl, Edmund 1970 (trans. David Carr 1970) *The Crisis of European Sciences and Transcendental Phenomenology* (Illinois: Northwestern University Press)

Hymes, Dell (ed.) 1964 *Language in Culture and Society* (New York: Harper & Row)

Ingarden, Roman 1960 (2nd ed.) *Das Literarische Kunstwerk* (Tubingen) (trans. 1973; Evanston: Northwestern University Press)

Iser, Wolfgang 1976 (trans. 1978) *The Act of Reading* (London: Routledge & Kegan Paul)

Jackson, Leonard 1969 'Radical Conceptual Change and the Design of Honours Degrees' *Higher Education Review* Summer 1969, in Open University 1971, 1977

Jackson, Leonard 1971 *A Transformational Theory of Context* (unpublished thesis London)

Jackson, Leonard 1974 'The Myth of Elaborated and Restricted Code' *Higher Education Review* Spring 1974, in Open University 1977

Jackson, Leonard 1976 'Squirrel Business' *Higher Education Review* Autumn 1976

Jackson, Leonard 1982 'The Freedom of the Critic and the History of the Text' in Barker et al, 1983

Jakobson, Roman and **Tynjanov, Jurij** 1928 'Problems in the Study of Language and Literature' in De George, 1972 Jakobson 1985

Jakobson, Roman, Fant, C., Gunnar, M. and **Halle, Morris** 1951 *Preliminaries to Speech Analysis* (Massachusetts: The M.I.T. Press)

Jakobson, Roman and **Halle, Morris** 1956 *Fundamentals of Language* (The Hague: Mouton)

Jakobson, Roman 1958 'Concluding Statement: Linguistics and Poetics' in Sebeok 1960

Jakobson, Roman and **Jones, Lawrence G.** 1970 *Shakespeare's Verbal Art in Th'Expence of Spirit* (The Hague: Mouton)

Jakobson, Roman 1973 *Main Trends in the Science of Language* (London: Allen & Unwin)

Jakobson, Roman 1976 (trans. 1978 John Mepham; original lectures 1942) *Sound and Meaning* (Six Lectures on) (Sussex: Harvester Press) 1978

Jakobson, Roman and **Waugh, Linda R.** 1979 *The Sound Shape of Language* (Sussex: Harvester Press)

Jakobson, Roman and **Pomorska, Krystina** 1980 'Dialogue on Time in Language and Literature' in Jakobson 1985

Jakobson, Roman 1985 (ed. Krystina Pomorska and Stephen Rudy) *Verbal Art, Verbal Sign, Verbal Time* (Oxford: Basil Blackwell)

Jameson, Frederick 1977 'Imaginary and Symbolic in Lacan' in Felman 1977a

Jaspers, Karl 1935 (trans. William Earle) 'Kierkegard and Nietzsche' in Kaufmann 1956

Johnson, Barbara 1977 'The Frame of Reference: Poe, Lacan, Derrida' in Felman 1977a

Joos, Martin (ed.) 1957 (4th ed. 1966) *Readings in Linguistics I: The Development of Descriptive Linguistics in America 1925–56* (Chicago: University of Chicago Press)

Kant, Immanuel 1787 (trans. J. M. Meiklejohn 1854) *Critique of Pure Reason* (London: J. M. Dent)

Kant, Immanuel 1790 (trans. J. C. Meredith, 1928) *Critique of Judgement* (Oxford: OUP)

Katz, Jerrold J. and **Fodor, Jerry A.** 1963 'The Structure of a Semantic Theory' in Fodor and Katz 1964

Kaufmann, Walter (ed.) 1956 *Existentialism from Dostoyevsky to Sartre* (New York: Meridian Books)

Kneebone, G. T. 1963 *Mathematical Logic and the Foundations of Mathematics* (London: Van Nostrand)

Kockelmans, Joseph J. (ed.) 1967 *Phenomenology* (New York: Doubleday and Co., Inc)

Koestenbaum, Peter 1978 *The New Image of the Person* (Connecticut/London: Greenwood Press)

Kojève, Alexandre 1969 *Introduction to the Reading of Hegel* (New York: Basic Books)

Korzybski, Alfred 1933 *Science and Sanity* (Lancaster, Pa: Science Press Printing Co.)

Kristeva, Julia 1969a *Semeiotike: Recherches pour une sémanalyse*: Essais (Paris: Editions du Seuil)

Kristeva, Julia 1969b *Semeiotike: Recherches pour une sémanalyse*: Points Extraits (Paris: Editions du Seuil)

Kristeva, Julia 1980 *Desire in Language: A Semiotic Approach to Literature and Art* (Oxford: Basil Blackwell)

Kristeva, Julia 1986 (various trans.: ed. Toril Moi) *The Kristeva Reader* (Oxford: Basil Blackwell)

Kristeva, Julia 1989 *Language: The Unknown: An Initiation into Linguistics* (Sussex: Harvester Press)

Kristeva, Julia 1971 'The Semiotic Activity' in *Signs of the Times*, (Cambridge: CUP) Reprinted *Screen Reader 2* 1981 (London: Society for Education in Film and Television)

Kristeva, Julia 1973 'The System and the Speaking Subject' *Times Literary Supplement* 12 Oct 1973, Sebeok 1975, Kristeva 1986

Kurzweil, Edith 1980 *The Age of Structuralism* (New York: Columbia)

Kwant, Remy C. 1966 *From Phenomenology to Metaphysics* (on Merleau-Ponty) (Duquesne University Press)

Labov, William 'The Logic of Non-Standard English' in Williams 1970

Lacan, Jacques 1953–4 (published 1975 France; trans. J. Forrester 1988) *The Seminar of Jacques Lacan,* Book 1, 1953–4 (Cambridge: CUP)

Lacan, Jacques 1954–5 (published 1978 France; trans. S. Tomaselli 1988) *The Seminar of Jacques Lacan*, Book II (Cambridge: CUP)

Lacan, Jacques 1959 (trans. in Felman 1977a) 'Desire and the Interpretation of Desire in Hamlet' *Yale French Studies* (55–6)

Lacan, Jacques 1966 (trans. Alan Sheridan; 1977) *Ecrits – A Selection* (London: Tavistock Publications)

Lacan, Jacques 1977 (trans. Alan Sheridan; originally given 1964) *The Four Fundamental Concepts of Psychoanalysis* (London: Penguin)

Lacan, Jacques and **members of Ecole Freudienne** 1982 (eds. and translator: Juliet Mitchell and Jacqueline Rose) *Feminine Sexuality: Jacques Lacan and the Ecole Freudienne* (London: Macmillan)

Ladefoged, Peter 1962 *Elements of Acoustic Phonetics* (Edinburgh: Oliver and Boyd)

Lakatos, Imre 1978a *Mathematics, Science and Epistemology* (Cambridge: CUP)

Lakatos, Imre 1978b *The Methodology of Scientific Research Programmes* (Cambridge: CUP)

Lakoff, George and **Johnson, Mark** 1980 *Metaphors We Live By* (Chicago: University of Chicago Press)

Lakoff, George 1987 *Women, Fire and Dangerous Things* (Chicago: University of Chicago Press)

Laplanche, J. and **Pontalis, J–B.** 1973 (trans. 1980) *The Language of Psychoanalysis* (London: The Hogarth Press)

Laruelle, Francois 1986 *Les Philosophies de la différence: introduction critique* (Paris: Presses Universitaires de France)

Lavers, Annette 1982 *Roland Barthes: Structuralism and After* (London: Methuen)

Leach, Edmund 1970 *Lévi-Strauss* (London: Collins/Fontana)

Leavis, F. R. 1932 *New Bearings in English Poetry* (London: Chatto and Windus)

Leavis, F. R. 1952 *The Common Pursuit* (London: Chatto & Windus)

Leavis, F. R. 1937 'Literary Criticism and Philosophy' in Leavis 1952

Lecercle, Jean-Jacques 1985 *Philosophy through the Looking Glass* (London: Hutchinson)

Lehmann, Winifred 1967 *A Reader in Nineteenth Century Historical Indo-European Linguistics* (Bloomington: Indiana University Press)

Lemaire, Anika 1970 (trans. David Macey 1977) *Jacques Lacan* (London: Routledge & Kegan Paul)

Lenin, V. I. 1908 *Materialism and Empirio-Criticism* (Collected Works 14) (London: Lawrence & Wishart)

Lenin, V. I. 1961 *Philosophical Notebooks* (Collected Works 38) (London: Lawrence & Wishart)

Lenneberg, Eric H. 1964 *New Directions in the Study of Language* (Massachusetts: The M.I.T. Press)

Lenneberg, Eric H. 1967 *Biological Foundations of Language* (New York: John Wiley)

Lentricchia, Frank 1980 *After the New Criticism* (Chicago: University of Chicago Press)

Lentricchia, Frank 1983 *Criticism and Social Change* (Chicago: University of Chicago Press)

Lévesque, Claude 1978 *L'étrangeté du texte* (Paris: Union Générale d'Editions)

Levinson, Stephen C. 1983 *Pragmatics* (Cambridge: CUP)

Lévi-Strauss, Claude 1949 (2nd ed. 1967; trans. R. Needham 1969) *The Elementary Structures of Kinship* (London: Eyre and Spottiswoode)

Lévi-Strauss, Claude 1958 (trans. Claire Jacobson etc. 1963) *Structural Anthropology* Vol I (London: Penguin/New York: Basic Books)

Lévi-Strauss, Claude 1960 (trans. Ortner 1967) *The Scope of Anthropology* (London: Jonathan Cape)

Lévi-Strauss, Claude 1962a (trans. R. Needham 1963) *Totemism* (London: Penguin)

Lévi-Strauss, Claude 1962b (trans. 1966) *The Savage Mind* (London: Weidenfeld & Nicolson)

Lévi-Strauss, Claude 1968 (trans. 1978 John and Doreen Weightman) *Introduction to a Science of Mythology: 1.The Raw and the Cooked. 2.From Honey to Ashes. 3.The Origin of Table Manners. 4.The Naked Man.* (London: Jonathan Cape)

Lévi-Strauss, Claude 1976 *Structural Anthropology* Vol 2 (London: Penguin)

Lewin, Roger 1987 *Bones of Contention* (New York: Simon and Schuster)

Lewis, C. S. 1942 *A Preface to Paradise Lost* (Oxford: OUP)

Lewis, C. S. 1954 *Oxford History of English Literature vol 3: English Literature in the Sixteenth Century, excluding Drama* (Oxford: OUP)

Lieberman, P. 1975 *On the Origins of Language* (New York and London)

Lieberman, P. et al 1972 'Phonetic Ability and Related Anatomy' *American Anthropologist*

Lieberman, P. 'Towards a Unified Linguistic Theory' *Linguistic Inquiry*, **1**, 307–22

Linsky, Leonard (ed.) 1952 *Semantics and the Philosophy of Language* (Urbana: University of Illinois Press)

Locke, John 1689 *An Essay Concerning Human Understanding* (London)

Lodge, D. (ed.) 1972 *20th Century Literary Criticism* (London: Longman)

Lodge, D. (ed.) 1988 *Modern Criticism and Theory* (London: Longman)

Luce, R. D., Bush, R. B. and **Galanter, E**. 1963 *Handbook of Mathematical Psychology vol II* (New York: John Wiley)

Luce, R. D., Bush, R. B. and **Galanter, E.** 1964 *Readings in Mathematical Psychology vol II* (New York: John Wiley)

Lyons, John 1981 *Language, Meaning, and Context* (London: Collins/Fontana)

McCabe, Colin (ed.) 1981 *The Talking Cure: Essays in Psychoanalysis and Language* (London: Macmillan)

Macdonell, Diane 1986 *Theories of Discourse* (Oxford: Basil Blackwell)

Macherey, Pierre 1966 (trans. Geoffrey Wall 1978) *A Theory of Literary Production* (London: Routledge & Kegan Paul)

Mackinnon, D. M. 1974 *The Problem of Metaphysics* (Cambridge: CUP)

Macksey, Richard and **Donato, Eugenio** 1970 *The Languages of Criticism and the Sciences of Man: the Structuralist Controversy* (Baltimore and London: Johns Hopkins University Press)

Mahaffy, John P. and **Bernard, John H.** 1889 *Kant's Critical Philosophy for English Readers* (London: Macmillan)

Malcolm, Janet 1982 *Psychoanalysis: the Impossible Profession* (London: Pan Books)

Malcolm, Janet 1984 *In the Freud Archives* (London: Jonathan Cape)

Malmberg, Bertil 1983 *L'analyse du language au XXe siècle: théories et méthodes* (Paris: Presses Universitaire de France)

Margolis, Joseph 1986 *Pragmatism without Foundations* (Oxford: Basil Blackwell)

Martinet, André and **Weinreich, Uriel** 1954 *WORD: Linguistics Today* (Columbia: Columbia University Press)

Marx, Karl 1840s – 1859 (trans. Rodney Livingstone and Greg Benton; intro. Colletti) *Early Writings* (London: Penguin)

Marx, Karl 1844 (trans. Martin Milligan 1959) *Economic and Philosophic Manuscripts of 1844* (Moscow: Progress Publishers)

Marx, Karl 1847 (trans. 1963) *The Poverty of Philosophy* (New York: International Publishers)

Marx, Karl 1859a (trans. 1976 Ben Fowles) *Capital Vol I* (London: Penguin)

Marx, Karl 1859b (trans. Moore and Aveling, ed. Engels, Untermann 1906) *Capital: A Critique of Political Economy* (New York: The Modern Library)

Marx, Karl and **Engels, Frederick** 1840s–90s (ed.) Lewis S. Feuer *Marx and Engels: Basic Writings on Politics and Philosophy* (London: Collins/Fontana)

Marx, Karl and **Engels, Frederick** 1965 *The German Ideology* (London: Lawrence & Wishart)

Marx, Karl and **Engels, Frederick** 1848 (trans. Samuel Moore 1888) *Manifesto of the Communist Party* (Moscow: Progress Publishers)

Matejka, L. and **Pomorska, J**. 1971 *Readings in Russian poetics: formalist and structuralist views* (Massachusetts: The M.I.T.Press)

Mays, Wolfe and **Brown, S. C.** 1972 *Linguistic Analysis and Phenomenology* (London: Macmillan)

McCawley, James D. 1981 *Everything that Linguists have Always Wanted to Know about Logic* (Oxford: Basil Blackwell)

McTaggart, John 1910 *A Commentary on Hegel's Logic* (New York: Russell and Russell)

Mepham, John and **Ruben, David–Hillel** (eds.) 1979 *Issues in Marxist Philosophy: 2 Materialism* (Sussex: Harvester Press)

Merleau–Ponty, M. 1955 *Adventures of the Dialectic* (London: Heinemann)

Merquior, J. G. 1986 *From Prague to Paris* (London: Verso)

Miller, J. Hillis 1979 'The Critic as Host' in Hartman 1979a

Miller, J. Hillis 1989 'The Function of Literary Theory at the Present Time' in Cohen 1989

Mohrmann, C., Sommerfelt, A. and **Whatmough, J.** 1961 *Trends in European and American Linguistics 1960* (Utrecht: Spectrum)

Moi, Toril 1985 *Sexual/Textual Politics* (London: Methuen New Accents)

Moore, Tim 1969 *Claude Lévi-Strauss and the Cultural Sciences* (Birmingham: University of Birmingham Centre for Contemporary Cultural Studies)

Morris, Terence (ed.) 1969 *British Journal of Sociology: Structuralism* Vol XX 3 Sept. (London: Routledge & Kegan Paul)

Muller, John P. and **Richardson, William J.** 1982 *Lacan and Language – a Reader's Guide to Ecrits* (New York: International Universities Press)

Newmeyer, Frederick 1986 *The Politics of Linguistics* (Chicago: University of Chicago Press)

Norris, Christopher 1982 *Deconstruction – Theory and Practice* (London: Methuen New Accents)

Norris, Christopher 1984 *The Deconstructive Turn – Essays in the Rhetoric of Philosophy* (London: Methuen University Paperbacks)

Norris, Christopher 1985 *The Contest of Faculties: Philosophy and Theory after Deconstruction* (London: Methuen University Paperbacks)

Norris, Christopher 1987 *Derrida* (London: Collins/Fontana)

Norris, Christopher 1988 *Paul de Man: Deconstruction and the Critique of Identity* (London: Routledge & Kegan Paul)

O'Malley, R. 1964 'One More Irrelevance' in Denys Thompson, ed.: *The Use of English* 1965

Open University 1971 *School and Society: a Sociological Reader* (London: Routledge & Kegan Paul)

Open University 1977 *School and Society*: 2nd edition (London: Routledge & Kegan Paul)

Parkinson, G. H. R. (ed.) 1968 *The Theory of Meaning* (Oxford: OUP)

Parrett, Hermann (ed.) 1976 *History of Linguistic Thought and Contemporary Linguistics* (Berlin and New York: de Gruyter)

Pateman, Trevor 1983 Review of Pécheux 1975 *Language, Semantics and Ideology*; in *Journal of Linguistics* **XIX** 2 Sept (Cambridge: CUP)

Pateman, Trevor 1988 Review of Newmeyer 1986 *The Politics of Linguistics*; in *Journal of Linguistics* **XXIV**, 1 (Cambridge: CUP)

Pécheux, Michel 1975 (trans. Nagpal 1982) *Language, Semantics and Ideology: Stating the Obvious* (London: Macmillan)

Peters, F. E. 1972 *The Harvest of Hellenism* (London: Allen & Unwin)

Pettit, Philip 1977 *The Concept of Structuralism: A Critical Analysis* (California: University of California Press)

Piaget, Jean 1965 (trans. Wolfe Mays 1972) *Insights and Illusions of Philosophy* (London: Routledge & Kegan Paul)

Piaget, Jean 1968 (trans. 1971 Chaninah Maschler) *Structuralism* (London: Routledge & Kegan Paul)

Piaget, Jean 1971 *Biology and Knowledge: . . Organic Regulations and Cognitive Studies* (Edinburgh: Edinburgh University Press)

Piaget, Jean and **Inhelder, Barbel** 1963 *The Early Growth of Logic: Classification and Seriation* (London: Routledge & Kegan Paul)

Pike, Kenneth L. 1967 *Language in Relation to a Unified Theory of Human Behaviour* (The Hague: Mouton)

Popper, Karl 1957 *The Poverty of Historicism* (London: Routledge & Kegan Paul)

Popper, Karl 1959 *The Logic of Scientific Discovery* (London: Hutchinson)

Popper, Karl 1963 *Conjectures and Refutations: the Growth of Scientific Knowledge* (London: Routledge & Kegan Paul)

Popper, Karl 1972 *Objective Knowledge: An Evolutionary Approach* (Oxford: OUP)

Popper, Karl 1974 *Unended Quest* (London: Collins/Fontana)

Pratt, Mary Louise 1977 *Toward a Speech-Act Theory of Literary Discourse* (Bloomington: Indiana University Press)

Prior, A. N. 1962 *Formal Logic* (Oxford: OUP)

Quine, Willard van Orman 1953 *From a Logical Point of View* (New York: Harper Torchbooks)

Quine, Willard van Orman 1960 *Word and Object* (Massachusetts: The M.I.T.Press)

Quine, Willard van Orman 1968 *Ontological Relativity and Other Essays* (Columbia: Columbia University Press)

Radford, Andrew 1981 *Transformational Syntax: A student's guide to the E.S.T.* (Cambrige: CUP)

Ragland-Sullivan, Ellie 1986 *Jacques Lacan and the Philosophy of Psychoanalysis* (London: Croom Helm)

Raglan, Lord 1936 *The Hero* (London: Watts/Thinkers Library)

Raglan, Lord 1940 *Jocasta's Crime* (London: Watts/Thinker's Library)

Ray, William 1984 *Literary Meaning* (Oxford: Basil Blackwell)

Reichenbach, Hans 1947 *Elements of Symbolic Logic* (New York: Free Press)

Riffaterre, Michael 1978 *Semiotics of Poetry* (London: Methuen)

Robins, R. H. 1967 *A Short History of Linguistics* (London: Longman)

Robinson, Ian 1975 *The New Grammarian's Funeral* (Cambridge: CUP)

Royce, Josiah 1919 *Lectures on Modern Idealism* (Yale: Yale University Press)

Runciman, W. G. 1969 'What is Structuralism?' in Morris (ed.) 1969 *British Journal of Sociology*

Russell, Bertrand 1905 'On Denoting' in Feigl and Sellars 1949

Russell, Bertrand 1967 *Autobiography, vol 1: 1872 – 1949* (London: Allen & Unwin)

Said, Edward W. 1983 *The World, The Text, and the Critic* (London: Faber & Faber)

Sallis, John (ed.) 1987 *Deconstruction and Philosophy: the Texts of Jacques Derrida* (Chicago: University of Chicago Press)

Sapir, Edward 1921 *Language* (New York: Harcourt, Brace & World, Inc.)

Sartre, Jean–Paul 1943 (trans. Hazel Barnes) *Being and Nothingness: an essay on Phenomenological Ontology* (New York: Philosophical Library)

Sartre, Jean–Paul 1945 (trans. Philip Mairet 1948) *Existentialism and Humanism* (London: Methuen)

Sartre, Jean–Paul 1948 (trans. Bernard Frechtman 1950) *What is Literature?* (London: Methuen)

Saussure, Ferdinand de 1916a (Critical edition, Tullio de Mauro 1972) *Cours de linguistique générale* (Paris: Payot)

Saussure, Ferdinand de 1916b (trans. Wade Baskin 1959) *Course in General Linguistics* (New York: McGraw-Hill)

Saussure, Ferdinand de 1916c (trans. Roy Harris 1983) *Course in General Linguistics* (London: Duckworth)

Saussure, Ferdinand de 1967 foll. (ed. R. Engler) *Edition Critique du Cours de Linguistique Générale de F. De Saussure* (Wiesbaden: Harrassowitz)

Schacht, Richard 1983 *Nietzsche* (London: Routledge & Kegan Paul)

Schneiderman, Stuart 1980 *Returning to Freud: Clinical Psychoanalysis in the School of Lacan* (Yale: Yale University Press)

Schneiderman, Stuart 1983 *Jacques Lacan: Death of an Intellectual Hero* (Harvard: Harvard University Press)

Scholes, Robert 1985 *Textual Power: Literary Theory and the Teaching of English* (Yale: Yale University Press)

Screen Reader, 2 1981 *Cinema and Semiotics* (London: The Society for Education in Film and Television)

Scruton, Roger 1974 *Art and Imagination* (London: Methuen)

Scruton, Roger 1981 *The Politics of Culture* (Manchester: Carcanet)

Scruton, Roger 1982 *Kant* (Oxford: OUP)

Scruton, Roger 1985 *Thinkers of the New Left* (London: Longman)

Searle, John 1969 *Speech Acts: An Essay in The Philosophy of Language* (Cambridge: CUP)

Searle, John 1977 'Reiterating the Differences – a Reply to Derrida' *Glyph 1 1977*

Searle, John 1984 *Minds, Brains, and Science* (London: BBC Publications Reith Lectures 1984)

Sebeok, Thomas A. 1960 *Style in Language* (Massachusetts: The M.I.T. Press)

Sebeok, Thomas A. 1975 *The Tell-Tale Sign: A Survey of Semiotics* (Netherlands: de Ridder)

Sedat, Jacques (ed.) 1981 *Retour à Lacan* (Paris: Fayard)

Selden, Raman 1985 *A Reader's Guide to Contemporary Literary Theory* (Sussex: Harvester Press)

Seung, T. K. 1982 *Structuralism amd Hermeneutics* (New York: Columbia University Press)

Shaffer, E. S. 1983 *Comparative Criticism* Vol 7 (Cambridge: CUP)

Shalvey, Thomas 1975 *Claude Lévi-Strauss: Social Psychotherapy and the Collective Unconscious* (Sussex: Harvester Press)

Sheridan, Alan 1980 *Foucault: the Will to Truth* (London: Tavistock Publications)

Shukman, Anne (ed.) 1983 *Bakhtin School Papers*: Russian Poetics in Translation 10

Silverman, David and **Torode, Brian** 1980 *The Material Word: some theories of language and its limits* (London: Routledge and Kegan Paul)

Skinner, B. F. 1957 *Verbal Behavior* (New York: Appleton Century Crofts)

Smith, Joseph H. and **Kerrigan, William** (eds.) 1983 *Interpreting Lacan* (Yale: Yale University Press)

Soll, Ivan 1969 *An Introduction to Hegel's Metaphysics* (Chicago: University of Chicago Press)

Soper, Kate 1986 *Humanism and Anti-Humanism* (London: Hutchinson)

Spanos, William V. 1976 *Martin Heidegger and the Question of Literature* (Bloomington: Indiana Press)

Spanos, William V., Bove, Paul A. and **O'Hara, Daniel** 1982 *The Question of Textuality* (Bloomington: Indiana University Press)

Sperber, Dan and **Wilson, Deirdre** 1986 *Relevance: Communication and Cognition* (Oxford: Basil Blackwell)

Staal, J. F. 1965 'Reification, Quotation and Nominalisation' in Tymieniecka 1965

Stam, James H. 1976 *Inquiries into the Origin of Language* (New York: Harper & Row)

Steinberg, Danny D. and **Jakobovits, Leon A.** 1971 *Semantics* (Cambridge: CUP)

Steiner, George 1978 *Heidegger* (London: Collins/Fontana)

Strawson, P. F. 1950 'On Referring', *Mind* 1950; in Flew 1956

Strawson, P. F. 1966 *The Bounds of Sense: An Essay on Kant's Critique of Pure Reason* (London: Methuen)

Strawson, P. F. 1967 *Philosophical Logic* (Oxford: OUP)

Sturrock, John (ed.) 1979 *Structuralism and Since* (Oxford: Opus)

Sturrock, John 1986 *Structuralism* (London: Paladin)

Tallis, Raymond 1988 *Not Saussure: A Critique of Post-Saussurean Literary Theory* (London: Macmillan)

Tarski, Alfred 1944 'The Semantic Conception of Truth', *Philosophy and Phenomenomolical Research* **4** (1944) and in Linsky 1952

Taylor, Charles 1975 *Hegel* (Cambridge: CUP)

Thody, Philip 1977 *Roland Barthes – A Conservative Estimate* (Atlantic Highlands, N.J.: Humanities Press)

Thompson, Denys (ed.) 1964 Summer; 1965 Spring *The Use of English* Vol XVI (London: Chatto and Windus)

Turkle, Sherry 1979 *Psychoanalytic Politics: Jacques Lacan and Freud's French Revolution* Burnett Books (London: Hutchinson/New York: Basic Books)

Tylor, E. B. 1871 *Primitive Culture* (London: J. Murray)

Tylor, E. B. 1881 *Anthropology* (2 vols) (London: Watts/Thinker's Library 2 vols 1930)

Tymieniecka, Anna–Teresa 1965 *Contributions to Logic and Methodology in Honor of J. M. Bochenski* (Amsterdam: North-Holland Publishing Co.)

Ulmer, Gregory L. 1985 *Applied Grammatology: post(e) pedagogy from Jacques Derrida . . .* (Baltimore: Johns Hopkins University Press)

Ungar, Steven 1983 *Roland Barthes: the Professor of Desire* (Lincoln: University of Nebraska Press)

Vachek, Josef 1966 *The Linguistic School of Prague* (Bloomington: Indiana University Press)

Walsh, W. H. 1963 *Metaphysics* (London: Hutchinson University Library)

Warnock, Mary 1970 *Existentialism* (Oxford: OUP)

Waterhouse, Roger 1981 *A Heidegger Critique* (Sussex: Harvester Press)

Wells, Rulon S. 1947 'De Saussure's System of Linguistics' in Joos 1957

White, Hayden 1989 'Figuring the nature of the times deceased', in Cohen 1989

Whorf, Benjamin Lee 1956 *Language, Thought and Reality: selected writings* (Massachusetts: The M.I.T. Press)

Widdowson, Peter (ed.) 1982 *Re-Reading English* (London: Methuen)

Wilden, Anthony 1972 *System and Structure: Essays in Communication and Exchange* (London: Tavistock Publications)

Wilden, Anthony 1986 (Orig. 1968 as *Language of the Self Speech and Language in Psychoanalysis* (Baltimore: Johns Hopkins University Press)

Williams, Frederick (ed.) 1970 *Language and Poverty: Perspectives on a Theme* (Markham Publishing Co.)

Winner, I. P. and **Umiker-Sebok, J.** (eds.) 1979 *Semiotics of Culture* (The Hague: Mouton)

Wiseman, Mary Bittner 1989 *The Ecstasies of Roland Barthes* (London: Routledge)

Wittgenstein, Ludwig 1922 *Tractatus Logico-Philosophicus* (London: Routledge & Kegan Paul)

Wittgenstein, Ludwig 1953 *Philosophical Investigations* (Oxford: Basil Blackwell)

Wuthnow, R., Hunter, J. D., Bergeson, A. and **Kurzweil, E.** 1984 *Cultural Analysis* (London: Routledge & Kegan Paul)

Indexes

INDEX OF NAMES
(and corresponding adjectives: e.g. Marx, Marxist)

INDEX OF TOPICS